Geoarchaeology in the Great Plains

Geoarchaeology in the Great Plains

Edited by *Rolfe D. Mandel*

UNIVERSITY OF OKLAHOMA PRESS • NORMAN

Library of Congress Cataloging-in-Publication Data

Geoarchaeology in the Great Plains / edited by Rolfe D. Mandel.
    p. cm.
    Includes bibliographical references and index.
    ISBN 0-8061-3261-2 (pbk. : alk. paper)
        1. Indians of North America—Great Plains—Antiquities.
    2. Archaeological geology—Great Plains. 3. Great Plains—Antiquities.
    I. Mandel, Rolfe D., 1952–

    E78.G73 G46 2000
    978'.01—dc21
                                                                00-041797

The paper in this book meets the guidelines for permanence and durability
of the Committee on Production Guidelines for Book Longevity of the
Council on Library Resources, Inc. ∞

1 2 3 4 5 6 7 8 9 10

We dedicate this book to the memory of our friend and colleague,

E. Mott Davis (1918–1998).

Mott, a true pioneer of archaeological studies on the Great Plains,

always welcomed geologic interpretations of his sites,

and he was a strong advocate of interdisciplinary archaeology.

We miss him.

Contents

List of Illustrations   ix

Preface   xiii

1. Introduction   3
   Rolfe D. Mandel

2. Historical Perspective on the Geoarchaeology of the
   Southern High Plains   10
   Vance T. Holliday

3. Geoarchaeology in the Southern Osage Plains:
   A Historical Perspective   44
   C. Reid Ferring

4. The History of Geoarchaeological Research in
   Kansas and Northern Oklahoma   79
   Rolfe D. Mandel

5. A Brief History of Geoarchaeology in the Eastern
   Plains and Prairies   137
   E. Arthur Bettis III

6. Geoarchaeological Research in Nebraska:
   A Historical Perspective   166
   David W. May

7. Resumé of Geoarchaeological Research on the
   Northwestern Plains   199
   John Albanese

8. Archaeology and the Earth Sciences on the
   Northern Plains   250
   Joe Alan Artz

9. The Past, Present, and Future: A Summary of
   Geoarchaeological Research in the Great Plains   286
   Rolfe D. Mandel

List of Contributors   296

Index   299

Illustrations

FIGURES

2.1. Stratigraphic chart for the gravel pit at the Clovis site
and the Anderson Basin 20

2.2. An Archaic age well at the Clovis site 22

2.3. A section of the valley fill in Yellowhouse Draw at
Lubbock Lake 23

2.4. The geocultural sequence of the Southern High Plains 25

2.5. Schematic illustration of depositional chronology and
relative dominance of environments in draws of the
Southern High Plains 28

3.1. Geologic diagram of the Frederick Locality 49

3.2. Dr. C. N. Ray, Brazos River, Abilene, ca. 1944 52

3.3. Dr. Ray pointing at deeply buried artifacts 52

3.4. Ray's section of the Gibson site 53

3.5. W. W. Crook's valley cross section of the Lewisville Site 56

3.6. Crook's profile for the Lewisville Site 56

3.7. Albritton's cross section of the Domebo Site 60

3.8. Group of Friends of the Pleistocene participants
bombarding Steve Hall with questions at Carnegie
Canyon, Oklahoma, 1987 63

4.1. Excavation units at the Coffey site, 1975 101

4.2. The east bank of the Buckner Creek site in south-
western Kansas 107

4.3. Buried soils and archaeological deposits exposed
at the Buckner Creek site 108

4.4. Bison skull discovered at the Burnham site, October 1986 117

4.5. Bone beds of *Bison antiquus* at the Cooper site in
northwestern Oklahoma 119

5.1.   Examining the discovery site of Minnesota Man   140

5.2.   Stratigraphic sequences and cultural associations in
       small Nebraska valleys   144

5.3.   High school students visiting the Turin site in
       western Iowa   145

5.4.   Ronald Ruppé and W. D. Frankforter examine a bone
       discovered at the Turin site   146

5.5.   Excavations at the Phipps site, Cherokee County, Iowa   150

5.6.   Excavations at the Cherokee Sewer site, Cherokee County,
       Iowa   152

5.7.   Diagram showing correlation of alluvial fan stratigraphic
       sequences in the Little Sioux Valley   153

5.8.   Investigations at the Rainbow site in Plymouth
       County, Iowa   154

5.9.   Chronogram for the thick loess region of the Middle
       Missouri basin   156

5.10. Conceptual model of burial with time of archaeological
       deposits of various cultural periods   157

6.1.   Excavations at the Lime Creek site, 1947   175

6.2.   Excavations at the Allen site, 1948   176

6.3.   Excavations at the Red Smoke site, 1951   177

6.4.   Cutbank at the Moffet Creek archaeological site, 1991   183

6.5.   View south of the La Sena site, 1994   186

6.6.   Drill rig owned by the Bureau of Reclamation being used
       at the La Sena site, 1991   188

7.1.   The Horner site, 1977   210

7.2.   Horner II bison bone bed excavated in 1977–78   211

7.3.   The Casper site   229

7.4.   Cross section A-A' at the Casper Site   230

7.5.   Stacked mammoth bone Pile No. 2 at the Colby Site   232

7.6.   Agate Basin site, view to the south   235

7.7.   Agate Basin site, Hell Gap bone bed   236

8.1.   A buried soil, the "Big Bend paleosol," in a cutbank at the
       Cattle Oiler site   257

8.2.   A 4.2-meter-high profile at the Flaming Arrow site,
       McLean County, North Dakota   264

8.3.   A geoclimatic model of the Oahe Formation   265

8.4.   Model of erosion processes in the Oahe Formation   267

MAPS

1.1.   Regions of the Great Plains   4

2.1.   Southern High Plains   12

3.1.   Southern Plains with Geoarchaeological Research Sites   46

3.2.   Physiographic Map of the Southern Plains   48

4.1.   Central Plains of Kansas and Northern Oklahoma   80

5.1.   Eastern Plains and Prairies   138

6.1.   Archaeological Sites in Nebraska   170

7.1.   Northwestern Plains   202

7.2.   Locations of Excavated Areas, Geologic Profile Trenches,
       and Cross Sections at the Horner Site   212

7.3.   Geologic Map of the Colby Site   231

7.4.   Map of the Agate Basin Site, cross section D-D'   234

8.1.   Northern Plains of North and South Dakota and
       Adjoining States and Provinces   253

TABLES

4.1   Archaeological Sites and Study Areas in
       Kansas and Oklahoma   82

4.2.   Geological Potential for Buried Archaeological
       Deposits in the Pawnee River Basin   109

7.1.   Sites Excavated During the 1970s in the
       Northwestern Plains   224

Preface

In 1992, I was asked to organize a geoarchaeology symposium for the fiftieth annual meeting of the Plains Anthropological Society to be held that year in Lincoln, Nebraska. The topic I selected was "Geoarchaeological Research in the Great Plains: A Historical Perspective." Given the significance of the Plains Anthropological Society's golden anniversary, it seemed fitting to reflect on the long history of collaboration between archaeologists and geoscientists in the midcontinent. This volume is an outgrowth of the symposium.

I extend my thanks and appreciation to Rob Bozell, Chair of the 1992 Plains Conference, for the opportunity to arrange the geoarchaeology symposium. Also, I thank everyone who participated in the symposium and contributed to this volume for their time and efforts, and for their cooperation and patience. All of the authors reviewed manuscripts, and I thank them for their help in this regard. I also thank Doug Bamforth (University of Colorado), Leland Bement (Oklahoma Archaeological Survey), David Benn (Bear Creek Archaeology, Inc.), E. Mott Davis (University of Texas at Austin), Wakefield Dort, Jr. (University of Kansas), George Frison (University of Wyoming), Jack Hofman (University of Kansas), Marlin Hawley (State Historical Society of Wisconsin), C. Vance Haynes, Jr. (University of Arizona), Marvin Kay (University of Arkansas), David Meltzer (Southern Methodist University), Dennis Toom (University of North Dakota), and Raymond Wood (University of Missouri at Columbia) for providing helpful reviews of manuscripts. I am grateful to Nora Ransom (Kansas State University) for serving as a technical editor.

I am indebted to John Drayton, Director of the University of Oklahoma Press, who agreed to publish this work and waited patiently for it to come together. I also appreciate Jean Hurtado, Acquisitions Editor, Jo Ann Reece, Associate Editor, and the technical staff of the Press for their collaborative efforts in bringing the book to completion.

ROLFE D. MANDEL

Lawrence, Kansas

Geoarchaeology in the Great Plains

CHAPTER ONE

Introduction

Rolfe D. Mandel

A number of scholars have addressed the history of geoarchaeology and archaeological geology (e.g., Daniel 1975; Gladfelter 1981; Butzer 1982; Rapp and Gifford 1982; Gifford and Rapp 1985a, 1985b; Haynes 1990; Rapp and Hill 1998:4–17). These historical accounts have been broad in geographic scope. None, however, has focused on a single region of North America. Yet one portion of the continent, the Great Plains, warrants such attention because for the most part geoarchaeology in the western hemisphere emerged and developed there. This observation recurs throughout this volume, especially in discussions of Paleoindian geoarchaeology. The list of geoscientists who have worked on archaeological projects in the Plains encompasses some of the most prominent figures to shape the discipline of geoarchaeology, among them Kirk Bryan, Ernst Antevs, Claude Albritton Jr., E. H. Sellards, C. Bertrand Schultz, and C. Vance Haynes Jr.

The term *geoarchaeology*, as used here, refers to the application of concepts and methods of geosciences to the study of archaeological deposits and the processes involved in the creation of the archaeological record. Geoarchaeologists employ techniques and concepts from geomorphology, pedology, sedimentology, stratigraphy, and geochronology to investigate and interpret the sediments, soils, and landforms in areas and at sites that are the focal points of archaeological studies (Waters 1992:3–4).

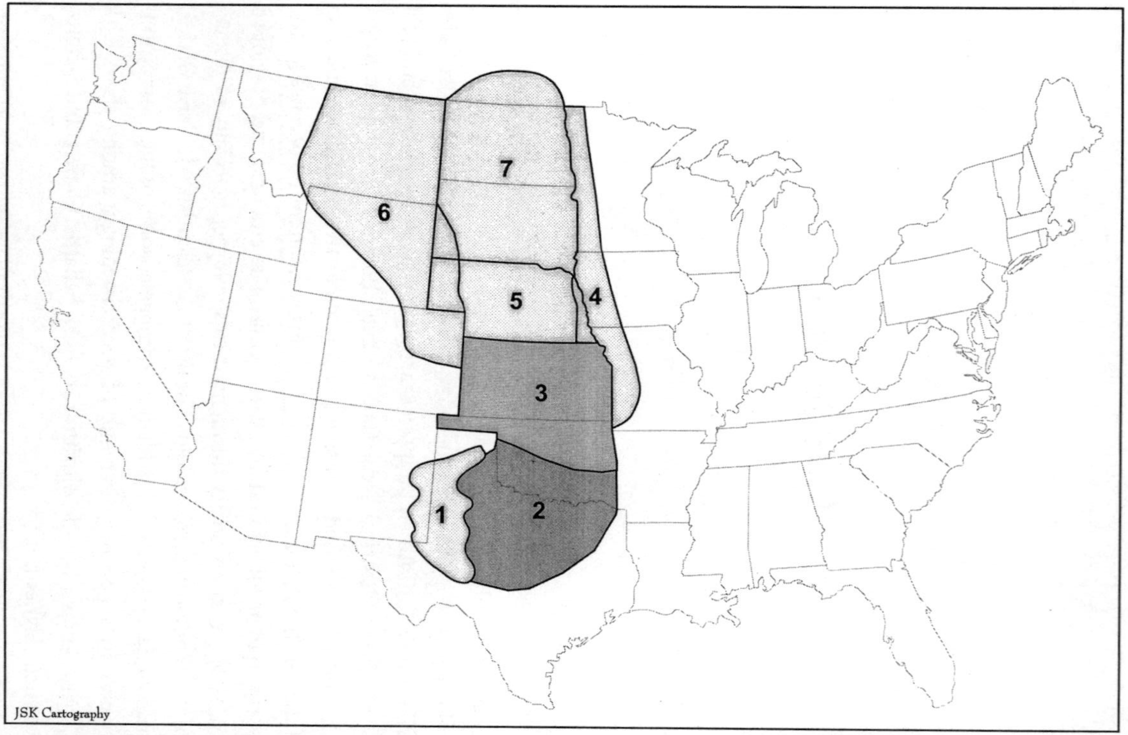

Map 1.1. Regions of the Great Plains, as reviewed in this volume. Region 1, the Southern High Plains, is discussed by Holliday in chapter 2. Region 2, the Southern Osage Plains, is discussed by Ferring in chapter 3. Region 3, the Central Plains of Kansas and northern Oklahoma, is discussed by Mandel in chapter 4. Region 4, the Eastern Plains and Praries, is discussed by Bettis in chapter 5. Region 5, the Great Plains of Nebraska, is discussed by May in chapter 6, and, in addition, Bettis (chapter 4) describes some of the research in extreme eastern Nebraska. Region 6, the Northwestern Plains, is discussed by Albanese in chapter 7, and May (chapter 6) and Artz (chapter 8) describe research in portions of the Northwestern Plains that extend into Nebraska and South Dakota, respectively. Region 7, the Northern Plains, is discussed by Artz in chapter 8.

JSK Cartography

The essays in this volume provide historical overviews of geoarchaeological research in different regions of the Great Plains (map 1.1). The authors go beyond chronicling this history by explaining the driving forces and research questions that for more than a century have brought geoscientists and archaeologists together in the Plains. Although the chapters describe the results of these collaborations, they focus primarily on the evolution of Plains geoarchaeology. It is not our intention to synthesize or correlate all of the data gleaned from geoarchaeological investigations in the region. Such a formidable task exceeds the objectives of this book and deserves a separate forum. Nevertheless, the book contains much substantive information about the late Quaternary geology and geomorphology of the Plains. Readers are exposed to all the major researchers, research projects and theoretical developments, and to important sites that contribute to the present state of geoarchaeological knowledge in the Plains. Also, because the book is framed as narrative, rather than data, nonspecialists in the earth sciences should find it approachable.

In Chapter 2, Vance Holliday focuses on the Southern High Plains. He points out that archaeologists and earth scientists have long been attracted to this region because it repeatedly yields discoveries of human artifacts with Pleistocene fauna in well-stratified deposits that provide evidence of past environments. Holliday frames his historical account of Paleoindian geoarchaeology around several world-class sites, including Clovis, Lubbock Lake, Plainview, Midland, Miami, and San Jon. He demonstrates that geoarchaeological studies in the Southern Plains were initially employed to establish cultural chronologies and for some environmental reconstructions, but that since the early 1970s, they have contributed to stratigraphic correlations, geochronologies, and regional paleoenvironmental reconstructions.

In Chapter 3, Reid Ferring describes the history of geoarchaeological research in the Southern Osage Plains of north-central Texas and southern Oklahoma. His essay begins with a reminiscence of the 1920s. During that time geoscientists were attracted to archaeological sites in the Southern Plains because of reported discoveries of artifacts and human skeletons with Pleistocene faunal remains. Ferring uses two controversial localities, the Lagow Sand Pit and Frederick sites, to illustrate how geologists were engaged in the debate over the antiquity of people in the New World. However, the geoarchaeology that emerged in the region during the 1920s was short-lived. Between 1930 and 1965, geoarchaeological development was almost negligible in the Southern Osage Plains, except for the contributions of avocational geoarchaeologists.

Ferring suggests that the paucity of reported in situ Paleoindian sites during the mid-1900s limited geoscientists' participation in archaeological projects. He explains how interdisciplinary archaeology evolved in the region during the late 1960s largely because of academic programs and research supported by the National Science Foundation (NSF). The strongest impetus for geoarchaeological research, however, came in the late 1970s as a result of federally mandated cultural resource management (CRM), which continues to be the driving force behind interdisciplinary archaeology in the region.

In Chapter 4, I review the history of geoarchaeological research in the Central Plains of Kansas and northern Oklahoma. Geoarchaeological research started late in this region and was sporadic until it developed fully in the 1980s. During the late 1800s and very early 1900s, geologists reported archaeological finds or visited suspected "Early Man" sites in Kansas and northern Oklahoma, but they did not collaborate with archaeologists. The first joint project between an archaeologist and a geologist occurred in the region in late 1937. At that time, Loren C. Eiseley and H. T. U. Smith, both at the University of Kansas, collaborated at the Spring Creek site in north-central Kansas. Unfortunately, Eiseley and Smith's interaction lasted only a short time and was followed by a long period when geologists were not involved in archaeological investigations in Kansas or northern Oklahoma. Although archaeologists conducted a number of surveys in the region during the 1950s and the following two decades, most focused on the Late Prehistoric and Protohistoric record. Because this record is at or near the land surface, archaeologists saw no need to seek help from geologists. The emergence of processual and environmental archaeology during the mid-1960s opened the door to interdisciplinary studies that included geoscientists. However, as was the case in many other areas of the United States, it was federally mandated CRM, which arrived during the late 1960s, that provided the funds to support these studies. By the mid-1970s, interdisciplinary research prompted by CRM was underway in full force in northern Oklahoma, and it was common in Kansas by the early 1980s.

The history of geoarchaeology in the Eastern Plains and Prairies is presented by Art Bettis in Chapter 5. Bettis stresses the late development of geoarchaeology in the region, noting that geoscientists and archaeologists collaborated little there before the 1970s largely because of a paucity of known Paleoindian sites. The discoveries of human remains in deposits that were considered late Pleistocene prompted some interdisciplinary research during the late 1800s and early 1900s. Also, a flurry of geologic studies at archaeological sites took place during the 1940s and 1950s. As Bettis points out, however, these studies and their application to archaeological problems did not go beyond the descriptive phase that was typical of earlier years. Nevertheless, despite its late development in the Eastern Plains and Prairies, during the late 1970s and early 1980s geoarchaeology quickly reached its present status. Bettis attributes its rapid evolution to the emergence of processual and environmental archaeology and federally mandated CRM. Regional studies aimed at determining the potential for buried archaeological deposits mark the latest phase in the development of geoarchaeology in the region.

In Chapter 6, David May reviews the development of geoarchaeology in Nebraska. He begins by describing how the search for paleontological sites by members of the Morrill Paleontological Expedition during the late 1920s and early 1930s led to the discovery of many archaeological sites in western Nebraska. The earliest interaction between geoscientists and archaeologists in Nebraska occurred at these sites. Collaborations continued into the 1940s and 1950s with the reservoir surveys and excavations at deeply buried Paleoindian sites along Lime and Medicine Creeks. The role of geoscientists, however, was usually restricted to assessing the age of the archaeological deposits. Paleontologist C. Bertrand Schultz and other personnel affiliated with the University of Nebraska State Museum conducted nearly all of the geoarchaeological research in Nebraska before 1955. May notes that geoarchaeology faltered in Nebraska after the early 1950s and did not reemerge until the 1970s. He attributes its resurgence to two factors: federal funding tied to the construction of reservoirs and associated canals in central Nebraska, and the discovery of several Paleoindian sites. Recent geoarchaeological research in Nebraska has involved physical geographers, soil scientists, and geologists associated with a variety of institutions, and most of it has been tied to CRM. May stresses that the roles of geoarchaeologists working in Nebraska are more varied than in the past. Today, they help determine where buried archaeological deposits might be found, and they are often called upon to infer the depositional environments at sites.

A summary of geoarchaeological research on the Northwestern Plains is presented by John Albanese in Chapter 7. The history of geoarchaeology in this region contrasts markedly with the historical development of geoarchaeology in the Eastern Plains and Prairies. Albanese stresses that from the time of the first geologic study of an archaeological site in the Northwestern Plains, at the Scottsbluff site in 1932, the primary driving force behind geoarchaeology in the region has been the investigation of Paleoindian sites. This is not surprising given the abundance of premier early sites, including Dent, Lindenmeier, MacHaffie, Ray Long, Horner, Claypool, and Hell Gap. During the early and mid-1900s, geoscientists were invited to these sites primarily to estimate the ages of the archaeological deposits. However, with the advent of radiocarbon dating in 1949, emphasis shifted to the study of geomorphic settings and sedimentary records at sites. Efforts also began to develop a regional alluvial chronology based, in part, on radiocarbon ages from archaeological sites in the Northwestern Plains. Albanese describes how multidisciplinary research at archaeological sites became more common during the 1960s. However, it was the CRM studies triggered by the energy boom of the 1970s and 1980s that resulted in a dramatic increase in both the number of geoarchaeological investigations and the number of geoscientists collaborating with archaeologists in the region. Sites other than those dating to the Paleoindian period suddenly attracted the attention of multidisciplinary research teams. Nevertheless, Paleoindian geoarchaeology has continued to overshadow other collaborations between geoscientists and archaeologists.

In the final essay, Joe Artz focuses on historic trends that marked the emergence and development of geoarchaeology in a portion of the Northern Plains that includes North Dakota, South Dakota, and southern Manitoba and Saskatchewan. He notes that little work resembling geoarchaeology was done in the northern Plains before the 1950s. Although archaeological investigations increased dramatically in the Dakotas during the mid-1930s, primarily because of support from the Works Progress Administration (WPA), these studies were not interdisciplinary. The lack of interaction between archaeologists and geoscientists continued into the 1940s, even as the River Basin Surveys promoted intensive and extensive archaeological investigations. Several studies in the 1950s combined archaeological and geological knowledge and expertise, but true interdisciplinary collaboration was infrequent before the 1960s and did not become commonplace until the 1970s. Artz stresses that what he calls the "threshold event" in the emergence of geoarchaeology in the Northern Plains was the development of a stratigraphic framework for the Holocene loess (Oahe Formation) that mantles the uplands. The Oahe Formation model, published by Lee Clayton and his colleagues in 1976, demystified the Holocene geologic record for archaeologists. This occurred at the same time that archaeologists developed a regional cultural chronology and began to explore the upland archaeological record. Artz concludes that geologists and archaeologists working in the Northern Plains were not ready to collaborate productively until their respective disciplines attained a level of knowledge in the region. That level was reached in the late 1970s.

I conclude the volume with a brief summary highlighting the driving forces that stimulated geoarchaeological research in the Great Plains over the past two decades, as well as current trends in Plains geoarchaeology. Finally, I look to the future and consider how Plains geoarchaeology may be affected by technological and methodological innovations and by changes in the types of research problems that are likely to bring geoscientists and archaeologists together.

REFERENCES

Butzer, K. W. 1982. Archaeology as human ecology: Method and theory for a contextual approach. Cambridge: Cambridge University Press.

Daniel, G. 1975. A hundred and fifty years of archaeology. London: Duckworth.

Gifford, J. A., and G. Rapp Jr. 1985a. The early development of archaeological geology in North America. In Drake, E. T., and W. M. Jordan, eds., Geologists and ideas: A history of North American geology. Boulder, Colo.: Geological Society of America, Centennial Special Volume 1:409–21.

————. 1985b. History, philosophy, and perspectives. In Rapp, G., Jr., and J. A. Gifford, eds., Archaeological geology, 1–23. New Haven: Yale University Press.

Gladfelter, B. G. 1981. Developments and directions in geoarchaeology. In Schiffer, M. B., ed., Advances in archaeological method and theory, 343–64. New York: Academic Press.

Haynes, C. V., Jr. 1990. The Antevs-Bryan years and the legacy of Paleoindian geochronology. In Laporte, L. F., ed., Establishment of a geologic framework for paleoanthropology. Boulder, Colo.: Geological Society of America, Special Paper 242:55–66.

Rapp, G., Jr. and J. A. Gifford. 1982. Archaeological geology. American Scientist 70:45–53.

Rapp, G., Jr., and C. L. Hill. 1998. Geoarchaeology: The Earth-science approach to archaeological interpretations. New Haven: Yale University Press.

Waters, M. R. 1992. Principles of geoarchaeology. Tucson: The University of Arizona Press.

CHAPTER TWO

Historical Perspective on the Geoarchaeology of the Southern High Plains

Vance T. Holliday

INTRODUCTION

Geoscientific studies have been an integral part of archaeological investigations on the Southern High Plains for more than sixty years. Few regions in North America have such a long history of geoarchaeological research at so many sites involving so many of the century's leading archaeologists and geoscientists. Their studies tended to focus on Paleoindian sites, but they addressed all cultural periods geoarchaeologically. This interdisciplinary research adds significantly to our understanding of cultural sequences and of people's relationships to their immediate surroundings, as well as our broader view of late Quaternary environments and environmental change.

There are several reasons for this long record of fruitful interdisciplinary research on the Southern High Plains. In the years immediately following the discoveries at the Folsom site, where from 1926 to 1928 the human association with extinct fauna in North America was finally confirmed, archaeologists were attracted to the Plains because it was the area that repeatedly yielded discoveries of human artifacts and Pleistocene fauna. Many of these archaeological sites have thick, well-stratified deposits that provide evidence of markedly different depositional environments than those found in the areas today, that is, meandering streams or perennial, freshwater lakes instead of dry valleys or dry lake basins. These striking contrasts drew the attention of archaeologists and earth scientists alike (Holliday 1997a).

Dating artifacts was one of the most immediate concerns of archaeologists in the early decades of Paleoindian studies. Geologists and paleontologists were called upon to provide age estimates of sites in the absence of radiometric dating methods (Hofman 1989:44; Ferring 1994; Holliday 1997a:21–30, 2000a; Rapp and Hill 1998:11–12). Much of the research was conducted by archaeologists with training or experience in geology or interdisciplinary research (E. B. Howard, Frank H. H. Roberts, Fred Wendorf, James J. Hester, Eileen Johnson) and, more commonly, geologists or paleontologists with an abiding interest in human prehistory, especially Paleoindian archaeology (E. H. Sellards, Glen L. Evans, Grayson E. Meade, Claude C. Albritton, F. Earl Green, C. Vance Haynes Jr.). For these scientists, geologic research was inseparable from their approach to archaeology. Finally, beginning in the 1950s, interdisciplinary research became more common in North American archaeology, and this development influenced work on the Plains (Holliday 1997a).

This chapter is a review, not an exhaustive discussion, of the history of geoarchaeological research on the Southern High Plains. It summarizes the chronology of earth science involvement in archaeology, highlights some of the more significant geoarchaeological contributions, and presents some of the current archaeologically significant interpretations based on the results of geoscientific research. Also included is a short chronology of geoarchaeological and related research in the region, identifying the major players and establishing timelines for the subsequent discussion of contributions in stratigraphy, soils, and paleoenvironments, as well as in studies of Paleoindian cultural chronology.

ENVIRONMENTAL SETTING AND REGIONAL GEOLOGY

The Southern High Plains or Llano Estacado ("stockaded plains") is a vast, level plateau covering approximately 130,000 km2 (map 2.1). The region has a warm, semiarid, continental environment (Lotspeich and Everhart 1962; Carr 1967). The natural vegetation is shortgrass prairie with scattered trees along the escarpments and in the valleys (Blair 1950; Wendorf 1975a). The Llano Estacado comprises the southernmost portion of the High Plains physiographic section

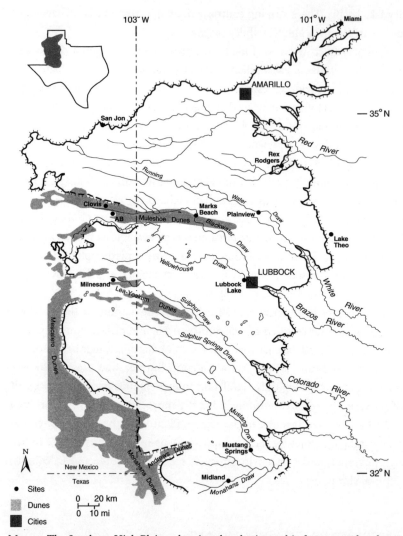

Map 2.1. The Southern High Plains, showing the physiographic features and archaeo-logical sites mentioned in the text (AB = Anderson Basin) and selected cities. Inset in upper left shows the location of the region in Texas.

(Hunt 1974) (map 2.1). The plateau is defined by escarpments along the west, north, and east sides. To the south, the surface of the Southern High Plains gradually merges with the Edwards Plateau province of central Texas (map 2.1).

The Southern High Plains is almost featureless, one of the most nearly level regions in the United States. Small basins, dry valleys, and dunes provide slight topographic relief (Reeves 1965, 1966, 1972, 1991; Wendorf 1975a; Hawley et al. 1976; Walker 1978; Holliday 1985a, 1995a) (map 2.1). Approximately 25,000 small (<5 km2) depressions dot the landscape and contain seasonal lakes or *playas* and about 40 larger (tens of km2) basins, also called playas or *salinas*. The playa and salina basins contain the only available, naturally impounded surface water on the Llano Estacado although the water is seasonal and sometimes brackish or saline. The dry valleys or *draws* are northwest-southeast trending tributaries of rivers on the Rolling Plains to the east (map 2.1). Today, the draws contain no flowing water and hold standing water only after heavy rain. Several large dune fields lie along the western Llano Estacado (map 2.1) with crescent-shaped dunes (*lunettes*) near some playas.

The draws, playas, dune fields, and lunettes are the sites of most late Quaternary sedimentation and, therefore, are also the areas where in situ archaeological deposits occur in stratified contexts. Virtually all geoarchaeological research in the region has focused on sites in one of these settings.

Extensive Cenozoic deposits that overlie Paleozoic and Mesozoic bedrock comprise most of the exposed sections and surficial deposits of the Southern High Plains. The bulk of these deposits are Miocene-Pliocene eolian and alluvial sediments of the Ogallala Formation, largely derived from mountains to the west in New Mexico (Hawley et al. 1976; Reeves 1972; Gustavson 1996; Reeves and Reeves 1996). The Ogallala Formation contains the economically significant Ogallala or High Plains aquifer. The upper Ogallala has a thick, highly resistant, pedogenic calcrete, known as the "caprock caliche" because it is a prominent ledge-forming unit near the top of the escarpments bordering the plateau. The Pliocene is represented by the Blanco Formation, an extensive lacustrine deposit of dolomite and some sand deposited in large basins cut into the Ogallala (Evans and Meade 1945; Harbour 1975; Hawley et al. 1976).

The modern surface of the Southern High Plains is composed of the Blackwater Draw Formation, which is a widespread eolian deposit derived from the Pecos River Valley (Reeves 1976; Holliday 1989a; Gustavson and Holliday 1999). This deposit blankets all older deposits and varies in thickness and texture from a thin veneer of sandy loam in the southwest to a thick deposit of clay loam in the northeast. Pleistocene lake sediments occur below, within, and inset against the Blackwater Draw Formation (Harbour 1975; Reeves 1976, 1991; Schultz 1986; Holliday et al. 1996).

Most of the rest of the archaeologically significant surficial deposits are the late Quaternary sediments found in the draws, lake basins, and dunes. The draws are inset into the Blackwater Draw Formation and locally cut into the Blanco or Ogallala Formations; they probably developed or at least took on their present shape during the late Pleistocene period (Holliday 1995b). Within these dry tributaries are a variety of late Pleistocene and Holocene lacustrine, paludal, alluvial, and eolian deposits (Holliday 1995a,b, 1997a). The playa and salina basins also are cut into the Blackwater Draw Formation or older deposits and contain late Quaternary lacustrine and paludal sediments (Reeves 1991; Holliday et al. 1996). The lunettes and dune fields rest on top of the Black-water Draw Formation. The lunettes contain late Pleistocene and Holocene eolian sediments deflated from adjacent playas, and the various dune fields consist primarily of Holocene sands (Huffington and Albritton 1941; Green 1961; Holliday 1985a, 1995a, 1997b). Archaeological sites are reported in all of this late Quaternary sediment, although sites in the draws have been the most intensively studied (archaeologically and geologically) and are the best known.

A Brief Chronology of Research

Geoarchaeology on the Southern High Plains had its inception in the 1930s with the archaeological research into the Paleoindian occupation of the Llano Estacado. In 1933, interdisciplinary archaeological work began in a gravel pit at the now famous Clovis site (Blackwater Draw Locality 1) (map 2.1). The work was jointly sponsored by the University of Pennsylvania Museum and the Academy of Natural Sciences of Philadelphia, led by E. B. Howard, an archae-ologist with advanced degrees in both anthropology and geology (Roberts 1943), and subsequently directed by archaeologist John L. Cotter (Antevs 1935, 1949; Howard 1935; Stock and Bode 1936; Cotter 1937, 1938; Patrick 1938). The research focused on valley fills with archaeological material (especially arti-facts in association with late Pleistocene fauna) along and in tributaries of the upper Blackwater Draw. The Clovis site is located in a basin that drains into the draw proper. The locality is one of the most significant archaeological sites in the region, and research, which continues to the present, has almost always been interdisciplinary. This is partly because of the rich, extensive, stratified Paleoindian and later archaeological remains, and partly because of its late Quaternary paleoecological record. Hester (1972) summarizes the history and results of the early research at Clovis and discusses the more significant geoar-chaeological contributions.

In 1937 geologist and paleontologist E. H. Sellards, under the auspices of the Texas Memorial Museum at the University of Texas at Austin, excavated the Miami site (Sellards 1938) (map 2.1). This was in a small playa and was one of the first archaeological sites where mammoth was excavated in North America (Holliday et al. 1994). The work at Miami marked the beginning of almost twenty-five years of research by Sellards into the Paleoindian archaeology and geology of the High Plains, with much of the fieldwork conducted by geologist G. L. Evans and paleontologist G. E. Meade (Holliday 1997a). Sellards's Paleoindian research grew out of a heated debate that he inadvertently became involved in early in the century (Meltzer 1983). In several papers (Sellards 1916, 1917), he presented evidence for the association of human bone with extinct animals at a site near Vero, Florida. He was apparently unprepared for the storm of criticism that followed his publications (e.g., Hrdlička 1918) and it affected him deeply (Evans 1986). The result, beginning several decades later when he was director of the Texas Memorial Museum (TMM), was his fieldwork in Texas and New Mexico aimed at proving that humans and extinct Pleistocene species were contemporaneous. Geology was a key component of these investigations, because Sellards was trained in geology and paleontology and because recognition of stratigraphy and various depositional environments was a key to dating and interpreting the sites.

Several other significant geoarchaeological investigations occurred just prior to the entry of the United States into World War II. Frank H. H. Roberts, a veteran field archaeologist for the Smithsonian Institution fresh from his fieldwork at the Lindenmeier Folsom site, was contacted in 1941 by Frank Hibben of the University of New Mexico regarding Paleoindian finds in another playa near San Jon, New Mexico (Roberts 1942; Hill et al. 1995) (map 2.1). Roberts tested the San Jon site in 1941 and, with geology graduate student Sheldon Judson, studied the stratigraphy at and near the site. Judson was a student at Harvard, and his involvement in the project was the result of his association with Kirk Bryan, noted for his interest in and research on geoarchaeological as well as geomorphological topics (Haynes 1990). The subsequent reports by Roberts (1942) and Judson (1953) discuss their work on the site's archaeology and geology and led to one of the first regional studies of playa origins and stratigraphy (Judson 1950). When the Works Progress Administration (WPA) began sponsoring archaeological research, the first of a series of investigations began at the Lubbock Lake site in Yellowhouse Draw. Joe Ben Wheat, another archaeologist with training in geology, conducted this investigation in 1939 and 1941 (Black 1974; Wheat 1974). Although geology was not a major component of these WPA studies, the stratigraphy at Lubbock Lake was obvious and played a key role in the archaeological interpretations (Wheat 1974).

In the decade after World War II, Sellards, Evans, and Meade worked at a number of archaeological sites on and off of the Southern High Plains. Their studies resulted in a remarkable body of research on Paleoindian archaeology and late Quaternary stratigraphy and geochronology (Holliday 1995b, 1997a). On the Llano Estacado, this work included the Clovis site (Evans 1951; Sellards 1952), Lubbock Lake (Sellards 1952), the Plainview site in Running Water Draw (Sellards et al. 1947), the Milnesand site in dunes on upper Sulphur Draw (Sellards 1955a), and the Midland (Scharbauer Ranch) site in dunes on Monahans Draw (Sellards 1955b) (map 2.1).

Sellards's work in the High Plains, in addition to his earlier research in Florida, resulted in several important publications. His summary of Paleoindian archaeology in the New World (Sellards 1952) is a classic because it was the most comprehensive study of the topic of its time and because it remains the only source of information for some of his fieldwork. Sellards and Evans's research also resulted in the first comprehensive summary of Paleoindian archaeology of the Llano Estacado (Sellards and Evans 1960). In both these works, Sellards employs a strong geoscience orientation, more so than in most subsequent reviews of Paleoindian archaeology.

Sellards also worked at the Midland site, but his investigations followed the more substantive geoarchaeological research of Wendorf et al. (1955) and Wendorf and Krieger (1959). This site, in a small dune field overlapping Monahans Draw, was studied and became well known because it yielded some human remains of late Pleistocene or early Holocene age (Holliday and Meltzer 1996). The dune stratigraphy is a key to dating the human bone, but the geochronology remains somewhat uncertain (Holliday and Meltzer 1996).

The initial work at the Midland site led to another significant development in late Quaternary research on the Llano Estacado in the late 1950s and early 1960s. Fred Wendorf and colleagues from the Museum of New Mexico, Texas Technological College (now Texas Tech University), and other institutions established the High Plains Paleoecology Project (HPPP). This interdisciplinary research program not only focused on reconstructing the late Pleistocene environment of the area, but included other aspects of late Quaternary history, such as archaeology and Holocene paleoenvironments (e.g., Wendorf 1961; Hester 1962; Hafsten 1964; Oldfield and Schoenwetter 1964, 1975; Wendorf and Hester 1975). The HPPP, which included work in the draws, playas, and dunes, was and remains one of the few regional studies of late Quaternary history in North America that incorporated archaeology, stratigraphy, geochronology, paleobotany, and paleontology. The principal outcomes of this research included the definition of a sequence of late Quaternary "climatic intervals" (Wendorf 1961) and "pollen-analytical episodes" (Oldfield 1975; Schoenwetter 1975), along with environmental reconstructions for various "intervals" and "episodes" (Oldfield and Schoenwetter 1975; Wendorf 1970, 1975b). Although some investigators criticized some of the interpretations of this work (Holliday 1987, 1995b, 1997a), the project nevertheless provided a model of interdisciplinary research strategies and environmental change, as well as a rich data base for subsequent investigators.

Other geoarchaeological research continued in association with the HPPP studies. F. E. Green (1962a,b, 1963) presented the first comprehensive discussion of the archaeology and geology of Lubbock Lake, and the most substantive discussion of geology, archaeology, and paleoenvironments at Clovis since the work of Howard, Cotter, and Evans. As a specific component of the HPPP and a direct outgrowth of the research at Midland, Green (1961) also summarized stratigraphic and paleoenvironmental research in the Monahans Dunes. His summary was the first comprehensive discussion of this extensive and archaeologically rich dune system. C. V. Haynes became involved in the later stages of the HPPP, which led to a long-term research program at the Clovis site and its environs. Haynes and Agogino (1966), Haynes (1975, 1995), and Stanford et al. (1990), among others, present extensive data on the stratigraphy and geochronology of the valley fill of upper Blackwater Draw in and near the Clovis site, research that is especially significant given the archaeological and paleoenvironmental data that came from the area.

Geoarchaeological research on the Southern High Plains essentially stopped from the middle 1960s to the early 1970s. Beyond some limited work at Clovis (Agogino and Rovner 1969; Stevens 1973; Agogino et al. 1976) and Marks Beach in middle Blackwater Draw (Honea 1980) (map 2.1), researchers carried out no large-scale archaeological investigations involving geoarchaeological studies.

In the 1970s, 1980s, and 1990s there were several new developments in geoarchaeological research on the Southern High Plains. The first began in 1972, with establishment of the Lubbock Lake Project under the auspices of the Museum of Texas Tech University. This was a continuing, interdisciplinary research program at the Lubbock Lake archaeological site, under the direction

of archaeologist and biologist Eileen Johnson and a succession of geoarchaeologists (C. A. Johnson, T. W. Stafford, and V. T. Holliday). Initially the project
focused on the record of human adaptation to late Quaternary environmental
change at the Lubbock Lake archaeological site (map 2.1). Building on earlier
work at the site by Wheat (1974), Evans (1949), Sellards (1952), Green (1962a),
and Kelley (1974), the research program included archaeology, geomorphology, pedology, paleontology, and paleobotany (e.g., Black 1974; C. Johnson 1974;
Johnson and Holliday 1980, 1981, 1986, 1989; Stafford 1981; Holliday 1985b,c,d,
1988; Holliday and Allen 1987; Johnson 1986, 1987) and yielded the most complete record of late Quaternary human occupation and paleoenvironments in
the south-central United States. The research broadened to encompass late
Quaternary studies throughout the Llano Estacado (e.g., Johnson 1986; Johnson
et al. 1982; Holliday 1985a,e, 1987, 1989b, 1997b; Holliday et al. 1996), including a
comprehensive investigation of the stratigraphy and paleoenvironmental record
of the fill in the draws (Holliday 1995b) and the Paleoindian geoarchaeology of
the region (Holliday 1997a).

Site-specific and regional archaeological and geoarchaeological studies
have continued on the Southern High Plains during the past several decades,
and the emphasis on Paleoindian sites has continued. In addition to Clovis
and Lubbock Lake, investigated sites included Miami (Holliday et al. 1994),
Midland (Holliday and Meltzer 1996), Milnesand (Johnson et al. 1986), and
Plainview (Holliday 1997a) on the Llano Estacado; Rex Rodgers (Willey et al.
1978) and Lake Theo (Johnson et al. 1982), just off of the Llano Estacado; and
Lipscomb in the northern Panhandle (Hofman et al. 1989) (map 2.1) (see also
Holliday 1997a). Investigators also addressed some of the non-Paleoindian geo-
archaeological records at some of these sites. Paleoenvironments and human
adaptations during the Early and Middle Archaic drew special attention at
Mustang Springs, on Mustang Draw (Meltzer and Collins 1987; Meltzer 1991)
(map 2.1). Regional geoarchaeological studies include work on lower Sulphur
Springs Draw (Frederick 1993a, 1994) (map 2.1) and, just north of the Llano
Estacado, in Palo Duro Creek (Caran 1991; Frederick 1993b).

The contributions of more than sixty years of geoarchaeology on the Southern High Plains fall into two broad categories: 1) stratigraphy, soils, and paleoenvironments, and 2) Paleoindian chronologies. As will become apparent, the
most immediate impact of this research—and by definition the aim of geoarchaeological research—has been on archaeological interpretations. Equally
important, however, and usually of equal concern to most geoarchaeologists

on the Southern High Plains, are the contributions of these investigations to the study of late Quaternary paleoenvironments. The studies of human prehistory and the Quaternary period on the Llano Estacado have been intimately linked, as they should be elsewhere.

STRATIGRAPHY, SOILS, AND PALEOENVIRONMENTS

Stratigraphic investigations and the reconstruction of paleoenvironments are probably two of the oldest contributions of earth science to archaeology. Certainly they are the first such contributions on the Southern High Plains and continue to be of primary importance in archaeological and broader late Quaternary studies. Most of the archaeological sites in the draws, dunes, and playas are in well-stratified contexts that invite geologic scrutiny. The bulk of the geoarchaeological studies in the region focused on draw localities (Clovis, Lubbock Lake, Midland, and Mustang Springs), but some playa localities (Miami and San Jon) are also worth noting.

An artificial exposure of the well-stratified archaeological record preserved in the draws led to the work at the Clovis site in 1933, heralding the long tradition of geoarchaeology on the Southern High Plains. In November 1932, E. B. Howard was led to the site by local collectors. There he observed "artifacts [including fluted projectile points] . . . as well as mammoth teeth, bison and horse bones . . . weathering out of . . . bluish-gray sands" (Howard 1935:81). These bluish sands contain most of the late Pleistocene and early Holocene archaeological and paleontological record at Clovis. Howard and company also identified similar deposits, which were rich in bone from extinct vertebrates and associated with stone artifacts, locally along Blackwater Draw proper, most notably downstream from the gravel pit in the area called "Anderson Lake" or "Anderson Basin" (Howard 1935; Stock and Bode 1936) (fig. 2.1). They immediately recognized the blue sand as an important geoarchaeological marker.

Howard and his associates focused their attention on the blue sand and underlying lighter (gray) sand—the "caliche" (Howard 1935). The blue sands consisted of several different layers: the lower blue sand included organic-rich, diatomaceous muds and local beds of pure diatomite, whereas the upper blue sand contained organic-rich silt and sand. Most subsequent workers divided the blue sands into two or four lithostrata (e.g., Haynes 1975:table 4-1). The

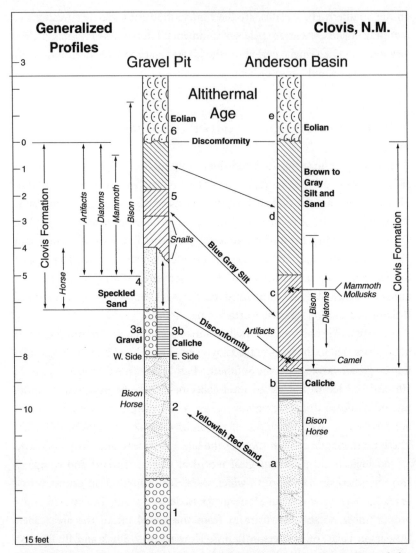

Fig. 2.1. Stratigraphic correlation chart for the gravel pit at the Clovis site and the Anderson Basin area, prepared by Ernst Antevs (Antevs 1949:186; with very slight modification). His "Blue Gray Silt" is the "Blue Sand" of Howard (1935) and Stock and Bode (1936), which contained most of the Paleoindian archaeology and much of the extinct fauna. Note also the identification of "Altithermal age" eolian sand at both sites.

archaeological investigations focused on the diatomaceous mud, diatomite, and gray sand, all of which produced fossils of extinct vertebrates, as well as stone tools with fluted lanceolate points. These strata indicated substantial changes in depositional environment. To further document these changes, several specialists became involved to study the geology and vertebrate paleontology (Stock and Bode 1936), diatoms (Lohman 1935; Patrick 1938), and mollusks (Howard 1935:89; Clarke 1938). The interpretations from these various lines of evidence were in basic agreement. The lower, pale gray sands were deposited by flowing water, which was fresh to slightly brackish. The blue sands accumulated first in a lake, and then under more marshy conditions. Initially the water was fresh during the deposition of blue sand, but later it became saline. The changing water conditions were interpreted as indicating gradual drying during the Paleoindian occupation, that is, from the Pleistocene into the Holocene period.

Antevs (1949, 186) identified "Altithermal age" eolian sand above the Paleoindian-age deposits at the Clovis site and in Anderson Basin (fig. 2.1) but did not elaborate on his interpretations. Presumably, he believed that the sands resulted from the "Altithermal drought" he proposed earlier (Antevs 1948).

The diatomaceous sediments and gray sands at Clovis were the expressed focus of E. H. Sellards as he directed the next phase of research in the gravel pit. His goal was to further document the association of humans and Pleistocene fauna. Paleoenvironmental data were important, but the archaeological considerations took precedence, in particular, the establishment of a cultural chronology. The TMM work did yield significant post-Paleoindian environmental clues in the discovery of Archaic wells (fig. 2.2). Evans's discussion of these striking features (1951) is an excellent case study in the use of stratigraphic principles for relative dating and, moreover, is a persuasive argument for viewing these features as a human adaptation to drought conditions.

The geoarchaeological significance of the diatomaceous earth and gray sand took on added importance with the discovery of a very similar geocultural record at Lubbock Lake (fig. 2.3). Extinct fauna and stone artifacts were found in diatomaceous mud, pure diatomite, and underlying gray sands (Sellards 1952). Sellards's geoarchaeological interests in Lubbock, as at Clovis, continued to be stratigraphic with the emphasis on building a cultural chronology (fig. 2.4). Sellards exemplifies this emphasis in his last writing on Clovis and Lubbock (Sellards and Evans 1960:643), in which he referred to geologic strata by their artifact content (e.g., the diatomite and diatomaceous muds are the

Fig. 2.2. One of the Archaic age wells (well F) found at the Clovis site by Glen Evans (1951). The well cuts through Units D and C of Haynes (1975, 1995) ("diatomaceous earth" and "gray sand," respectively, of Evans, 1951, and Sellards, 1952). The well was backfilled with a mixture of sediment removed during the Archaic excavation and then buried by Unit G1 of Haynes (1995), the "jointed sand" of Evans (1951), and Sellards (1952). Courtesy of the Texas Memorial Museum.

"Folsom stratum") (fig. 2.4). In this final writing, however, he made some very general interpretations concerning the paleohydrology of the two sites. Deposition of the basal gray sands was related to high spring discharge and runoff resulting in flow that "was greater during deposition of this stratum than at any subsequent time" (641). Based on the extensive lake deposits, climate during the Folsom occupation may have been wetter than today. Sellards also alludes to a dry interval between Clovis and Folsom occupations based on the recovery of Folsom artifacts on top of "older sand dunes" (643) on the uplands. He also invokes the purported dunes to account for the diatomite ponds with the sands choking the draws and impounding water (643). The location or physical characteristics of the "dunes" was never published but may include the sand sheet at the Mitchell Folsom locality at the Clovis site (Stratum II of Boldurian 1990; Stratum C of Holliday 1995b; the locality is also known as "Frank's Folsom site" by Stanford and Broilo 1981) and the pre-Folsom eolian sediments at Midland (Wendorf et al. 1955).

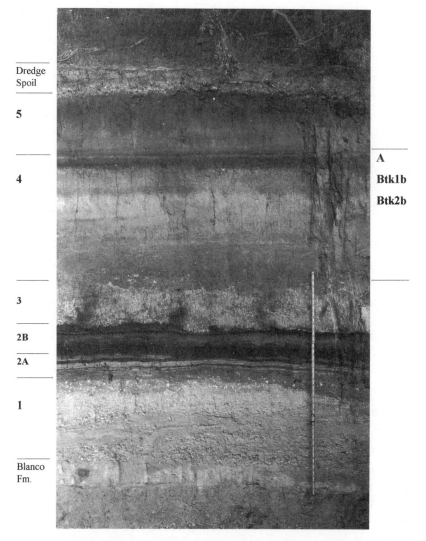

Dredge
Spoil

5

4

3

2B

2A

1

Blanco
Fm.

A

Btk1b

Btk2b

Fig. 2.3. A section of the valley fill in Yellowhouse Draw exposed at Lubbock Lake. The leveling rod at lower right is 3 meters long. The Blanco Formation is Pliocene bedrock. Numbers 1–5 at left are strata 1–5 of Stafford (1981) and Holliday (1985b). Stratum 1 is Clovis-age alluvium. Stratum 2 includes a bedded diatomaceous earth (Folsom) and overlying organic-rich mud (Plainview and Firstview) (lower and upper halves of stratum 2, respectively, in this photo). Stratum 3 (early Archaic) is marl (shown here) with a valley-margin sandy eolian facies. Stratum 4 (Middle Archaic) is primarily an eolian loam. Stratum 5 (Ceramic, Protohistoric, and Historic) includes mud along the valley axis with slope-wash gravel and eolian loam along the valley margin. The mud-loam interface is exposed here. Strata 3, 4, and 5 contain soils. In this section the best-expressed soil is the A-Btk profile in stratum 4 (the Lubbock Lake Soil of Holliday 1985b, c). Courtesy of the Lubbock Lake Landmark, Museum of Texas Tech University.

The TMM work at Plainview (Sellards et al. 1947) yielded a spectacular archaeological feature in well-stratified valley fill. The site was a *Bison antiquus* bone bed with dozens of associated Paleoindian stone artifacts, including the type specimens for the Plainview projectile point. Sellards and Evans (1960) discussed the site in the context of other stratified sites, but the Plainview strata were not incorporated into regional stratigraphic schemes (e.g., fig. 2.4) until several decades after Sellards's death. This was due to the absence of archaeological features, other than the bone bed with Plainview points, and the absence of distinctive stratigraphic markers such as diatomites and diatomaceous muds.

In the 1930s, Sellards's field crew at the Miami site found mammoth remains along with Clovis points in sediment filling a very small playa (Sellards 1938). The gray, clayey playa fill was devoid of stratigraphy with the notable exception of a light gray silt immediately below the bone level. Sellards eventually came to believe that the "loess" layer implied "drought and the absence of vegetation" (Sellards 1952:23).

Subsequent research at Miami (Holliday et al. 1994) confirmed a likely eolian origin of the silt layer. The Miami loess layer was one line of evidence used by Haynes (1991) to support his proposal of a "Clovis drought" in the western United States. Stratigraphic data from Clovis also were used to support this hypothesis, but there is no other obvious evidence to support such a drought on the Southern High Plains (Holliday 1995a,b, 1997a, 2000a). Haynes argued that this climatic event was in part responsible for the extinction of late Pleistocene megafauna.

The Miami excavations were followed by archaeological and geological investigations at another playa, the San Jon site (Roberts 1942; Judson 1953). Judson studied the fill in the lake basin and concluded that the San Jon Paleoindian occupation was associated with lake sediments and probably occurred when there was more moisture in the area than there is today. Later occupations at the site were associated with alternating layers of lake sediment, slopewash, and eolian sand, which were interpreted as representing environments alternating between increased moisture (lake sediments) and decreased moisture (slopewash and eolian sediments). Subsequent investigations at the site tend to confirm these conclusions (Hill et al. 1995).

Several years after Sellards's work at Lubbock Lake, during the final years of his studies at Clovis, stratigraphic studies again proved important in draw and dune contexts as research began at the Midland site (Wendorf et al. 1955;

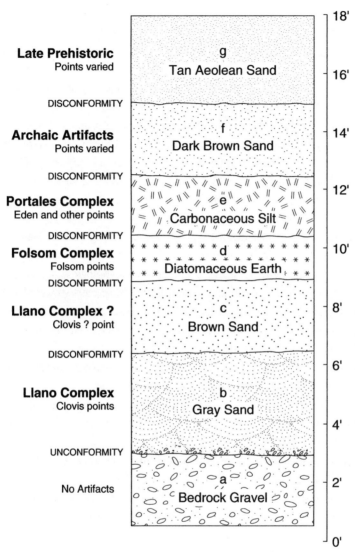

Late Prehistoric
Points varied

DISCONFORMITY

Archaic Artifacts
Points varied

DISCONFORMITY

Portales Complex
Eden and other points

DISCONFORMITY

Folsom Complex
Folsom points

DISCONFORMITY

Llano Complex ?
Clovis ? point

DISCONFORMITY

Llano Complex
Clovis points

UNCONFORMITY

No Artifacts

18'

16'

14'

12'

10'

8'

6'

4'

2'

0'

g
Tan Aeolean Sand

f
Dark Brown Sand

e
Carbonaceous Silt

d
Diatomaceous Earth

c
Brown Sand

b
Gray Sand

a
Bedrock Gravel

Fig. 2.4. The geocultural sequence of the Southern High Plains proposed by E. H. Sellards and Glen Evans (Sellards and Evans 1960:fig. 2; with very slight modification), based on geoarchaeological research at the Clovis and Lubbock Lake sites. This is the first geologically oriented cultural chronology for the region.

Wendorf and Krieger 1959). The resulting data were used for environmental reconstructions and to place the well-known human remains within a cultural chronology. The site is located in and next to Monahans Draw (map 2.1) where a small dune field overlaps the drainage. Three strata were identified: White Sand, Gray Sand, and Red Sand (oldest to youngest). The White Sand was interpreted as lacustrine and reflecting "cool, wet . . . pluvial conditions" (Wendorf et al. 1955:68, table 6; Wendorf and Krieger 1959:66). The Gray Sand, which contained the human remains, reflected a drying trend (Wendorf et al. 1955:68, table 6), and the overlying Red Sand represented a period of "extreme aridity" (Wendorf et al. 1955:98). Initial correlations dated all of these events to the Wisconsin glacial period, an interpretation that had substantial archaeological implications.

As an outgrowth of the work at Midland, the High Plains Paleoecology Project (HPPP) yielded environmental data that complemented the known late Quaternary geologic record in the draws. Palynology was a key component of the project, and samples were collected from most stratified archaeological sites (Clovis, Anderson Basin, Lubbock Lake, Plainview, San Jon). The results, combined with some new radiocarbon determinations, were used to define "climatic episodes" (Wendorf 1961, 1970, 1975b) and were a significant refinement of the more generalized environmental record proposed on the basis of geologic data from a few sites such as Midland.

Surprisingly, the HPPP did not incorporate regional stratigraphic investigations. The more localized work of Haynes and Green, however, did yield significant geoarchaeological results. Green provided the first comprehensive summary of the cultural and geological stratigraphy at Lubbock Lake, as well as additional data on wells at Clovis, and described the origin of dunes at the southern end of the Llano Estacado. Green (1962a) presented his Lubbock Lake record in a paper for a popular audience shortly after Sellards published his final work on the Llano Estacado (Sellards and Evans 1960). The interpretation of the site, based on its geology and paleontology, generally fit the scheme proposed by Antevs (1948) for the Desert West and Great Plains: a cool, humid late Pleistocene and early Holocene; a dry, warm middle Holocene "Altithermal"; and a return to cooler and more moist conditions in the late Holocene represented by today's environment. Variations in apparent intensity of occupation at the site were linked to these environmental fluctuations. Green's (1961) dune research expanded the sequence proposed for the Midland site and showed that the dune stratigraphy was more complex than previously thought. He also demonstrated that much of the record at Midland dated to the very late Pleistocene and most of the Holocene. These data and other work of the HPPP indicated that the Midland finds are younger than the Wisconsin glacial period (Wendorf 1961, 1975b). The dune research by Green (1961) also has proved useful for correlating and dating other archaeological sites associated with eolian sediments in the Midland region (e.g., Blaine 1968; Hofman et al. 1990; Holliday 1997a).

Haynes's studies included the first systematic geologic research at and around Clovis since Stock and Bode (1936), and added substantially to our understanding of the geoarchaeology of upper Blackwater Draw. In particular, Haynes (Haynes and Agogino 1966) documented the location and age of ancient springs along the "north bank" of the site that discharged into the old basin and resulted in deposition of the "gray Sand." Haynes then argued that the spring-laid deposits were time-transgressive but essentially pre-dated the earliest human occupation. The issue, however, is controversial. Green (1992:336) argues that "the gray sand in the north bank was of Clovis age in its entirety and may have represented the complete span of Clovis cultural activity on the southern High Plains." This point is significant because no site on the Great Plains is known to contain an in situ record of the "entire span of Clovis cultural activity." Haynes et al. (1992) point out, however, that most Clovis material comes from the upper gray sand or directly above it and that there is clear evidence for intrusion of Clovis artifacts deep into the gray sand and below it. The issue is likely to remain unresolved because the north bank of the site was destroyed by gravel mining.

Haynes (1968) was the first to correlate the geocultural stratigraphy of the Southern High Plains with other regions of North America. He fit the stratigraphy of the Clovis site into his "alluvial chronology," which had important implications for regional archaeological chronology, paleoenvironmental reconstructions, and landscape evolution.

Beginning with the work at Lubbock Lake, the resurgence of interdisciplinary archaeological investigations in the Southern High Plains in the 1980s and 1990s significantly expanded our understanding of regional stratigraphy, geochronology, and paleoenvironments. Several examples illustrate this point. The stratigraphic record preserved in the draws has long been used for correlation of archaeological sites and climatic episodes. Between 1988 and 1993, systematic investigations of the fill in the draws showed that the general stratigraphic sequence is remarkably similar along and between most of the draws

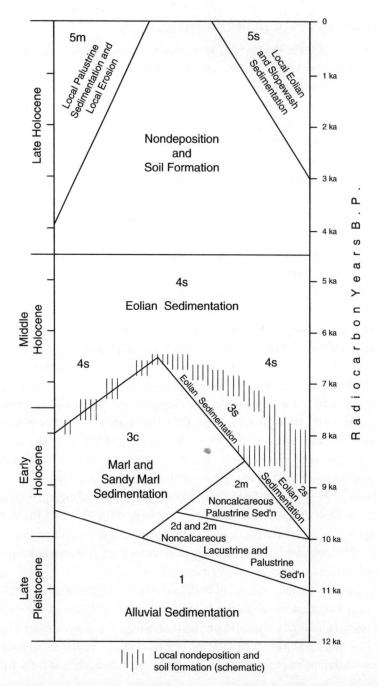

Fig. 2.5. Schematic illustration of depositional chronology (vertical scale) and relative dominance of depositional environments (horizontal scale) in draws of the Southern High Plains (from Holliday 1995b:fig. 19).

of the Brazos and Colorado systems (Holliday 1995b). The research also shows, however, that the stratigraphic units are time-transgressive (fig. 2.5), generally becoming younger down-draw. One discovery in this research is the very limited extent of sites with diatomite, diatomaceous earth, and muds of Paleoindian age. The presence of these deposits at such widely separated sites as Clovis, Lubbock Lake, and Mustang Springs (Meltzer and Collins 1987; Meltzer 1991) suggested that these sediments would be relatively common. This is not the case.

Correlation of the location of these lacustrine and paludal deposits with locations of historic springs, along with the time-transgressive nature of the valley fill, suggest that much of the stratigraphic record in the draws is related to spring discharge (Holliday 1995b). Stratified, multicomponent archaeological sites also seem to be associated with springs (Holliday 1995b, 1997a). The location of historic springs, therefore, may be a clue to archaeological sites with long, stratified records.

In 1983 renewed archaeological and geological research at the Clovis site resulted in several significant discoveries. Earlier mining of gravel at the site removed substantial quantities of archaeological material (Hester 1972), and the site was considered largely destroyed. Coring and excavation in 1983 and 1984 revealed, however, that a substantial body of archaeologically important late Quaternary valley fill is preserved in the outlet channel that connects the paleobasin with Blackwater Draw (Haynes 1995; Stanford et al. 1990). Stratigraphic mapping and radiocarbon accelerator-mass spectrometer (AMS) dating of this channel fill exposed in the walls of the gravel pit are significant. They document the relationship of lowland and upland facies, which aids in stratigraphic and archaeological correlation. They also show, locally, a major erosional disconformity between strata with Paleoindian debris and later Archaic-age deposits, as well as multiple early, middle, and late Holocene eolian deposits. Both conditions make within-basin stratigraphic and archaeological correlations more difficult but also clarify some long-standing issues of lithostratigraphy and chronostratigraphy at the site (Haynes et al. 1992; Haynes 1995).

Geoarchaeological studies in the 1980s and 1990s also focused on the environment of the early and middle Holocene. Previous investigators correlated Holocene deposits at specific sites with the geologic-climatic sequence proposed by Antevs (1948) for the western United States (Wendorf 1961; Green 1962a; Haynes 1975). Antevs's "Altithermal" drought was of particular interest. Subsequently, the occurrence of early to middle Holocene eolian sediments in

all dated stratigraphic records from draws, dunes, and playas in the region suggested that the Southern High Plains had, indeed, been subjected to drought
between 9000 and 4500 B.P. (Holliday 1989b, 1995a,b). Additional evidence for
the Altithermal on the Llano Estacado and human response to it was provided
by the artificially excavated wells found first at the Clovis site (Evans 1951;
Green 1962b) and later at the Mustang Springs site (Meltzer and Collins 1987;
Meltzer 1991). Evans (1951) recognized that the wells were a response to
drought, but did not place them in a regional climatic framework. Based on
his discovery of additional wells at Clovis and also on stratigraphic data, Green
(1962b) was the first to provide clear evidence that the Altithermal affected the
southern Great Plains (although Antevs 1949:186, inferred Altithermal conditions for the Clovis site; fig. 2.1). Mustang Springs yielded evidence for an
extensive well field (Meltzer and Collins 1987; Meltzer 1991), and Meltzer (1991)
used a variety of geologic arguments to support his contention that the pits
were not only artificially excavated, but were also related to drought-related
drops in the water table. Research on the Altithermal of the Southern High
Plains resulted in the development of a model for likely prehistoric responses
to such environmental conditions (Meltzer 1995, 1999).

The application of soil science has been an important methodological
development in geoarchaeology on the Llano Estacado. Buried "humus zones"
(buried A-horizons) were first noted in archaeological contexts in the region
during initial excavations at Lubbock Lake (1939 and 1941) (J. B. Wheat, field
notes on file, Museum of Texas Tech University; Wheat 1974). They were identified as marking stable land surfaces and utilized as stratigraphic markers.
Soils were similarly recognized and used for stratigraphic correlation at San
Jon (Judson 1953) and Midland (Wendorf et al. 1955), as well as in and around
Clovis (Haynes 1975). Wendorf et al. (1955) and Haynes (1975) also used soils
as environmental indicators (i.e., as indicators of more moist conditions following periods of relative aridity and eolian deposition). Systematic and widespread geoarchaeological application of soil science began with the Lubbock
Lake Project (C. Johnson 1974; Stafford 1981). Soils have proved very useful for
stratigraphic correlations, for age estimations of strata, and for reconstructing
paleoenvironments and site formation processes at Lubbock Lake (Holliday
1985b,d, 1988, 1992; Holliday and Allen 1987; Johnson and Holliday 1989) (fig.
2.3) and other localities throughout the region (Holliday 1985a,e, 1989b,
1995a,b, 1997a; Johnson et al. 1982).

PALEOINDIAN CHRONOLOGY

More than sixty years of geoarchaeological research on the Southern High Plains has contributed substantially to establishing the Paleoindian cultural chronology of the region. This research was also key in sorting out Great Plains cultural chronologies and contributing to a broader perspective of Paleoindian studies in North America.

Chronological differentiation of Clovis and Folsom occupations was first made at the Clovis site based on stratigraphic relationships. Following the initial Folsom discoveries in 1926–1928, Folsom points were recognized immediately as distinctive in technology and type. Formal differentiation between "Folsom" and "Clovis," however, took well over a decade to resolve. In the years following the Folsom finds, fluted points found in association with mammoth bones at Dent, Colorado (Figgins 1933), Clovis (Cotter 1937), and Miami (Sellards 1938) were differentiated from "True Folsom" by terms such as "Folsom-like," "Folsomoid," and "Generalized Folsom" (Wormington 1957:30). By the late 1930s, the typological and chronological distinctions between Clovis and Folsom points were all but formalized (Holliday and Anderson 1993; Holliday 2000a). In 1941, a symposium on Paleoindian terminology was held in Santa Fe (Howard 1943; Wormington 1948, 1957). The group decided to differentiate the various fluted types, thus defining the Folsom and Clovis types so familiar today.

Confirmation of the stratigraphic and relative chronologic relationship between Clovis and Folsom came with renewed excavations at Clovis by Sellards, Evans, and Meade. Folsom artifacts were consistently found in the diatomite and diatomaceous muds whereas Clovis material always came from the underlying sands (Sellards 1952:29–31, 54–58). Both Cotter (1938) and Sellards (1952) noted apparent faunal relationships (Clovis and mammoth, Folsom and bison) that were long considered characteristic of these early Paleoindian occupations. Subsequent work at Clovis and other sites shows this inferred relationship to be more complex than it first seemed (Hester 1972; Johnson 1986).

After the Folsom discoveries, one of the first stylistic differentiations noticed among Paleoindian projectile points was fluted versus unfluted (usually lanceolate) (e.g., Renaud 1931). In the 1940s, various lanceolate styles were found in sites in association with the remains of extinct bison. The Plainview artifact style, established by Sellards et al. (1947) on the basis of their work at the Plainview site, became the first unfluted Paleoindian point type to be formally described and proposed based on a sizeable collection. The age relationships of Plainview to other Paleoindian styles were unclear, however, because the site contained no archaeological features other than the bone bed with Plainview points and exposed no distinctive stratigraphic marker beds such as diatomites and diatomaceous muds. Sellards et al. (1947) believed that the Plainview style postdated Folsom on the basis of technological and morphological traits. Sellards and Evans (1960) supported this view based on several radiocarbon ages from Plainview and Lubbock Lake. This cultural chronological interpretation was correct, but the radiocarbon ages are questionable (Holliday and Johnson 1981; Holliday 1997a; Holliday et al. 1999).

Dating the Plainview site continues to be a vexing problem. The age of the Plainview occupation of the Southern High Plains has taken on added importance with the dating of the morphologically similar Goshen style to late Clovis or early Folsom time on the Northern Plains (Frison 1991, 1996) and the dating of Plainview-like artifacts to around 9000 B.P. at the Horace Rivers site just north of the Southern High Plains (Mallouf and Mandel 1997). An attempt was made to date bone associated with the Plainview-type collection using the AMS radiocarbon method, but the results are a frustratingly wide array of ages (Holliday et al. 1999). At other sites in the region, however, Plainview is clearly both locally late-Folsom and post-Folsom in age based on stratigraphy and radiocarbon dating (Dibble and Lorraine 1968; Dibble 1972; Harrison and Killen 1978; Johnson and Holliday 1980; Holliday and Johnson 1981). As of this writing, Plainview appears to date to 10,000±500 B.P., but may have continued to as late as 9000 B.P.

Along with determining the stratigraphic relationship of Clovis to Folsom, Sellards's crews at Clovis provided the first documentation of the stratigraphic and relative chronologic relationships of lanceolate styles to fluted forms. Excavations in several bone beds yielded a collection of lanceolate points that Sellards (1952) used to define the "Portales Complex." The points were recovered stratigraphically above Folsom features, establishing the unfluted Paleoindian styles as later than the fluted points (Sellards 1952).

Sellards's work at Clovis and Lubbock coincided with the development of radiocarbon dating. After the discovery of burned bone in the diatomaceous muds at Lubbock Lake in 1950, Sellards decided to submit a sample to Willard Libby, who was in the early stages of applying the radiocarbon method he had just developed. The bone was interpreted as coming from the same zone that yielded Folsom artifacts elsewhere in the site, and the resulting radiocarbon age (9883±350 B.P., C-558; Libby 1952:82) is one of the first applications of radiocarbon dating to Paleoindian archaeology and is thought to be the first date on the Folsom culture (Roberts 1951; Taylor 1985). Other investigators later questioned the date and the association with Folsom (Holliday and Johnson 1986), but determination and publication of the age were nevertheless landmarks in Paleoindian studies and brought Lubbock Lake into prominence.

CONCLUSIONS

Geoarchaeology has played an important role in archaeological research on the Southern High Plains for over a half century. Historically, researchers used geoarchaeology to establish cultural chronologies (Sellards 1952; Sellards and Evans 1960) and for some environmental reconstructions (Stock and Bode 1936; Sellards and Evans 1960; Green 1962b). More recently, geoarchaeological studies have made significant contributions in all of the traditional roles: stratigraphic correlations, dating, and paleoenvironmental reconstructions. Such research is best exemplified in the draws, where such site-specific geoarchaeological studies as the intensive and extensive work at Clovis (e.g., Haynes 1995) and Lubbock Lake (e.g., Holliday 1985b) were complemented by a regional stratigraphic study (Holliday 1995b). The resulting understanding of facies variations across the draws proved especially useful in placing the well-known human remains from the Midland site in a firmer chronological context (Holliday and Meltzer 1996) and in reconstructing the setting of Paleoindian occupations (Holliday 1997a). At a regional scale, this research provides a better understanding of paleoenvironmental changes in the draws. The depositional environments varied considerably from site to site in the late Pleistocene and early Holocene periods. The resulting lithostratigraphic units are asynchronous along the valleys. As a result, we must make time-stratigraphic correlations between archaeological sites in draws with considerable caution.

Although best known for providing geochronological or paleoenvironmental contexts for Paleoindian occupations, the past and present geoarchaeological investigations in the principal late Quaternary depositional environments (draws, dunes, and playas), integrated with other Quaternary studies, provide a better understanding of post-Paleoindian environments. Particular attention has focused on aridity during the early Archaic (the Altithermal) (Green 1962b; Meltzer and Collins 1987; Holliday 1989b, 1995b; Meltzer 1991; Quigg et al. 1994) and on environmental fluctuations during the Late Prehistoric and Historic periods (Holliday 1995b; Muhs and Holliday 1995).

Combining site-specific and regional geoscientific studies should provide a better understanding of how humans used the landscape although such studies are relatively rare (Hester 1975; Holliday 1997a, 2000b; Meltzer 1995, 1999). Moreover, geoarchaeological studies, inseparable from Quaternary research, provide a holistic view of the broader physical setting and the landscape and environmental evolution of the Southern High Plains throughout the past twelve thousand years of human occupation.

ACKNOWLEDGEMENTS

I thank Rolfe Mandel for organizing the symposium that led to this volume and for seeing the publication process through to the end. Mandel, C. Reid Ferring (University of North Texas), Marvin Kay (University of Arkansas), Marlin Hawley (State Historical Society of Wisconsin), C. Vance Haynes (University of Arizona), David J. Meltzer (Southern Methodist University), and Don Wyckoff (University of Oklahoma) provided helpful criticism of the manuscript. This chapter is dedicated to the memory of F. Earl Green (1925–1998).

REFERENCES

Agogino, G. A., and I. Rovner. 1969. Preliminary report of a stratified post-Folsom sequence at Blackwater Draw Locality No. 1. *American Antiquity* 34:175–76.

Agogino, G. A., D. K. Patterson, and D. E. Patterson. 1976. Blackwater Draw Locality No. 1, south bank: Report for the summer of 1974. *Plains Anthropologist* 21:213–23.

Antevs, E. 1935. The occurrence of flints and extinct animals in pluvial deposits near Clovis, New Mexico, part III: Age of Clovis lake beds. *Proceedings of the Philadelphia Academy of Natural Sciences* 87:304–11.

———. 1948. Climatic changes and pre-White Man. *In* The Great Basin with emphasis on glacial and postglacial times. *Bulletin of the University of Utah* 38, no. 20:168–91.

————. 1949. Geology of the Clovis sites. *In* Wormington, H. M., Ancient Man in North America, 185–92. Denver: Denver Museum of Natural History.

Black, C. C., ed. 1974. History and prehistory of the Lubbock Lake site. West Texas Museum Association, *The Museum Journal* 15:1–160.

Blaine, J. C. 1968. Preliminary report of an Early Man site in West Texas. Transactions of the Regional Archaeological Symposium for Southwestern New Mexico and Western Texas 3:1–11.

Blair, W. F. 1950. The biotic provinces of Texas. *Texas Journal of Science* 2:93–117.

Boldurian, A. 1990. Lithic technology at the Mitchell Locality of Blackwater Draw. Plains Anthropologist Memoir, vol. 24. Lincoln: Nebraska Anthropological Association.

Caran, S. C. 1991. Geomorphic analysis. *In* Peterson, J. A., ed., Prairie hinterland: The archaeology of Palo Duro Creek, Phase II: Testing, 343–97. Austin: Archaeological Research Inc.

Carr, J. T. 1967. The climate and physiography of Texas. Report 53. Austin: Texas Water Development Board.

Clarke, W. T., Jr. 1938. The occurrence of flints and extinct animals in pluvial deposits near Clovis, New Mexico, part VII: The Pleistocene mollusks from the Clovis gravel pit and vicinity. *Proceedings of the Philadelphia Academy of Natural Sciences* 90:119–21.

Cotter, J. L. 1937. The occurrence of flints and extinct animals in pluvial deposits near Clovis, New Mexico, part IV—Report on excavation at the gravel pit, 1936. *Proceedings of the Philadelphia Academy of Natural Sciences* 90:2–16.

————. 1938. The occurrence of flints and extinct animals in pluvial deposits near Clovis, New Mexico, part VI—Report on the field season of 1937. *Proceedings of the Philadelphia Academy of Natural Sciences* 90:113–17.

Dibble, D. S. 1970. On the significance of additional radiocarbon dates from Bonfire Shelter, Texas. *Plains Anthropologist* 15:251–54.

Dibble, D. S., and D. Lorrain. 1968. Bonfire Shelter: A stratified bison kill site, Val Verde County, Texas. Austin: Texas Memorial Museum Miscellaneous Papers 1.

Evans, G. L. 1949. Upper Cenozoic of the High Plains. *In* Cenozoic geology of the Llano Estacado and Rio Grande Valley. *West Texas Geological Society Guidebook* 2:1–22.

————. 1951. Prehistoric wells in eastern New Mexico. *American Antiquity* 17:1–8.

————. 1986. E. H. Sellards' contributions to Paleoindian studies. *In* Holliday, V. T., ed., Guidebook to the archaeological geology of classic Paleoindian sites of the Southern High Plains, Texas and New Mexico, 7–18. Guidebook for the 1986 Annual Meeting of the Geological Society of America. College Station, Tex.: Department of Geography, Texas A&M University.

Evans, G. L., and G. E. Meade. 1945. Quaternary of the Texas High Plains. Austin: The University of Texas Publication 4401, 485–507.

Ferring, C. R. 1994. The role of geoarchaeology in Paleoindian research. *In* Bonnichsen, R., and D. G. Steele, eds., Method and theory for investigating the
peopling of the Americas, 57–72. Orono, Maine: Center for the Study of
the First Americans, University of Maine.

Figgins, J. D. 1933. A further contribution to the antiquity of Man in America.
Denver: *Proceedings of the Colorado Museum of Natural History* 12:4–10.

Frederick, C. D. 1993a. Geomorphic investigations. *In* Quigg, J. M., C. D.
Frederick, and C. Lintz, Sulphur Springs Draw: Archaeological and geomorphological investigations at Red Lake dam axis, borrow area, and spill-
way, Martin County, Texas. Mariah Technical Report 873:36–49. Austin:
Mariah Associates, Inc.

———. 1993b. Geomorphology. *In* Quigg, J. M. and others. Historic and prehistoric data recovery at Paleo Duro Reservoir, Hansford County, Texas.
Mariah Technical Report 485:75–116. Austin: Mariah and Associates, Inc.

———. 1994. Late Quaternary geology of the Sulphur Draw Reservoir. *In*
Quigg, J. M., C. D. Frederick, and C. Lintz, Sulphur Springs Draw: Geoarchaeological and archaeological investigations at Sulphur Draw Reservoir, Martin County, Texas. Mariah Technical Report 776:29–82. Austin:
Mariah Associates, Inc.

Frison, G. C. 1991. Prehistoric hunters of the High Plains, 2d ed. New York:
Academic Press.

———., ed. 1996. The Mill Iron site. Albuquerque: University of New Mexico
Press.

Green, F. E. 1961. The Monahans Dunes area. *In* Wendorf, F., assembler, Paleoecology of the Llano Estacado. Fort Burgwin Research Center Publication 1:22–47. Santa Fe: The Museum of New Mexico Press.

———. 1962a. The Lubbock Reservoir site. West Texas Museum Association,
The Museum Journal 6:83–123.

———. 1962b. Additional notes on prehistoric wells at the Clovis site. *American Antiquity* 28:230–34.

———. 1963. The Clovis blades: An important addition to the Llano complex.
American Antiquity 29:145–65.

———. 1992. Comments on the report of a worked mammoth tusk from the
Clovis site. *American Antiquity* 29:331–37.

Gustavson, T. C. 1996. Fluvial and eolian depositional systems paleosols and
paleoclimate of the Upper Cenozoic Ogallala and Blackwater Draw Formations, Southern High Plains, Texas and New Mexico. Austin: University
of Texas at Austin, Bureau of Economic Geology report of Investigations
239.

Gustavson, T. C., and V. T. Holliday. 1999. Eolian sedimentation and soil development on a semiarid to subhumid grassland, Tertiary Ogallala and Quaternary Blackwater Draw Formations, Texas and New Mexico High Plains.
Journal of Sedimentary Research 69: 622–34.

Hafsten, U. 1964. A standard pollen diagram for the southern High Plains, USA, covering the period back to the early Wisconsin glaciation. Warsaw, Poland: 6th International Quaternary Congress, 1961, Report 2:407–20.

Harbour, J. 1975. General stratigraphy. *In* Wendorf, F., and J. J. Hester, eds., Late Pleistocene environments of the Southern High Plains. Taos, N.Mex.: Publications of the Fort Burgwin Research Center 9:33–55.

Harrison, B. R., and Killen, K. L. 1978. Lake Theo: A stratified, Early Man bison butchering and camp site, Briscoe County, Texas, Archeological Investigations Phase II. Canyon, Tex., Panhandle-Plains Historical Museum Special Archeological Report 1.

Hawley, J. W., G. O. Bachman, and K. Manley. 1976. Quaternary stratigraphy in the Basin and Range and Great Basin Provinces, New Mexico and western Texas. *In* Mahaney, W.C., ed., Quaternary stratigraphy of North America, 235–74. Stroudsburg, Pa.: Dowden, Hutchinson and Ross, Inc.

Haynes, C. V., Jr. 1968. Geochronology of late-Quaternary alluvium. *In* Morrison, R. B., and H. E. Wright Jr., eds., Means of correlation of Quaternary successions, 591–631. Salt Lake City: University of Utah Press.

———. 1975. Pleistocene and Recent stratigraphy. *In* Wendorf, F., and J. J. Hester, eds. Late Pleistocene Environments of the Southern High Plains. Taos, N.Mex.: Publication of the Fort Burgwin Research Center 9:57–96.

———. 1990. The Antevs-Bryan years and the legacy for Paleoindian geochronology. *In* Laporte, L. F., ed., Establishment of a geologic framework for paleoanthropology. Boulder, Colo.: The Geological Society of America, Special Paper 242:55–68.

———. 1991. Geoarchaeological and paleohydrological evidence for a Clovis-age drought in North America and its bearing on extinction. *Quaternary Research* 35:438–50.

———. 1995. Geochronology of paleoenvironmental change, Clovis type site, Blackwater Draw, New Mexico. *Geoarchaeology* 10:317–88.

Haynes, C. V., Jr., and G. A. Agogino. 1966. Prehistoric springs and geochronology of the Clovis site, New Mexico. *American Antiquity* 31:812–21.

Haynes, C. V., Jr., J. J. Saunders, D. Stanford, and G. A. Agogino. 1992. Reply to F. E. Green's comments on the Clovis site. *American Antiquity* 57:338–44.

Hester, J. J. 1962. A Folsom lithic complex from the Elida site, Roosevelt County, N.M. *El Palacio* 69:92–113.

———., compiler. 1972. Blackwater Locality no. 1: A stratified Early Man site in eastern New Mexico. Taos, N.Mex.: Publication of the Ft. Burgwin Research Center 8:1–239.

———. 1975. Paleoarchaeology of the Llano Estacado. *In* Wendorf, F., and J. J. Hester, eds., Late Pleistocene environments of the Southern High Plains. Taos, N.Mex.: Publication of the Ft. Burgwin Research Center 9:247–56.

Hill, M. G., V. T. Holliday, and D. J. Stanford. 1995. A further evaluation of the San Jon site, New Mexico. *Plains Anthropologist* 40:369–90.

Hofman, J. L. 1989. Prehistoric culture history—Hunters and gatherers in the Southern Great Plains. *In* Hofman, J., R. L. Brooks, J. S. Hays, D. W. Owsley, R. L. Jantz, M. K. Marks, and M. H. Manhein. From Clovis to Comanchero: Archeological overview of the Southern Great Plains. Fayetteville, Ark.: Archeological Survey Research Series 35:25–60.

Hofman, J. L., L. C. Todd, C. B. Schultz, and W. Hendy. 1989. The Lipscomb bison quarry: Continuing investigation at a Folsom kill-butchery site on the Southern Plains. *Bulletin of the Texas Archeological Society* 60:149–89.

Hofman, J. L., D. S. Amick, and R. O. Rose. 1990. Shifting Sands: A Folsom-Midland assemblage from a campsite in western Texas. *Plains Anthropologist* 35:221–53.

Holliday, V. T. 1985a. Holocene soil-geomorphological relations in a semi-arid environment: The Southern High Plains of Texas. *In* Boardman, J., ed., Soils and Quaternary landscape evolution, 325–57. New York: John Wiley and Sons.

———. 1985b. Archaeological geology of the Lubbock Lake site, Southern High Plains of Texas. *Geological Society of America Bulletin* 96:1483–92.

———. 1985c. Morphology of late Holocene soils at the Lubbock Lake site, Texas. *Soil Science Society of America Journal* 49: 938–46.

———. 1985d. Early Holocene soils at the Lubbock Lake archaeological site, Texas. *Catena* 12:61–78.

———. 1985e. New data on the stratigraphy and pedology of the Clovis and Plainview sites, Southern High Plains. *Quaternary Research* 23:388–402.

———. 1987. Re-examination of late-Pleistocene boreal forest reconstructions for the Southern High Plains. *Quaternary Research* 28:238–44.

———. 1988. Genesis of late Holocene soils at the Lubbock Lake archaeological site, Texas. *Annals of the Association of American Geographers* 23:594–610.

———. 1989a. The Blackwater Draw Formation (Quaternary): A 1.4-plus m.y. record of eolian sedimentation and soil formation on the Southern High Plains. *Geological Society of America Bulletin* 101:1598–1607.

———. 1989b. Middle Holocene drought on the Southern High Plains. *Quaternary Research* 31:74–82.

———. 1992. Soil formation, time, and archaeology. *In* Holliday, V. T., ed., Soils in archaeology: Landscape evolution and human occupation, 101–17. Washington, D.C.: Smithsonian Institution Press.

———. 1995a. Late Quaternary stratigraphy of the Southern High Plains. *In* Johnson, E., ed., Ancient peoples and landscapes, 289–313. Lubbock: Museum of Texas Tech University.

———. 1995b. Stratigraphy and paleoenvironments of late Quaternary valley fills on the Southern High Plains. Boulder, Colo.: The Geological Society of America, Memoir 186.

———. 1997a. Paleoindian Geoarchaeology of the Southern High Plains. Austin: University of Texas Press.

―――――. 1997b. Origin and evolution of lunettes on the High Plains of Texas and New Mexico. *Quaternary Research* 47:54–69.

―――――. 2000a. The evolution of Paleoiodian geochronology and typology on the Great Plains. *Geoarchaeology* 15: 227–90.

―――――. 2000b. folsom drought and episodic drying on the Southern High Plains from 10,900–10,200 ^{14}C yr B.P. *Quaternary Research* 53: 1–12.

Holliday, V. T., and B. L. Allen. 1987. Geology and soils. *In* Johnson, E., ed., Lubbock Lake: Late Quaternary studies on the Southern High Plains, 14–21. College Station: Texas A&M University Press.

Holliday, V. T., and A. B. Anderson. 1993. "Paleoindian", "Clovis" and "Folsom": A brief etymology. *Current Research in the Pleistocene* 10:79–81.

Holliday, V. T., and E. Johnson. 1981. An Update on the Plainview Occupation at the Lubbock Lake Site. *Plains Anthropologist* 26:251–53.

―――――. 1986. Re-evaluation of the First Radiocarbon Age for the Folsom Culture. *American Antiquity* 51:332–38.

Holliday, V. T., and D. J. Meltzer. 1996. Geoarchaeology of the Midland (Paleoindian) site. *American Antiquity* 61:755–71.

Holliday, V. T., E. Johnson, and T. W. Stafford Jr. 1999. AMS radiocarbon dating of the type Plainview and Firstview (Paleoindian) type assemblages. *American Antiquity* 64: 444–54.

Holliday, V. T., S. D. Hovorka, and T. C. Gustavson. 1996. Lithostratigraphy and geochronology of fills in small playa basins on the Southern High Plains. *Geological Society of America Bulletin* 108:953–65.

Holliday, V. T., C. V. Haynes Jr., J. L. Hofman, and D. J. Meltzer. 1994. Geoarchaeology and geochronology of the Miami (Clovis) site on the Southern High Plains of Texas. *Quaternary Research* 41:234–44.

Honea, K. 1980. The Marks Beach site, stratified Paleoindian site, Lamb County, Texas. *Bulletin of the Texas Archeological Society* 51:243–69.

Howard, E. B. 1935. Evidence of Early Man in North America. Philadelphia: University of Pennsylvania Museum, *The Museum Journal* 24:2–3.

―――――. 1943. The Finley site: Discovery of Yuma points, in situ, near Eden, Wyoming. *American Antiquity* 8:224–34.

Hrdlička, A. 1918. Recent discoveries attributed to Early Man in America. *Bureau of American Ethnology Bulletin* 66:1–67.

Huffington, R. M., and C. C. Albritton Jr. 1941. Quaternary sands on the Southern High Plains of western Texas. *American Journal of Science* 239:325–38.

Hunt, C. B. 1974. Natural Regions of the United States and Canada. San Francisco: W. H. Freeman.

Johnson, C. A. 1974. Geologic investigations at the Lubbock Lake site. *In* Black, C. C., ed., History and Prehistory of the Lubbock Lake site. West Texas Museum Association, *The Museum Journal* 15:79–105.

Johnson, E. 1986. Late Pleistocene and early Holocene paleoenvironments on the Southern High Plains (USA). *Geographie Physique et Quaternaire* 40:249–61.

————, ed. 1987. Lubbock Lake: Late Quaternary studies on the Southern High Plains. College Station: Texas A&M University Press.

Johnson, E., and V. T. Holliday. 1980. A Plainview kill/butchering locale on the Llano Estacado—the Lubbock Lake site. *Plains Anthropologist* 25:89–111.

————. 1981. Late Paleoindian activity at the Lubbock Lake site. *Plains Anthropologist* 26:173–93.

————. 1986. The Archaic record at Lubbock Lake. *Plains Anthropologist Memoir* 21:7–54.

————. 1989. Lubbock Lake: Late Quaternary cultural and environmental change on the Southern High Plains, USA. *Journal of Quaternary Science* 4:145–65.

Johnson, E., V. T. Holliday, and R. Neck. 1982. Lake Theo: Late Quaternary paleoenvironmental data and new Plainview (Paleoindian) date. *North American Archaeologist* 3:113–37.

Johnson, E., V. T. Holliday, J. Warnica, and T. Williamson. 1986. The Milnesand and Ted Williamson Paleoindian sites, east-central New Mexico. *Current Research in the Pleistocene* 3: 9–11.

Judson, S. 1950. Depression of the northern portion of the Southern High Plains of Eastern New Mexico. *Bulletin of the Geological Society of America* 61:253–74.

————. 1953. Geology of the San Jon site, eastern New Mexico. Washington, D.C.: Smithsonian Miscellaneous Collection 121:1–70.

Kelley, J. H. 1974. A brief resume of artifacts collected at the Lubbock Lake site prior to 1961. *In* Black, C. C., ed., History and prehistory of the Lubbock Lake site. West Texas Museum Association, *The Museum Journal* 15:15–42.

Libby, W. 1952. Radiocarbon Dating. Chicago: University of Chicago Press.

Lohman, K. E. 1935. Diatoms from Quaternary lake beds near Clovis, New Mexico. *Journal of Paleontology* 9:455–59.

Lotspeich, F. B., and M. E. Everhart. 1962. Climate and vegetation as soil forming factors on the Llano Estacado. *Journal of Range Management* 15:134–141.

Mallouf, R. J., R. D. Mandel. 1997. Horace Rivers: A Late-Plainview component in the northeastern Texas Panhandle. *Current Research in the Pleistocene* 14:50–52.

Meltzer, D. J. 1983. The antiquity of man and the development of American archaeology. *Advances in Archaeological Method and Theory* 6:1–51.

————. 1991. Altithermal archaeology and paleoecology at Mustang Springs, on the Southern High Plains of Texas. *American Antiquity* 56:236–67.

————. 1995. Modeling the prehistoric response to Altithermal climates on the Southern High Plains. *In* Johnson, E., ed., Ancient peoples and landscapes, 349–56. Lubbock: Museum of Texas Tech University.

————. 1999. Human responses to middle Holocene (Altithermal) climates on the North American Great Plains. *Quaternary Research* 52:404–16.

Meltzer, D. J., and M. B. Collins. 1987. Prehistoric water wells on the Southern High Plains: Clues to Altithermal climate. *Journal of Field Archaeology* 14:9–27.

Muhs, D. R., and V. T. Holliday. 1995. Active dune sand on the Great Plains in the 19th century: Evidence from accounts of early explorers. *Quaternary Research* 43:198–208.

Oldfield, F. 1975. Pollen-analytical results, part II. *In* Wendorf, F., and J. J. Hester, eds., Late Pleistocene environments of the Southern High Plains. Taos: N.Mex., Ft. Burgwin Research Center Publication 9:121-47.

Oldfield, F., and J. Schoenwetter. 1964. Late Quaternary environments of Early Man on the Southern High Plains. *Antiquity* 38:226–29.

———. 1975. Discussion of the pollen-analytical evidence. *In* Wendorf, F., and J. J. Hester, eds., Late Pleistocene environments of the Southern High Plains. Taos: N.Mex., Ft. Burgwin Research Center Publications 9:149–77.

Patrick, R. 1938. The occurrence of flints and extinct animals in pluvial deposits near Clovis, New Mexico, Part V: Diatom evidence from the mammoth pit. *Proceedings of the Philadelphia Academy of Natural Science* 90:15–24.

Quigg, J. M., C. D. Frederick, and C. Lintz. 1994. Sulphur Springs Draw: Geoarchaeological and archaeological investigations at Sulphur Draw Reservoir, Martin County, Texas. Mariah Technical Report 776. Austin: Mariah Associates, Inc.

Rapp, G., Jr., and C. L. Hill. 1998. Geoarchaeology: The earth-science approach to archaeological interpretation. New Haven: Yale University Press.

Reeves, C. C., Jr. 1965 Chronology of west Texas pluvial lake dunes. *Journal of Geology* 73:504–508.

———. 1966. Pluvial lake basins of west Texas. *Journal of Geology* 74:269–91.

———. 1972. Tertiary-Quaternary stratigraphy and geomorphology of west Texas and southeastern New Mexico. *In* Kelley, V., and F. D. Trauger, eds., Guidebook for East-Central New Mexico. Socorro, N.Mex.: New Mexico Geological Society Guidebook 24:108–17.

———. 1976. Quaternary stratigraphy and geological history of the Southern High Plains, Texas and New Mexico. *In* Mahaney, W. C., ed., Quaternary stratigraphy of North America, 213–34. Stroudsburg, Pa.: Dowden, Hutchinson and Ross.

———. 1991. Origin and stratigraphy of alkaline lake basins, Southern High Plains. *In* Morrison, R. B., ed., Quaternary nonglacial geology: Conterminous U.S. Boulder, Colo.: The Geological Society of America, Centennial Volume K-2:484–86.

Reeves, C. C., Jr. and J. A. Reeves. 1996. The Ogallala Aquifer (of the Southern High Plains), vol. 1: Geology. Lubbock, Tex.: Estacado Books.

Renaud, E. B. 1931. Prehistoric flaked points from Colorado and neighboring districts. Denver: *Proceedings of the Colorado Museum of Natural History* 10:24.

Roberts, F. H. H. 1942. Archaeological and geological investigations in the San Jon district, eastern New Mexico. Washington, D.C.: Smithsonian Miscellaneous Collections 3:1–39.

————. 1943. Edgar Billings Howard. *American Anthropologist* 45:452–454.

————. 1951. Radiocarbon dates and Early Man. *In* Johnson, F., assembler, Radiocarbon dating. *Memoirs of the Society for American Archaeology* 8:20–22.

Schoenwetter, J. 1975, Pollen-analytical results, part I. *In* Wendorf, F., and J. J. Hester, eds., Late Pleistocene environments of the Southern High Plains. Taos, N.Mex.: Ft. Burgwin Research Center Publication 9:103–20.

Schultz, G. E. 1986. Biostratigraphy and volcanic ash deposits of the Tule Formation, Briscoe County, Texas. *In* Gustavson, T. C., ed., Geomorphology and Quaternary stratigraphy of the Rolling Plains, Texas Panhandle. Austin: University of Texas, Bureau of Economic Geology Guidebook 22:82–84.

Sellards, E. H. 1916. Human remains and associated fossils from the Pleistocene of Florida. Tallahassee: Florida Geological Survey, 8th Annual Report, 123–60.

————. 1917. Further notes on human remains from Vero, Florida. *American Anthropologist* 19:239–51.

————. 1938. Artifacts associated with fossil elephant. *Geological Society of America Bulletin* 49:999–1010.

————. 1952. Early Man in America. Austin: University of Texas Press.

————. 1955a. Fossil bison and associated artifacts from Milnesand, New Mexico. *American Antiquity* 20:336–44.

————. 1955b. Further investigations at the Scharbauer site. *In* Wendorf, F., A. D. Krieger, A. D., and C. C. Albritton, Jr., The Midland Discovery, 126–32. Austin: University of Texas Press.

Sellards, E. H., and G. Evans. 1960. The Paleo-Indian cultural succession in the Central High Plains of Texas and New Mexico. *In* Wallace, A. F. C., ed., Men and cultures, 639–49. Philadelphia: University of Pennsylvania Press.

Sellards, E. H., G. L. Evans, and G. E. Meade. 1947. Fossil bison and associated artifacts from Plainview, Texas. *Geological Society of America Bulletin* 58:927–54.

Stafford, T. W. 1981. Alluvial geology and archaeological potential of the Texas Southern High Plains. *American Antiquity* 46:548–65.

Stanford, D., C. V. Haynes Jr., J. J. Saunders, G. A. Agogino, and A. T. Boldurian. 1990. Blackwater Draw Locality 1: History, current research, and interpretations. *In* Holliday, V. T., and Johnson, E., eds., Guidebook to the Quaternary history of the Llano Estacado, vol. 2., 105–28. Lubbock, Tex.: Lubbock Lake Landmark Quaternary Research Series.

Stevens, D. 1973. Blackwater Draw Locality No. 1, 1963–1972, and its relevance to the Firstview complex. Master's thesis. Portales: Eastern New Mexico University.

Stock, C. and F. D. Bode. 1936. The occurrence of flints and extinct animals in pluvial deposits near Clovis, New Mexico, part III: Geology and vertebrate paleontology. *Proceedings of the Philadelphia Academy of Natural Sciences* 88:219–41.

Taylor, R.E. 1985. The beginnings of radiocarbon dating in American Antiquity: A historical perspective. *American Antiquity* 50:309–25.

Walker, J. R. 1978. Geomorphic evolution of the Southern High Plains. Waco, Tex.: Baylor Geological Studies, Bulletin 35.

Wendorf, F., assembler. 1961. Paleoecology of the Llano Estacado. Santa Fe: The Museum of New Mexico Press, Ft. Burgwin Research Center Publication 1.

Wendorf, F. 1970. The Lubbock Subpluvial. *In* Dort, W., and J. K. Jones, eds., Pleistocene and Recent Environments of the Central Great Plains, 23–36. Lawrence: The University of Kansas Press.

———. 1975a. The modern environment. *In* Wendorf, F., and J. J. Hester, eds., Late Pleistocene environments of the Southern High Plains. Taos, N.Mex.: Ft. Burgwin Research Center Publication 9:1–12.

———. 1975b. Summary and conclusions. *In* Wendorf, F., and. J. J. Hester, eds., Late Pléistocene environments of the Southern High Plains. Taos, N.Mex.: Ft. Burgwin Research Center Publication 9:257-78.

Wendorf, F., and A. D. Krieger. 1959. New light on the Midland discovery. *American Antiquity* 25:66–78.

Wendorf, F., and J. J. Hester, eds. 1975. Late Pleistocene environments of the Southern High Plains. Taos, N.Mex.: Fort Burgwin Research Center Publication 9.

Wendorf, F., A. D. Krieger, C. C. Albritton Jr., and T. D. Stewart. 1955. The Midland Discovery. Austin: University of Texas Press.

Wheat, J. B. 1974. First excavations at the Lubbock Lake site. *In* Black, C. C., ed., History and prehistory of the Lubbock Lake site. West Texas Museum Association, *The Museum Journal* 15:15–42.

Willey, P. S., B. R. Harrison, T. J. Hughes. 1978. The Rex Rodgers site. *In* Hughes, J. T., and P. S. Willey, eds., Archaeology at MacKenzie Reservoir. Austin: Texas Historical Commission Archeological Survey Report 24:51–68.

Wormington, H. M. 1948. A proposed revision of Yuma point terminology. Denver: *Proceedings of the Colorado Museum of Natural History* 18.

———. 1957. Ancient Man in North America. 4th ed. Denver Museum of Natural History, Popular Series 4.

CHAPTER THREE

Geoarchaeology in the Southern Osage Plains

A HISTORICAL PERSPECTIVE

C. Reid Ferring

INTRODUCTION

For almost seventy years, researchers interested in the archaeology of the Southern Osage Plains have studied late Quaternary sediments. In recounting the history of these investigations, it was necessary to come upon an organizational framework that would not only provide the reader with a chronicle of the researches, but also would assess their development. In other words, I sought something other than a soporiphic annotated bibliography organized by decade.

Queries yielded possible organizational themes. Were there cumulative trends in the kinds of research conducted that showed changing (improving?) patterns of interaction between geologists and archaeologists? Were innovations in research concepts or methods made in this region? What role did institutions, including universities, museums, and funding agencies, play in the history of combined archaeologic and geologic research? Perhaps most important, how did the number and kind of geologic investigations relate to the intensity of archaeological research and to the problems that archaeologists were addressing?

After considerable reflection, I decided that certain trends could be identified, but that no clearly expressed pattern of cumulative disciplinary growth became evident until perhaps the last decade, when the number of people involved in geoarchaeology increased noticeably. Therefore, I organized the following review around a set of themes. Some of the themes are developmental segments of the historical story, while others are time-transgressive and nondevelopmental.

THE SOUTHERN OSAGE PLAINS

The geographic focus of this chapter is the southern part of the Osage Plains (Fenneman 1938), which here includes the portion of that physiographic province south of the Canadian River (map 3.1). Mandel considers the northern part of that province in this volume. The Southern Osage Plains is a broad expanse of low relief prairies. This region is bounded by the caprock escarpment of the High Plains on the west and the rugged, forested Ouachita Mountains and Ozark Plateau to the east (map 3.1). The southern boundary is the Edwards Plateau of Texas, a tableland formed on resistant Cretaceous limestone. The southeastern boundary is the indistinct transition to the Gulf Coastal Plain.

Except for the uplifted Wichita and Arbuckle Mountains of Oklahoma, the region is characterized by gentle relief; rolling terrain and low, hilly landforms have formed on differentially resistant sedimentary rocks. This landscape is broken primarily by the valleys of the east and southeast flowing rivers. The Canadian, Red, Brazos, and Colorado Rivers are the principal streams that flow across the entire region. These not only facilitated travel across the plains, but also promoted westward extension of vegetation communities into the plains from the moister eastern woodlands. Extensive dune fields are common along the northern or eastern margins of the valleys. Karstic features are common in the areas where Permian evaporites are present at or below the surface (Gustavson 1986; Caran and Baumgardner 1990; Gustavson et al. 1991), although the playa lakes common to the High Plains are very rare in the Southern Osage Plains (Madole et al. 1991). Studies of alluvial geology have been conducted on many smaller drainages, as discussed below, yet relatively little work has been done on the alluvial histories of larger rivers (Madole et al. 1991).

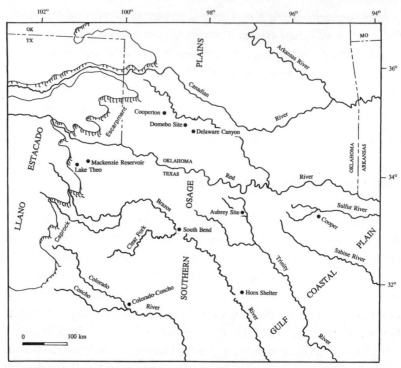

Map 3.1. Map of the Southern Plains, with locations of sites mentioned in the text.

This region has a subtropical climate. Precipitation deceases from west to east and is usually concentrated in the fall and spring (Bomar 1983). Winters are usually mild but with brief cold and wet periods. Southwesterly winds not only desiccate the soils, but also promote eolian transport of sand and silt, mainly in the western part of the region (Gustavson et al. 1991). Climatic gradients are registered in the vegetation associations, which shift from short-grass prairies in the west to mixed-grass prairies in the east, along the border of the eastern woodlands (Blair and Hubbell 1938; Blair 1950). Locally, vegetation and soil associations in this region usually correspond with bedrock lithology. For example in north-central Texas, calcareous soils supporting prairies occur over Cretaceous marls and limestones. Adjacent outcrops of sandstones with deep, well-drained sandy soils are covered by oak-hickory forests that are called the Cross Timbers (Hill 1901; Blair 1950).

There have been no attempts at a comprehensive archaeological overview of the whole region like Wedel's (1961) in recent years. Useful summaries include

Hofman et al. (1989) for the western part of the region, Bell (1984) and Bell and Baerreis (1951) for Oklahoma, and Story (1990) for the eastern part of the region. Ferring (1990a) discussed the archaeological geology of the whole Southern Plains, including the region considered here.

EARLY CONTROVERSIES AND AN ODD NUMBER OF GEOLOGISTS

Several localities discovered in the Southern Osage Plains in the 1920s were quickly added to the raging debates about the age of the initial human occupation of the New World. Moreover, the agenda for many subsequent arguments between and among geologists and archaeologists concerning archaeological associations and dating was exemplified by many of the sometimes-raucous debates over these sites.

In 1920 quarry workers unearthed a human skeleton from the sidewall of the Lagow Sand Pit on the Trinity River in Dallas (map 3.1). The site was soon visited by Ellis Shuler (1923) and the father of Texas geology, Robert T. Hill. Although all human bones had been removed, Shuler and Hill found no evidence for disturbance of the sediments. They concluded that the bones had been in situ below the thick soil B-horizon in the alluvium of the terrace, approximately fifty feet above the flood plain. Later, Lull (1921) identified a rich Pleistocene fauna from the same locality that included horse, mammoth, camel, and saber-toothed cat. Shuler (1923) used analyses of phosphate and calcium content of the human and animal bones to support the claim that they were contemporaneous. Shuler held to this interpretation for many years; although he did not allude to the human materials in a discussion of the ages of the Trinity River terraces in 1935 (Shuler 1935), he was nonetheless adamant about the probable early entry via Beringia about the same time (Shuler 1934). Subsequent chemical analysis of the bones by Oakley and Howells (1961) showed that the human material was much younger than the vertebrate fossils. Shuler's appraisal of the geologic context of materials that were recovered by quarry workers was soon paralleled at a locality in Oklahoma, where the debate intensified over the antiquity of humans in North America.

The 1926 discovery of a rich Pleistocene fauna and artifacts in a gravel pit owned by a Mr. Holloman, near Frederick, Oklahoma, was quickly brought to the scientific arena (map 3.2) Dr. F. G. Priestly, a local physician, referred the

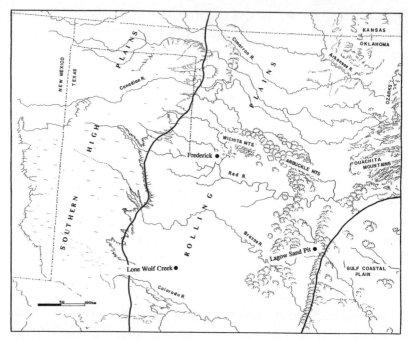

Map 3.2. Physiographic map of the Southern Plains, with locations of sites investigated in early phase of geoarchaeology.

case to the editor of the *Scientific American,* which had recently published articles on discoveries at Lone Wolf Creek, Texas (Figgins 1927; Cook 1927b; Cook and Hay 1930) (map 3.2) Word was sent to J. Figgins at the Denver Museum, who was of course on the track of the 1926 discovery at Folsom, New Mexico. He in turn sent Harold Cook to Frederick to investigate. Cook (1927a) described flint tools and apparent grinding stones associated with the bones of extinct animals in gravels at the Holloman quarry, combining his release on these "remarkable finds of ancestral man" with descriptions of discoveries in Nebraska. Cook's initial geologic appraisal of Frederick suggested a case of inverted topography, with the fossil-encasing channel gravels standing at the crest of the present landform (fig. 3.1). Cook (1927b) added detail to this geologic description of the association as part of an article that placed Frederick as the oldest of three localities (followed by Lone Wolf Creek and Folsom, respectively) that confirmed a long and continuous presence of humans in America.

The reported association of artifacts with Pleistocene fossils at these localities began a remarkable stir in the scientific community and an active (and

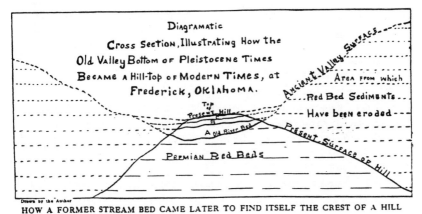

HOW A FORMER STREAM BED CAME LATER TO FIND ITSELF THE CREST OF A HILL

Fig. 3.1. Geologic diagram of the Frederick Locality, drawn by Cook (1927a). This diagram illustrates Cook's view that the site has inverted topography. Courtesy of Scientific American.

indeed continuing) debate concerning the dating of the arrival of humans to the New World. The debate over Frederick quickly established patterns of argument that were to characterize many subsequent debates in geoarchaeology. Most apparent is the early expression of a priori skepticism, and the second is the geologic assessment of physical/stratigraphic association, in this case artifacts, in the same sediments with early Pleistocene fossils. Unlike Shuler's (1923) seemingly ignored claim for a Pleistocene human skeleton at Lagow, Cook's interpretation of Frederick began intense debates that lasted for many years.

The immediate response to Cook's (1927b) claim for Frederick came from anthropologist Leslie Spier (1928a), who noted the incongruity between the apparent age of the artifacts and the fossils and also expressed concern for whether the reported manos were actually artifacts. Spier suggested that the blades would be of Neolithic age, or at the earliest Solutrean, but certainly not early Pleistocene. He suggested that Hay was not aware of this problem. Further, Spier cast doubt on the association because no scientist was present at the time of discovery, and he was "told" that artifacts also occurred on the surface at the locality. Spier (1928b) had a later opportunity to examine the manos and concluded that they were indeed real. However, during his visit to the site with Frank Melton, they found artifacts on the surface but none in situ. He concluded that Cook and Hay were simply wrong about the association. Hay's response to Spier set geologic conclusion against archaeological rebuttal in quite certain terms:

> Our anthropologists are forced to admit that the age of human bones and artifacts is to be determined by geology, but they insist on making their own geology. When the geology appears to be opposed to their view a variety of agencies are invoked to account for the apparent occurrences of Pleistocene man under the circumstances. (Hay 1928)

As the debate progressed, Gould (1929a,b) supported the association, and Hay (1929) set out a long argument that the anthropologist's rejection of the association was based on comparisons with Old World technologies and was inappropriate. Evans (1930) rejected the claim, invoking arguments that included 70–100 feet of post-Pleistocene uplift of western Oklahoma. Cook (1931) quite firmly rejected that possibility. At last the services of E. H. Sellards (1932) came into play. His ten days of fieldwork there in 1931 and 1932 led him to define the deposits as a remnant of a high terrace of the Red River. Sellards accepted the contextual descriptions made by Mr. Holloman and, therefore, the validity of the locality as an archaeological site. Notably, this "last word" on Frederick has been ignored in all subsequent literature on the antiquity of humans in North America, except for such historical reviews as the present discussion.

The debates about Frederick are early illustrations of issues that have remained pertinent to geoarchaeology. The fact that scientists did not make the discovery was critical to some. Incongruities of archaeological data with established cultural chronologies were also invoked. More pertinent to the geoarchaeological issues, however, was that investigations at Frederick stood as precedent to contemporary discussions of site formation processes. Many of the debates centered on those agencies that could possibly have mixed in young artifacts with older fossils. For example, Hay and Cook (1930) questioned quite reasonably why younger fossils or bones of modern animals were not mixed with the early Pleistocene forms. Sellards (1932) made astute observations on the mechanisms of bone deterioration, transport, and possible redeposition; indeed, his points are still extremely valid. At times the arguments slipped into sarcasm, as when Hay (1928) responded to the proposition that a whirlwind may have been involved by agreeing that a "mighty wind" could well have hurled Comanchean implements into the quarry face. Shortly after the close of the intense Frederick discussions, Shuler (1934) made the following suggestion to those who might join him in the search for artifacts associated with fossil elephants:

> If artifacts should be discovered associated with skeleton bones do not move them. Photograph and have pictures sworn by a Notary Public. Send for an odd number of geologists so that you can get a decision.

Clearly, the field of geoarchaeology, as applied to controversial problems such as the antiquity of humans in the New World, and with all its academic and personal warts, was partly born in the Southern Plains.

AVOCATIONAL GEOARCHAEOLOGISTS

Almost as soon as geologists began to study archaeological sites in this region, avocational archaeologists appreciated the importance of those geologic studies and began reporting on the stratigraphy and soils of their sites. This tradition has continued essentially since the first publications of Dr. Cyrus N. Ray of Abilene, who devoted almost two decades to archaeological fieldwork and publication in the Abilene area. Although his investigations began in the late 1920s, Ray's geologic descriptions did not begin to appear until 1930 and were produced up until the end of World War II (Ray 1930, 1938, 1940, 1942, 1944). Because most of the sites he investigated contained deeply buried materials, he was unable to conduct many excavations. Rather, he spent much time examining stream channel cuts, measuring sections, and recording the artifacts and features that he observed and collected (figs. 3.2, 3.3).

The profiles that Ray described included stratigraphic subdivisions based on lithology as well as soil properties, including humus content, rubification, and pedogenic carbonate accumulation (fig. 3.4). Concerning one buried A-horizon, Ray (1944) noted a high density of hearths. He astutely interpreted this as signifying that the old surface:

> either remained stationary longer than any of the others, or it represents a period when there was much more abundant rainfall which produced more vegetation and heavier staining of the old ground level.

Ray's work soon attracted the attention of professionals. In 1934, his field area was visited by E. B. Sayles, as well as by Ernst Antevs and M. M. Leighton.

Fig. 3.2. Photograph of C. N. Ray, taken along Brazos River near Abilene, around 1944. Courtesy of the Texas Archaeological Society.

Fig. 3.3. Ray pointing at deeply buried artifacts, now thought to be Archaic. Courtesy of the Texas Archaeological Society.

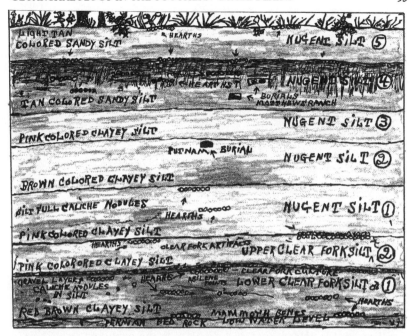

Fig. 3.4. Ray's (1945) section of the Gibson site. Note buried soils that Ray used to infer either a stable surface or a climate change to moister conditions. He found concentrations of hearths in the upper, thick buried soil A-horizon. Redrawn courtesy of the Texas Archaeological Society.

The latter published a report on the observations made during the short trip (Leighton 1936) that included naming of soil-stratigraphic units previously identified by Ray, but with new names and with no citation of Ray's publications. Ray (1944) responded to this rather unprofessional treatment and clarified a number of inaccuracies in Leighton's descriptions.

Leighton (1937) later published on the sites in the Abilene area, as part of an interesting discussion of pedology and archaeology. Incidentally, this report included results of petrographic study of soil samples by R. E. Grim of the Illinois Geological Survey; this is, if not the earliest, one of the earliest applications of soil micromorphology to archaeology. Unfortunately Leighton made no reference at all to Ray's contributions in that paper. He would have done well to consider Ray's work, since Ray's late Pleistocene dating of mammoth-bearing deposits was considerably more accurate than Leighton's Sangamon designation.

With all due respect to Frank Roberts (Roberts 1944), the most notable visitor to Ray's area was Kirk Bryan. In addition to studying Ray's (1938) work, Bryan collaborated with Ray (Ray and Bryan 1938; Bryan and Ray 1938) on a study of the McLean Site, which consisted of mammoth remains and a Clovis point, both of which appear to have been redeposited (Bryan 1941; Wormington 1957:115; Sellards 1952:36).

A contemporary of Ray's, Adolf Witte of Henrietta, Texas, was also active in making geologic observations at sites along the Red River and its tributaries (Witte 1935, 1936, 1937, 1942). Although he noted sites with deep stratigraphy, Witte excavated at late Prehistoric sites that were not as deeply buried. He found a number of these to be on eroded Permian clays and above the flood plains of the larger streams, such as the Little Wichita (map 3.1). He concluded that the sites had not been flooded during occupations and burial by sands reflected eolian deposition (Witte 1936).

Wilson Crook, an avocational archaeologist from Dallas, Texas, became known through his extensive investigations of sites along the Trinity River and in other areas of northern Texas. Most of his investigations were done in partnership with King Harris, one of the most able and published researchers in the history of Texas archaeology. Crook and Harris focused their survey and excavation efforts along the terraces of the Trinity River near Dallas (e.g., Crook and Harris 1955) but also teamed on sites in other parts of the region, such as the Acton Site in Hood County (Blaine et al. 1968). Crook developed a geomorphic and stratigraphic framework that was used not only for archaeological work, but was also incorporated in local paleontological investigations by Bob Slaughter, Elmer Cheatum, and others (Slaughter et al. 1962).

Certainly the best known of Crook and Harris's work was at the Lewisville Site, on the Elm Fork of the Trinity (Crook and Harris 1957). There they recovered a Clovis point, several other lithic artifacts, and a late Pleistocene fauna. These were associated with a number of large burned areas interpreted as hearths. This discovery achieved notoriety when two charcoal samples yielded essentially "dead" carbon, both reported as more than 37,000 years B.P. (Crook and Harris 1958). Especially after other Clovis sites were radiometrically dated (Haynes 1967), the ages from Lewisville were viewed with great skepticism. Later investigations (Stanford 1982) showed that the samples contained lignite, and the Clovis materials are within the same terminal Pleistocene age range as other Clovis sites. While this conclusion calmed many archaeologists, it left questions concerning the geology of the site, as reported by Crook. By his interpretation, the artifacts were contained in situ in sediments (the "Upper Shuler Formation") that comprised the fill of a terrace that was approximately twenty meters above the Trinity River flood plain (figs. 3.5, 3.6). Later studies (Ferring 1986b, 1989a, 1990a,c, 1993) showed that Crook's interpretation would require that the valley had been incised some forty meters, and then filled again with Holocene alluvium about twenty meters thick in a scant 11,000 years. Further, the faunas from other localities on the Trinity all appeared to be older than Clovis (Slaughter et al. 1962). Although Crook's interpretations have been substantially replaced, his appreciation for the importance of geologic investigations, as well as his numerous efforts to improve archaeological research, remain as testaments to his goals.

One last avocational geoarchaeologist who deserves mention is Al Redder, who has excavated at Horn Shelter, a stratified Paleoindian site located in the middle Brazos River Valley (map 3.1). In addition to excellent archaeological descriptions, Redder (1985) has done an admirable job of documenting the stratigraphy of the site, which includes probable Clovis material, as well as Folsom and San Patrice-like occupations, along with well-preserved faunas and an early Holocene human burial. Collins (1991) has argued very well for the systematic study of shelter deposits, which are quite common in this region.

No Elephant, No Geologist

Between 1940 and 1965, the development or application of geoarchaeology in the Southern Osage Plains was almost negligible, except for these avocational contributions. After the war years, in fact, archaeology in this region was practically dominated by avocational investigators. Although limited Works Progress Administration (WPA) funds were available for projects associated with reservoir construction (Albert 1984), most professionals were academics who relied on scant funds from the National Park Service or the River Basin Survey (RBS). Scant funds were sometimes very scant indeed. For example, the total archaeological effort associated with construction of Lake Grapevine in north-central Texas consisted of a ten-day survey by Robert Stephenson (Ferring 1986b).

The availability of Quaternary geoscientists was also very limited. In this region, postwar educational efforts were geared toward the petroleum industry. Major petroleum geology programs at the University of Texas at Austin

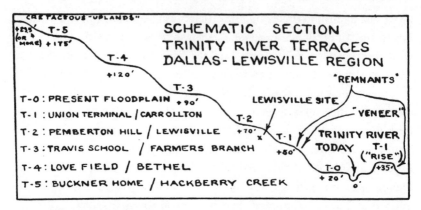

Fig. 3.5. W. W. Crook's (1958) valley cross section for the Lewisville Site. Courtesy of the Society for American Archaeology.

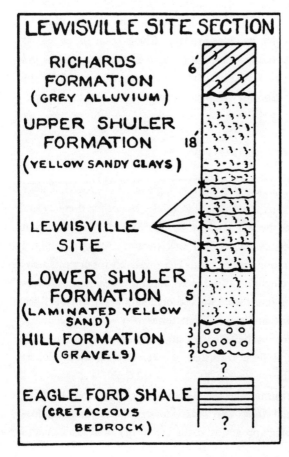

Fig. 3.6. Crook's site profile. Note the use of the names of local geologists for stratigraphic units (which are mainly soil horizons). Courtesy of the Society for American Archaeology.

and Oklahoma University grew rapidly, and even at private universities such as Southern Methodist and Baylor, petroleum geology was paramount in the postwar years. Soils programs at Texas A&M University and Oklahoma State University did not provide homes for Quaternary specialists.

During these years, another factor seems to have limited geologists' participation in archaeological projects: no elephants. Up to 1965, and even after that, Quaternary geologists tended (as would be expected) to collaborate on projects that had significant research potential. In many cases this meant that ancient or early occupations were involved, and those were also sites where geologic dating would be required. Thus most geologic investigations in the southern mid-continent were focused on Paleoindian sites (Ferring 1990a). Between 1940 and 1962, no in situ Paleoindian sites were discovered in the Southern Osage Plains. A burial found in a terrace of the Trinity River near Dallas raised hopes of a Paleoindian age. Geologic investigations by Albritton and Patillo (1940), however, showed that it was within an intrusive pit.

But this is not at all to say that these quiet years represent total avoidance of collaboration on the part of geologists. The discipline of archaeology, especially as applied to post-Paleoindian research problems, was focused on questions associated with its own theoretical-methodological evolution, which placed interdisciplinary approaches, including geoscience, on the back burner for much of this period.

FOCUS ON THE PATTERNS OF PHASES

McKern's (1939) Midwestern Taxonomic System provided archaeologists with a means of ordering archaeological sites into cultural-historical groupings, to meet the objective of assessing cultural affiliations of sites and layers within sites. Trait lists, filled with ceramic varieties, projectile point types, house plans, and burial patterns, were the modus operandi of this distinctly descriptive phase of archaeological research. Fieldwork was designed basically to recover artifacts from sites, and often from six-inch levels within five-by-five-foot squares, so that trait lists within and between sites could be employed to define the foci, aspects, phases, patterns, and cultures as outlined by the McKern system. This approach is explicitly reported in syntheses like that of Bell and Baerreis (1951) for Oklahoma. Dating was important but was difficult before radiocarbon methods. Krieger's (1946) *Culture Complexes and*

Chronology in Northern Texas relied on cross-dating of sites to the southwest through analysis of imported ceramics but nonetheless fulfilled the descriptive goals of the McKern System. Eight years later, the *Introductory Handbook of Texas Archaeology* (Suhm et al. 1954) provided an exhaustive lexicon of pottery and projectile point types sites in the state. They chose those artifact categories because "they provide the best clues to the presence of particular culture complexes in the state" (Suhm et al. 1954:3). As noted by Haag (1986), even screening was a late addition to field methodologies because it was not needed to find "diagnostic" artifacts. It was only adopted when "ecological" approaches were borrowed from Old World archaeologists.

Walter Taylor's (1948) *A Study of Archaeology* critiqued archaeologists' obsession with chronology and proposed a "conjunctive" approach that stressed analysis and interpretation of ways of life through comparison of artifacts, features, and ecofacts in their site context. The contextual emphasis signaled a potentially significant shift in archaeological methodologies, but Taylor's ideas and approach were slow to be accepted by American archaeologists (Willey 1968), including those in the Southern Osage Plains. Ten years later, Willey and Phillips (1958) further nudged archaeology towards problem-oriented, interdisciplinary archaeology by stressing comparison of archaeological data with a goal of establishing cultural-historical units that had many more adaptive-technological parameters than those used previously. Nonetheless, their approach was still largely descriptive and only gently promoted interdisciplinary efforts, such as those required by studying plant domestication.

Fortunately, several developments led to the potential application of interdisciplinary archaeology, although none was manifest in this region as early as in other areas. Some of these developments were fiscal; others were conceptual. The use of National Science Foundation (NSF) funds for archaeological research enabled the funding of specific, high-potential projects. Passage of the Historic Preservation Act of 1966, the National Environmental Policy Act in 1969, and the Moss-Bennett Act in 1974 enabled federal projects to expend funds on archaeology, beginning the stage of cultural resources management (CRM) and creating a major influx of monies for archaeological research (Fowler 1986).

More importantly, the 1960s and early 1970s were times of major change in archaeological theory and method. Butzer's (1964, 1971) synthesis of interdisciplinary archaeology, with a strong emphasis on dating, stratigraphy, pedology, and environmental reconstruction, had a progressive impact on archaeological

methodologies. The publication of *Archaeology as Human Ecology* strength-
ened his influence and it became a mainstay reference for geoarchaeology
(Butzer 1982). This came at a time when cultural ecology and cultural evolution were also gaining popularity, and people such as Julian Steward, Michael
Coe, Stewart Struever, and Kent Flannery were attracting large audiences in
the discipline.

Large interdisciplinary projects, funded by the National Science Foundation, had a remarkable impact on the archaeological community—and the
emphasis was indeed on science. Braidwood's project in Iraq and MacNeish's
project in the Tehuacan Valley, both focused on the origins of agriculture, generated interest and spawned followers of interdisciplinary approaches that
included geology as an essential component of the research. At about the same
time, the ecological approaches of the British, such as J. G. D. Clark, and the
explicitly geologic aspects of "La Methode Bordes" exemplified the increasing
Old World influences on New World archaeological concepts and methods.

Last, but certainly not least, the impact of the "New Archaeology," driven
primarily by Lewis Binford (e.g., Binford and Binford 1968), led to the widespread application of "prefieldwork thinking" by archaeologists. Not all of
them took an explicitly interdisciplinary approach, and many did not build
geology into their research designs. Yet thereafter most archaeologists were
required to have a research design, and this played an important role in the
shift towards interdisciplinary research strategies. True, the impact of geology
on archaeology (beyond excavating Paleoindian sites) was slow in coming, but
within a few years of the changes noted, articles concerning geoarchaeology,
including work by Gladfelter (1977) and Hassan (1978,1979), registered the
increasing interest in the discipline.

INTERDISCIPLINARY, INCLUDING GEOLOGY

Interdisciplinary archaeology essentially began in this region in the 1960s,
significantly influenced by Fred Wendorf's projects on the High Plains (see
Holliday, this volume); but his work was out of the region immediately at issue.
A flagship project in the Southern Osage Plains was the NSF-supported research
at the Domebo Clovis site in Oklahoma, funded by NSF and led by Adrian
Anderson and Marvin Tong of the Museum of the Great Plains (Leonhardy
1966). They, with significant contributions from Robert E. Bell (Oklahoma

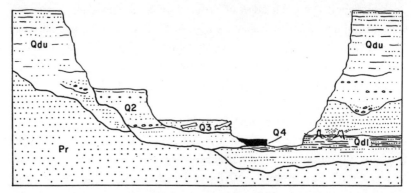

Figure 3.7. Albritton's (1966) cross section of the Domebo Site, Oklahoma: Pr = Rush Springs Formation; Qdl and Qdu = lower and upper members of the Domebo Formation; Q2, Q3, Q4 = younger alluvial deposits. Courtesy of the Museum of the Great Plains.

University) assembled a notable team of specialists who thoroughly established the geologic and paleoenvironmental context of the mammoth and its associated Clovis points. Albritton (1966) conducted stratigraphic studies, and Retallick (1966) established the geomorphic setting of the site (fig. 3.7). Since that time, the well-dated locality has been of stratigraphic importance to the study of other Paleoindian sites in the mid-continent (Haynes 1984, 1991). Hofman and Brackenridge (1988) have continued those stratigraphic investigations in southwestern Oklahoma, building on Albritton's base.

Not far from the Domebo site, a mammoth had been discovered near Cooperton, Oklahoma, in 1961. This site was thoroughly investigated as a possible archaeological site, since large stones that were found with the mammoth skeleton appeared to be manuports, and a number of the bones were fractured (Anderson 1975). Geologic study by Albritton (1975) and detailed soils analysis by Nichols (1975) of the Soil Conservation Service, were important components of dating and environmental reconstruction. Dated to around 19,000 B.P., the site has not been widely accepted as a pre-Clovis archaeological locality. However, the kinds of geoscientific studies that Anderson directed represented the full concern for contextual analyses demanded by the situation.

These two projects cannot be called the start of a rapid increase in the application of geoscience to archaeological investigations in this region, because it would be some years before that would occur. During the subsequent interval, however, a few academic programs within and outside the region began to support the kinds of curricula and research that could advance geoarchaeological studies. This education and training needed to be addressed not only to geoscientists but also to archaeologists.

ACADEMIC SEEDS

Although none of the universities within or near the Southern Osage Plains developed a program in geoarchaeology before the late 1980s, Southern Methodist University (SMU) made good strides towards advancing geoarchaeological concepts. There faculty such as Fred Wendorf and Garth Sampson actively promoted interdisciplinary concepts in their teaching and applied them to their research projects. Geologists at SMU during the 1960s and 1970s included Claude Albritton Jr. (a student of Kirk Bryan) and C. Vance Haynes Jr. While Albritton and Haynes were very actively engaged in geoarchaeology in the New World and in northeast Africa, only Albritton conducted work in the Southern Osage Plains. The only geomorphology degree granted during that period was to Mary Rainey (1974), who worked on the Sulfur River in northeast Texas. The pedologist David Pheasant was at SMU for a short period after Haynes returned to Arizona, but when Pheasant left so did Quaternary geology. But the academic impact of the archaeologists and geoscientists at SMU was noticeable, and a number of SMU graduates later applied interdisciplinary concepts in their research. Among them Fekri Hassan, Don Henry, Britt Bousman, and I all earned degrees in Old World Prehistory at SMU, and later went on to participate in or actually conduct geoarchaeological research. The latter three of us worked in the Southern Plains, although most of Don Henry's work was in northern Oklahoma (see Mandel, this volume).

At the University of Texas at Austin (UT), the large geology program never supported a strong geomorphology program. Victor Baker did not, to my knowledge, engage in geoarchaeology, although he did on occasion use archaeological data to date flood events. Stephen Hall joined the geography faculty at UT in the early 1980s, as did Karl Butzer. Butzer trained Mike Blum, whose contributions to geoarchaeology are referenced later. Hall was trained in palynology at Michigan but began doing geomorphology in the Southern Plains in the 1970s. He worked on a number of projects as a palynology-malacology-geomorphology consultant and produced summary papers of those efforts (Hall 1982, 1988).

Mike Collins, trained in both archaeology and geology and affiliated with UT through the Texas Archaeological Research Laboratory, has conducted notable geoarchaeological research. Geologists at the Bureau of Economic Geology (a branch of the UT System), notably Tom Gustavson, Chris Caran, and Robert Baumgardner, have conducted prodigious geomorphic investigations, including intensive work on the Texas Rolling Plains segment of the Osage Plains (Gustavson 1986; Caran and Baumgardner 1990; Gustavson et al. 1991). Caran has collaborated with archaeologists on a variety of projects, including several in north-central Texas (Caran 1990a,b).

Texas A&M has a strong, well-known program in archaeology and archaeobotany, developed under the leadership of Vaughn Bryant. However, despite large programs in geology and geography they lacked a geoarchaeological component to their program until they hired Vance Holliday. After Holliday left for the University of Wisconsin, A&M hired Mike Waters, a student of Vance Haynes from Arizona. Lee Nordt (now at Baylor Univeristy) taught pedology at A&M in the department of soil and crop sciences. Overall, A&M has the strongest interdisciplinary program in the region. Although there are large soils and/or geology programs at schools such as Texas Tech and the University of Oklahoma, they do not have geoarchaeologists. However, research by archaeologists at Oklahoma University (and those associated with the Oklahoma Archaeological Survey) increasingly included geological studies. Notable in this respect is the excellent synthesis of alluvial and eolian geology and site formation processes at two sites in central Oklahoma by Don Wyckoff (1984). Brian Carter and I, at Oklahoma State University and the University of North Texas respectively, practice geoarchaeology but do not have enough colleagues at our campuses to claim full programs.

This brief "bestiary" of academic geoarchaeologists is intended to sum up the history of the academic aspect of the discipline in this region. As the following discussions will show, the individuals mentioned above account for the vast majority of geoarchaeology done in the Southern Osage Plains. Except for brief invasions of our territory by people trained and living elsewhere, such as Rolfe Mandel, a small group of people has conducted most of the geoarchaeology in this region since about 1975. However, the contributions of geoarchaeology have increased dramatically for the two reasons mentioned above: first, trained geologists and archaeologists interested in geoarchaeology became available, and second, federal, state, and local agencies had both the desire and the money to support that work in a context of Cultural Resources Management (CRM)

Fig. 3.8. A group of Friends of the Pleistocene participants bombarding Steve Hall with questions at Carnegie Canyon, Oklahoma, in 1987.

projects. Before moving to that, however, I must briefly mention an organization that has probably done more than any university curriculum to advance the quality and quantity of geoarchaeology in this region.

THE FOP CONNECTION

The Friends of the Pleistocene (FOP), an informal organization, is spread across the United States in a number of cells, with no charter, no rules, no officers or dues, and no journal. It has one function: to bring Quaternary scientists together each spring on a field trip (Goldthwait 1989). These trips are offered by people who are willing to donate their effort to organize the trip, prepare guidebooks, arrange for banquets, and suffer the relentless questions of the participants. The apparent mode of these trips is for all participants—students and professionals from different disciplines—to learn by asking on the spot. The trips are "live and unrehearsed" opportunities to learn about geomorphology, soils, archaeology, and whatever else is being presented. All questions are regarded as fair, and none are considered naive (fig. 3.8).

The FOP was brought to the Southern Plains in 1983 by Vance Holliday and Eileen Johnson (Holliday 1983). Their three-day trip on the High Plains of Texas, which included presentations by John Hawley, Lee Gile, and C. C. Reeves, brought about one hundred people from geology and archaeology together in a new and exciting learning environment. Many archaeologists (the author included) came away with fresh enthusiasm for Quaternary geology and new ideas on how that could be brought into archaeological investigations.

Since that first FOP, the Southern Cell has had annual trips that cumulatively have brought well over a thousand participants together in the field. Many people who now communicate and work together were introduced on these trips, and the exchange of ideas and problems between archaeologists and geologists has been remarkable. The trips have ranged from the prairies of southwest Oklahoma (Ferring 1987) at Domebo and Delaware Canyons with neotectonic stops in the Wichitas, to the Hill Country of Central Texas (Blum et al. 1989), to deep, wet alluvial exposures in South Texas (Mandel and Caran 1992), to the Lava Creek Ash exposures of northwest Oklahoma (Carter and Ward 1991), and Fort Hood, near Killeen, Texas (Carlson 1996), to name a few. Undoubtedly, the in-field illustrations of research for diverse audiences that always include students, establishes the FOP as a major historical factor in the development of geoarchaeology in this region.

GEOARCHAEOLOGY IN FORCE: THE CRM INITIATIVE

Having discussed trends in North American archaeological method and theory and described the academic situation in this region from the 1970s to the present, I will next consider the CRM role in geoarchaeology as the last factor in this historical review. This is not a phase of research, linked by common goals and means, but rather a chronicle of quite rapidly changing agency policies and professional approaches to geoarchaeological investigations in a CRM context.

Geoscience has certainly not always been a part of CRM investigations but rather has become an increasingly important part of them since the late 1970s in the Southern Osage Plains. But geoscience has not simply become more common in these investigations, it has changed from an interdisciplinary (or multidisciplinary in most cases) appendage to a fully integrated geoarchaeological component of research. These changes seem to have come about over the past two decades as a result of an influx of freshly trained archaeologists into policy and implementation roles in both regulatory and operations branches of the diverse CRM structure. The personnel that have drawn up regulatory guidelines and have played oversight roles in CRM, including the National Advisory Council for Historic Preservation and the State Historic Preservation Officers, have gradually increased their demands for geoarchaeological investigations as part of CRM projects. In some cases, their regulations and standards actually emulated practices instigated at the operations level by contracting officers who saw both practical and scientific advantages to geoarchaeological studies. These patterns of change in policy and practice are evident in the CRM investigative history in the Southern Osage Plains.

After passage of the Moss-Bennett Act in 1974, federal funding allocations for archaeology increased dramatically nationwide. Lacking national standards for contract performance, agencies and districts set their own contracting standards, which allowed considerable leeway in the "problem" orientation of mitigative investigation, as well as in methods for survey and testing. Competition for contracts was often based strictly on cost. In this region in the 1970s, however, the National Park Service set cost ceilings within scopes-of-work and evaluated proposals on their technical merit. It quite soon became clear that interdisciplinary research proposals were successful. Examples include mitigation efforts at Hog Creek, Texas, (Henry et al. 1980) and Delaware Canyon, Oklahoma (Ferring 1982, 1986a). At Delaware Canyon, study of geology and soils (Pheasant 1982) were integrated into the research design and were added as contributions to the technical report. At about the same time, the Army Corps of Engineers was also funding geologic investigations on their contracts, but only at the mitigation phase and usually at too low a level to make substantial contributions to the projects.

By the mid-1980s, the situation had changed considerably. In 1985, for example, the Fort Worth District of the Corps of Engineers contracted with the University of North Texas to prepare an assessment of and a long-range management plan for cultural resources sites within the standard project flood area (100-year event) for the Upper Trinity River basin (Ferring 1986b). Through the insight of Robert "Skipper" Scott, this contract called for preparation of a geologic model of site occurrence in the project area and provided funds for fieldwork, laboratory analyses, and interviews with scientists who had worked in the area. The planning document is still used today as a means to predict potential impacts to buried sites resulting from the now rampant development of the flood plain. In this case, the Corps saw practical benefit in applying geoarchaeology in advance of any "traditional" archaeological surveys. The Corps has been able to advise land developers of potential archaeological sites (and the implied costs associated with those potential sites) and also has been able to better design strategies to avoid sensitive sites.

The Corps, in coordination with the State Historic Preservation Officer (SHPO), followed this experience with a major contract to conduct a priori geologic studies at the Cooper Reservoir (Bousman et al. 1988) that identified geologic contexts of sites and developed strategies for finding and mitigating them. Bousman and Collins were able to inspect many natural cuts and excavate numerous backhoe trenches to describe and sample profiles. Using an extensive radiocarbon dating program, they developed a sound chronology for the sedimentary units and periods of soil development. In the same project area, Robert Darwin conducted intensive resistivity profiling, which proved to be extremely useful for defining the geometry of buried alluvial and geomorphic features (Darwin et al. 1990).

These efforts do not simply register an intent to do science, but rather they signify the tremendous shift in overall archaeological research strategies from the descriptive, assemblage-based analyses of the 1930s through the 1960s to the processual and ecological approaches of more recent archaeological research. For the former, a surface survey designed to find shallow sites with dense accumulations of artifacts was the normal procedure to ensure success. The latter required stratified sites with lower densities of artifacts in well-preserved contexts, associated with faunal-floral remains and amenable to detailed behavioral and environmental analyses. To find and study these sites geology is essential before survey, as well as during testing and excavation, to assess site formation processes (see Butzer 1982). The Corps was clearly ready to fund such studies, as documented by the excellent papers on site modification processes in a Corps-sponsored symposium (Mathewson 1989).

Lee Nordt has done intensive geomorphic and pedologic studies at Fort Hood, Texas, as part of a long-term Corps-supported CRM project (Nordt 1992, 1995). At the southern margin of the Osage Plains, this limestone-dominated landscape was a challenge to researchers comparing larger stream alluvial sequences with those from tributaries and with the extensive colluvial sediments in the area. In addition to developing a detailed framework for the archaeological studies, Nordt conducted isotopic analyses of detrital and pedogenic carbonates to explain soils-genesis/morphology and to construct a soils chronosequence. He expanded these studies into an isotopic analysis of soil organics used for paleoenvironmental reconstruction (Nordt et al. 1994). Humphrey and Ferring (1994) took a similar approach in their isotopic analyses of carbonates and organics from the Aubrey Clovis Site. Other work being done at Fort Hood includes sourcing of lithic materials (Frederick and Ringstaff 1994); Larry Bank's (1990) landmark study of lithic raw materials has assisted work in the entire region.

The Corps also supported the author's geoarchaeological investigations as part of archaeological projects at Lake Ray Roberts and Lake Lewisville, Texas (Ferring 1989a, 1990a, 1990c). This included the geology and geoarchaeology of the Aubrey Clovis Site, a deeply buried locality with abundant artifacts and faunal remains (Ferring 1989b, 1990b, 1995). This happens to be one of the few in situ Paleoindian sites discovered as part of a federally supported CRM project.

The Corps of Engineers is not the only agency responsible for these changes in CRM practice, although it seems fair to say that the staff at the Fort Worth District (including Robert Scott, Jay Newman, Karen Scott, and Dan McGregor) have been independently aggressive in this regard. In both Texas and Oklahoma, the State Archaeologists and the SHPO (of which the latter has oversight on public archaeology) have been strong advocates for similar use of geoarchaeology on public archaeology projects. In Oklahoma, for example, Robert Brooks and Don Wyckoff have been instrumental in supporting geoarchaeology, both within the office of the State Archaeologist and within the Oklahoma Archaeological Survey (OAS). An example is the excellent study of buried site potentials in a survey in central Oklahoma that was supported by the OAS, the Office of Historic Preservation, and the National Park Service (Hofman and Drass 1990). Geomorphologist Robert Brackenridge and pedologist Brian Carter worked with the archaeologists to develop a model of site preservation contexts.

In Texas, the SHPO and the Department of Antiquities Protection (which issues permits for appropriate state or municipal projects) have explicitly built geoarchaeology into their permit requirements. In collaboration with the Corps of Engineers, they have assisted in the implementation of geoarchaeological studies at non-federal projects, such as at Justiceberg Reservoir on the Colorado-Concho Rivers in the southwestern part of the Osage Plains (map 3.1). There Mike Blum completed an intensive study of the geomorphology, sedimentary environments, and soils that resulted in site prediction and site formation models (Blum 1989; Blum and Valastro 1992, 1989; Blum et al. 1992). His detailed analysis of sediment-soil profiles, including laboratory work, indicates his excellent training under Karl Butzer and also his own aggressive initiative in both geology and geoarchaeology.

Rolfe Mandel, working with Texas A&M archaeologists at the South Bend Project on the Brazos River (Mandel 1992) and at the Valley Branch Project in the Red River Valley (Mandel 1994) also considered landform, sediments, and soils to establish the late Quaternary geologic history and determine the archaeological implications (map 3.1). Both he and Mike Blum used their data to assist in paleoenvironmental reconstruction. Mandel also worked with SMU at Cooper Reservoir on the Sulfur River, doing detailed profile descriptions and analyses at Finley Fan.

Overall, it seems clear that in this region, CRM work has increasingly employed geoarchaeology. This has met agency goals in several ways. First, it has improved their site detection and site prediction capabilities significantly. Second, it has allowed implementation of research designs that consider site formation processes and environmental reconstruction, improving the research designs and helping reach the goal of minimizing adverse impact. In CRM studies, archaeologists have in the past employed geoscientists who drew the standard, oversimplified valley cross-sections, made sweeping generalizations about the sections without detailed soils descriptions or sedimentary-soils labwork, and then fit these data into long-held conceptions about past climates. But the new generation of geoarchaeologists should put an end to those pseudointerdisciplinary investigations, which, in CRM contexts, one might refer to as the Geologic Appendix phase of geoarchaeology. The research now being done in CRM work is current in method and theory and is advancing the field of archaeology far beyond what it used to be.

CONCLUSIONS

Geoarchaeology in the Southern Osage Plains has a long tradition that mirrors many of the developments within associated disciplines in other regions of the country. The early involvement of geologists engrossed in debates over the antiquity of humans in the New World, which entailed their concern not only for dating but also for the validity of assorted claims, is well illustrated by the work of Cook, Hay, Sellards, and others. Their debates with anthropologists such as Spier were also part of nationwide disputes that set geologic observation against failed cultural-historical expectations.

As archaeology settled in, and less controversial issues were addressed, geologic participation waned. Archaeologists, working within the frame of current theoretically driven goals, did not need geologists for much of this period, which Willey (1968) called the "descriptive-historical" phase of American archaeology. Archaeologists needed artifacts and features, not geologic profiles, to do their work. Even as archaeology moved into the "comparative-historical" period of Willey (1968) geology was practiced on a limited scale, and hardly at all in this region, except by spirited avocational geoarchaeologists such as Ray, Witte, and Crook. In other arenas, however, people like Antevs and Bryan continued their study of both Paleoindian and younger sites as part of an interest in climate change and human adaptations (see Haynes 1990).

Cultural resources management programs, with funding and projects in hand, set geoarchaeology off on a new phase of disciplinary growth. It has developed (either in coevolutionary or codependent fashion, depending on one's view) into a vital discipline, linked to contemporary theory and methods in archaeology. The days when geoscientists are brought in to draw profiles and sent home to write brief reports appear to be over. In this region, geoscience has become fully integrated into the entire process of archaeology— from survey through excavation and lithic analysis. Though teamwork is still involved, this is what geoarchaeology should be.

The academic side of the discipline has been, and will be, integral to maintaining geoarchaeology and to ensuring that it continues to grow in contact with, or as part of, archaeology in general. Geoarchaeology demands well-educated and well-trained participants; universities will need both geoscience and archaeology as supporting disciplines to prepare future scientists. With respect to past and future geoarchaeology in the Southern Osage Plains, things look pretty good.

ACKNOWLEDGEMENTS

I am grateful to Rolfe Mandel for the invitation to participate in the symposium and to prepare this chapter. I thank him, Vance Holliday, Christopher Caran, Marlin Hawley, Marvin Kay, and Don Wyckoff for thorough reviews and very useful comments on draft versions of the paper. Despite all of their excellent suggestions to improve the paper, I assume responsibility for its present condition.

REFERENCES

Albert, L. 1984. Survey of archaeological activity in Oklahoma. *In* Bell, R. E, ed., The prehistory of Oklahoma, 45–63. New York: Academic Press.

Albritton, C. C., Jr. 1966. Stratigraphy of the Domebo site. *In* Leonhardy, F. C., ed., Domebo: A Paleo-Indian mammoth kill in the Prairie-Plains, 10–13. Lawton, Okla.: Museum of the Great Plains, Contributions 1.

———. 1975. Stratigraphy of the Cooperton site. *Great Plains Journal* 14, no. 2:133–39.

Albritton, C. C., Jr., and L. G. Patillo Jr. 1940. A human skeleton found near Carrollton, Texas. *Field and Laboratory* 8, no. 2:59–64.

Anderson, A. D., ed. 1975. The Cooperton mammoth: An early man bone quarry. *Great Plains Journal* 14, no. 2:130–64.

Banks, L. D. 1990. From mountain peaks to alligator stomachs: A review of lithic sources in the trans-Mississippi south, the Southern Plains, and adjacent southwest. Norman, Okla.: Anthropological Society Memoir no. 4.

Bell, R. E., ed. 1984. Prehistory of Oklahoma. Academic Press: New York.

Bell, R. E., and D. A. Baerreis. 1951. A survey of Oklahoma archaeology. *Bulletin of the Texas Archeological and Paleontological Society* 22:7–100.

Binford, S. R., and L. R. Binford, eds. 1968. New perspectives in archaeology. Chicago: Aldine.

Blaine, J. C., R. K. Harris, W. W. Crook, and J. L. Shiner. 1968. The Acton site: Hood County, Texas. *Bulletin of the Texas Archaeological Society* 39:45–94.

Blair, W. F. 1950. The biotic provinces of Texas. *The Texas Journal of Science* 2, no. 1:93–117.

Blair, W. F., and T. H. Hubbell. 1938. The biotic districts of Oklahoma. *The American Midland Naturalist* 20:425–55.

Blum, M. D. 1989. Geoarchaeological investigations. *In* Boyd, D. K., M. D. Freeman, M. D. Blum, E. R. Pruitt, and J. M. Quigg. Phase I cultural resources investigations at Justiceburg Reservoir on the Double Mountain Fork of the Brazos River, Garza and Kent Counties, Texas. Austin: Prewitt and Associates, Report of Investigations 66:81–106.

Blum, M. D., J. T. Abbott, and S. Valastro Jr. 1992. Evolution of landscapes on the Double Mountain Fork of the Brazos River, West Texas: implications for preservation and visibility of the archaeological record. *Geoarchaeology* 7, no. 4:339–70.

Blum, M. D., J. F. Peterson, and R. S. Toomey III. 1989. Geomorphology, Quaternary stratigraphy, and paleoecology of central Texas. Guidebook,

7th Annual Meeting, Friends of the Pleistocene, South-Central Cell. Austin: Department of Geography, University of Texas at Austin.

Blum, M. D., and S. Valastro Jr. 1992. Quaternary stratigraphy and geoarchaeology of the Colorado and Concho rivers, West Texas. *Geoarchaeology* 7, no. 5:419–48.

Bomar, G. 1983. Texas weather. Austin: University of Texas Press.

Bousman, B., M. Collins, and T. Perttula. 1988. Quaternary geology at Cooper basin: A framework for archaeological inquiry, Delta and Hopkins Counties, Texas. Austin: Pruitt and Associates, Inc., Reports of Investigations no. 55.

Bryan, K. 1938. Deep sites near Abilene, Texas. *Bulletin of the Texas Archeological and Paleontological Society* 10:248–62.

————. 1941. Geologic antiquity of man in America. *Science* 93, no. 2422:505–14.

Bryan, K., and C. N. Ray. 1938. Long channeled point found in alluvium beside bones of *Elephas columbi*. *Bulletin of the Texas Archeological and Paleontological Society* 10:263–68.

Butzer, K. W. 1964. Environment and archaeology: An introduction to Pleistocene geography. Chicago: Aldine.

————. 1971. Environment and archaeology: An ecological approach to prehistory. Chicago: Aldine.

————. 1982. Archaeology as human ecology. Cambridge: Cambridge University Press.

Caran, S. C. 1990a. Geomorphology of lower Village Creek, Tarrant County, Texas. *In* Andrews, S. L., and S. C. Caran, Archaeological investigation of the proposed Green Oaks Boulevard extension from IH30 to Fielder Road, Tarrant County, Texas, A1–A34. Fort Worth: Freese and Nichols, Inc.

————. 1990b. Geomorphology of Village Creek, Tarrant County, Tex's. *In* Andrews, S. L. and S. C. Caran, Archaeological investigation of the proposed Green Oaks Boulevard extension from U.S. Highway 80 to Meadowbrook Drive, Tarrant County, Texas. Fort Worth: Freese and Nichols, Inc.

Caran, S. C., and R. W. Baumgardner Jr. 1990. Quaternary stratigraphy and paleoenvironments of the Texas Rolling Plains. *Geological Society of America Bulletin* 102:768–85.

Carlson, D. L., ed. 1996. Upland, lowland and in between— landscapes in the Lampasas Cut Plain. Friends of the Pleistocene, South-Central Cell, Field Trip Guidebook. College Station, Tex.: Department of Anthropology.

Carter, B. J., and P. A. Ward, III, eds. 1991. A prehistory of the Plains border region. Guidebook, 9th Annual Meeting, South-Central Friends of the Pleistocene. Stillwater: Agronomy Department, Oklahoma State University.

Cliff, M. D., D. Shanabrook, S. M. Hunt, and S. N. Allday. 1993. Testing and evaluation of archaeological sites in the vicinity of the Lowrance Pumping Station, Area X, Red River Chloride Control Project, King County, Texas. Plano, Tex.: Geo-Marine Inc., Miscellaneous Report of Investigations 37.

Collins, M. B. 1991. Rockshelters and the early archaeological record in the Americas. *In* Dillehay, T. D., and D. L. Meltzer, eds., The first Americans: Search and research, 157–82. Boca Raton, Fla.: CRC Press.

Cook, H. J. 1927a. New trails of ancient man. *Scientific American* 137, no. 2: 114–17.

———. 1927b. New geological and paleontological evidence bearing on the antiquity of man in America. *Natural History* 27, no. 3:240–47.

———. 1928. Further evidence concerning man's antiquity at Frederick, Oklahoma. *Science* 67, no. 1736:371–73.

———. 1931. The antiquity of man as indicated at Frederick, Oklahoma: A reply. *Journal of the Washington Academy of Sciences*, 21, no. 8:161–66.

Crook, W. W. Jr. and R. K. Harris. 1955. Scottsbluff points in the Obshner Site near Dallas, Texas. *Bulletin of the Texas Archaeological Society* 26:75–100.

Crook, W. W., Jr., and R. K. Harris. 1957. Hearths and artifacts of early man near Lewisville, Texas and associated fauna. *Bulletin of the Texas Archeological Society* 28:7–97.

Crook, W. W., Jr., and R. K. Harris. 1958. A Pleistocene campsite near Lewisville, Texas. *American Antiquity* 23, no. 3:233–46.

Darwin, R., C. R. Ferring, and B. Ellwood. 1990. Geoelectric stratigraphy and subsurface evaluation of Quaternary stream sediments at Cooper Basin, NE Texas. *Geoarchaeology* 5, no. 1:53–79.

Dunnell, R. C. 1986. Five decades of American archaeology. *In* Meltzer, D. J., D. D. Fowler, and J. A. Sabloff, eds., American archaeology past and future, 23–52. Washington, D.C.: Smithsonian Institution Press.

Evans, O. F. 1930. Probable history of the Holloman gravel pit. *Proceedings of the Oklahoma Academy of Science* 10:77–79.

Fenneman, N. M. 1938. Physiography of eastern United States. New York: McGraw-Hill Book Company, Inc.

Ferring, C. R., ed. 1982. The late Holocene prehistory of Delaware Canyon Oklahoma. Denton: Institute of Applied Sciences, University of North Texas.

Ferring, C. R. 1986a. Late Holocene cultural ecology in the Southern Plains: Perspectives from Delaware Canyon, Oklahoma. *Plains Anthropologist* 31, no. 114:55–82.

———. 1986b. Late Quaternary geology and environments of the upper Trinity basin. *In* Yates, B. C. and C. R. Ferring, eds., An assessment of the cultural resources in the Trinity basin, Dallas, Tarrant and Denton Counties, Texas, 32–112. Denton: North Texas State University, Institute of Applied Sciences.

Ferring, C. R., assembler. 1987. Late Quaternary stratigraphy, neotectonics and geoarchaeology of southwestern Oklahoma. Friends of the Pleistocene South-Central Cell Field Trip Guidebook. Denton: North Texas State University, Institute of Applied Sciences.

Ferring, C. R. 1989a. Field guide to the archaeological geology of the upper Trinity River drainage basin. Geological Society of America, South Central Section Field Trip Guidebook. Arlington: University of Texas at Arlington.

———. 1989b. The Aubrey Clovis site: A Paleoindian locality in the upper Trinity River basin, Texas. *Current Research in the Pleistocene* 6:9–11.

———. 1990a. Archaeological geology of the Southern Plains. *In* Lasca, N. P. and J. Donahue, eds., Archaeological geology of North America, 253–66. Boulder, Colo.: Geological Society of America, Centennial Special Volume no. 4.

———. 1990b. The 1989 investigations at the Aubrey Clovis site, Texas. *Current Research in the Pleistocene* 7: 10–12.

———. 1990c. Late Quaternary geology and geoarchaeology of the upper Trinity River basin, Texas. Guidebook 11, Geological Society of America. Dallas: Dallas Geological Society,

———. 1991. Upper Trinity River drainage basin, Texas. *In* Morrison, R., ed., Quaternary non-glacial geology: Conterminous United States. Decade of North American Geology, vol. K-2:526–31. Denver: The Geological Society of America.

———. 1993. Late Quaternary geology of the upper Trinity River drainage basin, north-central Texas. Ph.D. diss., Dallas, University of Texas at Dallas.

———. 1995. Middle Holocene environments, geology and archaeology in the Southern Plains. *In* Bettis, E. A. III, ed., Archaeological geology of the Archaic period in North America, 21–35. Boulder, Colo.: The Geological Society of America Special Paper no. 297:21-35.

Figgins, J. D. 1927. The antiquity of man in America. *Natural History* 27, no. 3:229–39.

Fowler, D. D. 1986. Conserving American archaeological resources. *In* Meltzer, D. J., D. D. Fowler, and J.A. Sabloff, eds., American Archaeology Past and Future, 135–62. Washington, D.C.: Smithsonian Institution Press.

Frederick, C. D., and C. Ringstaff. 1994. Lithic resources at Fort Hood: Further investigations. *In* Trierweiler, W. N., ed., Archaeological investigations on 571 prehistoric sites at Fort Hood, Bell and Coryell Counties, Texas. Austin: Mariah Associates, Inc., U.S. Army Fort Hood, Archaeological Resource Management Series Research Report 31:125–81.

Gladfelter, B. G. 1977. Geoarchaeology: The geomorphologist and archaeology. *American Antiquity* 45:519–38.

Goldthwait, R. P. 1989. Friends of the Pleistocene: Recollections of fifty annual reunions, 1934–1988. Columbus: Byrd Poler Research Center, The Ohio State University.

Gould, C. N. 1929a. Fossil bones and artifacts at Frederick. *University of Oklahoma Bulletin* 9:90–92.

———. 1929b. On the recent finding of another flint arrow-head in the Pleistocene deposit at Frederick, Oklahoma. *Journal of the Washington Academy of Sciences* 19, no. 3:66–68.

Gustavson, T. C., ed. 1986. Geomorphology and Quaternary stratigraphy of the Rolling Plains, Texas Panhandle. Austin: Bureau of Economic Geology, Guidebook no. 22.

Gustavson, T. C., R. W. Baumgardner, S. C. Caran, V. T. Holliday, H. H. Mehnert, J. M. O'Neill, and C. C. Reeves. 1991. Quaternary geology of the Southern Great Plains and an adjacent segment of the Rolling Plains. *In* Morrison, R., ed., Quaternary non-glacial geology: Conterminous United States. Decade of North American Geology, vol. K-2:477–501. Denver: The Geological Society of America.

Haag, W. G. 1986. Field methods in archaeology. *In* Meltzer, D. J., D. D. Fowler, and J. A. Sabloff, eds., American Archaeology Past and Future, 63–76. Washington, D.C.: Smithsonian Institution Press.

Hall, S. A. 1982. Late Holocene paleoecology of the Southern Plains. *Quaternary Research* 17:391–407.

Hall, S. A. 1988. Environment and archaeology of the central Osage Plains. *Plains Anthropologist* 33, no. 120:203–18.

Hassan, F. A. 1978. Sediments in archaeology: Methods and implications for paleoenvironmental and cultural analysis. *Journal of Field Archaeology* 5:197–213.

————. 1979. Geoarchaeology: The geologist and archaeology. *American Antiquity* 44:267–70.

Hay, O. P. 1927. Early man in America. *Science News Letter* 12: 215–16.

————. 1928. On the antiquity of relics of man at Frederick, Oklahoma. *Science* 67, no. 1739:442–44.

————. 1929. On the recent discovery of a flint arrow-head in early Pleistocene deposits at Frederick, Oklahoma. *Journal of the Washington Academy of Sciences* 19, no. 5:93–-98.

Hay, O. P., and H. J. Cook. 1930. Fossil vertebrates collected near, or in association with human artifacts at localities near Colorado, Texas, Frederick, Oklahoma, and Folsom, New Mexico. *Proceedings of the Colorado Museum of Natural History* 9, no. 2:4–40.

Haynes, C. V. Jr. 1967. Geochronology of Late-Quaternary alluvium. *In* Morrison, R. B. and Wright, H. E., eds., Means of correlation of Quaternary successions, 591–631. Salt Lake City: University of Utah Press.

————. 1984. Stratigraphy and Late Pleistocene extinction in the United States. *In* Martin, P. S and R. G. Klein, eds., Quaternary extinctions, a prehistoric revolution, 345–53. Tucson: The University of Arizona Press.

————. 1990. The Antevs-Bryan years and the legacy for Paleoindian geochronology. *In* L. F. Laporte, ed., Establishment of a geologic framework for paleoanthropology, 55–68. Boulder, Colo.: The Geological Society of America, Special Paper no. 242.

————. 1991. Geoarchaeological and paleohydrological evidence for a Clovis-age drought in North America and its bearing on extinction. *Quaternary Research* 35:438–51.

Henry, D. O., F. E. Kirby, S. B. Justen, and T. R. Hays. 1980. The prehistory of Hog Creek: An investigation of Bosque and Coryell Counties, Texas. Tulsa: University of Tulsa, Laboratory of Archaeology.

Hill, R. T. 1901. Geography and geology of the Black and Grand Prairies, Texas, with detailed description of the Cretaceous formations and special reference to artesian waters. United States Geological Survey, 21st Annual Report, Part 7—Texas.

Hofman, J. L., and G. R. Brackenridge. 1988. Geoarchaeological Investigation of the lower member of the Domebo Formation in western Oklahoma. Program and Abstracts of the Tenth Biennial Meeting, American Quaternary Association.

Hofman, J. L., and R. R. Drass, eds., 1990. A survey of archaeological resources and an evaluation of buried site potential in northwestern Oklahoma County, Oklahoma. Norman: Oklahoma Archaeological Survey, The University of Oklahoma.

Hofman, J. L., R. L. Brooks, J. S. Hays, D. W. Owsley, R. L. Jantz, M. K. Marks, and M. H. Manhein. 1989. From Clovis to Comanchero: Archaeological overview of the southern Great Plains. Fayetteville: Arkansas Archaeological Survey, Research Series no. 35.

Holliday, V. T., ed. 1983. Guidebook to the central Llano Estacado. Friends of the Pleistocene, South-Central Cell Field Trip Guidebook. Lubbock: The Museum, Texas Tech University.

Hughes, J. T. and P. S. Willey. 1978. Archaeology at MacKenzie Reservoir. Austin: Texas Historical Commission, Archaeological Survey Report no. 24.

Humphrey, J. D., and C. R. Ferring. 1994. Stable isotopic evidence for late Pleistocene to Holocene climate change, north-central Texas. *Quaternary Research* 41:200–13.

Krieger, A. D. 1946. Culture complexes and chronology in northern Texas. Austin: University of Texas, Publication no. 4640.

Leighton, M. M. 1936. Geological aspects of findings of primitive man near Abilene, Texas. Gila Pueblo, Globe, Ariz.: Medallion Papers, no. 24.

———. 1937. The significance of profiles of weathering in stratigraphic archaeology. *In* MacCurdy, G. G., ed., Early man, 163–72. Philadelphia: J.B. Lippincott Co.

Leonhardy, F. C., ed. 1966. Domebo: A paleo-indian mammoth kill in the prairie-plains. Lawton, Okla.: Museum of the Great Plains, Contributions no. 1.

Lull, R. S. 1921. Fauna of the Dallas sand pits. *American Journal of Science* 2:159–76.

McKern, W. C. 1939. The midwestern taxonomic method as an aid to archaeological culture study. *American Antiquity* 4:301–13.

Madole, R. F., C. R. Ferring, S. A. Hall, W. C. Johnson, and C. J. Sorenson. 1991. Quaternary geology of the Osage Plains and Interior Highlands. *In* Morrison, R. B., ed., Quaternary non-glacial geology: Conterminous United

States. Boulder, Colo.: The Geological Society of America Geology of North America, vol. K-2: 503–46.

Mandel, R. D. 1992. Geomorphology. *In* Saunders, J. W., C. S. Mueller-Wille, and D. L. Carlson, eds., An archaeological survey of the proposed South Bend Reservoir area: Young, Stephens and Throckmorton Counties, Texas, 53–83. College Station: Archaeology Research Laboratory, Texas A&M University.

———. 1994. Geomorphology and soil stratigraphy of 41MU55. *In* Thoms, A. V., ed., The valley branch archaeological project: Excavations at an Archaic site (41MU55) in the Cross-Timbers uplands, north-central Texas. College Station: Texas A&M University, Archaeological Research Laboratory, Reports of Investigations, no. 15:41–50.

Mandel, R. D., and S. C. Caran, eds. 1992. Late Cenozoic alluvial stratigraphy and prehistory of the inner Gulf Coastal Plain, south-central Texas. Series 4 Guidebook, 10th Annual Meeting, South-Central Friends of the Pleistocene. Lubbock: Lubbock Lake Landmark Quaternary Research Center.

Mathewson, C. C., ed. 1989. Interdisciplinary workshop on the physical-chemical-biological processes affecting archaeological sites. Contract Report EL-89-1. Vicksburg, Miss.: U.S. Army Engineers Waterways Experiment Station.

Nichols, J. D. 1975. Soils at the Cooperton site. *Great Plains Journal* 14, no. 2:139–43.

Nordt, L. C. 1992. Archaeological geology of the Fort Hood military reservation. Ft. Hood, Texas. College Station: Archaeology Research Laboratory, Texas A&M University.

———. 1995. Geoarchaeological investigations of Henson Creek: A low-order tributary in central Texas. *Geoarchaeology* 10:205–21.

Nordt, L. C., T. W. Boutton, C. T. Hallmark, and M. R. Waters. 1994. Late Quaternary vegetation and climate changes in central Texas based on isotopic composition of organic carbon. *Quaternary Research* 41:109–20.

Oakley, K. P., and W. W. Howells. 1961. Age of the skeleton from the Lagow sand pit, Texas. *American Antiquity* 26:543–45.

Pheasant, D. 1982. Soils analyses from Delaware Canyon. *In* Ferring, C. R., ed., The late Holocene prehistory of Delaware Canyon, Oklahoma, 64–94. Denton: Institute of Applied Sciences, University of North Texas.

Rainey, M. 1974. The Quaternary stratigraphy of the North Sulfur River. Master's thesis, Dallas, Southern Methodist University.

Ray, C. N. 1930. Report on some recent archeological researches in the Abilene section. *Bulletin of the Texas Archeological and Paleontological Society* 2:45–58.

———. 1938. New evidences of ancient man in Texas, found during professor Kirk Bryan's visit. *Bulletin of the Texas Archeological and Paleontological Society* 10:269–73.

————. 1940. The deeply buried Gibson Site. *Bulletin of the Texas Archeological and Paleontological Society* 12:223–37.

————. 1942. Ancient artifacts and mammoth's teeth of the McLean site. *Bulletin of the Texas Archeological and Paleontological Society* 14:137–38.

————. 1944. Stream bank silts of the Abilene region. *Bulletin of the Texas Archeological and Paleontological Society* 16: 117–47.

Ray, C. N., and K. Bryan. 1938. Folsomoid point found in alluvium beside a mammoth's bones. *Science* 88: 257–58.

Redder, A. J. 1985. Horn shelter no. 2: The south end. *Central Texas Archaeologist* 10:37–65.

Retallick, H. J. 1966. Geomorpholoy of the Domebo site. *In* Leonhardy, F. C., ed., Domebo: A paleo-indian mammoth kill in the prairie-plains. Lawton, Okla.: Museum of the Great Plains, Contributions in Archaeology 1:3–10.

Roberts, F. H. H. Jr. 1944. A deep burial on the Clear Fork of the Brazos River. *Bulletin of the Texas Archeological and Paleontological Society* 16:9–30.

Sellards, E. H. 1932. Geologic relations of deposits reported to contain artifacts at Frederick, Oklahoma. *Bulletin of the Geological Society of America* 43:783–96.

————. 1952. Early man in America. Austin: University of Texas Press.

Shuler, E. W. 1923. Occurrence of human remains with Pleistocene fossils, Lagow Sand Pit, Dallas. *Science* 57:333–34.

————. 1934. Collecting fossil elephants at Dallas, Texas. *Bulletin of the Texas Archeological and Paleontological Society* 6:75–79.

————. 1935. Terraces of the Trinity River, Dallas County, Texas. *Field and Laboratory* 3:44–53.

Slaughter, B. H., W. W. Crook Jr., R. K. Harris, D. C. Allen, and M. Seifert. 1962. The Hill-Shuler local faunas of the upper Trinity River, Dallas and Denton Counties, Texas. Austin: Bureau of Economic Geology, The University of Texas, Report of Investigations 48.

Spier, L. 1928a. Concerning man's antiquity at Frederick, Oklahoma. *Science* 67:160–61.

————. 1928b. A note on reputed ancient artifacts from Frederick, Oklahoma. *Science* 68:184.

Stanford, D. J. 1982. A critical review of archaeological evidence relating to the antiquity of human occupation of the new world. *In* Ubalaker, D. H. and H. J. Viola, eds. Plains Indian studies: A collection of essays in honor of John C. Ewers and Waldo Wedel, 208–18. Washington, D.C.: Smithsonian Institution Press.

Story, D. A. 1990. Culture history of the native Americans. *In* Story, D. A., ed., The archaeology and bioarchaeology of the Gulf Coastal Plain, vol. 1:163–366. Fayetteville: Arkansas Archaeological Survey, Research Series 38.

Suhm, D. A., A. D. Krieger, and E. B. Jelks. 1954. An introductory handbook of Texas archaeology. *Bulletin of the Texas Archaeological Society* 25:1–562.

Taylor, W. W. 1948. A study of archaeology. Carbondale: Southern Illinois Press.

Wedel, W. R. 1961. Prehistoric man on the Great Plains. Norman: University of Oklahoma Press.

Willey, G. R. 1968. One hundred years of American archaeology. *In* Brew, J. O., ed., One hundred years of anthropology, 29–53. Cambridge: Harvard University Press.

Willey, G. R., and P. Phillips. 1958. Method and theory in American archaeology. Chicago: University of Chicago Press.

Witte, A. H. 1935. Archeology of a section of upper Red River drainage. *Bulletin of the Texas Archeological and Paleontological Society* 7:47–56.

———. 1936. Kitchen middens of the upper Red River drainage. *Bulletin of the Texas Archeological and Paleontological Society* 7:71–86.

———. 1937. Buried middens in the floodplain of Little Wichita River. *Bulletin of the Texas Archeological and Paleontological Society* 9:222–26.

———. 1942. Channeled points from Clear Fork sites in north Texas. *Bulletin of the Texas Archeological and Paleontological Society* 14:27–31.

Wormington, H. M. 1957. Ancient man in North America. Denver: Denver Museum of Natural History.

Wyckoff, D. G. 1984. The Bethel and Rose Creek sites: Clues to Archaic occupations in central Oklahoma. *In* Kawecki, P. L. and D. L. Wyckoff, eds., Contributions to Cross Timbers prehistory. Duncan, Okla.: Cross Timbers Heritage Association, Studies in Oklahoma's Past 12:231–341.

CHAPTER FOUR

The History of Geoarchaeological Research in Kansas and Northern Oklahoma

Rolfe D. Mandel

INTRODUCTION

Geoarchaeological research has a long, rich history in portions of the Great Plains, especially in the southern and western High Plains (see Holliday, this volume; Albanese, this volume). However, the story of collaboration between geoscientists and archaeologists in Kansas and northern Oklahoma is relatively short. The main reason for this brief history is simple: few trained archeologists worked in the region before 1937. Before the early 1920s, universities and government agencies in these states employed no archaeologists. Also, because it is located in the interior of North America, this region was not readily accessible to scholars at the Smithsonian, the American Museum of Natural History, Harvard University, and other institutions east of the Mississippi River that were engaged in archaeological research during the late nineteenth and early twentieth centuries.

Other factors also delayed archaeological exploration in Kansas and northern Oklahoma. Wedel (1975, 1982) noted that during the late nineteenth century and well into the twentieth century, many archaeologists had no interest in the Central Plains because they believed that the region had been uninhabited by people before the reintroduction of the horse in the sixteenth century. In short, the myth of the Great American Desert was strongly entrenched

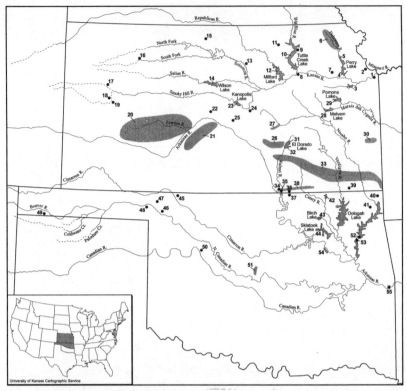

Map 4.1. The Central Plains of Kansas and northern Oklahoma, showing the localities mentioned in the text (keyed to table 4.1).

among eastern scholars. Wedel (1975) also emphasized that most of the anthropologists who ventured into the region during the late nineteenth century focused on the living inhabitants, the Plains Indians, instead of the artifacts of former occupants. Although a few anthropologists, ethnologists, and trained archaeologists investigated prehistoric sites in the region during the early twentieth century, most of their studies consisted of sporadic observations with little systematic fieldwork, much less any geoarchaeological research.

Interactions between archaeologists and geoscientists were sporadic in Kansas during the mid-1900s, and it was not until the 1980s that archaeological geology was frequently employed in the region. Once the archaeological community, especially those involved in cultural resource management (CRM), recognized the benefits of interdisciplinary research, geomorphology, stratigraphy, and pedology became essential components of archaeological investigations.

This chapter describes the history of geoarchaeological research in Kansas and the area of Oklahoma north of the Canadian River (map 4.1 and table 4.1). My review is organized around a set of themes used to trace the emergence and development of geoarchaeology in this region. First, I discuss how geologists and paleontologists conducted most of the earliest archaeological investigations in Kansas and Oklahoma. While these cursory studies did not include geologic assessments of archaeological sites, they demonstrated that an archaeological record existed in a region that many considered uninhabitable during prehistoric times. Next, I report on how geologists working in Kansas at the turn of the nineteenth century became involved, both intentionally and unintentionally, in the debate over human antiquity in the New World. At the time, the primary role of geologists in this controversy was to sort out the stratigraphy and chronology of early sites. This discussion is followed by a review of the few collaborations between archaeologists and geoscientists in the region from 1937 to 1965. Most of the summary focuses on the interactions of archaeologist Loren C. Eiseley and geologist H. T. U. Smith at the Spring Creek site in north-central Kansas. The last half of the chapter is devoted to the recent, substantive history of geoarchaeological research and the driving forces behind it: processual archaeology, CRM, and an academic environment that promotes interdisciplinary research.

GEOLOGISTS AS ARCHAEOLOGISTS: 1870–1900

In the years immediately following the Civil War, as geographical and geological explorations pushed west across Kansas along with the advancing frontier, the material remains of Native Americans attracted greater attention. However, few trained archaeologists were in the region at the time. Thus, the burden of recording and reporting archaeological sites often fell to geologists and naturalists (Wedel 1961:82). During the late 1800s several prominent geologists, including Benjamin F. Mudge, Charles N. Gould, Johan A. Udden, and Samuel W. Williston, became well known for their interest in the traces of prehistoric people in Kansas. Although none of them practiced geoarchaeology, their role as "archaeologists" warrants consideration.

In 1864, Benjamin Franklin Mudge addressed the Kansas state legislature on the geology of the state. Legislators were so impressed that they appointed him state geologist and director of the newly established Geological Survey of

Table 4.1 Archaeological Sites and Study Areas in Kansas and Oklahoma Mentioned in Text

Study Area or Site	Map Ref.[1]	Geoscientist	References(s)
Lower Mill Creek valley	1	R. D. Mandel	Mandel 1994c
Lansing Man Site	2	T. C. Chamberlin, G. F. Wright, N. H. Winchell, W. Upham, B. Shimek, R. D. Salisbury, S. W. Williston[2]	Williston 1902a, 1905b; Upham 1902a, 1902b; Winchell 1902, 1903; Chamberlin 1902a, 1902b; Shimek 1903
Clinton Lake	3	R.E. Mandel	Schmits et al. 1987
Perry Lake	4	R. D. Mandel	Mandel 1987a
Upper Parry Lake	5	W. Johnson	Johnson 1989
Upper Delaware River Basin	6	R. D. Mandel	Mandel et al. 1991
Sutter Site	7	W. Dort, Jr.	Dort 1974
Site 14RY38	8	R. D. Mandel	Mandel 1993
Coffey site	9	L. Schmits[3]	Schmits 1976, 1978, 1980
Tuttle Creek Lake	10	R. D. Mandel	Schmits et al. 1987
Unnamed site in Riley County, KS	11	B. F. Mudge	Mudge 1896
Milford Lake	12	R. D. Mandel	Mandel and Schmits 1984
Unnamed site in Cloud County, KS	13	B. F. Mudge	Mudge 1896
Wilson Lake	14	D. May	May 1986
Spring Creek site	15	H. T. U. Smith	Smith 1936; Eisley 1939
Penokee	16	S. W. Williston	Williston 1879
12 Mile Creek site	17	S. W. Williston, R. A. Rogers	Williston 1902a; Rogers 1984a; Rogers and Martin 1984
El Cuartelejo	18	S. W. Williston	Williston 1899; Williston and Martin 1900
Norton Bone Bed	19	W. C. Johnson	Hofman et al. 1995
Pawnee River Basin	20	R. D. Mandel	Mandel 1988a, 1992
Great Bend Prairie	21	A. Arbogast, W. Johnson	Logan et al. 1983
Unnamed site in Rice County, KS	22	B. F. Mudge	Mudge 1896

Table 4.1 Archaeological Sites and Study Areas in Kansas and Oklahoma Mentioned in Text (*continued*)

Study Area or Site	Map Ref.[1]	Geoscientist	References(s)
Kanopolis Lake	23	R. D. Mandel	Mandel 1989b, 1992
Paint Creek Village site	24	J. Udden	Udden 1900, 1919
Serpent Intaglio	25	A. E. Bettis III	Mallam 1985
Whitewater River Basin	26	R. D. Mandel	Mandel 1992
Doyle Creek Basin	27	R. D. Mandel	Mandel 1992
Melvern Lake	28	R. D. Mandel	Mandel and Schmits 1984
Pomona Lake	29	R. D. Mandel	Mandel and Schmits 1984
Fort Scott Lake	30	R. D. Mandel	Schmits et al. 1983
East Branch Walnut River	31	J. A. Artz	Artz 1983
El Dorado Lake	32	D. L. Drew	Drew 1979, 1984
Southeast Kansas Highway Corridor	33	R. D. Mandel	Mandel 1993a
Lower Walnut River valley	34	R. D. Mandel	Mandel 1993a, 1994a, 1994b
Arkansas City Country Club site	35	C. N. Gould	Gould 1898b
Maple City chert quarries	36	C. N. Gould	Gould 1898a, 1898b, 1899
Timbered Mounds	37	C. N. Gould	Gould 1898a, 1899
Highway 166 Corridor	38	R. D. Mandel	Mandel 1993b
Stigenwalt site (14LT351)	39	R. D. Mandel	Mandel 1990
Peoria Quarry or "Spanish Diggings"	40	W. H. Holmes	Holmes 1894; Bryan 1950
Afton Springs	41	W. H. Holmes	Holmes 1903
Copan Lake	42	S. A. Hall, J. A. Artz	Hall 1977a, 1977b, 1977c; Artz and Reid 1984
Birch Lake	43	S. A. Hall	Henry et al. 1979
Skiatook Lake	44	J. A. Artz	Artz 1988
Burnham site	45	B. J. Carter, R. Brakenridge, W. Dort, L. Martin	Wyckoff et al. 1990; Wyckoff and Carter 1994

Table 4.1 Archaeological Sites and Study Areas in Kansas and Oklahoma Mentioned in Text (*continued*)

Study Area or Site	Map Ref.[1]	Geoscientist	References(s)
Cooper site	46	B. J. Carter	Bement 1994; Carter and Bement 1995
Waugh site	47	B. J. Carter	Hofman and Carter 1991; Hofman et al. 1992
Laverty Ditch	48	D. G. Wyckoff[a]	Wyckoff 1985b
Nall site	49	G. L. Evans	Baker et al. 1957
Hajny site	50	B. J. Carter	Wyckoff et al. 1992
Deer Creek	51	B. Carter, R. Brackenridge	Carter 1990; Brakenridge 1990
Packard site	52	D. G. Wyckoff[a]	Wyckoff 1964, 1985a, 1989
Cherokee Turnpike	53	J. C. Dixon	Kay and Dixon 1990
Jenks/Bixby	54	J. C. Dixon	Odell et al 1990
Coppie Mound	55	F. C. Leonhardy	Leonhardy 1989

1. Kayed to map 4.1.

2. None of these geoscientists collaborated with archaeologist Gerald Fowke, who excavated the Lansign man site.

3. Primarily an archaeologist, but has considerable training in the geosciences.

Kansas (Page 1984). Mudge left the survey in 1865 and became professor of natural science at Kansas State Agricultural College in Manhattan (now Kansas State University). Mudge rapidly attained a reputation for collecting fossil vertebrates in Kansas and for collaborating with world-famous paleontologists, including Edward Cope and O. C. Marsh (Page 1984). He also gained some renown for his involvement in archaeological research. In a paper presented in 1873 at the sixth annual meeting of the Kansas Academy of Science, Mudge reported three localities where he had seen potsherds and other archaeological materials (Mudge 1896). One site was near the Santa Fe Trail crossing of Cow Creek in Rice County; another was near a spring in the extreme northeast corner of Riley County; and the third was near Asher Creek and the Solomon River in Cloud County. He considered the site in Cloud County the most significant of the three, noting that it had "much clay mixed with straw," as well as "fragments of what appeared to be ovens in which the pottery had been baked." However, despite his professional experience in geology, Mudge did not consider the geologic contexts of the sites.

Among the best archaeological investigations conducted in Kansas during the nineteenth century was the work carried out by Johan Udden from 1883 to 1888 at the Paint Creek Village site near Lindsborg (map 4.1). At the time, Udden was a natural science and civics instructor at Bethany College in Lindsborg, Kansas. One of his students told him there were mounds at Paint Creek (Underwood 1992). During the next five years, he spent a considerable amount of his own time and money excavating and studying the mounds (Udden 1909). His meticulous investigations at the Paint Creek Village yielded an abundance of pottery, a variety of stone and bone artifacts, a fragment of chain mail, and some glass beads. Based on the archaeological evidence, Udden suggested that the site had been occupied by semihorticulturalists and that it had been visited by Spaniards, perhaps even by members of the Coronado expedition (Udden 1900, 1909). Notably, the tentative conclusions reached by Udden, a geologist with no training in archaeology, were later confirmed by professional archaeologists, including Waldo Wedel (see Wedel 1935, 1959).

Udden left Kansas in 1888 and joined the faculty at Augustana College in Rock Island, Illinois. Although he continued to write about the Paint Creek Village, there are no records indicating that Udden worked at other archaeological sites after his departure from Kansas. Instead, he focused his research on important geological problems, such as the origin of loess (Hansen 1985). Udden eventually became the director of the Bureau of Economic Geology and Technology at the University of Texas, where he gained a reputation as a pioneer geologist (Lungstrom 1992). Wedel (1959:86) commented: "Despite Udden's disclaimer to the designation of archaeologist, one wonders whether archaeology was not the loser when his career led him into full-time geologic studies."

Working in Kansas during the late 1800s, Charles Gould, like Udden, was an emerging geologist with interests in archaeology. In 1897 and 1898, Gould investigated two clusters of mounds: the Timbered Mounds on the Kaw Reservation about eight miles south of Maple City, Kansas, in what is now Kay County, Oklahoma, (Gould 1898a) and a group of mounds in and around Maple City (Gould 1899) (map 4.1). The mounds in both areas consisted of a mixed matrix of soil, limestone cobbles, and chert fragments. Although Gould thought that some of the mounds appeared to be collapsed structures, his friend and colleague, Samuel W. Williston, rightfully convinced him that they were tailings from Native American chert quarries (Gould 1898a, 1899). Gould actually made an important geoarchaeological observation when he noted that the nodular chert occurring in these quarries also occurred as artifacts in mounds at the present-day Arkansas City Country Club site (14CO3), thirty-two kilometers to the west-northwest (map 4.1). (Gould 1898a, 1898b, 1899). His interpretation was based, in part, on fossil inclusions in the chert. Gould left Kansas in 1900 and in 1908 became the first director of the newly established Oklahoma Geological Survey. While working as a professional geologist in Oklahoma, he continued to engage in archaeological research, including investigations at the controversial Frederick site in extreme southwestern Oklahoma (see Ferring, this volume).

Samuel Wendell Williston stands out as a late nineteenth-century American geologist who made significant and lasting contributions to Kansas archaeology. However, these contributions are often overshadowed by his other accomplishments (Reynolds 1992). Williston was, in the words of Shor (1971) a "complete scientist." His interests and expertise spanned several scientific fields, including geology, medicine, paleontology, entomology, and archaeology. During the 1870s and 1880s, Williston collected fossil bones in western Kansas, Colorado, and Wyoming for O. C. Marsh of the Peabody Museum of Natural History at Yale University. Through this experience, he became familiar with large areas of the High Plains and amassed an impressive collection of fossil vertebrates. Williston also documented some archaeological finds while he was in the field, including an outline of a human figure more than sixty feet long on a bluff overlooking the South Fork of the Solomon River near Penokee, Kansas (Williston 1879:16) (map 4.1). The figure, which consists of small cobbles laid out in a human shape, was relocated by professional archaeologists in 1977 (Witty 1978). Williston's early report provides evidence supporting the argument that the Penokee figure was constructed by Native Americans (Reynolds 1992).

Williston joined the faculty of the University of Kansas (K.U.) in 1890 and remained there for twelve years. During his tenure he served as professor of geology and anatomy and as the first dean of the school of medicine. Although Williston was a prolific writer, only forty-five of his more than four thousand pages of published scientific research were devoted to archaeology (Reynolds 1992). However, in retrospect, it is clear that his brief archaeological papers report on three of the most significant sites in North America: the El Cuartelejo Pueblo ruin in Scott County, Kansas; the 12 Mile Creek Site in Logan County, Kansas; and the Lansing Man site in Doniphan County, Kansas.

Williston published the first account of the El Cuartelejo ruin soon after visiting it in 1898 (Williston 1899). The site is near Ladder Creek in what is now Lake Scott State Park in northern Scott County (map 4.1). Williston initially thought it was a Spanish settlement constructed during the early nineteenth century (Williston 1899:113). Recognizing the possible significance of the site, he and his field assistant, Handel T. Martin, excavated the seven-room pueblo (Williston and Martin 1900:126). Their efforts yielded numerous artifacts, including pottery, metates, and objects of chipped and ground stone, plus a large quantity of burned maize (Williston and Martin 1900; Martin 1909). Based on the architecture and other features, Frederick W. Hodge, an anthropologist at the U.S. National Museum (Smithsonian Institution) Bureau of American Ethnology (BAE), determined that the ruins actually date to the late seventeenth and early eighteenth century (Hodge 1900). He suggested that it was the pueblo of El Cuartelejo occupied by Pueblo Indians who fled from New Mexico to avoid Spanish oppression. More recent investigations documented evidence of Apache occupation near the pueblo and extending for several miles up and down Ladder Creek (Gunnerson 1968). Although there is still debate among archaeologists as to the true location of El Cuartelejo, the archaeological evidence affirms the ruins at Lake Scott State Park as the only pueblo structure in association with a Plains Apache village at the proper time in history for the El Cuartelejo settlement (Witty 1971). While Williston's initial interpretation of the age of the site was incorrect, his excavation techniques and documentation were commendable for the time.

One of the earliest archaeological investigations in Oklahoma was conducted by William Henry Holmes, a multitalented individual with training and experience in art, geology, and archaeology (Noelke 1974; Gifford and Rapp 1985:412–13). Holmes was on the staff of the U.S. Geological Survey (USGS) from 1872 to 1889. In the late 1870s he began contributing archaeological studies to the BAE, and in 1889 he finally switched from the USGS to the BAE. In 1891, Holmes conducted some minor excavations at the flint quarries located near Peoria, Oklahoma (map 4.1). The quarries, commonly known as the "Spanish Diggings," were brought to Holmes's attention by geomorphologist G. K. Gilbert of the USGS (Bell 1987). Holmes (1894) reported that evidence of quarries in the form of pits were scattered over four or five acres. He also noted many locations where the flint had been worked. According to Holmes (1894), there was an abundance of flakes, cores, roughed-out quarry blocks, unfinished materials, and hammerstones, but he claimed that no finished specimens were found.

SEARCHING FOR THE FIRST AMERICANS: 1895–1915

The late nineteenth and early twentieth century was a time of considerable debate over human antiquity in the New World (Haynes 1969, 1990; Meltzer 1983, 1991). Discoveries during the late 1850s revealed that people in Europe lived at the same time as fauna that became extinct at the end of the Pleistocene period (Grayson 1983:79). These finds caused researchers to look for similar evidence of early human inhabitants in America (Wilmsen 1965; Meltzer 1983, 1991). As was the case in European controversy, the role of geologists in the American debate was to interpret the stratigraphy of early sites and estimate their age (Waters 1992).

Some of the initial observations that suggested peopling of America during the Pleistocene were made by Lyell (1863), Koch (1857), and Whitney (1880). However, it was Charles Abbott's claim of discovering "Paleolithic" artifacts that launched the search for Pleistocene traces of the first Americans (Meltzer 1991). Abbott, a physician and naturalist, reported that he had found artifacts deeply buried in Pleistocene sediments of the Delaware River near Trenton, New Jersey

(Abbott 1876a). Noting that the artifacts were "rude" in form, Abbott and his close friend, Frederic Ward Putnam of the Peabody Museum at Harvard, concluded that they were Paleolithic implements like those that had been found in Pleistocene contexts in Europe (Abbott 1876a, 1876b, 1877, 1892; Putnam 1888).

Initially, archaeologists and geologists almost universally accepted the idea of Paleolithic people in America (Meltzer 1991). Between 1880 and 1890, researchers reported similar "Paleolithic" discoveries throughout North America (see summaries in Hrdlička 1907; McGee and Thomas 1905; Holmes 1919; Jenness 1933:93). However, the American Paleolithic was soon challenged by some of the most distinguished scholars of the time, including William Henry Holmes, Ales Hrdlička, and Thomas C. Chamberlain (Holmes 1890, 1892, 1893; Hrdlička 1902; Chamberlain 1897). By the turn of the nineteenth century, most archaeologists and geologists had dismissed the American Paleolithic, and new discoveries of American paleoliths had virtually ceased. Exceptions to this trend were reports of paleoliths in Kansas (Winchell 1912, 1913) and extreme western Missouri (Owen 1907, 1909).

In 1912 Newton Horace Winchell, a founder of the *American Geologist* and the Geological Society of America, reported the discovery of "Paleolithic" artifacts in east-central Kansas (Winchell 1912). The artifacts were collected on the land surface, either on uplands or a high terrace in the Kansas River valley. Winchell (1912) provided a fairly detailed description of the geology and geomorphology of the area where the artifacts were found. In addition, he used a geologic concept to account for the antiquity of the paleoliths. Specifically, Winchell proposed that strongly weathered artifacts, which displayed distinct patination, were considerably older than less weathered artifacts, which he referred to as "semi-patinated" specimens (Winchell 1912, 1913). He closed his 1912 paper with the following line of reasoning:

> The argument of this article is based on the fact (which is well known by geologists) that siliceous rocks, such as quartzite, jaspilite, flint and chert, are particularly indestructible under atmospheric agents. The boulders of red quartzite found near Topeka, in the Kansan moraine, are entirely intact, whereas those of granite can be crushed in the hand. Therefore chipped chert, whenever it has a weathered scale of decay [patinated], must be older than the Kansan moraine (Winchell 1912:178).

Although Winchell did not understand patination rates, nor did he realize the great antiquity of the "Kansan moraine," he was ahead of his time in using a weathering index to infer the age of artifacts. However, like other geologists who proposed Paleolithic finds in America during the early 1900s (e.g, Owen 1907, 1909), Winchell attracted little attention from the archaeological community.

One of the most important discoveries relevant to the debate over human antiquity in America occurred in Kansas about twenty years after the Trenton find. In 1895, while collecting vertebrate fossils in western Kansas, H. T. Martin and one of Samuel Williston's other assistants, T. R. Overton, found a small fluted projectile point in direct association with a complete skeleton of a bison (Williston 1902a, 1905a). The site was located on the bank of 12 Mile Creek, a small tributary of the Smoky Hill River in Logan County (map 4.1). Based on descriptions of the bison bones, Williston concluded that they were from "an extinct form" (Williston 1902a:313). He immediately recognized the potential significance of the find and instructed Martin and Overton to proceed with excavations at the site. They eventually recovered the remains of twelve bison that were sealed beneath approximately 5.5 meters of sediment (Hill 1996; Hill et al. 1997). Williston examined the bison bones and initially identified them as the extinct species *Bison antiquus* Leidy (Williston 1902a). However, according to Williston (1902a:313), "Mr. Lucas of the National Museum, after an exhaustive study of the known species of fossil bisons of America, recognized the species as new, and gave to it the name *Bison occidentalis*, known otherwise only from a fragmentary skull collected in Alaska." Although debate continues about which bison species are represented at 12 Mile Creek, it is clear that it is a late Pleistocene form (Hill 1996).

A brief description of the geologic context of the bone bed at the 12 Mile Creek site was included in H. T. Martin's field notes and later published by Williston (1902a:315):

> Overlying this [bone bed] there were twenty feet of the so-called plains-marl. Below the bone layer there was a four-inch thick layer of a sandy conglomerate, which rested directly upon the Niobrara chalk, here forming a bluff to the north of the bone deposit.

Williston's interpretation of Martin's description of the geology is as follows:

> The material covering the skeletons was the wide-spread upland marl, doubtless in part of wind origin. In the same material, and not far distant from the place where the bones were exhumed, I have obtained bone of *Elephas primigenius*, a species characteristic of the Equus Beds (Williston 1902a: 315).

Recent studies have established that the 12 Mile Creek site is a Paleoindian-age bison bone bed. Apatite and collagen fractions from one of the bones recovered during the 1895 excavation yielded radiocarbon ages of 10,435±260 B.P. and 10,245±335 B.P., respectively (Rogers 1984a; Rogers and Martin 1984). Hill (1996) reported a radiocarbon age of 10,520±70 B.P. determined by AMS dating of the KOH-collagen fraction from another bone in the 12 Mile Creek collection.

It is important to stress that Williston recognized the great antiquity of the 12 Mile Creek site without the benefit of radiocarbon dating. In addition to associating a human artifact with extinct forms of bison, Williston affirmed that the bone layer was in the Equus Beds, a geologic unit that he considered late Pleistocene in age (Williston 1897; 1898:90–91). Hence, Williston's 1902 report on 12 Mile Creek is the earliest description of a Native American projectile point in association with the bones of extinct animals in undisturbed Pleistocene-age deposits. Moreover, the find predates by thirty years the unequivocal discovery at Folsom, New Mexico, of other distinctive points with Pleistocene fauna.

Despite its significance, Williston's report was largely ignored by the anthropological community (Rogers and Martin 1984; Hawley 1992a). However, other scientists, especially paleontologists, regarded 12 Mile Creek as an important Pleistocene locality with an indisputable human component (Figgins 1927; Sellards 1940, 1952; McClung 1908; Osborn 1910). It is puzzling that the 12 Mile Creek site did not enter the debate over human antiquity in the New World. Some scholars questioned the Pleistocene dating of the site, contending that *Bison occidentalis* may have survived into the Holocene (e.g., Romer 1933). However, this argument is invalid given the fact that the geologic unit that yielded the bison remains at 12 Mile Creek also contained Pleistocene fauna, including elephant, at a nearby locality (Schultz and Eiseley 1935:312). Wedel (1959:89) was pragmatic when he considered the skepticism among anthropologists who doubted the antiquity of the 12 Mile Creek site: "Here, as elsewhere in America at the time, I suppose there would have been no question about the Pleistocene dating of the site had there not been evidence of human associations."

In 1901, William Henry Holmes reported finds of Native American artifacts with elephant bones in a spring near Afton Springs, Indian Territory (northeastern Oklahoma) (map 4.1). From his brief excavations at the Afton Springs site, Holmes (1903) concluded that the spring's flow was mixing artifacts from an uppermost deposit with mammoth and mastodon bones from an earlier, lower one. He suggested that Osage Indians deposited the artifacts in the spring as offerings at a shrine. Bell (1958:6–7) subsequently determined that the spearpoints illustrated by Holmes are Afton points dating to approximately 4000–3500 B.P.

The search for the first Americans changed direction at the beginning of the twentieth century with several discoveries of human skeletal remains in deposits presumed to be late Pleistocene in age (Meltzer 1991; Bettis, this volume). Notable among these were two skeletons—an adult male and a child—found in February 1902 during the excavation of a root cellar near Lansing, Kansas (map 4.1). The skeletons were enclosed in rocky talus beneath twenty feet of silty sediment at the mouth of a small tributary to the Missouri River. News of the discovery quickly spread, prompting William Henry Holmes to dispatch Gerald Fowke to Lansing. Fowke excavated a deep exploratory trench adjacent to the root cellar in order to better understand the geology of the site and to search for artifacts and additional human remains. By the end of 1902, the locality had been visited by a "who's who" of Quaternary geologists of the time, including Thomas C. Chamberlin (University of Chicago), G. Frederick Wright (U.S. Geological Survey), Newton Horace Winchell (University of Minnesota), Warren Upham (U.S. Geological Survey), Bohumil Shimek (University of Iowa), and Rollin D. Salisbury (University of Chicago). However, Samuel Williston published the first geologic note on the locality. In his August 1, 1902, *Science* paper, "A Fossil Man from Kansas," he concluded that the human bones were sealed in alluvium that was deposited during early postglacial times, but that they were contemporaneous with mammoth, mastodon, extinct bison, camel, and other ancient forms found in the Equus Beds (Williston 1902b). Williston's paper was quickly followed by claims that the silts above the skeletal remains were Iowan-age (Wisconsinan) loess deposits (Upham 1902a; Winchell 1902). This set off a fierce debate largely aired through a series of papers in the nation's prominent geological journals (e.g., Upham 1902b; Winchell 1903; Chamberlin 1902a, 1902b; Shimek 1903; Williston 1905b).

Questions concerning the antiquity of the Lansing skeletons centered on whether the sediments overlying the human remains were actually loess, and therefore of glacial age, or deposits reworked in recent (Holocene) times from older loess formations. Compounding the argument was the long-standing conflict over whether loess was wind or water derived, and all of Pleistocene age (Meltzer 1991:24). Ultimately, Chamberlin's interpretation that the silts above the skeletons were not primary loess, and that, therefore, the human remains postdated the glacial period, won the approval of Samuel Calvin, Rollin Salisbury, and Bohumil Shimek, the loess experts of the day (letters in Chamberlin 1902a:777–79; Shimek 1903). The principal archaeologists involved in the debate, William Holmes and Gerald Fowke, also agreed with Chamberlin's interpretation (Holmes 1902; Fowke 1926–1927).

The debate over the antiquity of the Lansing skeletons took another turn when Ales Hrdlička became involved in the controversy. At the time many of the anthropologists who were interested in the prehistory of Native Americans, including Hrdlička, were substituting anatomical or morphological dating for geologic dating (Stewart 1949). Hrdlička had an opportunity to study the skull of the adult skeleton from Lansing soon after he joined the staff of the U.S. National Museum. His interpretation was as follows:

> The Lansing skeleton is practically identical with the typical male skeleton of a large majority of present Indians of the Middle and Eastern states. Any assumption that it is thousands of years old would carry with it not only the comparatively easily acceptable assumption of so early an existence of man on this continent, but also the very far more difficult conclusion that this man was physically identical with the Indian of the present time, and that his physical characteristics during all the thousand of years assumed to have passed have undergone absolutely no important modification (Hrdlička 1903:328–29).

The debate over Lansing, like other early sites in America, became stalemated with neither side changing its position (Hill et al.1996). By 1910 much of the controversy had subsided, and by the late 1950s, Lansing Man was "an obscure fossil which appeared only in old books or as a question on doctoral examinations" (Bass 1973:101).

It was not until 1965 that the antiquity of the Lansing skeletons was resolved. William M. Bass, a physical anthropologist at the University of Kansas, submitted bones from the adult skeleton to three laboratories for radiocarbon dating. The bones yielded four radiocarbon ages: 4610±200, 4750±250, 5785±105, and 6970±200 B.P. (Bass 1973). An average of all four ages is 5529 B.P., which suggests that the skeletons date to the early Middle Archaic. The radiocarbon data are supported by the results of a recent skeletal analysis. Bass (1973) determined that the skull of the adult from the Lansing site is morphologically closer to the Early Archaic populations than to the later Protohistoric or Historic Plains Indian populations. Thus, while Hrdlička was correct in doubting that the Lansing skeletons were those of Paleoindians, he was wrong in assuming that the adult skeleton was very similar to male skeletons of modern Native Americans (Bass 1973:103).

A FEW BRIEF INTERACTIONS: 1937–1965

Archaeological studies in Kansas during the first several decades of the twentieth century followed the trend set in the late nineteenth century: they were sporadic and rarely conducted by trained archaeologists. However, 1937 marked a turning point in Kansas archaeology. Waldo Wedel's archaeological investigations for the U.S. National Museum (Smithsonian) were initiated in the state that year and continued until 1940 (Wedel 1959:98). Also, Loren C. Eiseley was hired by the University of Kansas (K.U.) sociology department in 1937, making him the state's first academically employed anthropologist/ archaeologist (Hawley 1992b). With the exception of a few years between 1944 and 1946, K.U. maintained the tradition of having a professional archaeologist on its faculty.

Although Eiseley's career at K.U. was brief and generally unremarkable, he was responsible for what may well be the first case of interdisciplinary research directed on an archaeological site in the Central Plains (Hawley 1992b:12). Several months after he arrived at K.U., Eiseley heard about a deposit of ash and bone on the banks of Spring Creek (Christianson 1990:187). The locality, which became known as the Spring Creek site (14SM308), is in Smith County, Kansas, about twenty miles south of the Kansas-Nebraska border (map 4.1). Eiseley visited the site on weekends and eventually discovered charcoal, fragmentary bison remains, chert flakes, and other evidence of human occupation about ten feet below the surface of an alluvial terrace. He was intrigued by the great depth of the cultural deposits and thought that he was on to something quite old, perhaps a Folsom site (Christianson 1990:187). Being a strong advocate of interdisciplinary research, Eiseley sought the help of geologist Harold T. U. Smith to reconstruct the alluvial history of the site (Hawley 1992b:10).

Harold Smith served on the faculty at K.U. from 1935 to 1956. A specialist in geomorphology, he received his Ph.D. from Harvard and had studied under Kirk Bryan, one of the most prominent geologists of the time. Bryan was himself heavily involved in studies of early sites in North America, including several Folsom occupations in the Plains (see Holliday, this volume; Albanese, this volume). Through his interactions with Bryan, Smith had gained an appreciation for geoarchaeological research.

Eiseley and Smith worked at the Spring Creek site on weekends during the winter of 1937–38 and in August 1938. They were assisted by Ivan Phetteplace, a local amateur archaeologist, and several students from K.U. Smith (1938) described the geomorphic setting of the site as "a 21-foot cut-and-fill terrace." An area 1 yard wide was excavated to a depth of 10.5 feet below the surface of the terrace. They recovered "fossilized bones" (mostly bison), numerous flakes, a few scrapers, and a single projectile point (Eiseley 1939:221). The point, discovered by Phetteplace, dashed Eiseley's hopes (Christianson 1990:187). Eiseley noted that although it predated "by a considerable margin" the appearance of agriculture in the Central Plains, it was neither Folsom nor any other Pleistocene type (Eiseley 1939:221).

Smith's geomorphic evaluation of the Spring Creek site supported Eiseley's interpretation that the cultural deposits did not date to the Pleistocene. Using estimated rates of post-Wisconsinan erosion and deposition for glaciated regions of the Midwest, Smith concluded that the accumulation of 10.5 feet of sediment above the cultural deposits, subsequent downcutting by Spring Creek, and the development of the modern floodplain all could have occurred in the "latter half or third of postglacial time" (Smith 1938). Taking a liberal view of Smith's assessment, Eiseley suggested that the site dated to approximately 5000 B.P. and that it could be older (Eiseley 1939). As it turned out, a conservative estimate would have been more appropriate. Charcoal recently recovered from the deepest cultural horizon at the Spring Creek site yielded a radiocarbon age of 2940 ± 70 B.P. (Hawley 1994).

Although the Spring Creek site was not a Folsom occupation, its suspected age made it a significant discovery even by today's standards. However, Eiseley never undertook full-scale excavations, and the site was underreported in scientific journals (Hawley 1992b:12). Eiseley's lack of enthusiasm may be attributed to his desire to find something much older, preferably a Folsom occupation (Christianson 1990:188). Another explanation may be that the relationship between Eiseley and Smith was strained. Letters between Carroll Clark (chairman of the K.U. Department of Sociology) and Eiseley indicate that they did not trust Smith (Hawley 1992b:12). Eiseley and Smith discontinued their cooperative efforts after the Spring Creek excavations, and Eiseley left K.U. in 1944 to become chair of the Department of Sociology at Oberlin College, Ohio. Sadly, an archaeologist and a geologist would not collaborate again in Kansas until the early 1960s.

The paucity of interaction between archaeologists and geoscientists in Kansas and northern Oklahoma between 1939 and 1965 may be largely attributed to the research interests of the archaeologists who were working in the region at that time. Carlyle S. Smith, who had been trained as an archaeologist under the direction of William Duncan Strong, joined the K.U. faculty in 1947. Although Smith appreciated interdisciplinary research, he was primarily interested in late prehistoric and historic archaeology (Smith 1992). Because the cultural deposits associated with the Pawnee occupations he studied are at or very near the land surface, Smith's investigations did not demand the help of a geologist.

Waldo Wedel, who was periodically involved in Kansas archaeology between 1934 and the time of his death in 1995, is regarded by many as one of the most influential archaeologists to work in the Central Plains. It seems odd that Wedel never sought the help of a geoscientist on projects in Kansas, although he was one of the strongest proponents of interdisciplinary research (e.g., Wedel 1941). However, like Carlyle Smith, Wedel focused on surficial Late Prehistoric and Protohistoric sites that simply did not require geologic evaluation (Wedel 1959, 1961, 1986).

At the same time, some archaeologists seemed to resent the growing involvement of geologists in archaeological investigations during the 1940s. George S. Metcalf, a well-known archaeologist who participated in River Basin Surveys throughout the Great Plains from 1947 to 1953 (Gunnerson and Gunnerson 1977), echoed some of this irritation in a letter to Carlyle Smith:

> For the life of me I cannot find the connection between archaeology and loess geology, and the more that Ried and Ted White and other authorities lecture us on it the less use I can see in it. What do you think of the program for the [Sixth] Plains Conference? Personally I think that it is top heavy on the side of geology. I don't think that I will attend much of it. I aim to be there and see people, but I am damned if I am going to waste time sitting through boring talks on dirt. If I wanted any of that I would attend a conference on geology. To hell with it. I think that archaeology should attend to archaeology and let geologists work in geology (G. S. Metcalf to C. S. Smith, November 4, 1948).

With the exception of a study at the Nall site (Baker et al. 1957), there was no collaboration between archaeologists and geoscientists at sites in northern Oklahoma before the mid-1970s. Instead they worked independently of each other. For example, in 1942 Kirk Bryan conducted a study of the "Spanish Diggings" in northeastern Oklahoma (map 4.1). As noted earlier, this chert quarry was first described by William Henry Holmes, who had collected numerous lithic materials from the site (Holmes 1894). Bryan was puzzled by Holmes's report that his large collection of artifacts from the quarry did not include a single piece that "could be called an implement." Bryan set out on his own to prove that Holmes was wrong. His mission proved successful when he recovered numerous retouched flakes and other tools, including a projectile point (Bryan 1950).

The Nall site, a multicomponent prehistoric occupation on the High Plains surface of the western Oklahoma Panhandle, was investigated by William E. Baker, T. N. Campbell, and Glen L. Evans during the late 1950s (Baker et al. 1957) (map 4.1). Baker was a self-trained avocational archaeologist from Boise City, Oklahoma, who often worked with professional archaeologists, including Campbell. At the time of the Nall study, Campbell was on the faculty at the University of Texas at Austin. Evans, a Quaternary geologist with a strong interest in archaeology, worked closely with E. H. Sellards (University of Texas at Austin) and is best known for his geologic investigations at the Lubbock Lake and Midland sites (Holliday 1997:30–33, 40). The Nall site is in a dune field south of the North Canadian (Beaver) River and was exposed by wind erosion during the 1930s (Baker et al. 1957). Despite Evans's involvement in the study, a detailed geologic investigation was not conducted at Nall. Instead, Baker and his colleagues (Baker et al. 1957) focused on the rich assemblage of Paleoindian through late Prehistoric projectile points collected from the surface. They noted that the Paleoindian points were eroding from a clay-rich buried horizon exposed in the blowout. Unfortunately, no additional stratigraphic information was provided.

In summary, professional archaeologists made great strides in the Central Plains of Kansas and northern Oklahoma between 1937 and 1965. However, they did not quickly adopt the concept of interdisciplinary research, which archeologists elsewhere in the Plains grasped during this period (see Albanese, this volume; May, this volume). Although geoarchaeology had a promising start at the Spring Creek site, it quickly faltered with Eiseley's departure from Kansas in 1944. Nearly forty years would pass before another archaeological study in the region would involve collaboration between an archaeologist and a geologist. However, the driving force behind the resurgence of geoarchaeology was not due to the influence of a prominent archaeologist like Loren Eiseley or Waldo Wedel. Instead, it was driven by federal mandates for cultural resource management (CRM).

PROCESSUAL ARCHAEOLOGY AND CRM-DRIVEN GEOARCHAEOLOGY: 1965–PRESENT

In the mid-1960s researchers witnessed a major change in archaeological methods and theory with the appearance of processual or "new" archaeology (Hill et al. 1996). Lewis Binford, who led the processual movement, wanted archaeology to become more scientific and involve hypothesis testing (Binford 1968). As Bettis (this volume) points out, the growing concern for the scientific method of investigation, plus the emergence of the environmental approach to archaeology in the 1960s, caused archaeologists to seek specialists to determine the environmental context of cultural deposits. However, archaeologists often lacked resources to support their own research, much less provide funds for special studies. This changed with the passage of three pieces of federal legislation: the National Historic Preservation Act of 1966, the National Environmental Policy Act of 1969, and the Moss-Bennett Bill of 1974. Together these laws secured funding for preservation of historical and archaeological data in areas affected by federal construction projects, thereby establishing the basis for CRM programs (Hill et al. 1996:33).

The most important factor contributing to the rapid development of geoarchaeology over the past twenty-five years has been the growth of the CRM industry. According to Grosser (1981), more than 95 percent of the archaeological fieldwork conducted in the Great Plains since the late 1960s has been tied to federally supported CRM projects. This fieldwork has generally focused on locating archaeological deposits in proposed project areas. Faced with large areas to assess, such as reservoirs and major highways, archaeologists have turned to geoscientists to help focus their surveys and identify localities with high potential for buried cultural deposits. Once the cultural resources are located, they must consider the site significance and the formation of the archaeological record. Here again, archaeologists have sought the help of geoscientists, especially in addressing site-formation processes, paleoenvironmental conditions, and geologic filtering of the archaeological record.

Some of the best early examples of CRM-driven interdisciplinary research are the investigations prompted by the construction of impoundments on tributaries in the Verdigris River basin in northeastern Oklahoma. Most of these investigations were conducted by the University of Tulsa Laboratory of Archaeology between 1976 and 1988. The project areas included Copan Lake on the Little Caney River (Henry 1977a; Keyser and Farley 1979, 1980; Prewitt 1980;

Kay 1981; Reid and Artz 1984; Artz 1985); Birch Lake on Birch Creek (Henry 1977b; Henry et al. 1979); and Skiatook Lake on Hominy Creek (Henry 1978, 1980; Artz 1988) (map 4.1). The research designs of the archaeological investigations stressed the development of a cultural chronology for archaeological sites in conjunction with the recovery of paleoenvironmental information. Donald O. Henry, who directed most of the studies, emphasized the integration of cultural and paleoenvironmental evidence in an attempt to better understand the prehistoric human ecology of the project areas. He brought in Stephen A. Hall, a physical geographer on the faculty at North Texas State University (now at the University of Texas at Austin; see Ferring, this volume), to conduct the geomorphological and paleoenvironmental investigations. In June 1981 Joe A. Artz, an archaeologist with considerable training in the geosciences, was hired by the Laboratory of Archaeology and served as project geomorphologist until August 1983.

Hall's (1977a) study of the Little Caney River near Copan Lake was the first detailed investigation of Holocene valley fills in the Verdigris drainage system of Oklahoma. He identified three major alluvial units beneath a low, broad terrace of the Little Caney River: Units A, B, and C. Unit C is the oldest of the three, considered early or mid-Holocene in age. Unit B, which aggraded during the late Holocene, is the dominant valley fill and unconformably overlies Unit C. Hall also identified a thick, dark buried soil (Copan paleosol) that can be traced throughout northeastern Oklahoma. The Copan paleosol is at the top of Unit B and at the top of Unit C where Unit B is missing. Using radiocarbon ages determined on charcoal above and below the soil, he bracketed formation of the Copan paleosol between approximately 1900 and 900 years B.P. After formation of the Copan paleosol and before around 850 B.P., the Little Caney River downcut. By 850 B.P., alluviation was underway and the Copan paleosol was buried in the central portion of the valley by Unit A (Hall 1977a).

Hall (1977b) studied the geomorphology of Birch Creek in conjunction with archaeological investigations at Birch Creek Reservoir. He identified two stratigraphic units beneath the valley floor and correlated them with units A and B in the Little Caney River valley (Hall 1977b:12). Hall (1977b:13) also recognized the Copan paleosol in Birch Creek valley.

Hall (1977c) and Henry (1978, 1980) studied the Holocene alluvial stratigraphy and chronology of tributaries in Hominy Creek basin in the area of Skiatook Lake, Oklahoma. Artz (1988) collected additional data, subsequently refining the stratigraphic framework and depositional sequence presented in the previous studies.

Hall's investigations in Hominy Creek basin and Birch Creek valley are particularly significant because they included reconstruction of late Holocene paleoenvironments. He inferred climatic change from pollen and land snail evidence in several rockshelters (Hall 1977b, 1980, 1982). These were the first studies in the Central Plains that integrated paleoenvironmental data into archaeological investigations.

The stratigraphic framework presented in Hall's investigation of the Little Caney River, Birch Creek, and Hominy Creek basin has appeared in many archaeological studies that consider the Holocene stratigraphy in northeastern Oklahoma. Specifically, his lithostratigraphic units (A, B, and C) and pedostratigraphic unit (Copan paleosol) have been radiocarbon dated and/or described by other researchers (e.g., Nials 1977; Keyser and Farley 1979, 1980; Prewitt 1980; Kay 1981; Salisbury 1980; Saunders 1980; Lees et al. 1982; Artz and Reid 1984; Odell et al. 1990). Artz and Reid (1984) refined the alluvial chronology of the Little Caney River system, and Artz (1985) identified soil-geomorphic relationships in the valleys of the Little Caney and one of its major tributaries, Cotton Creek. Going one step further, Artz (1985) demonstrated how the soil-geomorphic relationships could be used to guide the search for buried Late Archaic archaeological deposits (Artz 1985).

Two archaeological surveys conducted in northeastern Oklahoma in 1990 included geomorphological investigations: the Cherokee Turnpike Project in Mayes County, and the Jenks/Bixby Project near Tulsa (map 4.1). John Dixon, a geomorphologist in the geography department at the University of Arkansas, was involved with both of these CRM projects. The Cherokee Turnpike Project focused on a small portion of the Neosho River valley in the area of what is now Fort Gibson Reservoir (Kay and Dixon 1990). Soils and sedimentological information were used to distinguish Pleistocene valley fill from Holocene alluvium. Based on the inferred ages of the alluvial deposits, Kay and Dixon (1990) determined where buried archaeological materials are likely to occur in the project area.

The Jenks/Bixby Project was conducted along the western bluffline of the Arkansas River between the communities of Jenks and Bixby, Oklahoma (Odell et al. 1990). Although the archaeological survey focused on high positions of the valley landscape, John Dixon examined and described a low Holocene terrace and the modern floodplain of the Arkansas River. Most of

Fig. 4.1. Excavation units at the Coffey site during the 1975 field season. Localities I and II are in the background and foreground, respectively. The Big Blue River is on the west (left) side of the site. Photo by Martin Stein, 1975, photo no. 14PO1-14, courtesy of the Kansas State Historical Society.

the geomorphic information was gleaned from the Tulsa County Soil Survey. However, two cores were taken on the valley floor of the Arkansas River. The history of Holocene landscape evolution in the project area was inferred from limited sedimentological and soil-geomorphic data (Odell et al. 1990:24–25).

As in Oklahoma, CRM projects associated with reservoirs were responsible for the emergence of geoarchaeology in Kansas during the 1970s. The funding level for these projects was initially inadequate to support special studies. Nevertheless, geologic assessments were incorporated into some projects, as demonstrated in the mitigation of one of the most significant prehistoric sites in Kansas, the Coffey site.

Coffey is located on the east bank of the Big Blue River in northeastern Kansas (map 4.1 and fig. 4.1). Mett Shippee and Ralph S. Solecki first recorded this site as 14PO1 during their 1952 survey of the proposed Tuttle Creek Lake (Solecki 1953). Their investigation was part of the Smithsonian Institution's River Basin Surveys. At the time, Shippee and Solecki described 14PO1 as consisting of a ten-acre surface scatter on a slope leading to the Big Blue River (Solecki 1953). The site was tested in 1957 by the University of Kansas under the direction of Caryle S. Smith, but the investigation was discontinued when cultural material was found to be confined to the plow zone (Johnson 1973).

In 1970 Ed Coffey, a local landowner, brought 14PO1 to the attention of the University of Kansas field crew conducting a shoreline survey of Tuttle Creek Reservoir. He had discovered artifacts eroding from the river bank on the west side of the site. Test excavations revealed several cultural strata of Middle Archaic affiliation located between 2.75 and 3.25 meters below the surface of an alluvial terrace. Patricia O'Brien continued the work at Coffey with students from Kansas State University during the fall of 1971 and spring of 1972 (O'Brien et al. 1973). During the summer of 1972 full-scale excavation of the site was undertaken by the K.U. Museum of Anthropology, and it continued for the next three field seasons with support from the National Park Service and U.S. Army Corps of Engineers (fig. 4.1). Based on surface collections and excavated material, a cultural sequence consisting of Paleoindian, repeated Archaic, and possible Late Woodland occupations was established for the site (Schmits 1980, 1981).

Larry J. Schmits, who was working on his Ph.D. in the K.U. anthropology department, supervised the excavations at Coffey. Schmits recognized that an analysis of the geology and sediments of the site was a prerequisite to understanding the complex alluvial stratigraphy and archaeological deposits at Coffey (Schmits 1981:1). Since funds were not available to hire a consulting geomorphologist, he trained himself by taking geomorphology, soils, and sedimentology courses at K.U. The result of his efforts is an excellent assessment of the fluvial history and depositional environments at the Coffey site (Schmits 1976, 1978, 1980, 1981). Schmits reconstructed the sedimentary environments through detailed study of the physical and chemical properties of the alluvium (Schmits 1980, 1981). He also provided a precise alluvial and cultural chronology spanning the period from around 6300 to 2300 B.P. (Schmits 1980, 1981). Despite the fact that Schmits is not a geoscientist, his work at Coffey represents the first explicit geoarchaeological investigation in Kansas.

In 1977, the U.S. Army Corps of Engineers contracted with the K.U. Museum of Anthropology to conduct a four-phase study of cultural resources at the proposed site of El Dorado Lake in southeastern Kansas (map 4.1). According to Leaf (1979:1), the research design called for "an interdisciplinary program to retrieve data and test models of paleoenvironments useful for the study of prehistoric cultural ecological relationships." However, as with the Tuttle Creek Lake project, funding was insufficient to hire a geomorphologist. Instead Darrell Drew, a graduate student with training in geology, was placed in charge of assessing the late Quaternary history and paleogeography of the project area (Alfred E. Johnson, personal communication, 1997). Drew's contribution to the contract report was largely a literature review (Drew 1979). Although an attempt was made to recover pollen at two prehistoric sites in the project area, James E. King (Illinois State Museum) determined that none of the deposits at these sites contained pollen (King 1979).

In 1982 the U.S. Army Corps of Engineers had plans to construct Fort Scott Lake on the Marmaton River in southeastern Kansas (map 4.1). They contracted with Environmental Systems Analysis, a private company owned by Larry J. Schmits, to conduct an archaeological and geomorphological inventory and evaluation of 10 percent of project area. Schmits brought me into the project as a private consultant to attend to the geomorphological analyses. At the time, I was coordinator of the environmental research program at the K.U. Center for Public Affairs. My involvement with the Fort Scott Lake project included mapping Holocene landforms throughout the area that was going to be affected by the proposed reservoir (Schmits et al. 1983:fig. 5). The distribution of these landforms was determined from soil surveys, air photos, and topographic maps. This task was followed by field investigations that focused on sites discovered during the archaeological survey. Alluvial deposits and associated surface and buried soils were described in stream-bank exposures and backhoe trenches. Unfortunately, no funds were available to establish a radiocarbon-based alluvial chronology. Hence, the ages of alluvial deposits were inferred from diagnostic artifacts at archaeological sites and from the morphology of soils in the project area (Schmits et al. 1983: 99–107). Finally, I compared the Holocene alluvial stratigraphy in the project area with other stratigraphic records in the region (Schmits et al. 1983:107–109).

In retrospect, the investigation at Fort Scott Lake was unique. It was the first time a professional geomorphologist was hired as part of research team involved in an archaeological study in Kansas. The use of consulting geomorphologists, as well as other specialists, would soon become a standard practice.

Cultural resource surveys and testing projects were conducted at seven reservoirs in Kansas from 1982 to 1988. Most of these projects involved National Register evaluation of archaeological sites on public lands threatened by erosion. The U.S. Army Corps of Engineers contracted with Environmental Systems Analysis to inventory and evaluate sites at Milford, Melvern, Pomona, Tuttle Creek, and Perry Lakes in northeastern Kansas (map 4.1). Geomorphological investigations were included in all of these studies, but they were limited to general terrain analysis and descriptions of soil profiles at archaeological sites (Mandel and Schmits 1984; Mandel 1987a; Schmits et al. 1987). Again, funds were unavailable for developing precise alluvial chronologies in the project areas. Instead, radiocarbon dating was restricted to features at a few archaeological sites. This aspect of CRM in Kansas would change with the Wilson Lake project.

In 1985 the U.S. Army Corps of Engineers contracted with Donald J. Blakeslee (Wichita State University) to conduct a cultural resource survey and testing along the shoreline of Wilson Lake in north-central Kansas (map 4.1). David W. May, a physical geographer on the faculty at Northern Iowa University, was brought in as a private consultant to assess the geomorphology of the project area. And Steven Bozarth, who at the time was a graduate student in the geography department at K.U., was hired to reconstruct Holocene paleoenvironments from the phytolith record. May (1986) described Holocene deposits and associated buried soils exposed in two cutbanks at the north end of Wilson Lake. Sediment samples collected from the cutbanks were analyzed for particle-size distribution and organic-carbon content. In addition bulk samples were collected from buried soils for radiocarbon dating of the humates. The collection of temporal data critical to understanding landscape evolution finally moved away from archaeological sites!

The results of the geomorphological investigation at Wilson Lake were used to reconstruct the Holocene alluvial history of the lower Saline River (May 1986). This information, combined with the results of the phytolith analysis, was used to infer late Holocene climatic change. It also explained gaps in the archaeological record of the project area. Specifically, May (1986) determined that most of the geomorphic surfaces around Wilson Lake are late Holocene in age. This finding helps to explain why early sites were not recorded during the archaeological survey (Blakeslee 1986:95).

In 1986 Brad Logan, an archaeologist at the K.U. Museum of Anthropology, was awarded a U.S. Army Corps of Engineers contract to evaluate twenty-seven prehistoric sites in the area of Clinton Lake (map 4.1). Funding was sufficient to hire several specialists, including Steven Bozarth (phytolith analysis), Mary Adair (macrofloral analysis), Glen Fredlund (microbotanical analysis), and me (geomorphology). Although part of the geomorphological investigation involved describing soil profiles at archaeological sites, considerable resources and effort were devoted to defining late Quaternary landform sediment assemblages and establishing a radiocarbon-based alluvial chronology for the lower Wakarusa River (Mandel 1987b). This information was used to interpret spatial and temporal variability in the archaeological record at Clinton.

Perry Lake was the focus of another round of archaeological testing in 1988. Brad Logan directed this project, which included three specialists: William C. Johnson (geomorphology), Steven Bozarth (phytolith analysis), and Mary Adair (macofloral analysis). Johnson (1990) addressed the taphonomy of archaeological sites through an examination of the geomorphology of the Delaware River valley in the Perry Lake project area, particularly the northern portion (map 4.1). The geomorphic investigation involved both field and laboratory analyses and focused on landforms, soils, soil-geomorphic relationships, and sediments (Johnson 1990:22). Because of the limited scope of the study, a well-defined alluvial chronology was not established.

Although nearly all of the CRM-driven geoarchaeological investigations conducted in Kansas during the mid- to late 1980s were associated with reservoir projects, one investigation focused on a site that is not on public lands adjacent to a lake. This study was at the Stigenwalt site (14LT351) in southeastern Kansas (map 4.1). Archaeological salvage excavations carried out by the Kansas State Historical Society in late 1986 at Stigenwalt included a detailed investigation of soils and stratigraphy (Mandel 1990). This site, which is located on Big Hill Creek downstream from Big Hill Lake, was discovered as the result of a U.S. Army Corps of Engineers–funded emergency channelization project. Deeply stratified Early Archaic deposits dating from approximately 8800 to 7400 B.P. were exposed when a new channel for Bill Hill Creek was excavated across the midsection of a small alluvial/colluvial fan (Thies 1990). The primary objective of the geomorphological investigation was to place the cultural deposits, which included large earth ovens and many hearths, into a geologic context. Stratigraphic units and buried soils were defined and described, and numerical time relationships were established for the fan deposits (Mandel 1990). Also, site formation processes were considered in order to account for the remarkable preservation of the Early Archaic record at Stigenwalt (Mandel 1990).

The first regional CRM project in Kansas that included a geomorphological investigation was conducted in June 1986. It was a Phase II archaeological survey of thirty-nine proposed watershed structures scattered throughout the Pawnee River Basin in southwestern Kansas (map 4.1). The Pawnee River and its tributaries drain an area of approximately 3,975 km^2 into the Arkansas River; it is the largest watershed planning district in Kansas.

Robert D. Timberlake, an archaeologist with the Kansas State Historical Society, was in charge of the Pawnee River Basin survey. Through his previous research experience as a graduate student in Iowa, Timberlake learned that archaeological deposits are often deeply buried in alluvial settings and cannot be detected with traditional surface survey methods. Faced with the same problem in southwestern Kansas, he asked me to determine the geologic potential for buried cultural deposits in late Quaternary deposits of the Pawnee River and its tributaries.

At the time of the Pawnee River Basin survey, I was working on my Ph.D. in Quaternary Studies at K.U. under the direction of Wakefield Dort Jr. Having served as a geoarchaeologist on a number of CRM projects that were restricted to reservoirs or individual sites, I wanted to advance into a large basin-wide cultural resource survey that required a landscape approach. The Pawnee River Basin survey presented that opportunity.

I adopted my strategy for the geomorphic investigation from Dean M. Thompson and E. Arthur Bettis's watershed studies in western Iowa (e.g., Thompson and Bettis 1980; Bettis and Thompson 1981, 1982). Intensive and extensive radiocarbon dating, combined with a basin-wide alluvial stratigraphic investigation, determined whether deposits of certain ages are differentially preserved in the Pawnee River Basin (Mandel 1988a, 1992a). The investigation also focused on buried Holocene soils as indicators of former stable landscapes in alluvial settings (figs. 4.2, 4.3). Information gleaned from this investigation was used to predict where buried archaeological deposits dating to each cultural period are likely to be found in the drainage network (Mandel 1988a, 1991a) (table 4.2).

My work in the Pawnee River Basin continued for five years and evolved into the topic of my dissertation (Mandel 1991a). It also led to the first joint publication between the Kansas Geological Survey and the Kansas State Historical Society (Mandel 1994a).

The Kansas State Historical Preservation Office was pleased with the interdisciplinary approach employed in the Pawnee River Basin survey. It was clear that a three-dimensional analysis of landform sediment assemblages could be used to detect, and thereby protect, buried cultural resources. As a result the preservation office encouraged other agencies, including the Kansas City District of the Army Corps of Engineers, the Kansas Department of Transportation, and the U.S. Department of Agriculture's Soil Conservation Service (now the Natural Resources Conservation Service), to request geologic studies in conjunction with archaeological investigations when proposed construc-

Fig. 4.2. The Buckner Creek site (14HO306) on the east bank of Buckner Creek in southwestern Kansas. The vehicle is parked above the cutbank shown in fig. 4.3. The site was discovered in 1986 during a systematic geoarchaeological survey of the Pawnee River basin (Mandel 1988a). This survey was the first of its kind in Kansas.

tion projects might affect buried cultural resources. These agencies responded favorably to the request. By 1987 the scopes-of-work for many CRM projects in Kansas called for detailed geomorphological investigations, including deep subsurface exploration (coring, trenching, and cutbank inspection) and radiocarbon dating of deposits and associated buried soils. It is likely that the agencies responsible for funding CRM projects recognized that the information gleaned from geomorphological investigations could be used to concentrate archaeological survey and testing efforts in potentially productive areas. Hence, geoarchaeology became a cost-effective approach to CRM.

Three major geomorphological investigations were conducted in association with archaeological surveys in Kansas between 1988 and 1991: one in the lower Smoky Hill River Basin at and near Kanopolis Lake in north-central Kansas (Mandel 1988b, 1992a); another in the upper Delaware River Basin in northeastern Kansas (Mandel et al. 1991); and the third in the Doyle Creek watershed and the Whitewater River Basin in southeastern Kansas (Mandel 1991b) (map 4.1). The studies were basin-wide in scope and focused on alluvial stratigraphy in different sized drainage elements within the project areas. The results were used to determine the potential for buried cultural deposits.

Fig. 4.3. Buried soils and archaeological deposits exposed in the cutbank at the Buckner Creek site (Mandel 1992a:fig. 2-13). Plains Woodland materials, including a hearth, are associated with the Buckner Creek Paleosol (BCP). The Hackberry Creek Paleosol (HCP) contains stratified Late Archaic deposits at depths of 3.9 to 5.3 meters below land surface. Courtesy of the Smithsonian Institution Press.

In 1991 the Kansas Department of Transportation (KDOT) funded two large projects that involved geomorphological investigations in advance of the archaeological surveys: the Southeast Kansas Highway Corridor Project and the U.S Highway 166 Corridor Project. The Southeast Kansas Highway Corridor originally was presented as an enormous study area, beginning as a narrow band near Augusta in Butler County and widening to the south and east to take in entire counties along a 250-km route to the Kansas-Missouri border (Weston 1993). The U.S Highway 166 Corridor Project also began as a large project area. It was about 80 km long and 5 km wide, straddling the present route of U.S. Highway 166 between Arkansas City and Sedan, Kansas (Hawley 1993a). The geomorphological investigations focused on the alluvial stratigraphy of stream valleys in both project areas (Mandel 1993a, 1993b). I inspected many cutbanks along creeks and rivers in order to describe and sample thick sections of valley fill. Intensive radiocarbon dating allowed development of a sound chronology for the sedimentary units and buried soils. My strategy was to locate areas with high geologic potential for buried archaeological deposits.

Table 4.2   Geologic potential for Buried Archaeological Deposits in the Pawnee River Basin (from Mandel 1991a: table 26)

Cultural Periods	Large Valleys			Small Valleys	
	T-0	T-1	T-2	T-0	T-1
Paleoindian	—	+++	+++	—	—
Early Archaic	—	+++	+++	—	—
Middle Archaic	—	+++	+++	—	—
Plains Woodland	+	+++	+++	—	+++
Historic	+++	+++	—	+++	+

+   Low Potential
++   Moderate Potential
+++ High Potential
—   Impossible
* Applies only to the T-2 terrace in the lower reaches of fourth-oder steams near their confluence with the Pawnee river

This information, combined with data on recorded archaeological sites in the project areas, was used to recommend highway routes that would minimize impact on cultural resources.

A geomorphological investigation conducted in 1992 actually led to a major site mitigation project. While surveying Kansas Highway 177 for the KDOT, the Kansas State Historical Society documented a very sparse lithic scatter at site 14RY38 near Manhattan, Kansas (map 4.1). The site is on the valley floor of a small, unnamed stream near its confluence with the Kansas River. Based on the surficial evidence, 14RY38 did not warrant additional study. However, the historical society requested a geomorphological investigation to determine the potential for buried cultural materials. A four-meter-deep backhoe trench exposed three buried soils developed in late Holocene alluvium valley fill (Mandel 1992b). Two of the buried soils contained in situ Early Ceramic materials and features. Because 14RY38 was directly in the path of a proposed roadway, KDOT authorized the Kansas State Historical Society to excavate the site (Benison et al. 2000).

In 1993 archaeological testing was conducted by the K.U. Museum of Anthropology, Augustana College Archeology Laboratory, and the Kansas State Historical Society at sites in lower Mill Creek valley near Kansas City (map 4.1). The project area was along the construction route of proposed wastewater facility improvements. Geomorphological investigations were coordinated with the testing of nine prehistoric sites located on a Holocene terrace that dominates the valley floor of Mill Creek (Mandel 1993c, 1994b). The objectives

110 ROLFE D. MANDEL

of these investigations were to describe the soils and stratigraphy at the sites and determine the geologic potential for deeply buried cultural deposits. Stratigraphic data were collected from numerous cores, backhoe trenches, and stream cutbanks (Mandel 1993c, 1994b). Buried soils discovered during the geomorphic investigation were targeted for deep archaeological testing. The Mill Creek study stands out as an excellent example of a geomorphological investigation steering a major component of a CRM project.

In 1992 the KDOT, in coordination with the Tulsa District of the U.S. Army Corps of Engineers, awarded the Kansas State Historical Society a long-term contract to conduct archaeological testing and mitigation within portions of the proposed Arkansas City bypass. The proposed highway would bend around the east side of Arkansas City, crossing a large segment of the valley floor of the lower Walnut River (map 4.1). Even before the work began, it was known that areas affected by the new highway and associated levee include portions of some of the richest and most important archaeological sites in the state (Hawley and Haury 1994:1). These sites, affiliated with the Great Bend Aspect (the prehistoric and protohistoric Wichita Indians), bear the remains of a vast village complex, dating from the early 1300s and possibly as late as the mid-1700s (Hawley 1993b). Given the great significance of these sites, the scope-of-work called for interdisciplinary investigations, including geologic studies. The project team, under the direction of Marlin H. Hawley, began the field investigations at Arkansas City in the summer of 1992 and periodically tested and mitigated sites until the end of 1996. As a consulting geologist on the team, I was responsible for describing the geomorphology, soils, and stratigraphy at and near the sites. Subsurface information was gleaned from cores, backhoe trenches, archaeological test units, and excavation blocks. In addition to yielding new information about Holocene landscape evolution in the lower Walnut River valley, the geomorphological investigations provided a detailed soil-stratigraphic framework for the cultural deposits that were found in the project area (Mandel 1994c, 1994d, 1994e). The potential for buried archaeological materials also was assessed and eventually corroborated. For example, a buried soil in the upper part of the T-1 terrace fill was considered to have high potential for containing Plains Woodland materials (Mandel 1994d: 63). This potential was realized at sites 14CO331 and 14CO385, which have buried Early to Middle Ceramic components.

The vast assemblage of archaeological, geomorphological, and paleoenvironmental data collected during the five years of testing and mitigation at Arkansas City is currently being analyzed. A suite of nearly one hundred radiocarbon ages will be used to develop a precise chronology for the sedimentary units and buried soils, and my previous descriptions of the alluvial stratigraphy of the lower Walnut River valley will be refined.

GEOARCHAEOLOGY AS ACADEMIC RESEARCH: 1960–PRESENT

While CRM has been the primary force behind geoarchaeological research in Kansas and Oklahoma, geoscientists and archaeologists affiliated with universities have also fostered interdisciplinary archaeological studies in their teaching and academic research. Geoscientists at the University of Kansas who have been actively engaged in archaeological investigations include Wakefield Dort Jr., Larry D. Martin, and William C. Johnson. Dort, a geomorphologist, was hired by the K.U. geology department in 1957 to replace H. T. U. Smith. Although in Kansas Dort focused his research on glacial and fluvial landscapes, he was involved in studies at many important archaeological sites outside of the state, including the Shriver site (Missouri), the Wasden site (Idaho), and the Midvale site (Idaho). He also participated in geoarchaeological investigations at the Burnham site in northwestern Oklahoma.

In 1968 Dort worked with Paul R. Katz at the Sutter site (14JN309) in northeastern Kansas (map 4.1). At the time, Katz was a graduate student in the K.U. anthropology department. The site was discovered when a bulldozer exposed bison bones during construction of a private pond on small stream that joins the West Fork of Muddy Creek. The landowner contacted the Kansas State Historical Society, which in turn notified the K.U. Museum of Anthropology. Katz and Dort visited the site and found stratified Early Archaic deposits in clay-rich alluvium 7.5 to 10.5 meters below the land surface (Katz 1971). The artifact and faunal assemblages indicated a primary emphasis on bison killing and processing activities, supplemented by gathering and processing of wild flora (Katz 1971). In addition to describing the stratigraphy of the site, Dort secured funding for radiocarbon analyses (Katz 1973; Dort 1974). Radiocarbon ages determined on charcoal from burned-rock features ranged between approximately 8000 and 7650 B.P., making Sutter one of the oldest statified sites documented in Kansas.

Dort retired from K.U. in 1995, but he is still actively involved in research. Perhaps Dort's greatest contribution to Kansas archaeology was his promotion of interdisciplinary concepts through his teaching. Several of his students, including Richard Rogers, Joe Artz, and me, went on to conduct geoarchaeological research in Kansas.

Larry Martin, trained in both geology and paleontology under the direction of C. Bertrand Schultz, took a faculty position at the K.U. Museum of Natural History in 1972. Martin has worked on a number of archaeological projects in the Central Plains as a faunal specialist and, like Dort, has promoted interdisciplinary concepts in his teaching. During the past twenty years, he has collaborated with Richard Rogers and Don Wyckoff.

William Johnson joined the geography faculty at K.U. in the late 1970s. He was trained in geomorphology at the University of Wisconsin at Madison under the direction of James C. Knox. Johnson initially focused on the Holocene fluvial histories of streams in Kansas and adjacent states. He used chronologic and soil stratigraphic data largely gleaned from archaeological projects to produce summary papers (Johnson and Martin 1987; Johnson and Logan 1990). In 1992 and 1993 Johnson worked with archaeologist Jack Hofman (University of Kansas) at the Norton Bone Bed site (14SC6), a Late Paleoindian occupation in northwestern Kansas (Hofman et al. 1995) (map 4.1). More recently he has concentrated on the paleoenvironmental history of the Central Plains as a means of understanding the cultural history of the region (Johnson and Park 1996). Johnson has also turned his attention to Holocene and late Pleistocene eolian deposits that may contain archaeological deposits. For example, some of his recent research has focused on the geoarchaeology of dune fields in the Great Bend Prairie of central Kansas (Johnson 1991; Logan et al. 1993) (map 4.1). In 1998 Johnson took his research experience into the classroom by developing the first geoarchaeology course at K.U.

Two students, Joe A. Artz and Richard A. Rogers, completed graduate programs in the K.U. Department of Anthropology with strong backgrounds in geoarchaeology. In addition, Darrell L. Drew, who conducted the geoarchaeological investigations at El Dorado Lake (Drew 1979), earned a graduate degree in Special Studies at K.U.

Joe Artz assembled an interdisciplinary thesis committee that included William Johnson and Curtis Sorenson (pedologist) from the geography department, and he worked closely with Wakefield Dort. His thesis focused on alluvial soils and landforms of the East Branch Walnut valley in southeastern Kansas (map 4.1), and he used soil-geomorphic relationships to infer paleoenvironmental change during the late Holocene (Artz 1983). Although Artz's thesis deals primarily with pedologic, geomorphic, hydrologic, and climatic phenomena, archaeological data contributed to all stages of his analysis. The most important of these contributions was providing a chronological framework. The relative and numerical ages of archaeological deposits from various soil-stratigraphic and soil-geomorphic contexts contributed to the definition of soil-stratigraphic units and to the establishment of an alluvial chronology. Also, much of the geomorphic data used to document regional geomorphic responses to climatic change relied on chronological and stratigraphic data gleaned from archaeological contexts. While Artz relied heavily on archaeological data to address soil-geomorphic and soil-stratigraphic issues, archaeology certainly benefited from this study. For example, he assessed the relationship between soil phosphorous and preservation of bone at two archaeological sites, and he considered prehistoric human ecology and site selection in the East Branch Walnut valley.

Richard Rogers worked primarily under the direction of Wakefield Dort while completing his Ph.D. in Anthropology during the early 1980s. His dissertation is a synthetic analysis of archaeological site location and terrace systems for the Arkansas River and, to a lesser extent, the Kansas River (Smoky Hill River) drainages (Rogers 1984a). He used archaeological and paleontological evidence to infer the age of geomorphic surfaces (terraces) in river valleys. Rogers (1984a) noted a dramatic difference in terrace ages between the Arkansas and Kansas river systems and suggested tectonics, rather than climatic or other causes, were responsible for terrace formation and the disparity in terrace ages. His geoarchaeological research in Kansas has largely focused on the Paleoindian period (Rogers 1984b, 1987; Rogers and Martin 1982, 1983, 1984), and he has been a strong proponent of pre-Clovis occupation in the Central Plains (Rogers 1984c).

Darrell Drew worked under the direction of Wakefield Dort while completing his master's thesis in Special Studies. His thesis focuses on paleogeographical and predictive archaeology (Drew 1984). Using the area of El Dorado Lake as an example, Drew described how three-dimensional landscape analysis is needed to determine the potential for buried archaeological deposits. Although Drew identifies some alluvial deposits that could contain prehistoric cultural materials, a predictive model was not developed.

Most of my geoarchaeological research in the Central Plains has been linked to CRM. I drew heavily from this experience while I was an assistant professor at the University of Nebraska-Omaha (1989–1994), and I continue to do so as an adjunct professor in the geography department at K.U. Much of my academic research has focused on geologic filtering of the archaeological record, especially in river basins of Kansas and adjoining states (Mandel 1992a, 1994d, 1995). I have also considered the archaeological geology of Paleoindian sites in Kansas (Mandel 1996). I recently conducted a subsurface investigation at the 12 Mile Creek site in conjunction with Jack Hofman's efforts to relocate the buried bison bone bed representing the Paleoindian horizon, and I am currently studying alluvial fills in southern and western Kansas that are yielding early archaeological deposits.

There is only one example of an archaeologist and a geoscientist from academic institutions outside the region collaborating on a research project in Kansas. In November 1982 the late R. Clark Mallam, an archaeologist on the faculty at Luther College in Iowa, investigated a serpent-shaped intaglio (site 14RC102) on the ridge of a hilltop in Rice County, Kansas. Arthur Bettis, who had just started his career at the Iowa Geological Survey Bureau (University of Iowa), was invited to study the soils at the site. Bettis took hand cores along four transects that crossed the intaglio and adjacent ridge. He also examined soil profiles in trenches excavated across the central portion of the intaglio. Bettis concluded that the original soil had been removed down to the Bt horizon within the intaglio area and that some soil was mounded up in the area of the serpent's "head" (Mallam 1985). He also determined that the feature was of human origin and was constructed in four stages. Although the pedological investigation was critical to the interpretation of the intaglio, Bettis did not contribute a chapter to the report. Instead, Mallam referred to Bettis's findings (Mallam 1985).

Few geoscientists affiliated with academic institutions were involved with archaeological investigations in northern Oklahoma before the 1980s. Oren F. Evans, a professor in the geology department at the University of Oklahoma during the early to mid-1900s, briefly described geomorphic factors that may have influenced the settlement patterns of prehistoric people in central Oklahoma (Evans 1952). He also considered how geologists and archaeologists might help each other through collaboration (Evans 1957). However, Evans was never involved with an archaeological investigation.

In 1962 and 1963 Don G. Wyckoff directed excavations at the deeply stratified Packard site (map 4.1), one of fifteen sites studied along a segment of northeastern Oklahoma's Grand (Neosho) River that is now flooded by Lake Hudson. At the time of the excavation, Wyckoff was principal archeologist of the Oklahoma River Basin Survey, a research unit at the University of Oklahoma. Although Wyckoff was trained as an archaeologist, he developed skills in pedology, stratigraphy, and geochronology while completing his Ph.D. through a Quaternary Studies option in the anthropology department at Washington State University. He applied these skills at the Packard site (Wyckoff 1964, 1985a, 1989), as well as at other localities in Oklahoma, including the Laverty Ditch.

The Laverty Ditch is located in eastern Beaver County in the Oklahoma Panhandle (map 4.1). It is a narrow, sickle-shaped furrow extending for nearly half a mile across a terrace of the Beaver River. Because of its close proximity to several Panhandle Aspect sites, investigators considered it possible that the Laverty Ditch was an irrigation channel constructed by Native Americans who occupied the region between approximately 1200 and 1500 A.D. (Wyckoff 1985). To test this hypothesis, Wyckoff conducted a detailed geomorphic and stratigraphic investigation at Laverty in 1982. He concluded that the "ditch" is an alluvial feature created by the Beaver River; there was no evidence indicating that it is of human origin (Wyckoff 1985).

Established at the University of Oklahoma in 1968, the Oklahoma Archaeological Survey (OAS) has played a formative role in the history of geoarchaeological and paleoenvironmental research. A strong interdisciplinary program was developed under the leadership of the survey's first director, Don Wyckoff (Bell 1984). Wyckoff recognized that archaeologists and geoscientists needed to collaborate at all phases of archaeological investigations. Pedologist Brian J. Carter (Department of Agronomy, Oklahoma State University) was brought in as a principal investigator on several major OAS projects, and Wyckoff often sought guidance from Wakefield Dort and Larry Martin. Geomorphologist Robert Brakenridge (Department of Geography, Dartmouth College) also participated in several OAS investigations.

One of the first interdisciplinary archaeological projects sponsored by OAS was the 1982 excavations at Copple Mound. Copple forms part of the Spiro Mound Group on the south side of the Arkansas River in extreme eastern Oklahoma (map 4.1). Wyckoff encouraged Frank C. Leonhardy to work at Copple and, more specifically, to define the stratigraphy of the mound. At the time, Leonhardy was a faculty member in the anthropology department at the University of Idaho. Like Wyckoff, Leonhardy had considerable training in the geosciences while completing his Ph.D in anthropology at Washington State University. In 1978 Leonhardy worked with Guy Muto on testing the Paris Mound in Sequoyah County, Oklahoma; as a result, he was already familiar with complex mound stratigraphy. Leonhardy defined four stages of mound construction at Copple, and he demonstrated that the microstratigraphy was extremely variable laterally, vertically, and radially (Leonhardy 1989).

Members of the OAS and the Oklahoma State University Department of Agronomy undertook cooperative interdisciplinary investigations in northwestern Oklahoma during the late 1980s. The primary objective of these studies was to assess Pleistocene localities that had potential for containing archaeological deposits (Wyckoff et al. 1987). Two of these localities, the Hajny and Burnham sites, were targeted for intensive investigations that included studies of landforms, alluvial stratigraphy, soils, paleontology, gastropods, and dating methods (Wyckoff et al. 1987; Wyckoff et al. 1992; Wyckoff and Carter 1994).

The Hajny site is located on a terrace of the Canadian River in Dewey County, Oklahoma (map 4.1). Mammoth remains were discovered in spring sediments during quarrying of gravel at the site. Apatite from bone fragments recovered during a preliminary investigation yielded a radiocarbon age of approximately 8900 B.P., whereas snails from associated sediments yielded an age of around 27,900 B.P. (Wyckoff et al. 1987). Because the age determined on the bone was potentially relevant to a time when Paleoindians were in the Central Plains, the site was excavated during the 1985 and 1986 field seasons. It was Oklahoma's first extensively studied Ice Age site since the 1962 interdisciplinary investigation at the Domebo locality (Wyckoff 1992:1; see Ferring, this volume). The research team included Don Wyckoff (site stratigraphy), Brian Carter (pedology and geomorphology), Larry Martin (paleontology), Peggy Flynn (paleontology), and James Theler (malacology). Although they found no traces of humans, the site contained a small, but intriguing, assemblage of fauna that inhabited the region during the late Pleistocene (Wyckoff et al. 1992). Also, the careful exposure of partially disarticulated mammoths at Hajny yielded important clues to the natural processes that create ancient bone beds.

In May 1986, as soils and geomorphological investigations were being completed at the Hajny site, a Woods County rancher reported to OAS that some large bones were being uncovered during construction of a small farm pond. The locality, which became known as the Burnham site, is about five kilometers north of the Cimarron River in northwestern Oklahoma (map 4.1). Don Wyckoff, Wakefield Dort, and Larry Martin visited the site in June 1996 and discovered many snails and some horse, mammoth, and bison bones in a gray sediment exposed in the bulldozer-scraped slopes (Wyckoff and Carter 1994:7). Among the faunal remains was a bison skull with a massive horn core (fig. 4.4). Larry Martin's initial impression was that it could be *Bison latifrons*, the big-horned bison thought to be early to middle Wisconsinan in age (Wyckoff et al.

Fig. 4.4. The bison skull discovered at the Burnham site in October 1986. Although not identifiable as *Bison latifrons*, the skull is considered a precursor to *Bison antiquus* (Wyckoff and Carter 1994:9). Photo by Don Wyckoff.

1987). Based on these finds, the site was considered potentially important for its vertebrate and invertebrate faunal record.

Brief testing at the Burnham site in October 1986 recovered the bison skull, which is now believed to be *Bison alleni* or *B. cheneyi*, and a few bones of other mammals and reptiles (Wyckoff et al. 1987). However, a dramatic discovery was made when all of the sediment surrounding the skull was waterscreened. In addition to containing numerous snails and small bones, the gray sediment yielded several resharpening flakes (Wyckoff et al. 1990). The presence of human artifacts next to the remains of bison that were known to be much older than those hunted by Clovis people changed the significance of the Burnham site. With financial support from the National Science Foundation, the National Geographic Society, and numerous private citizens, the Oklahoma Archaeological Survey launched a major geoarchaeological study of the site (Wyckoff and Carter 1994).

Excavations were conducted at the Burnham site in 1988, 1989, 1991, and 1992. A team of geoscientists, including Brian Carter, Wakefield Dort, Larry Martin, and Robert Brakenridge, collaborated with Don Wyckoff and other specialists (Wyckoff et al. 1990; Wyckoff and Carter 1994). Through extensive coring and trenching, nearly four hectares were explored to determine the age and stratigraphic context of the archaeological materials. Initially Wyckoff and his colleagues concluded that some artifacts were mixed in ponded sediments that date to approximately 25,000 B.P. (Wyckoff et al. 1990; Wyckoff and Carter 1994:41). A radiocarbon age of around 10,200 B.P. determined on a small piece of charcoal from an artifact-bearing stratum was considered evidence that people were there at least that long ago (Wyckoff and Carter 1994:77). More recently they concluded that the charcoal sample came from alluvial fill that washed into the area near the bison skull and artifacts while the excavation blocks were open; hence the age of the charcoal has no bearing on the age of the archaeological deposits (Don Wyckoff, personal communication, 1998). Also, they now suspect that the artifacts were redeposited when the pond deposit formed about 30,000 years ago. Regardless of the age of the archaeological deposits, Burnham yielded a tremendous amount of paleoenvironmental information. The significance of the interdisciplinary approach taken at Burnham was articulated by Wyckoff and Carter (1994:77):

> Although the Burnham site does not prove that Native Americans were on this continent before Clovis times, the site does demonstrate the need for careful, well documented, interdisciplinary research at fossil-bearing locations older than 12,000 years. Even if no such locations ever yielded unquestionable evidence for a much earlier presence of humans, these kinds of sites can tell us much about the plants, animals, and habitats that existed before the arrival of people. Without this kind of substantial information, how will archaeologists ever really assess the impacts of the first human inhabitants of this land?

While the archaeological record at Burnham is problematic, interdisciplinary OAS-sponsored investigations at the Waugh and Cooper sites in northwestern Oklahoma yielded indisputable evidence of in situ Folsom occupations. The Waugh site is located on a tributary of Buffalo Creek, which drains into the Cimarron River (map 4.1). The site was excavated in 1991, 1992, 1993, and 1996 under the direction of Jack Hofman. Waugh includes a bone bed with the remains of at least five *Bison antiquus* and a nearby camping area probably related to the bone bed (Hofman et al. 1992; Hofman 1995). Two Folsom points were found in the bone bed (Hofman et al. 1992:24). Brian Carter was brought in from Oklahoma State University to assess the soils and stratigraphy at the site. Carter confirmed the integrity of the bison bone bed and con-

Fig. 4.5. Bone beds composed of *Bison antiquus* exposed in the walls of an arroyo at the Cooper site in northwestern Oklahoma. Photo by Leland Bement.

cluded that the faunal remains are in a sandy alluvial fill associated with a large arroyo cut into Permian sandstone high in the landscape (Hofman and Carter 1991; Hofman et al. 1992).

The Cooper site is located along the floodplain margin of the North Canadian River (map 4.1) (Bement 1994, 1999). Leland Bement (OAS) excavated Cooper during the 1993 and 1994 field seasons, and Brian Carter studied the soils and stratigraphy of the site during all stages of the excavation. Three bone beds composed of *Bison antiquus* were found in alluvium at the head of a steep-sided arroyo cut into bedrock (Carter and Bement 1995; Bement 1999). The bone deposits are stacked one on top of the other, and all are associated with Folsom occupations (fig. 4.5). A radiocarbon age of 10,050±210 years B.P. was determined on sediments below the lowest bone bed (Carter and Bement 1995).

Collaboration between OAS archaeologists and geoscientists was not limited to site-specific studies; it occurred during archaeological surveys and testings. A good example of a multidisciplinary study is the archaeological reconnaissance survey and subsurface testing along portions of Deer Creek basin in northwestern Oklahoma County (map 4.1). This investigation was conducted in the winter of 1987–1988 under the direction of Jack Hofman (now at the University of

Kansas) and Richard Drass (Hofman and Drass 1990a). It was complemented by detailed pedological and geomorphological studies. Brian Carter focused on the physical and chemical properties of surface and buried soils in the study area (Carter 1990). In addition, Bob Brakenridge described the late Quaternary geomorphic and pedogenic history of Deer Creek basin and considered the implications of this history for buried archaeological site location (Brakenridge 1990). The record of Holocene erosion and alluviation helped explain the evidence for prehistoric and historic sites in the study area (Hofman and Drass 1990b:59–62).

SUMMARY AND CONCLUSIONS

Geoarchaeological research started late in Kansas and northern Oklahoma and was sporadic until it fully developed during the 1980s. Pioneering geologists of the late nineteenth century reported archaeological sites as they explored the region, but they rarely considered the geologic context of the cultural materials. Ironically, one of the most important archaeological finds in North America, the 12 Mile Creek site, was made by paleontologists working in western Kansas at the end of the nineteenth century. Most archaeologists ignored the report of a projectile point in direct association with extinct Pleistocene fauna at 12 Mile Creek, perhaps because the messenger, Samuel Williston, was a geologist.

During the early 1900s, geoscientists were drawn into the debate over the antiquity of humans in the New World. Without the benefit of numerical dating techniques, archaeologists often turned to geologists to resolve the age of suspected early sites through stratigraphic methods. This was the case at the Lansing Man site in northeastern Kansas, where several of the most prominent geologists of the time were called upon to determine whether two human skeletons were sealed in Pleistocene loess. At Lansing the geologists visited the site independently after the archaeological investigation was completed. They did not collaborate with the archaeologists involved in the subsequent excavation of the site, and they were soon engaged in an argument over the nature of the geologic deposits (primary or reworked loess?) and age of the sediments (Pleistocene or Post-Glacial?). Although geologists played an important role at Lansing, their involvement can hardly be called geoarchaeological research in the sense of geologists collaborating with archaeologists.

The first collaboration between an archaeologist and geologist did not occur in the region until Loren C. Eiseley and H. T. U. Smith worked together at the Spring Creek site in north-central Kansas during the late 1930s. Although the investigation at Spring Creek stands out because of Smith's involvement, Eiseley's motive for inviting Smith was not unusual for the times. Eiseley suspected that Spring Creek was an early occupation, perhaps Folsom, and he needed a geologist to determine the age of the artifact-bearing deposits. As was the case elsewhere in North America, a potential Paleoindian site was one of the few places where archaeologists welcomed geologists.

Eiseley and Smith's interaction was short-lived and followed by a long period when geologists were not involved in archaeological investigations in the region. Once the boundaries of anthropology (which absorbed archaeology), geology, and other sciences crystallized during the early 1900s, jumping the boundaries was frowned upon except·when Paleoindian sites were involved. Also, as archaeological surveys expanded in Kansas and northern Oklahoma during the 1950s and the following two decades, most the investigations focused on the Late Prehistoric and Protohistoric record. Because this record is at or near the land surface, archaeologists saw no need to seek help from geologists.

The emergence of processual and environmental archaeology during the mid-1960s opened the door to interdisciplinary studies that included geoscientists. However, it was federally mandated CRM, which arrived during the late 1960s, that provided the funds to support these studies. By the mid-1970s, CRM-driven interdisciplinary research was underway in full force in northeastern Oklahoma, and it was common in Kansas by the early 1980s.

Initially, geoscientists working on CRM projects described soil profiles at archaeological sites and/or provided terrain analysis for survey areas. By the mid-1980s, their roles were expanded to what they are today. Earth-science specialists are often called upon to map landform sediment assemblages and to determine the geologic potential for buried archaeological deposits. At individual sites, they are usually expected to interpret depositional environments, site-formation processes, and postdepositional modification of archaeological deposits and sediments.

Despite its brief history in Kansas and northern Oklahoma, much geoarchaeological research has been conducted in the region. Geoarchaeology has advanced from its developmental stage of the early- and mid-1900s, when it was characterized by geoscientists trying to determine the age of suspected early sites, to its present level of collaborative, multidisciplinary research in a wide variety of archaeological and geological contexts. Moreover, the science of archaeological geology has proceeded far beyond the descriptive stage by providing archaeologists with knowledge about the relationship between prehistoric people and the landscape they occupied.

ACKNOWLEDGEMENTS

I want to thank Marlin Hawley for opening his private library to me and providing a wealth of historical information that was essential to the preparation of my paper. This manuscript benefited greatly from thoughtful and stimulating reviews by Marlin Hawley, Wakefield Dort Jr., Leland Bement, Jack Hofman, and Don Wyckoff. I greatly appreciate their efforts and suggestions. Thanks goes to Jennifer Smith for producing map 4.1. Finally, I want to thank Art Bettis for encouraging me to look at the "big picture" as I pursued my interests in geomorphology and geoarchaeology.

REFERENCES

Abbott, C. C. 1876a. The stone age in New Jersey. Washington, D.C.: Smithsonian Institution annual report for 1875:246–380.
———. 1876b. Western worked flakes and the New Jersey rude implements. *The American Naturalist* 10:431–32.
———. 1877. On the discovery of supposed Paleolithic implements from glacial drift in the valley of the Delaware River, near Trenton, New Jersey. *Peabody Museum Annual Report* 10:30–43.
———. 1892. Paleolithic man in America. *Science* 20:270–71.
Artz, J. A. 1983. The soils and geomorphology of the East Branch Walnut Valley: Contexts of human adaptation in the Kansas Flint Hills. Master's thesis, Lawrence, University of Kansas.
———. 1985. A soil-geomorphic approach to locating buried Late-Archaic sites in northeast Oklahoma. *American Archaeology* 5:142–50.
———. 1988. Geomorphic setting and alluvial stratigraphy. *In* Haury, C. H., ed., The prehistory and paleoenvironment of Hominy Creek Valley: Excavations at Copperhead Cave (34OS85) and archaeological overview of investigations in Hominy Creek valley. Tulsa, Okla.: University of Tulsa Laboratory of Archaeology *Contributions in Archaeology* 15:5–23.

Artz, J. A., and K. C. Reid. 1984. Geoarchaeological investigations in Cotton Creek Valley. *In* Reid, K. C. and J. A. Artz, eds., Hunters of the forest edge: Culture, time, and process in the Little Caney Basin. Tulsa, Okla.: University of Tulsa, Laboratory of Archaeology *Contributions in Archaeology* 14:97–186.

Baker, W. E., T. N. Campbell, and G. L. Evans. 1957. The Nall site: Evidence of Early Man in the Oklahoma Panhandle. *Bulletin of the Oklahoma Anthropological Society* 5:1–20.

Bass, W. M. 1973. Lansing Man: A half century later. *American Journal of Physical Anthropology* 38:99–104.

Bell, R. E. 1958. Guide to the identification of certain American Indian projectile points. Oklahoma Archaeological Society Special Bulletin 1.

Bell, R. E. 1984. Prehistory of Oklahoma. New York: Academic Press.

Bell, R. E. 1987. The development of archaeology in Oklahoma. *Bulletin of the Oklahoma Anthropological Society* 36:1–13.

Bement, L. C. 1994. The Cooper site: A stratified Paleoindian bison kill in northwestern Oklahoma. *Current Research in the Pleistocene* 11:7–9.

———. 1999. Bison Hunting at Cooper Site: Where Lightning Bolts Drew Thundering Herds. Norman: University of Oklahoma Press.

Benison, C. J., W. E. Banks, and R. D. Mandel. 2000. Phase IV archaeological investigations at 14RY38: A multicomponent Early Ceramic period campsite near Manhattan, Kansas. Topeka: Kansas State Historical Society, Contract Archaeology Publication no. 22.

Bettis, E. A. III, and D. M. Thompson. 1981. Holocene landscape evolution in western Iowa—concepts, methods, and implications for archaeology. *In* Anfinson, S. F., ed., Current directions in midwestern archaeology: Selected papers from the Mankato Conference. St. Paul, Minn.: Minnesota Archaeological Society Occasional Papers in Minnesota Archaeology 9:1–14.

Bettis, E. A. III, and D. M. Thompson. 1982. Interrelations of cultural and fluvial deposits in northwest Iowa. Vermillion, S.Dak.: Association of Iowa Archaeologists, Fieldtrip Guidebook.

Binford, L. R. 1968. Archaeological perspectives. *In* Binford, S. R., and L. R. Binford, New perspectives in archaeology, 5–32. Chicago: Aldine.

Blakeslee, D. J. 1986. Discussion. *In* Blakeslee, D. J., R. Blasing, and H. Garcia, eds., Along the Pawnee Trail: Cultural resource survey and testing at Wilson Lake, Kansas, 94–95. Kansas City, Mo.: U.S. Army Corps of Engineers.

Brakenridge, G. R. 1990. Quaternary geomorphology of northwestern Oklahoma County: Implications for Geoarchaeology. *In* Hofman, J. L., and R. R. Drass, eds., A survey of archaeological resources and an evaluation of buried site potential in northwestern Oklahoma County, Oklahoma. Norman: University of Oklahoma, Oklahoma Archaeological Survey, Archaeological Resource Survey Report no. 36:45–57.

Bryan, K. 1950. Flint quarries—the source of tools and, at the same time, the factories of the American Indian. Papers of the Peabody Museum of American Archaeology and Ethnology, Harvard University 17, no. 3:1–40.

Carter, B. J. 1990. Soils within the Deer Creek flood plain. In Hofman, J. L., and R. R. Drass, eds., A survey of archaeological resources and an evaluation of buried site potential in northwestern Oklahoma County, Oklahoma. Norman: University of Oklahoma, Oklahoma Archaeological Survey, Archaeological Resource Survey Report no. 36:31–43.

Carter, B. J., and L. C. Bement. 1995. Soil investigations at the Cooper site. Current Research in the Pleistocene 12:109–11.

Chamberlin, T. C. 1897. Editorial. Journal of Geology 5:637–38.

———. 1902a. The geologic relations of the human relics of Lansing, Kansas. Journal of Geology 10:745–77.

———. 1902b. Editorial on the atiquity of man. Journal of Geology 10:793.

Christianson, G. E. 1990. Fox at the wood's edge. New York: Holt and Company.

Dort, W., Jr. 1974. Archaeogeology of the Sutter site, Jackson County, Kansas. Lawrence, Kans.: Program and abstracts of the annual meeting of the Kansas Academy of Science.

Drew, D. L. 1979. Late Quaternary History and paleogeography of the El Dorado Lake area, Kansas. In Leaf, G. R., ed., Finding, managing, and studying prehistoric cultural resources at El Dorado Lake, Kansas (Phase I). Lawrence, Kans.: University of Kansas Museum of Anthropology, Research Series no. 2:108–202.

Drew, D. L. 1984. A case study in paleogeographical archaeology and predictive archaeology: El Dorado Lake, Kansas. Master's thesis, Lawrence, University of Kansas.

Eiseley, L. C. 1939. Evidence of a Pre-Ceramic culture in Smith County, Kansas. Science 89:221.

Evans, O. F. 1952. Some factors that controlled the location of the villages of the pre-historic people of central Oklahoma. Proceedings of the Oklahoma Academy of Sciences 33:320–22.

———. 1957. Related problems of archaeology and geology. Bulletin of the Oklahoma Anthropological Society 5:21–22.

Figgins, J. D. 1927. The antiquity of man in America. Natural History 27:229–39.

Fowke, G. 1926–1927. The Lansing skeleton. Washington, D.C.: Bureau of American Ethnology 44th Annual Report:471–84.

Gifford, J. A., and G. Rapp Jr. 1985. The early development of archaeological geology in North America. In Drake, E. T., and W. M. Jordan, eds., Geologists and ideas: A history of North American geology. Boulder, Colo.: Geological Society of America Centennial Special Volume 1:409–21.

Gould, C. N. 1898a. The Timbered Mounds of the Kaw reservation. Transactions of the Kansas Academy of Science 15:78–79.

————. 1898b. Prehistoric mounds in Cowley County. *Transactions of the Kansas Academy of Science* 15:79–80.

————. 1899. Additional notes on the Timbered Mounds of the Kaw reservation. *Transactions of the Kansas Academy of Science* 16:282.

Grayson, D. K. 1983. The establishment of human antiquity. New York: Academic Press.

Grosser, R. D. 1981. Federal involvement in Great Plains archaeology. *In* Johnson, A. E., and L. J. Zimmerman, eds., Methods and theory in Plains archaeology: A volume dedicated to Carlyle S. Smith. Vermillion, S.Dak.: Special Publications of the South Dakota Archaeological Society, no. 8:57–64.

Gunnerson, J. H. 1968. Plains Apache archaeology: A review. *Plains Anthropologist* 13:167–89.

Gunnerson, D. A., and J. H. Gunnerson. 1977. George Stephen Metcalf, 1900–1975. *Plains Anthropologist* 22:75–83.

Hall, S. A. 1977a. Geology and palynology of archaeological sites and associated sediments. *In* Henry, D. O., ed., The prehistory of the Little Caney River, 1976 season. Tulsa, Okla.: University of Tulsa Laboratory of Archaeology *Contributions in Archaeology* 1:13–41.

————. 1977b. Geological and paleoenvironmental studies. *In* Henry, D. O., ed., Prehistory and paleoenvironment of Birch Creek valley. Tulsa, Okla.: University of Tulsa Laboratory of Archaeology *Contributions in Archaeology* 3:11–31.

————. 1977c. Holocene geology and paleoenvironmental history of the Hominy Creek valley. *In* Henry, D. O., ed., Prehistory and paleoenvironment of Hominy Creek valley. Tulsa, Okla.: University of Tulsa Laboratory of Archaeology *Contributions in Archaeology* 2:12–42.

————. 1980. Paleoenvironmental synthesis of Hominy Creek valley: Pollen and land snail evidence. *In* Henry, D. O., ed., The prehistory and paleoenvironment of Hominy Creek valley, 1978 Season. Tulsa, Okla.: University of Tulsa, Laboratory of Archaeology *Contributions in Archaeology* 6:44–66.

————. 1982. Late Holocene paleoecology of the Southern Plains. *Quaternary Research* 17:391–407.

Hansen, W. R. 1985. Dust in the wind: J. A. Udden's turn-of-the-century research at Augustana. *In* Drake, E. T., and W. M. Jordan, eds., Geologists and ideas: A history of North American geologists. Boulder, Colo.: The Geological Society of America, Centennial Special Volume 1:203–14.

Hawley, M. F. 1992a. Preface. *The Kansas Anthropologist* 13:i–ii.

————. 1992b. Loren C. Eiseley KU Years: 1937–1944. *The Kansas Anthropologist* 13:5–22.

————., ed. 1993a. Cultural resource investigations for the U.S. Highway 166 corridor. Topeka: Kansas State Historical Society, Contract Archeology Publication no. 11.

————., ed. 1993b. Archaeological and geomorphological investigations of sites in the vicinity of Arkansas City, Cowley County, Kansas. Topeka: Kansas State Historical Society.

————. 1994. Additional notes on Loren Eiseley's years at the University of Kansas. *The Kansas Anthropologist* 15:17–22.

Hawley, M. F., and C. E. Haury. 1994. Lower Walnut Great Bend: Investigations of sites near Arkansas City, Kansas, background and preliminary results. *The Kansas Anthropologist* 15:1–45.

Haynes, C. V., Jr. 1969. The earliest American. *Science* 166:709–15.

————. 1990. The Antevs-Bryan years and the legacy for Paleoindian geo-chronology. *In* Laporte, L. F., ed., Establishment of a geologic framework for paleoanthropology. Boulder, Colo.: The Geological Society of America, Special Paper 242:55–68.

Henry, D. O. 1977a. The prehistory of the Little Caney River, 1976 field season. Tulsa, Okla.: University of Tulsa, Laboratory of Archaeology *Contributions in Archaeology* 1.

————. 1977b. The prehistory and paleoenvironment of Birch Creek valley. Tulsa, Okla.: University of Tulsa, Laboratory of Archaeology *Contributions in Archaeology* 3.

————. 1978. The prehistory and paleoenvironment of Hominy Creek valley, 1977 field season. Tulsa, Okla.: University of Tulsa, Laboratory of Archaeology *Contributions in Archaeology* 4.

————. 1980. The prehistory and paleoenvironment of Hominy Creek valley, 1978 field season. Tulsa, Okla.: University of Tulsa, Laboratory of Archaeology *Contributions in Archaeology* 6.

Henry, D. O., B. H. Butler, and S. A. Hall. 1979. The Late Prehistoric human ecology of Birch Creek Valley, northeastern Oklahoma. *Plains Anthropologist* 24:207–38.

Hill, M. E., Jr. 1996. Paleoindian bison remains from the 12 Mile creek site in western Kansas. *Plains Anthropologist* 41:359–72.

Hill, M. E., J. L. Hofman, and K. K. Kinsey. 1996. A history of archaeological research on the Central Plains. *In* Hofman, J. L., ed., Archeology and paleoecology of the Central Great Plains. Fayetteville, Ark.: Arkansas Archaeological Survey Research Series no. 48:29–40.

Hodge, F. W. 1900. Pueblo ruin in Kansas. *American Anthropologist* 2:778.

Hofman, J. L. 1995. Dating Folsom occupations in the Southern High Plains. *Journal of Field Archaeology* 22:421–37.

Hofman, J. L., and B. J. Carter. 1991. The Waugh site: A Folsom occupation in northwestern Oklahoma. *In* Carter, B. J., and A. Ward III, eds., A prehistory of the Plains border region, 24–37. Stillwater: Oklahoma State University, Agronomy Department, South-Central Cell Friends of the Pleistocene Guidebook.

Hofman, J. L., and R. R. Drass, eds. 1990a. A survey of archaeological resources and an evaluation of buried site potential in northwestern Oklahoma County, Oklahoma. Norman: University of Oklahoma, Oklahoma Archaeological Survey, Archaeological Resource Survey Report no. 36.

―――. 1990b. Summary. *In* Hofman, J. L., and R. R. Drass, eds., A survey of archaeological resources and an evaluation of buried site potential in northwestern Oklahoma County, Oklahoma. Norman: University of Oklahoma, Oklahoma Archaeological Survey, Archaeological Resource Survey Report no. 36:59–62.

Hofman, J. L., B. J. Carter, and M. Hill. 1992. Folsom occupation at the Waugh site in northwestern Oklahoma. *Current Research in the Pleistocene* 9:22–24.

Hofman, J. L., M. E. Hill Jr., C. W. Johnson, and D. T. Sather. 1995. Norton: An Early-Holocene bison bone bed in western Kansas. *Current Research in the Pleistocene* 12:19–21.

Holliday, V. T. 1997. Paleoindian geoarchaeology of the Southern High Plains. Austin: University of Texas Press.

Holmes, W. H. 1890. A quarry workshop of the flaked stone implement makers in the District of Columbia. *American Anthropologist* 3:1–26.

―――. 1892. Modern quarry refuse and the Paleolithic theory. *Science* 20:295–97.

―――. 1893. Gravel man and the Paleolithic culture: A preliminary word. *Science* 20:295–97.

―――. 1894. An ancient quarry in Indian territory. Washington, D.C.: Smithsonian Institution, Bureau of Ethnology, Bulletin 21.

―――. 1902. Fossil human remains found near Lansing, Kansas. *American Anthropologist* 4:743–52.

―――. 1903. Flint implements and fossil remains from a sulphur spring at Afton, Indian Territory. Washington, D.C.: Report for the U.S. National Museum for 1901:237–52.

―――. 1919. Handbook of aboriginal American antiquities, Part I. Washington, D.C.: Bureau of American Ethnology Bulletin 60.

Hrdlička, A. 1902. The crania of Trenton, New Jersey, and their bearing upon the antiquity of Man in that region. *American Museum of Natural History Bulletin* 16:23–62.

―――. 1903. The Lansing skeleton. *American Anthropologist* 5:320–30.

―――. 1907. Skeletal remains suggesting or attributed to early man in North America. Washington, D.C.: Bureau of American Ethnology Bulletin 33.

Jenness, D., ed. 1933. The American aboriginies: Their origins and antiquities. Toronto: University of Toronto Press.

Johnson, A. E. 1973. Archaeological investigations at the Budenbender site, Tuttle Creek Reservoir, North-Central Kansas. *Plains Anthropologist* 18:271–99.

Johnson, W. C. 1989. Geomorphology of the Perry Lake project area. *In* Logan, B., ed., Archaeological investigations in the Perry Lake project area, northeast Kansas: National Register evaluation of 17 sites, 22–48. Kansas City, Mo.: U.S. Army Corps of Engineers.

————. 1991. Buried soil surfaces beneath the Great Bend Prairie of central Kansas and archaeological implications. *Current Research in the Pleistocene* 8:108–10.

Johnson, W. C., and B. Logan. 1990. Geoarchaeology of the Kansas River basin, Central Great Plains. *In* Lasca, N. P., and J. Donahue, eds., Archaeological geology of North America. Boulder, Colo.: The Geological Society of America, Centennial Special vol. 4:267–300.

Johnson, W. C., and C. W. Martin. 1987. Holocene alluvial- stratigraphic studies from Kansas and adjoining states of the east-central Plains. *In* Johnson, W. C., ed., Quaternary environments of Kansas. Lawrence: Kansas Geological Survey, Guidebook Series 5:109–22.

Johnson, W. C., and K. Park. 1996. Late Wisconsinan and Holocene environmental history. *In* Hofman, J. L., ed., Archeology and paleoecology of the Central Great Plains. Fayetteville, Ark.: Arkansas Archaeological Survey, Research Series no. 48:3–28.

Katz, P. R. 1971. Archaeology of the Sutter site, northeastern Kansas. *Plains Anthropologist* 16:1–19.

————. 1973. Radiocarbon dates from the Sutter site, northeastern Kansas. *Plains Anthropologist* 18:167–68.

Kay, M. 1981. Little Caney River prehistory: 1979 field season. Tulsa, Okla.: University of Tulsa Laboratory of Archaeology *Contributions in Archaeology* 8.

Kay, M., and J. Dixon. 1990. Archaeology and geomorphology of the Cherokee Turnpike Project, Mayes County, Oklahoma. *Bulletin of the Oklahoma Anthropological Society* 39:57–101.

Keyser, J. D., and J. A. Farley. 1979. Little Caney River prehistory, 1977 field season. Tulsa, Okla.: University of Tulsa Laboratory of Archaeology *Contributions in Archaeology* 5.

Keyser, J. D., and J. A. Farley. 1980. Jackson-Fall Leaf: A multi-component occupation site in northeastern Oklahoma. *Plains Anthropologist* 25:247–264.

King, J. E. 1979. Preliminary survey for palynological sites in the El Dorado Lake area. *In* Leaf, G. R., ed., Finding, managing, and studying prehistoric cultural resources at El Dorado Lake, Kansas (Phase I). Lawrence: University of Kansas Museum of Anthropology, Research Series no. 2:203–208.

Koch, A. K. 1857. Mastodon remains in the State of Missouri, together with evidence of the existence of man contemporaneously with the mastodon. *Transactions of the Kansas Academy of Science* 1:61–64.

Leaf, G. R. 1979. A research design for impacted archaeological sites at El Dorado Lake, Butler County, Kansas. *In* Leaf, G. R., ed., Finding, managing, and studying prehistoric cultural resources at El Dorado Lake, Kansas

(Phase I). Lawrence: University of Kansas Museum of Anthropology, Research Series no. 2:1–30.

Lees, W. B., Mandel, R. D., and P. E. Brockington Jr. 1982. ETSI pipeline project cultural resources report. Topeka, Kans.: Soil Systems, Inc., Report no. 5.

Leonhardy, F. C. 1989. Physical stratigraphy of Copple Mound. *In* Rogers, J. D., D. G. Wyckoff, and D. A. Peterson, eds., Contributions to Spiro archaeology: Mound excavations and regional perspectives. Norman: Oklahoma Archaeological Survey, University of Oklahoma, Studies in Oklahoma's Past, no. 16:15–26.

Logan, B., A. F. Arbogast, and W. C. Johnson. 1993. Geoarchaeology of the Kansas Sand Prairie. Lawrence: University of Kansas, Museum of Anthropology, Project Report Series no. 83.

Lungstrom, L. 1992. Recognition of three pioneer scientists of Swedish descent. *Transactions of the Kansas Academy of Science* 93:171–76.

Lyell, C. 1863. The geological evidences of the antiquity of man, with remarks on theories of the origin of species by variation. London: John Murray.

McClung, C. E. 1908. Restoration of the skeleton of *Bison occidentalis*. *Kansas University Bulletin* 4:249–52.

McGee, W. J., and C. Thomas. 1905. Prehistoric North America. Philadelphia: G. Barrie and Sons.

Mallam, R. C. 1985. Site of the serpent: A prehistoric life metaphor in south central Kansas. Lyons, Kans.: Occasional Publications of the Coronado-Quivira Museum, no. 1.

Mandel, R. D. 1987a. Environmental setting. *In* Schmits, L. J., ed., Archaeological survey and testing at Perry Lake, Jefferson County, Kansas. Shawnee Mission, Kans.: Environmental Systems Analysis, Inc, Publications in Archaeology, no. 2:3–9.

———. 1987b. Geomorphology of the Wakarusa River valley, northeastern Kansas. *In* Logan, B., ed., Archaeological investigations in the Clinton Lake project area, northeastern Kansas: National Register evaluation of 27 prehistoric sites. Kansas City, Mo.: U.S. Army Corps of Engineers:20–34.

———. 1988a. Geomorphology of the Pawnee River valley, southwest Kansas. *In* Timberlake, R. D., ed., Phase II archaeological and geomorphological survey of the proposed Pawnee River watershed covering subwatersheds 3 through 7, Ness, Ford, Lane, and Finney Counties, southwest Kansas, 79–134. Topeka, Kansas State Historical Society, unpublished manuscript on file.

———. 1988b. Geomorphology of the Smoky Hill River valley at Kanopolis Lake. *In* Schmits, L. J., ed., An archaeological and geomorphological survey of Kanopolis Lake, north-central Kansas, 49–72. Kansas City, Mo.: U.S. Army Corps of Engineers.

———. 1990. Geomorphology and stratigraphy of the Stigenwalt site. *In* Thies, R., ed., The archeology of the Stigenwalt site, 14LT351. Topeka: Kansas State Historical Society Contract Archeology Series Publication no. 7:138–45.

————. 1991a. Holocene landscape evolution in the Pawnee River Valley, southwestern Kansas. Ph.D. diss., Lawrence, University of Kansas.

————. 1991b. Geologic potentials for buried archaeological sites in the White-water River and Doyle Creek watersheds, Southeast Kansas. Topeka, Kansas State Historical Society, unpublished manuscript on file.

————. 1992a. Soils and Holocene landscape evolution in central and south-western Kansas: Implications for archaeological research. In Holliday, V. T., ed., Soils in archaeology, 41–117. Washington, D.C.: Smithsonian Institution Press.

————. 1992b. Preliminary geomorphological investigation of site 14RY38, Riley County, Kansas. Topeka, Kansas State Historical Society, unpublished manuscript on file.

————. 1993a. Geomorphology. In Weston, T., ed., Phase II cultural resource survey of high potential areas within the southeast Kansas highway corridor. Topeka: Kansas State Historical Society Contract Archeology Series Publication no. 10:44–121.

————. 1993b. Geomorphology. In Hawley, M. F., ed., Cultural resource investigations for the U.S. Highway 166 corridor. Topeka: Kansas State Historical Society Contract Archeology Publication no. 11:24–75.

————. 1993c. Geomorphology and stratigraphy of site 14JO359. In Ritter-bush, L. C, ed., Archeological investigations of 14JO359, Johnson County, Kansas. Lawrence: University of Kansas, Museum of Anthropology, Project Report Series no. 82:10–24.

————. 1994a. Holocene landscape evolution in southwestern Kansas. Lawrence: Kansas Geological Survey and Kansas State Historical Society, Bulletin 236.

————. 1994b. Geomorphology and stratigraphy of lower Mill Creek valley, Johnson County, Kansas. In Gillen, T. V., R. P. Winham, E. J. Lueck, and L. A. Hanus, eds., Archeological test excavations at six prehistoric sites within the lower Mill Creek valley, Johnson County, Kansas. Sioux Falls, S.Dak.: Augustana College, Archeology Laboratory, Archeology Contract Series no. 99:96–125.

————. 1994c. Geomorphology and alluvial stratigraphy of the Walnut River valley at Arkansas City, Kansas: Implications for archeological research. Tulsa, Okla.: U.S. Army Corps of Engineers.

————. 1994d. Geoarchaeology of the lower Walnut River valley at Arkansas City, Kansas. The Kansas Anthropologist 15:46–69.

————. 1994e. Geomorphology and alluvial stratigraphy of the Walnut River valley. In Hawley, M. F., ed., Archaeological and geomorphological investigations of sites in the vicinity of Arkansas City, Cowley County, Kansas, 35–72. Topeka: Kansas State Historical Society.

————. 1995. Geomorphic Controls of the Archaic Record in the Central Plains of the United States. In Bettis, E. A., III, ed., Archaeological Geology of the Archaic period in North America. Boulder, Colo.: The Geological Society of America, Special Paper 297:37–66.

———. 1996. Geomorphic controls of the Paleoindian record in the Central Plains of Kansas. Abstracts of the 61st Annual Meeting of the Society for American Archaeology, New Orleans.

Mandel, R. D., J. D. Reynolds, B. G. Williams, and V. A. Wulfkuhle. 1991. Upper Delaware River and tributaries watershed: Results of geomorphological and archeological studies in Atchison, Brown, Jackson, and Nemaha Counties, Kansas. Topeka: Kansas State Historical Society, Contract Archeology Publication no. 9.

Mandel, R. D., and L. J. Schmits. 1984. Geomorphology and landscapes of the Milford, Melvern and Pomona Lake areas. *In* Schmits, L. J., ed., Archaeological inventory and evaluation at Milford, Melvern and Pomona Lakes, eastern Kansas, 23–40. Kansas City, Mo.: U.S. Army Corps of Engineers.

Martin, H. T. 1909. Further notes on the pueblo ruins of Scott County. *Kansas University Science Bulletin* 5, no. 2:11–22.

May, D. W. 1986. Geomorphology. *In* Blakeslee, D. J., R. Blasing, and H. Garcia, eds., Along the Pawnee Trail: Cultural resource survey and testing at Wilson Lake, Kansas, 72–86. Kansas City, Mo.: U.S. Army Corps of Engineers.

Meltzer, D. J. 1983. The antiquity of man and the development of American archaeology. *Advances in Archaeological Method and Theory* 6:1–52.

———. 1991. The problem of "paradigms" and "paradigm bias" in controversies over human antiquity in America. *In* Dillehay, T. D., and D. J. Meltzer, eds., The first Americans, 13–14. Boca Raton, Fla.: CRC Press, Inc.

Mudge, B. F. 1896. Traces of moundbuilders. *Transactions of the Kansas Academy of Science* 2:69–71.

Nials, F. 1977. Geology of resources area Cowden Laterals Watershed Site no. 8. Oklahoma City: Oklahoma Conservation Commission.

Noelke, V. H. M. 1974. The origin and early history of the Bureau of American Ethnology, 1879–1910. Ph.D. Diss., Austin, The University of Texas.

O'Brien, P. J., P. Hixon, B. Miller, D. Rowlison, P. Tribble, D. Vitt, and J. P. Young. 1973. A most preliminary report of the Coffey site, 14PO1: A Plains Archaic site in Pottawatomie County. *Kansas Anthropological Association Newsletter* 18:1–38.

Odell, G. H., J. C. Dixon, K. E. Dickerson, and K. L. Shingleton Jr. 1990. An archaeological investigation of the Arkansas River bluffline between Jenks and Bixby, eastern Oklahoma. Tulsa, Okla.: University of Tulsa, Department of Anthropology, *Contributions in Archaeology* 17.

Osborn, H. F. 1910. The age of mammals in Europe, Asia, and North America. New York: MacMillan.

Owen, L. A. 1907. A Paleolithic implement from the loess. *Records of the Past* 5:289–92.

Owen, L. A. 1909. Another Paleolithic implement and possibly an eolith from northwestern Missouri. *Records of the Past* 8:108–11.

Page, L. E. 1984. Benjamin F. Mudge: The first Kansas geologist. *Earth Sciences History* 3:103–11.

Prewitt, T. J. 1980. Little Caney River prehistory (Copan Lake): 1978 field season. Tulsa, Okla.: University of Tulsa Laboratory of Archaeology *Contributions in Archaeology 7.*

Putnam, F. W. 1888. Comparison of Paleolithic implements. *Proceedings of the Boston Society of Natural History* 23:421–24.

Reid, K. C., and J. A. Artz. 1984. Hunters of the forest edge: Culture, time, and process in the Little Caney Basin (1980, 1981, and 1982 field seasons). Tulsa, Okla.: University of Tulsa, Laboratory of Archaeology *Contributions in Archaeology* 14.

Reynolds, J. D. 1992. Samuel Wendell Williston KU years: 1890–1902. *The Kansas Anthropologist* 13:1–4.

Rogers, R. A. 1984a. Kansas prehistory—an alluvial geomorphological perspective. Ph.D. diss., Lawrence, University of Kansas.

———. 1984b. Distinctive bifacial artifacts from Wisconsin terraces in Kansas. *Current Research in the Pleistocene* 1:33–34.

———. 1984c. The Donahue locality: Evidence suggesting a pre-Wisconsin human presence in North America. *Current Research in the Pleistocene* 1:19–20.

———. 1987. Frequency of occurrence of Paleoindian sites in the Neosho River drainage of Kansas—a geomorphological analysis. *In* Johnson, W. C., ed., Quaternary environments of Kansas. Lawrence: Kansas Geological Survey, Guidebook Series 5:197–99.

Rogers, R. A., and L. D. Martin. 1982. A Clovis projectile point from the Kansas River. *Transactions of the Kansas Academy of Sciences* 85:78–81.

———. 1983. American Indian artifacts from the Kansas River. *Transactions of the Nebraska Academy of Sciences* 11:13–18.

———. 1984. The 12 Mile Creek site—A reinvestigation. *American Antiquity* 49:757–64.

Romer, A. S. 1933. Pleistocene vertebrates and their bearing on the problems of human antiquity. *In* Jenness, D., ed., The American Aborigines: Their origins and antiquities, 49–84. Toronto: University of Toronto Press.

Salisbury, N. E. 1980. Soil-geomorphic relationships with archaeological sites in the Keystone Reservoir area, Oklahoma. *In* Moore, B. M., ed., A cultural assessment of the archaeological resources in the Keystone Lake project area, north-central Oklahoma. Norman: University of Oklahoma, Archaeological Research Associates Report no. 23:59–98.

Saunders, J. 1980. Reassessment of certain archeological sites in the Candy Lake area, Oklahoma. Norman: University of Oklahoma Archeological Research Associates Research Report no. 22.

Schmits, L. J. 1976. The Coffey site: Environment and cultural adaptation at a prairie Plains Archaic site. Lawrence: University of Kansas Museum of Anthropology.

———. 1978. The Coffey site: Environmental and cultural adaptation at a prairie Plains border Archaic site. *Midcontinent Journal of Archaeology* 3:69–185.

———. 1980. Holocene fluvial history and depositional environments at the Coffey site, Kansas. *In* Johnson, A. E., ed., Archaic prehistory on the Prairie-Plains border. Lawrence: University of Kansas Publications in Anthropology 12:79–105.

———. 1981. Archaeological and geological investigations at the Coffey site, Tuttle Creek Lake, Kansas. Lawrence: University of Kansas Museum of Anthropology.

Schmits, L. J., J. E. Donahue, and R. D. Mandel. 1983. Archaeological and geomorphological inventory and evaluation at the proposed Fort Scott Lake project, Southeast Kansas. Overland Park, Kans.: Environmental Systems Analysis, Inc., Cultural Resource Management Report no. 12.

Schmits, L. J., R. D. Mandel, J. McKay, and J. G. Hedden. 1987. Archaeological and historical investigations at Tuttle Creek Lake, eastern Kansas. Kansas City, Mo.: U.S. Army Corps of Engineers.

Schultz, C. B., and L. C. Eiseley. 1935. Paleontological evidence for the antiquity of the Scottsbluff bison quarry and its associated artifacts. *American Anthropologist* 37:306–19.

Sellards, E. H. 1940. Early Man in America: Index to localities, and selected bibliography. *Bulletin of the Geological Society of America* 51:373–432.

———. 1952. Early man in America: A study of prehistory. Austin: The University of Texas Press.

Shimek, B. 1903. The loess and Lansing Man. *American Geologist* 32:353–69.

Shor, E. N. 1971. Fossils and flies: The life of a complete scientist, Samuel Wendell Williston (1851–1918). Norman: University of Oklahoma Press.

Smith, C. S. 1992. Carlyle S. Smith KU years: 1947–1980. *The Kansas Anthropologist* 13:58–72.

Smith, H. T. U. 1938. Geomorphic evidence relating to the antiquity of man in north-central Kansas. *Abstracts of the Geological Society of America* 49:1901.

Solecki, R. S. 1953. Appraisal of the archaeological and paleontological resources of the Tuttle Creek Reservoir, Marshall, Pottawatomie, and Riley counties, Kansas. Washington, D.C.: Smithsonian Institution.

Stewart, T. D. 1949. The development of the concept of morphological dating in connection with early man in America. *Southwestern Journal of Anthropology* 5:1–16.

Thies, R., ed. 1990. The archeology of the Stigenwalt site, 14LT351. Topeka: Kansas State Historical Society, Contract Archeology Series Publication no. 7.

Thompson, D. M., and E. A. Bettis III. 1980. Archaeology and Holocene land-
    scape evolution in the Missouri Drainage of Iowa. *Journal of the Iowa
    Archeological Society* 27:1–60.

Udden, J. A. 1900. An old Indian village. Rock Island, Ill.: Augustana Library
    Publication no. 2.

———. [1909] 1969. Memories of my sojourn in Lindsborg. *In* Bildt, R. B.,
    ed., The Smoky Valley in after years, 80–84. Reprint, Lindsborg, Kans.:
    Lindsborg News-Record.

Underwood, J. R., Jr. 1992. The life of Johan August Udden, geologist, teacher,
    inventor: Through the Kansas years. *Transactions of the Kansas Academy
    of Science* 93:177–91.

Upham, W. 1902a. Glacial man in Kansas. *American Anthropologist* 4:566–68.

———. 1902b. Man and the Ice Age at Lansing, Kansas and Little Falls, Min-
    nesota. *American Geologist* 30:135–50.

Waters, M. R. 1992. Principles of geoarchaeology: A North American perspec-
    tive. Tucson: University of Arizona Press.

Wedel, W. R. 1935. Reports on field work by the archaeological survey of the
    Nebraska State Historical Society, 1934. *Nebraska History Magazine* 14, no.
    3:132–255.

———. 1941. Environment and native subsistence economies in the Central
    Great Plains. Washington, D.C.: Smithsonian Institution Miscellaneous
    Collections 101, no. 3:1–29.

———. 1959. An introduction to Kansas archeology. Washington, D.C.:
    Smithsonian Institution, Bureau of American Ethnology 174.

———. 1961. Prehistoric Man on the Great Plains. Norman: University of
    Oklahoma Press.

———. 1975. Some Euro-American perceptions of the Great Plains and their
    influence on anthropological thinking. *In* Blouet, B. W., and M. P. Lawson,
    eds., Images of the Plains: The role of human nature in settlement, 13–20.
    Lincoln: University of Nebraska Press.

———. 1982. Toward a history of Plains archeology. *In* Wedel, W. R., ed.,
    Essays in the history of Plains archeology. Lincoln, Nebr.: J & L Reprints,
    Reprints in Anthropology 24:78–131.

———. 1986. Central Plains prehistory: Holocene environments and culture
    change in the Republican River basin. Lincoln, University of Nebraska
    Press.

Weston, T. 1993. Phase II cultural resource survey of high potential areas within
    the southeast Kansas highway corridor. Topeka: Kansas State Historical
    Society Contract Archeology Series Publication no. 10.

Whitney, J. D. 1880. Auriferous gravels of the Sierra Nevada of California. *Pub-
    lication of the Museum of Comparative Zoology, Harvard College* 6:288–321.

Williston, S. W. 1879. Indian figures in western Kansas. *Kansas City Review of
    Science* 3:16.

————. 1897. The Pleistocene of Kansas, vol. 2:299–308. Lawrence: The University Geological Survey of Kansas [Kansas Geological Survey].

————. 1898. The Pleistocene of Kansas. *Transactions of the Kansas Academy of Science* 15:90–94.

————. 1899. Some prehistoric ruins in Scott county, Kansas. Lawrence: *Kansas University Quarterly*, series B, vol. 7:109–14.

————. 1902a. An arrowhead found with bones of *Bison occidentalis* Lucas, in western Kansas. *American Geologist* 30:313–15.

Williston, S. W. 1902b. A fossil man from Kansas. *Science* 16:195–96.

————. 1905a. On the occurrence of an arrow-head with bones of an extinct bison. Proceedings of the International Congress of Americanists, Thirteenth Session:335–37.

————. 1905b. On the Lansing Man. *American Geologist* 35:342–46. Williston, S. W., and H. T. Martin. 1900. Some Pueblo ruins in Scott County, Kansas. *Transactions of the Kansas State Historical Society* 6:124–30.

Wilmsen, E. 1965. An outline of early man studies in the United States. *American Antiquity* 31:172–92.

Winchell, N. H. 1902. The Lansing skeleton. *American Geologist* 30:189–94.

————. 1903. The Pleistocene geology of the Concannon farm, near Lansing, Kansas. *American Geology* 31:263–308.

————. 1912. Paleolithic artifacts from Kansas. *Records of the Past* 11:174–78.

————. 1913. The weathering of aboriginal stone artifacts. St. Paul, Minn.: Minnesota Historical Society.

Witty, T. A., Jr. 1971. Archeology and early history of the Scott Lake State Park area. *Kansas Anthropological Association Newsletter* 16, no. 5:1–5.

————. 1978. The Penokee stone Indian. *Kansas Anthropological Association Newsletter* 23:6–9.

Wyckoff, D. G. 1964. The cultural sequence at the Packard site, Mayes County, Oklahoma. Norman: University of Oklahoma Research Institute, Oklahoma River Basin Survey Project, Archaeological Site Report no. 2.

————. 1985a. The Packard complex: Early Archaic, Pre-Dalton occupations on the parairie-woodlands border. *Southeastern Archaeology* 4:1–26.

————. 1985b. The Laverty Ditch: Prehistoric irrigation in the Oklahoma Panhandle? *Bulletin of the Oklahoma Anthropological Society* 34:147–78.

————. 1989. Accelerator dates and chronology at the Packard site, Oklahoma. *Current Research in the Pleistocene* 6:24–26.

————. 1992. Introduction. *In* Interdisciplinary studies of the Hajny mammoth site, Dewey County, Oklahoma. Norman: Oklahoma Archaeological Survey, University of Oklahoma, Studies in Oklahoma's Past no. 17:1–6.

Wyckoff, D. G., and B. J. Carter. 1994. Geoarchaeology of the Burnham site: 1992 investigations at a "Pre-Clovis site" in northwestern Oklahoma. Norman: Oklahoma Archaeological Survey, University of Oklahoma, Special Publication.

Wyckoff, D. G., P. Flynn, B. J. Carter, and B. A. Branson. 1987. Research on the late Pleistocene in Oklahoma. *Current Research in the Pleistocene* 4:41–43.

Wyckoff, D. G., B. J. Carter, P. Flynn, L. D. Martin, B. A. Branson, and J. L. Theler. 1992. Interdisciplinary studies of the Hajny mammoth site, Dewey County, Oklahoma. Norman: Oklahoma Archaeological Survey, University of Oklahoma, Studies in Oklahoma's Past no. 17.

Wyckoff, D. G., B. J. Carter, Wakefield Dort Jr., G. R. Brakenridge, L. D. Martin, J. L. Theler, and L. C. Todd. 1990. Northwestern Oklahoma's Burnham site: Glimpses beyond Clovis. *Current Research in the Pleistocene* 7:60–63.

CHAPTER FIVE

A Brief History of Geoarchaeology in the Eastern Plains and Prairies

E. Arthur Bettis III

*So often these things you fellows call archaeological laws turn
out not to be laws of human behavior, but examples of the
physical processes involved in the formation of sites. And son,
those are no more than the products of geological laws.*
—the Old Timer to the Born Again Philosopher (Flannery 1982)

INTRODUCTION

In North America, archaeological geology is a relatively new discipline that
has a foot in both archaeology and geology. Early studies in the Southwest
and Southern Plains, discussed elsewhere in this volume, laid the ground-
work for the development of the discipline in the United States. For the most
part, the eastern Plains and Prairies (roughly the area between the Missouri,
Minnesota, and Mississippi River valleys; map 5.1) are relative latecomers as
far as collaborations among archaeologists and earth scientists are concerned,
and archaeological geology has risen to prominence in this region only since
the 1980s. The slow development of archaeological geology in the Eastern
Plains and Prairies has been attributed to a paucity of known Paleoindian
sites, and the long-standing, but usually unstated, assumption by archaeologists that deep burial or complex natural stratigraphy is a problem associated
primarily with older sites (Bettis et al. 1985). Thus, archaeologists in this area

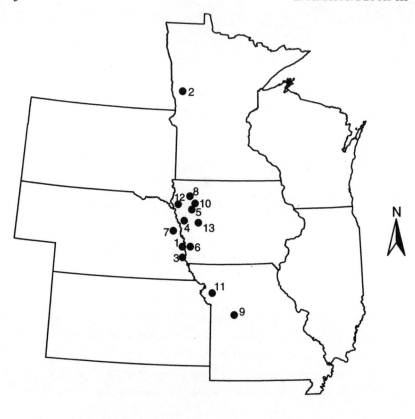

Map 5.1. The Eastern Plains and Prairies, showing the localities discussed in the text: 1) Guilder Mound near Florence, Nebraska; 2) Minnesota Man site; 3) Walker Gilmore site; 4) Turin site; 5) Simonson site; 6) Hill site; 7) Logan Creek site; 8) Mill Creek Project; 9) Truman Reservoir; 10) Cherokee site; 11) Little Platte Drainage; 12) Rainbow site; 13) MAD sites.

had no strong impetus for establishing interactions with geologists, soil scientists, paleontologists, and paleobotanists, and the few early attempts at such interactions did not proceed very far.

The brief history of archaeological geology in this region does not reflect a lack of interest on the part of earth scientists regarding environmental history and human prehistory. The Upper Midwest has long been a center of Pleistocene studies because of its spectacular record of glacial and interglacial episodes (Chamberlin 1895; Kay 1931; Leighton 1960; Ruhe 1969), and it is the area where many key concepts in pedology, including the inseparability of geomorphology and soil genesis, were developed (Hilgard 1892; Marbut 1935; Ruhe 1956). Many early Midwestern earth scientists were also keenly interested in and involved with studies investigating the duration of the human presence on the continent.

The history of archaeology and earth science interactions in the Eastern Plains and Prairies can be organized into three chronologically overlapping periods that differ in the nature, goals, and level of the interaction. This short history of the interaction of earth scientists and archaeologists provides a perspective on the way science gets done and demonstrates how, after several false starts, archaeological geology has arrived as a partner with archaeology in the pursuit of the human past.

EARLY PERIOD: THE ANTIQUITY OF HUMAN PRESENCE

Several discoveries of human skeletal remains enclosed in deposits presumed to date from the last (Wisconsin) glacial period were made during the late 1800s and early 1900s. Notable among these was the discovery, during excavation of a root cellar, of the remains of two individuals in rocky talus beneath silts at the mouth of a small tributary of the Missouri River near Lansing, Kansas (see Mandel, this volume). Following the discovery and interpretation of the "Lansing Man," the antiquity of humans remained of great interest, and the remains of other supposed "loess men" were reported from the eastern Plains and Prairies. An interesting case, because it involved remains associated with an excavated mound, is the "Nebraska Loess Man" found on a bluff overlooking the Missouri River near Florence, Nebraska (map 5.1; Barbour and Ward 1906; Barbour 1907a; Gilder 1908). During excavation of Gilder Mound, R. F. Gilder and E. H. Barbour found two distinct layers of human remains, the lower of which contained "five primitive skulls" and was within "original undisturbed loess" (Barbour 1907b:327). This report prompted Bohumil Shimek, professor of botany at the State University of Iowa (University of Iowa) and a staff member of the Iowa Geological Survey, to investigate the nature of the "undisturbed loess" in order to ascertain whether this was a valid claim for great antiquity of human presence in the

Fig. 5.1. Examining the discovery site of Minnesota Man in northwestern Minnesota. Debates about the stratigraphic associations of the human remains and glacial lake sediments prompted visits by prominent geologists. Pictured here, left to right, are two unidentified individuals, archaeologist A. Jenks, and geologists M. Leighton, G. Kay, and G. Theil (from Kay and Leighton 1938:fig. 1). Courtesy of the University of Chicago Press.

area. After a thorough study of the mound, he concluded that the human remains were within mound fill rather than loess (Shimek 1908). He concurred with Barbour's observation that the mound contained burials representing two distinct periods but concluded that the interments both postdated the loess and dated from well within the postglacial period.

Discoveries of human remains presumably associated with deposits dating to the last glaciation continued during the first four decades of the twentieth century. Notable among these was a series of discoveries in northwestern Minnesota (e.g., Minnesota Man; map 5.1, fig 5.1) that gained the attention of a number of prominent geologists (Antevs 1935; Bryan 1935; Kay and Leighton 1938). As with the earlier discoveries, human remains contained within glacial deposits (in this case outwash and glaciolacustrine sediments) were discovered and removed by archaeologists; then geologists were called in to assess the geologic context of the remains (Jenks 1932; 1936; fig. 5.1). In the case of the Minnesota finds, it was generally agreed (with the exception of a dissenting opinion by geologist Ernst Antevs) that the geologic deposits were in place and attributable to the last glacial period and that the human remains were directly associated with them (Bryan 1935; Bryan and MacClintock 1938; Jenks 1936; Kay and Leighton 1938; Antevs 1938).

Interest in early man by earth scientists and engineers was highlighted at a conference convened in Chicago by the National Research Council in 1931. The conference focused on recent discoveries in North America and what measures should be taken to aid in the discovery and documentation of new finds (Leighton 1932). Further discussion of these issues continued at the International Symposium on Early Man, held at the Philadelphia Academy of Sciences in March 1937 (Kay and Leighton 1938). Apparently, during this period, earth scientists were very interested in the antiquity of human presence on the continent and agreed that geologic proof was the key to demonstrating antiquity or lack thereof (Winchell 1902; Chamberlin et al. 1902; Leighton 1932, 1933). On the other side of the coin, archaeologists during this period seemed to view geologic information as being important only in situations where great antiquity was suspected. Information transfer was unidirectional—geologists told archaeologists how old certain archaeological deposits (those suspected of being very ancient) were in order to validate or dismiss claims of early human presence on the continent.

MIDDLE PERIOD: MORE THAN
BONES AND ARTIFACTS?

In all disciplines there are a few people who gain perspectives too advanced to become widely incorporated in existing theory and methodology. This is the story of the middle period, a time when the great importance of geologic context in all archaeological studies was almost realized, then all but forgotten when Midwestern archaeology focused on the salvage operations of the River Basins Survey.

The most important group of studies occurred early in this period at the Walker-Gilmore site (25CC28) along Sterns Creek in southeastern Nebraska (map 5.1). F. H. Sterns reported the site in 1915 and undertook a detailed study of the stratified locality as part of his doctoral dissertation in Anthropology at Harvard University (Sterns 1915). Exposures in the banks of deeply entrenched Sterns Creek revealed buried Woodland (Sterns Creek Phase) archeological deposits 1.8 to 8.2 meters below the land surface. Also, a younger, near-surface Nebraska Phase component occurred on a higher terrace along the creek. Sterns made remarkable observations regarding the stream channel and the alluvial deposits exposed along the creek and encountered in hand auger borings (Sterns 1915). He identified two lithologically distinct alluvial fills and concluded that the modern entrenched stream channel was narrower than that present during the Woodland occupations and that the former course of the stream was different from the modern one. It is obvious that at this early date Sterns realized that significant landscape changes had occurred in the not-too-distant past and that those changes influenced archaeological interpretations of the Woodland occupations.

Further investigations at Walker-Gilmore by W. D. Strong, A. T. Hill, and John Champe in the 1930s and 1940s corroborated Sterns's observations and broadened the case for significant landscape change in valleys during the last few millennia (Strong 1935; Champe 1946). As early as 1935, Strong envisioned the need for an interdisciplinary study to elucidate man-land relationships during the Woodland period:

> First of all, the place calls for an extended period of cooperative research on the part of both anthropologists and geographers . . . Meanwhile the course of the older stream as indicated by gravel and clay deposits could be mapped in by the geographers. Also the extent and relationship of the different types of soil would be diagrammed. The combined results of such a survey would be an accurate series of maps showing the old dwelling places in relation to the former stream, to the various soil deposits, and to the present gully of Sterns Creek (Strong 1935:197).

Investigations at other localities in eastern Nebraska (e.g., Hill and Kivett 1940) and northwest Missouri (Wedel 1943) revealed associations of archaeological deposits and alluvial stratigraphy reminiscent of Sterns Creek. Champe elaborated on some of these localities in his 1946 report on Ash Hollow Cave (1946:66–82). He concluded that small valleys of the region contain a sequence of two alluvial fills with distinct archaeological associations: 1) an older fill that occurs beneath a low terrace (T_1) with buried pre-ceramic and Woodland and Nebraska Phase surface and near-surface archaeological associations; and 2) a younger fill beneath the flood plain (T_0) with buried Woodland archaeological associations. He realized the importance of these associations in the context of the regional archaeological record and the need for interdisciplinary cooperation to help discover and properly interpret the archaeological record (fig. 5.2). Champe astutely observed that "the benefit . . . need not be too one-sided in favor of archaeology" (Champe 1946:8).

A session devoted to geologic reports bearing on the nature of site burial at the 1948 Sixth Plains Conference for Archaeology indicated how interested some archaeologists were in the geologic context of sites (Jennings 1950). The focus on the predictability of geologic settings rather than specific sites and the regional scope of some of these papers indicate a level of geoarchaeological awareness that has not been matched until quite recently.

Aside from the flurry of innovation associated with Nebraska archaeologists, little changed in approaches to geoarchaeology from 1940 to 1950. That is not to say that there were not several important archaeological discoveries that involved geologic interpretations, but the geologic studies and their application to archaeological problems did not go beyond the descriptive phase characteristic of the early period.

Four investigations in which W. D. Frankforter, a geologist associated with the Stanford Museum in Cherokee, Iowa, evaluated the geologic context typify the scope and approach of most geoarchaeological studies during the middle period. The most famous of the sites discovered during this period is Turin (13MN2), located at the junction of the Maple and Missouri valleys in Monona County, Iowa (map 5.1, fig. 5.3). Late in the summer of 1955 the State University of Iowa received a report from the Monona County Coroner that human physical remains had been found by a gravel pit operator (Fisher et al. 1985). Over the course of a few weeks four skeletons were found, two during archaeological excavations under the scrutiny of a number of specialists who had been summoned to the site, including archaeologists H. M. Wormington, Waldo R. Wedel, E. Mott Davis, John Champe, Marvin Kivett, Franklin Fenenga, and G. Hubert Smith (Ruppé 1956). Archaeologists were very interested in the site because the context of the human remains was interpreted as "silty loess" believed to be of late-glacial age (Ruppé 1956; Frankforter and Agogino 1959). Ruppé, then the state archaeologist of Iowa, believed the site was of "extreme importance" (Ruppé 1955:31), and, thanks in large part to the media savvy of the gravel pit operator, the site received national publicity with a feature article in *Life* magazine (1955) entitled "Bones Found in Iowa Sand Pit May be Oldest American Skeleton" (fig. 5.3, 5.4). The excitement surrounding the Turin discovery slowly subsided, especially following the release of radiocarbon ages

TIME DIVISIONS		STRATIFIED SITES					SITES IN TERRACES			
		ASH HOLLOW	SIGNAL BUTTE	POTTTORF	SONDERGAARD	WHITE RIVER	WALKER GILMORE	BAKENHUS	DK-3	SKULL CREEK
HISTORIC	1700 A.D	SURFACE								
CERAMIC Late	1500 A.D.	A DISMAL RIVER	SIGNAL BUTTE3 DISMAL RIVER & UPPER REPUBLICAN							
CERAMIC Middle	1300 A.D.	B UPPER REPUBLICAN		UPPER REPUBLICAN	UPPER REPUBLICAN		NEBRASKA	UPPER REPUBLICAN	NEBRASKA	NEBRASKA
CERAMIC Early	1000 A.D	C WOODLAND D		WOODLAND	WOODLAND	WOODLAND	WOODLAND	WOODLAND	WOODLAND	WOODLAND
	600 A.D.	E		STRATUM C		TERRACE T1				
Intermediate	300 A.D.	F								
	1 A.D.	G				5 SOIL ZONES				
LITHIC	3000 B.C.		SIGNAL BUTTE 2							
Early	8000 B.C.		SIGNAL BUTTE 1			TERRACE T2 YUMA				

A Tentative Stratigraphic Sequence And Comparison Of Central Plains Sites

TENTATIVE STRATIGRAPHIC SEQUENCE AND COMPARISON OF CENTRAL PLAINS SITES

Fig. 5.2. Stratigraphic sequences and cultural associations in small Nebraska valleys as depicted by Champe in his 1946 monograph on Ash Hollow Cave (Champe 1946). His proposition that there was a regional association of alluvial fills and cultural deposits made little impact on archaeology at the time, but would later be resurrected and, beginning in the late 1970s, would play a significant role in CRM and anthropological archaeology. Courtesy of the University of Nebraska at Lincoln.

Fig. 5.3. Publicity surrounding the presumed discovery of human remains in a Late Glacial loess deposit at the Turin site in western Iowa drew many visitors to the site. Pictured here is a visit by a group of high school students. Photograph on file at the Office of the State Archaeologist, University of Iowa.

on one of the human skeletons (skeleton number 3; 4720±250 B.P., Frankforter and Agogino 1959) and on bison bone found 2.7 meters below the human skeletal material (6080±300 B.P.; Crane and Griffin 1960). These ages indicated that the burials were Middle Archaic and therefore enclosed in Holocene rather than late-glacial deposits (Ruhe 1969; Fisher et al. 1985).

Frankforter also investigated the geology of three other sites in the region: the Simonson site (13CK61) in the Little Sioux Valley of northwest Iowa (map 5.1; Frankforter 1959; Frankforter and Agogino 1959; Agogino and Frankforter 1960); the Hill Site (13ML62) along Pony Creek in southwestern Iowa (map 5.1; Frankforter 1959; Frankforter and Agogino 1959); and the Logan Creek site (25BT3) in northeastern Nebraska (map 5.1; Kivett 1962; Frankforter and Agogino 1959). All of these were buried pre-ceramic sites where a geologist

Fig. 5.4. Ronald Ruppé, State Archaeologist of Iowa (left), and geologist W. D. Frank-forter examine a bone discovered by eight-year-old Jonathan Davis at the Turin site. Davis, son of archaeologist E. Mott Davis and great-grandson of geologist William Morris Davis, would become a respected geoarchaeologist before his untimely death in 1990. Courtesy of the Office of the State Archaeologist, University of Iowa.

was consulted because the archaeological deposits were deeply buried and presumed old. Unfortunately, geological aspects of these investigations only consisted of cursory statements about the landforms and depositional context for the archaeological deposits. Little or no attention was focused on the details of stratigraphy or soil geomorphology, thus severely limiting the usefulness of the geologic studies to the archaeological field studies and subsequent interpretations.

Although there were many archaeological investigations during the middle period, few included the service of a geologist and, judging from published reports from the period, most were concerned more with cultural chronology than with site formation processes or environmental settings (e.g., Brown 1967). Perhaps this was a product of the focus on high-profile Late Prehistoric village and earth lodge localities by archaeologists working with the Smithsonian Institution's River Basin Surveys, where a keen interest in use of the Direct Historical Method for evaluating the archaeological record was popular (see Artz, this volume). Those working with Late Prehistoric sites usually labored under the assumption that the present configuration of the landscape was more or less unchanged from that of the Late Prehistoric, and therefore the landscape contexts of archaeological sites were readily interpreted without the need for an earth science specialist.

Exceptions to this general disinterest in collaborating with earth scientists occurred on the eastern edge of the Prairies in northeast Iowa and southwestern Wisconsin, where soil scientists from Iowa State University and archaeologists from the State University of Iowa joined efforts on investigations of Woodland mounds (Parsons 1962; Parsons et al. 1962). Two-way information transfer characterized these studies; soil scientists provided archaeologists with information on the source of the materials used to construct the mounds, and archaeologists provided the soil scientists with age information essential for determining rates of soil development in mound fill. During the early 1900s geologist Morris Leighton had suggested that the degree of soil-profile development in mounds could serve to determine the relative age of mounds (Leighton 1929). Using techniques and insights gained from mound studies during the middle period, Hurley (1971) was able to apply Leighton's suggestion to the benefit of archaeology by chronologically ordering late Woodland mounds in southwestern Wisconsin on the basis of the degree of soil development in the mounds' fill.

In sum, geoarchaeology in the Eastern Plains and Prairies came into its own during the early part of the middle period with a series of studies that addressed the landscape context of archaeological sites. In spite of its promising start, however, geoarchaeology languished during most of this period, and despite the strong urging of prominent archaeologists such as Waldo Wedel (1941) and John Champe, little in the way of interdisciplinary studies occurred. With the exception of studies of Woodland mounds on the eastern fringe of the Prairies, what had been learned at the start of the middle period was forgotten in the flurry of River Basin Surveys salvage investigations.

THE LAST THREE DECADES: THE
EMERGENCE OF LANDSCAPE CONTEXT

Undoubtedly, the most important events for geoarchaeology's present status were the passage of the National Historic Preservation Act of 1966, the
National Environmental Policy Act of 1969, and the Moss-Bennett Act of 1974.
These pieces of legislation, along with subsequent laws and implementing regulations, established federal mandates for large-scale cultural resource surveys
and for the mitigation of significant cultural resources. The present cultural
resource management (CRM) industry, in which geoarchaeology has come to
prominence, is a product of these acts. Geoarchaeology owes its resurgence in
the Eastern Plains and Prairies to the "New Archaeology" and its concern for
the scientific method of investigation (i.e., hypothesis testing; Binford 1968).
This, combined with a blossoming of the environmental approach to archaeology in the 1960s, encouraged archaeologists to search out specialists to provide the environmental context for archaeological deposits. The sourcing of
lithic materials (usually chert) was one important interdisciplinary endeavor
that resulted from the environmental approach to archaeology, providing
archaeologists with new insights into prehistoric trade networks and movement ranges (Clayton et al. 1970; Anderson 1978; Ballard 1984; Morrow 1994;
Ray 1983; Reid 1984). Two notable studies, in which a wide range of specialists
participated in addressing environmental archaeology questions, were the University of Wisconsin and University of Nebraska's Mill Creek Culture study in
northwestern Iowa and the Harry Truman Dam and Reservoir Project in the
Pomme de Terre Valley of central Missouri (map 5.1).

Funded by the National Science Foundation, the Mill Creek Culture Study
began in the early 1960s and continued off and on until the end of the decade
(Henning 1968, 1969). One of the major objectives of the Mill Creek Study was
to test climate models proposed by climatologist Reid A. Bryson and associates at the University of Wisconsin (Bryson and Wendland 1967; Bryson et al.
1970; Baerreis and Bryson 1965) with paleoenvironmental data gathered from
archaeological sites in northwestern Iowa and adjacent parts of South Dakota
(Bryson and Baerreis 1968). Although no geologist participated in the project,
the incorporation and integration of paleoecological studies to elucidate cultural response to climate change was a big step forward in demonstrating the
utility of contributions by other disciplines for interpreting the archaeological
record. This study also pointed out that significant and abrupt climatic change

had occurred in the not-too-distant past and shook the foundation upon which the view of a static near past was founded (fig. 5.5). The climate models of Bryson and associates, tested and refined in part with data from the Mill Creek Culture Study, have had a strong influence on earth science and Quaternary geology in particular. The notion of climate change as rapid transitions between periods of climate stability joined with Schumm's (1980) concept of geomorphic thresholds in the 1970s to provide a robust model for explaining behavior of Holocene fluvial systems (Knox 1976, 1983; Schumm and Brackenridge 1987; Van Nest and Bettis 1990).

The initial intent of the archaeological geology study in the Truman Reservoir Project was interpretation of the stratigraphy and landscape context of Rogers Shelter, identified during R. Bruce McMillan's 1960s excavations as a key locality for interpreting Ozark prehistory (McMillan 1971; (map 5.1). The possibility of Paleoindian occupation and the presence nearby of localities where mastodon remains had been discovered prompted W. Raymond Wood, director of River Basin Surveys at the University of Missouri-Columbia, to invite geologist C. Vance Haynes Jr. (University of Arizona) to participate in the project (Haynes 1985). Several other environmental specialists were also involved with the project, including palynologists Peter Mehringer Jr. (Washington State University) and James King (University of Arizona), and soil-geomorphologist Donald Johnson (University of Illinois). Originally the specialists focused on the terminal Pleistocene and early Holocene record in order to reconstruct the environment and landscape setting of the area's mastodon-bearing spring deposits and earliest inhabitants (Haynes 1985; Wood and McMillan 1976; Mehringer et al. 1968), but as the project progressed, emphasis shifted to the Holocene record (Johnson 1983; Brackenridge 1981; King 1982; Wood and McMillan 1976). Though the Truman Reservoir Project took place outside the Plains and Prairies, it had a significant effect on the development of geoarchaeology in the region because, as a successful interdisciplinary study whose scope went beyond archaeological sites, it demonstrated that environmental reconstruction was important for interpretation of the whole of the archaeological record, not merely the earliest chapters.

The Mill Creek Culture Study and the Truman Reservoir Project also affected the academic front in anthropology. David Baerreis at Wisconsin and W. Raymond Wood at Missouri were among the prominent educators involved. Many students who worked on these projects and saw the benefit of

Fig. 5.5. Excavations at the Phipps site, Cherokee County, Iowa. This site was one of the key localities in the Mill Creek Culture Study. Palynological studies conducted on sediments from Phipps were used to demonstrate relationships among climate change and Mill Creek Culture human adaptations. Courtesy of the Office of the State Archaeologist, University of Iowa.

interdisciplinary studies would later become educators or hold influential positions in research institutions and government agencies overseeing CRM work. Thus, archaeology was "primed" for cooperative ventures in the study of the human past.

The 1970s witnessed several cultural resource investigations that incorporated geoarchaeological approaches. These ranged from site-specific studies, such as the excavations at the Cherokee Sewer Site (13CK405) in northwest Iowa (map 5.1 and fig. 5.6; Anderson and Semken 1980: fig. 5) to basin-wide studies, such as that of the Little Platte River in Missouri (map 5.1; McHugh et al. 1982). In the case of the Cherokee Sewer Site, the archaeological investigations focused on stratified Paleoindian and Archaic archaeological deposits in a single alluvial fan, but the accompanying geology, pedology, and palynology studies ranged beyond the site boundaries to place the archaeological remains in an environmental and landscape context (Hoyer 1980a,b; Van Zant 1979; fig. 5.7). The geoarchaeological approach pursued in the Little Platte Drainage was to document the stratigraphy and chronology of the basin in an attempt to understand the surficial distribution of archaeological sites and to assess the potential distribution of buried archaeological deposits (Gardner and Donahue 1985). With studies such as these, geoarchaeology began to go beyond the descriptive stage to provide archaeologists with insights about the nature of the archaeological record.

Since 1980 geoarchaeology has become commonplace in CRM studies in the region. Some archaeologists are geoarchaeologists, and others, who make no such claim, still incorporate earth science concepts and observations in their work. The stratigraphic context of sites is often required information in many contract reports, and professional associations of archaeologists in some states have recognized the importance of geoarchaeology to the point of adopting guidelines for its practitioners (Association of Iowa Archaeologists 1993).

Regional studies aimed at determining the potential for buried archaeological deposits are the hallmark of this latest period in the development of geoarchaeology in the eastern Plains and Prairies. Ironically, the regional approach to assessment of preservation potential stemmed from a site-specific study at the Rainbow Site (13PM91) in northwestern Iowa (map 5.1). In 1978 Interagency Archaeological Services (Denver) contracted with Luther College Archaeological Research Center (Decorah, Iowa) to undertake salvage investigations of a deeply buried, stratified Woodland site soon to be affected by construction of an erosion-control structure in a small valley in northwestern Iowa (Benn 1990; fig. 5.8). I was included as the geomorphologist in the project team, which was under the direction of archaeologist David W. Benn (a graduate of the University of Wisconsin-Madison trained in the "environmental approach to archaeology"). At that time I was a graduate student in agronomy at Iowa State University (Ames). While researching the geology of western Iowa, I found studies of Holocene alluvial stratigraphy that had been

Fig. 5.6. Excavations at the Cherokee Sewer site in Cherokee County, Iowa, were the first in Iowa to make extensive use of earth-moving equipment. In this photo the project director, Richard Schutler (in foreground with back to camera), monitors excavation of a backhoe trench into Cultural Horizon 1, subsequently dated to the middle Holocene.

conducted in southwestern Iowa by Raymond B. Daniels of the Soil Conservation Service in the late 1950s (Daniels et al. 1963; Daniels and Jordan 1966). After studying the reports of Daniels and co-workers and examining some of their southwestern Iowa localities, I concluded that the sequence of Holocene alluvial fills that they had documented in southwestern Iowa was also present in northwestern Iowa at the Rainbow Site (Benn 1990). This suggested an extensive regional sequence of Holocene alluvial fills in the thick loess region of the middle Missouri River basin. This was important to archaeologists because the fills appeared to have accumulated during several temporally discrete episodes and possessed distinct lithologic properties and archaeological associations.

The year following the Rainbow Site investigation, the Mahaphy, Akers, Denison (MAD) sites (13CF101, 13CF102) were discovered during earth-moving operations for the city of Denison's wastewater treatment facility in the Boyer River Valley of western Iowa (map 5.1). At that time I was employed by

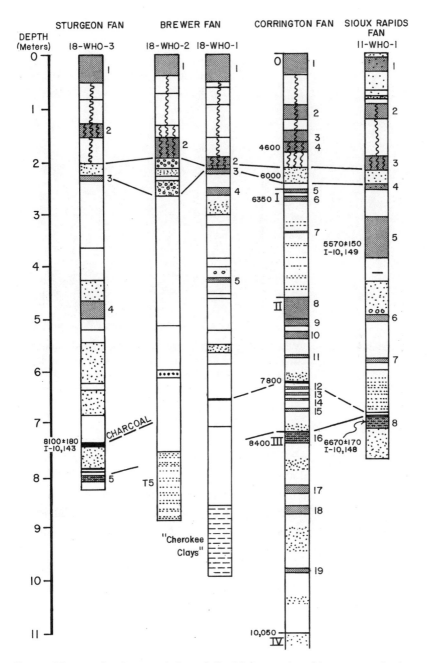

Fig. 5.7. Diagram showing correlation of alluvial fan stratigraphic sequences in the Little Sioux Valley, including that from the Cherokee Sewer site (Corrington Fan). Regional studies by geologist Bernie Hoyer in conjunction with excavations at the Cherokee Sewer site pointed to the presence of regional sedimentation patterns that could significantly influence the preservation and discovery potential of early and middle Holocene archaeological sites (Hoyer 1980a).

Fig. 5.8. Investigations at the Rainbow site in Plymouth County, Iowa, demonstrated that deep burial was also an issue with parts of the Late Prehistoric archaeological record. In this photo project director David Benn (left) and two crew members (Art Hoppin and Bob Peterson) ponder a Late Woodland house floor buried more than two meters below the floor of a small valley. Photo by Art Bettis.

the Iowa State Historic Preservation Office to inventory the geologic setting of known archaeological sites in western Iowa, and I undertook a geoarchaeological study of this large valley locality as part of a mitigation effort under the direction of David Benn (Luther College). With the results of the Rainbow and MAD investigations in hand, Benn and I concluded that geological processes exert a strong influence on site formation processes and control the subsequent preservation and visibility of archaeological deposits (Benn 1990). The ideas of Sterns, Strong, and Champe that had gone into eclipse during the 1950s were now reemerging. Clearly, a significant number of archaeological sites in the region were buried in alluvium and could not be located in adequate numbers for sampling without employing geological procedures.

The Rainbow and MAD investigations directly resulted in the first and most ambitious of the regional geoarchaeology studies in the eastern Plains and Prairies. This study was undertaken as part of a U.S.D.A. Soil Conservation Service (SCS; now the Natural Resources Conservation Service) watershed protection plan that focused on small valleys in the thick loess region of

western Iowa. The three-year program, spearheaded by then SCS archaeologist Dean M. Thompson and employing me (then a research soil scientist
at Iowa State University) as the project geomorphologist, aimed to delimit
areas with high potential for containing buried archaeological deposits. These
areas could then be avoided and, if possible, not damaged or destroyed by soil-
erosion and flood-control measures (Thompson and Bettis 1980; Bettis and
Thompson 1982). The western Iowa studies resulted in the development of several significant concepts: First, many archaeological deposits are buried and
not detectable using traditional archaeological discovery methods of surface
survey and shovel testing (Thompson and Bettis 1981). Second, alluvial fills (as
well as the archaeological deposits contained therein) are differentially preserved through the drainage network (Thompson and Bettis 1981; Bettis and
Thompson 1982; fig. 5.9). And third, the Holocene alluvial fill sequence of
western Iowa (the DeForest Formation) is also present in adjacent areas of
Nebraska and Missouri, and that the archaeological associations and implications are regional in scope (Thompson and Bettis 1980, 1981; Bettis 1992;
Mandel and Bettis 1995). The western Iowa project culminated in a field trip,
sponsored by the Association of Iowa Archaeologists, to localities in northwest
Iowa where archaeologists, soil scientists, and geologists viewed and discussed
relationships among alluvial stratigraphy, archaeological deposits, and interpretations of the archaeological record (Bettis and Thompson 1982).

The western Iowa project stimulated interest by archaeologists in geologic
contexts and the influence of geologic processes on the archaeological record.
A product of this interest has been many studies focused on the depositional
context of the archaeological record across much of the region. These studies
have provided archaeologists and planners with detailed models for assessing
relationships among Holocene geologic history and the distribution of known
sites (Bettis and Benn 1984, 1989; Bettis and Littke 1987; Bettis 1992; Bettis and
Hajic 1995; Benn et al. 1988; Artz 1985; Mandel 1985, 1994; Fosha and Mandel
1991). As Champe suggested in 1946, this upswing in geoarchaeological studies
has been "not too one sided in favor of archaeology." Geoarchaeological studies have increased knowledge of the chronology, distribution, properties, and
pedology of Holocene alluvium in the region far beyond what earth science
studies would have done without the mandate and monetary impetus provided by CRM (Hoyer 1980a,b; Bettis and Hoyer 1986; Bettis and Littke 1987;
Bettis et al. 1992; Van Nest and Bettis 1990; Bettis 1995; Mandel 1997). Knowledge of the properties and chronology of alluvial fills derived from decades of

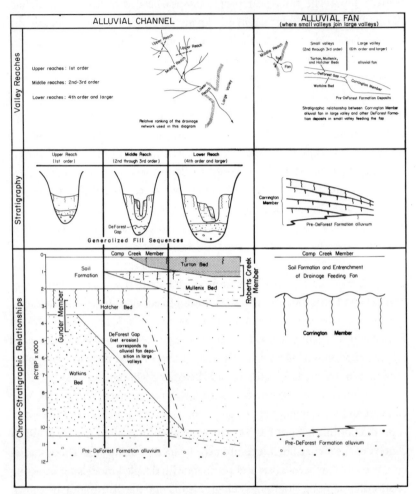

Fig. 5.9. Chronogram for the thick loess region of the Middle Missouri basin (from Bettis and Hajic 1995:fig. 12, 104).

regional studies has also allowed archaeologists and their geoarchaeologist colleagues to recognize deposits that may contain a record of humans' first occupation of the region (Ray et al 1998).

During the last decade geoarchaeological investigations have also begun to assess archaeological deposits in upland settings. In the past most upland landscapes were assumed to be relatively stable or eroding during the Holocene, and therefore not likely to contain intact buried archaeological deposits. This

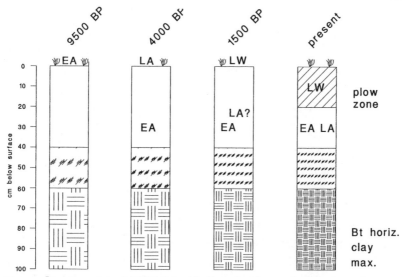

Fig. 5.10. Conceptual model of burial with time of archaeological deposits of various cultural periods in loess-mantled upland soils with biomantles (from Van Nest 1997:fig. 74, 320). Shown is a soil with clay-depleted upper sola that is 40 cm thick. EA, LA, and LW represent Early Archaic, Late Archaic, and Late Woodland cultural deposits, respectively.

assumption was challenged by archaeologist Larry R. Abbott as a result of field studies in the late 1970s and 1980s in Iowa (Abbott 1980; Abbott and Tiffany 1986). Field studies and the theories of Donald L. Johnson and his associates have laid the foundation for subsequent work on the pedologic mechanisms responsible for the burial of archaeological deposits in upland settings (Wood and Johnson 1978; Johnson and Watson-Stegner 1987, 1990; Van Nest 1997; fig. 5.10). What was once considered a relatively stable part of the landscape with an archaeological record much disturbed by cultivation now appears to harbor a significant buried archaeological record (Artz 1991, 1993, 1995; Van Nest 1993; Hajic 1992; Bettis and Hajic 1995).

Geoarchaeology has graduated from something done only by a specialist at an old or deeply buried site to a cooperative effort among archaeologists and earth-science specialists (often with archaeological training) in a wide variety of archaeological contexts. New techniques and approaches are helping to refine archaeologists' understanding of site formation processes, while regional models of landscape evolution now permit estimates of an area's potential for harboring buried deposits of each culture period and for realizing what part of the past record has been destroyed by earth surface processes. Geologic information contributes to a better understanding of anthropological parameters by helping to distinguish between patterns that reflect human behavior and those produced by earth surface processes. This is a prerequisite for interpreting the physical record of archaeology in anthropological terms of human activities and choices.

ACKNOWLEDGMENTS

Many people have contributed information and clarifications relating to the development of geoarchaeological approaches to the archaeological record of the Eastern Plains and Prairies. Comments on an earlier draft by Joe Artz, David Benn, E. Mott Davis, and Rolfe Mandel were especially helpful. David Gradwohl introduced me to the archaeology of the region and made me aware that archaeology is more than anthropology. David Benn and Dean Thompson conceived of and executed projects that revolutionized geoarchaeology in the region. I have been very fortunate to be associated with these two archaeologists. My "dirt brothers" Rolfe Mandel and Ed Hajic have been a constant source of ideas, data, help, and good humor. Finally, I'd like to thank my wife, Brenda Nations, and my family for putting up with my absences and obsession with the record of the human past.

REFERENCES

Abbott, Larry R. 1980. Upland soil development in Iowa. Paper presented at the Iowa Academy of Science Annual Meeting, Simpson College, Indianola, Ia.

Abbott, L. R., and J. A. Tiffany. 1986. Archaeological context and upland soil development: The Midwest U.S.A. example. Iowa City, Office of the State Archaeologist, unpublished manuscript on file.

Agogino, G. A. and W. D. Frankforter. 1960. A Paleo-Indian bison kill in northwestern Iowa. *American Antiquity* 25:414–15.

Anderson, D. C. 1978. Aboriginal use of Tongue River silica in northwest Iowa. *Plains Anthropologist* 23:149–57.

Anderson, D. C., and H. A. Semken Jr., eds. 1980. The Cherokee excavations: Holocene ecology and human adaptation in Northwest Iowa. New York: Academic Press.

Antevs, E. 1935. The spread of aboriginal man to North America. *Geographical Review* 25:302–309.

———. 1938. Was "Minnesota Girl" buried in a gully? *Journal of Geology* 46:293–95.

Artz, J. A. 1985. A soil-geomorphic approach to locating buried Late Archaic sites in northeast Oklahoma. *American Archeology* 5:142–50.

———. 1991. Site formation processes and soil evolution: A case study from southeastern Iowa. Paper presented at the 49th Plains Anthropological Conference, Lawrence, Kans.

———. 1993. Geoarchaeological observations on buried archaeological components in loess-mantled terrains of Iowa. Paper presented at the 38th Midwest Archaeological Conference, Milwaukee, Wisc.

———. 1995. Geological contexts of the early and middle Holocene archaeological record in North Dakota and adjoining areas of the Northern Plains. *In* Bettis, E. A., III, ed., Archaeological geology of the Archaic period in North America. Boulder, Colo.: The Geological Society of America, Special Paper 297:67–86.

Association of Iowa Archaeologists. 1993. Guidelines for geomorphological investigations in support of archaeological investigations in Iowa. *Journal of the Iowa Archaeological Society* 40:1–19.

Baerreis, D. A. and R. A. Bryson. 1965. Climatic episodes and the dating of the Mississippian cultures. *The Wisconsin Archaeologist* 14:105–16.

Ballard, D. N. 1984. Cherts of the upper Skunk River Valley, Story County, Iowa. *Iowa Archaeological Society Newsletter* 10:4–7.

Barbour, E. H. 1907a. Evidence of man in the loess of Nebraska. *Science* 25:110–12.

———. 1907b. Evidence of loess man in Nebraska. Lincoln: *Nebraska Geological Survey* 2:331–48.

Barbour, E. H. and H. B. Ward. 1906. Discovery of an early type of man in Nebraska. *Science* 24:628–29.

Benn, D. W., ed. 1990. Woodland cultures on the Western Prairies. Iowa City: Office of the State Archaeologist of Iowa, Report 18.

Benn, D. W., E. A. Bettis III, and R. C. Vogel. 1988. Archaeology and geomorphology in Pools 17–18, upper Mississippi River. Springfield, Mo.: Center for Archaeological Research, Southwest Missouri State University, Report No. 714.

Bettis, E. A., III. 1992. Soil morphologic properties and weathering zone characteristics as age indicators in Holocene alluvium in the Upper Midwest. *In* Holliday, V. T., ed., Soils in archaeology, 119–44. Washington, D. C.: Smithsonian Institution Press.

———. 1995. The Holocene stratigraphic record of entrenched streams in thick loess regions of the Mississippi River Basin. Ph.D. diss., Iowa City, University of Iowa.

Bettis, E. A. III, and D. W. Benn. 1984. An archaeological and geomorphological survey in the central Des Moines River Valley, Iowa. *Plains Anthropologist* 29:211–27.

————. 1989. Geologic context of Paleoindian and Archaic occupations in a
portion of the Mississippi Valley, Iowa and Illinois. *Current Research in
the Pleistocene* 6:85–86.

Bettis, E. A., III, and E. R. Hajic. 1995. Landscape development and the location of evidence of Archaic cultures in the Upper Midwest. *In* Bettis,
E.A., III, ed., Archaeological geology of the Archaic period in North America. Boulder, Colo.: The Geological Society of America, Special Paper
297:87–113.

Bettis, E. A., III, and B. E. Hoyer. 1986. Late Wisconsinan and Holocene landscape evolution and alluvial stratigraphy in the Saylorville Lake area, central Des Moines River valley, Iowa. Iowa City: Iowa Geological Survey,
Open File Report 86-1.

Bettis, E. A., III, and J. P. Littke. 1987. Holocene alluvial stratigraphy and landscape development in Soap Creek Watershed, Appanoose, Davis, Monroe,
and Wapello counties, Iowa. Iowa City: Iowa Department of Natural
Resources, Geological Survey Bureau, Open File Report 87-2.

Bettis, E. A., III, and D. M. Thompson. 1982. Interrelations of cultural and fluvial deposits in Northwest Iowa. Iowa City: Association of Iowa Archaeologists Fieldtrip Guidebook.

Bettis, E. A., III, D. W. Benn, and M. J. O'Brien. 1985. The interaction of archeology and the earth sciences in the American Midwest. *American Archeology* 5:120–26.

Bettis E. A., III, R. G. Baker, W. Green, M. K. Whelan, and D. W. Benn. 1992.
Late Wisconsinan and Holocene alluvial stratigraphy, paleoecology, and
archaeological geology of East-Central Iowa. Iowa City: Iowa Department of Natural Resources, Guidebook Series No. 12.

Binford, L. R. 1968. Archaeological perspectives. *In* Binford, S.R., and Binford,
L.R., eds., New perspectives in archaeology, 5–32. Chicago: Aldine.

Brackenridge, G. R. 1981. Late Quaternary floodplain sedimentation along the
Pomme de Terre River, southern Missouri. *Quaternary Research* 15:62–76.

Brown, L. A. 1967. Pony Creek archeology. Publications in salvage archeology
no. 5. Washington, D.C.: Smithsonian Institution Press.

Bryan, K. 1935. Minnesota Man—a discussion of the site. *Science* 82:170–171.

Bryan, K. and P. MacClintock. 1938. What is implied by "disturbance" at the
site of Minnesota Man? *Journal of Geology* 46:279–92.

Bryson, R., and D. A. Baerreis. 1968. Introduction and project summary. *In*
Henning, D., ed., Climatic change and the Mill Creek culture of Iowa,
Part I. *Journal of the Iowa Archaeological Society* 15:1–34.

Bryson, R. A., D. A. Baerreis, and W. M. Wendland. 1970. The character of late-
glacial and post-glacial climate changes. *In* Dort, W., Jr., and J. K. Jones Jr.,

eds., Pleistocene and recent environments of the Central Great Plains, 53–74. Lawrence: University of Kansas Press.

Bryson, R. A., and W. M. Wendland. 1967. Tentative climatic patterns for some late-glacial and post-glacial climatic episodes in North America. *In* Mayer-Oakes, W. J., ed., Life, land and water, Lake Agassiz region, 271–98. Winnipeg: University of Manitoba Press.

Chamberlin, T. C. 1895. The classification of American glacial deposits. *Journal of Geology* 3:270–77.

Chamberlin, T. C., S. Calvin, and R. D. Salisbury. 1902. The geologic relations of the human relics of Lansing, Kansas. *Journal of Geology* 10:745–79.

Champe, J. L. 1946. Ash Hollow Cave: A study of stratigraphic sequence in the Central Great Plains. Lincoln: University of Nebraska Studies, New Series no.1.

Clayton, L., W. B. Bickley Jr., and W. J. Stone. 1970. Knife River flint. *Plains Anthropologist* 15:282–90.

Crane, H. R., and J. B. Griffin. 1960. University of Michigan radiocarbon dates VI. *Radiocarbon* 3:113.

Daniels, R. B., and R. H. Jordan. 1966. Physiographic history and the soils, entrenched streams systems, and gullies, Harrison County, Iowa. Washington, D.C.: U.S. Department of Agricuture Technical Bulletin 1348.

Daniels, R. B., M. Rubin, and G. H. Simonson. 1963. Alluval chronology of the Thompson Creek watershed, Harrison County, Iowa. *American Journal of Science* 261:473–84.

Fisher, A. K., D. C. Anderson, and J. A. Tiffany. 1985. Turin: A Middle Archaic burial site in western Iowa. *Plains Anthropologist* 30:195–218.

Flannery, K. V. 1982. The golden Marshalltown: A parable for the archeology of the 1980s. *American Anthropologist* 84:265–78.

Fosha, M. R., and R. D. Mandel. 1991. Cultural resources investigations, Phase I survey, West Fork Big Creek watershed, Decatur and Ringgold counties, Iowa, and Harrison and Daviess Counties, Missouri. Lawrence: University of Kansas, Museum of Anthropology, Project Series no. 72.

Frankforter, W. D. 1959. A pre-ceramic site in western Iowa. *Journal of the Iowa Archaeological Society*.8:47–72.

Frankforter, W. D., and G. A. Agogino. 1959. Archaic and Paleo-Indian archaeological discoveries in western Iowa. *The Texas Journal of Science* 11:482–91.

Gardner, G. D. and J. Donahue. 1985. The Little Platte drainage, Missouri: A model for locating temporal surfaces in a fluvial environment. *In* Stein, J. K, ed., Archaeological sediments in context, 69–89. Orono, Maine: Center for the Study of Early Man, Peopling of the Americas Edited Volume Series, vol. 1.

Gilder, R. F. 1908. Recent excavations at Long's Hill, Nebraska. *American Anthropologist* 10:60–73.

Hajic, E. R. 1992. Geomorphological testing results. *In* Hickson, R. N., and S. R. Katz, eds., Progress report on the FAP 407 Route 336 archeological survey and prehistoric site testing along the priority Quincy to Mendon alternate segment in Adams County, Illinois. Kampsville, Ill.: Center for American Archeology, Report of Investigation 197c: 180–86.

Haynes, C. V., Jr. 1985. Mastodon-bearing springs and late Quaternary geochronology of the lower Pomme de Terre Valley, Missouri. Boulder, Colo.: The Geological Society of America, Special Paper 204.

Henning, D. R., ed. 1968. Climate change and the Mill Creek culture of Iowa I. *Journal of the Iowa Archaeological Society* 15:1–192.

Henning, D. R. 1969. Climate change and the Mill Creek culture of Iowa II. *Journal of the Iowa Archaeological Society* 16: 192–358.

Hill, A. T. and M. F. Kivett. 1940. Woodland-like manifestations in Nebraska. *Nebraska History Magazine* 21:146–243.

Hilgard, E. W. 1892. A report on the relations of soil to climate. Washington, D.C.: U.S. Department of Agriculture, Weather Bulletin no. 3:1–59.

Hoyer, B. E. 1980a. Geomorphic history of the Little Sioux River valley. Iowa City: Geological Society of Iowa, Fieldguide no. 34.

———. 1980b. The geology of the Cherokee Sewer site. *In* Anderson, D. C., and H. A. Semken Jr., eds., The Cherokee excavations: Holocene ecology and human adaptations in Norhthwestern Iowa, 21–26. New York: Academic Press.

Hurley, W. M. 1971. Rates of soil development at two Wisconsin effigy mound sites. Iowa City: University of Iowa, Office of the State Archaeologist, Prehistoric Investigations no. 3.

Jenks, A. E. 1932. Pleistocene man in Minnesota. *Science* 75:607–608.

———. 1936. Pleistocene man in Minnesota. Minneapolis: University of Minnesota Press.

Jennings, J. D., ed. 1950. Proceedings of the Sixth Plains Archaeological Conference (1948). Salt Lake City, University of Utah, Anthropological Papers 11.

Johnson, D. L. 1983. Soils and soil-geomorphic investigations in the lower Pomme de Terre Valley. *In* Wood, W. R., ed., Cultural resources survey, Harry S. Truman Dam and Reservoir project, vol. 10:63–143. Columbia: University of Missouri, Department of Anthropology.

Johnson, D. L., and E. Watson-Stegner. 1987. Evolution model of pedogenesis. *Soil Science* 143:349–66.

Johnson, D. L., and D. Watson-Stegner. 1990. The soil evolution model as a framework ffor evaluating pedoturbation in archaeological site formation. *In* Lasca, N. P., and J. Donahue, eds., Archaeological geology of North America. Boulder, Colo.: The Geological Society of America, Centennial Special vol. 4:541–60.

Kay, G. F. 1931. Classification and duration of the Pleistocene period. *Geological Society of America Bulletin* 42:425–66.

Kay, G. F., and M. M. Leighton. 1938. Geological notes on the occurrence of "Minnesota Man". *The Journal of Geology* 46:268–78.

King, F. B. 1982. Vegetational reconstruction and plant resources prediction. *In* Kay, M., ed., Holocene adaptation within the lower Pomme de Terre River valley, Missouri, 81–106. Springfield: Illinois State Museum, Report to the U.S. Army Corps of Engineers, Kansas City District, under contract no. DACW41-76-C-0011.

Kivett, M. F. 1962. The Logan Creek Complex. Lincoln, Nebr.: Paper presented at the 20th Annual Meeting of the Plains Anthropological Society.

Knox, J. C. 1976. Concept of the graded stream. *In* Melhorn, W. N., and R. C. Flemal, R.C., eds., Theories of landform development, 169–98. Binghamton, N.Y.: Publications in Geomorphology, State University of New York at Binghamton.

———. 1983. Responses of river systems to Holocene climates. *In* Wright, H. E., Jr., ed., Late Quaternary environments of the United States: Vol. 2, the Holocene, 26–41. Minneapolis: University of Minnesota Press.

Leighton, M. M. 1929., Geology of the Indian mounds. *Illinois State Academy of Science Transactions* 22:65–71.

———. 1932. Did prehistoric men live in the Middle West? *The Scientific Monthly* 34:77–79.

———. 1933. Some observations on the antiquity of man in Illinois. *Transactions of the Illinois State Academy of Science* 26:83.

———. 1960. The classification of the Wisconsin stage of North Central United States. *Journal of Geology* 68:529–52.

McHugh, W. C., G. D. Gardner, and J. Donahue. 1982. Before Smith Mills: Archaeological and geological investigations. Kansas City, Mo.: Report to the Kansas City District Corps of Engineers under contract no. DACW41-78-C-0121.

McMillan, R. B. 1971. Biophysical change and cultural adaptation at Roger's Shelter, Missouri. Ph.D. diss., Boulder, University of Colorado, Department of Anthropology.

Mandel, R. D. 1985. Geomorphology of the Little Blue Drainage Basin. *In* Schmits, L. J., ed., Prehistory of the Little Blue River valley, 35<46>. Overland Park, Kans.: Environmental Systems and Analysis, Inc., ESA Cultural Resources Management Report no. 29, prepared for the U.S. Army Corps of Engineers, Kansas City District.

———. 1994. A Geomorphological investigation of the Council Bluffs Industrial Park, Council Bluffs, Iowa. Cresco, Iowa: Bear Creek Archaeology, Inc., Report no. 343.

———. 1997. Geomorphological investigation in support of the Phase I archaeological survey of the Highway 60 corridor, Northwest Iowa. Waterloo, Iowa, RUST Environment and Infrastructure, Inc., unpublished manuscript on file.

Mandel, R. D. and E. A. Bettis III. 1995. Late Quaternary landscape evolution and stratigraphy in eastern Nebraska. *In* Flowerday, C. A., ed., Geologic field trips in Nebraska and adjacent parts of Kansas and South Dakota. Lincoln, 29th Annual Meeting of the North-Central and South-Central Sections of the Geological Society of America. Lincoln: Conservation and Survey Division, University of Nebraska, Guidebook no. 10:77–90.

Marbut, C. F. 1935. The soils of the United States. *In* Atlas of American Agriculture, Part 3, Advance Sheets no.8. Washington, D.C.: U.S. Department of Agriculture.

Mehringer, P. J., Jr., C. E. Schweger, W. R. Wood, and R. B. McMillan. 1968. Late-Pleistocene boreal forest in the western Ozark Highlands. *Ecology* 49:567–68.

Morrow, T. 1994. A key to the identification of chipped-stone raw materials found on archaeological sites in Iowa. *Journal of the Iowa Archaeological Society* 41:108–29.

Parsons, R. B. 1962. Indian mounds of northeast Iowa as soil genesis benchmarks. *Iowa Archaeological Society Journal* 12: 1–70.

Parsons, R. B., W. H. Scholtes, and F. F. Riecken. 1962. Soils of Indian mounds in northeast Iowa as benchmarks for studies of soil science. *Soil Science Society of America Proceedings* 26:491–96.

Ray, J. H. 1983. Excello chert: An undescribed chert resource in north central Missouri. *Missouri Archaeological Society Newsletter* nos. 375–79:9–14.

Ray, J. H., N. H. Lopinot, E. R. Hajic, and R. D. Mandel. 1998. The Big Eddy site: A multicomponent Paleoindian site on the Ozark border, southwest Missouri. *Plains Anthropologist* 43:73–81.

Reid, K.C. 1984. Fusilinacean sourcing of late Paleozoic cherts in the western Midwest. *In* Butler, B. M., and E. E. May, eds., Prehistoric chert exploitation: Studies from the midcontinent. Carbondale: Southern Illinois University, Center For Archaeological Investigations, Occasional Paper no. 2:253–70.

Ruhe, R. V. 1956. Geomorphic surfaces and the nature of soils. *Soil Science* 82:441–55.

———. 1969. Quaternary landscapes in Iowa. Ames: Iowa State University Press.

Ruppé, R. J. 1955. Cherokee and Turin, Iowa: Archaeological investigations reveal more knowledge about prehistoric man. *State University of Iowa Staff Magazine*, Nov. 16–20:30–31.

———. 1956. Archaeological investigations of the Mill Creek culture of northwestern Iowa. *American Philosophical Society Yearbook 1955*:335–39.

Schumm, S. A. 1980. Geomorphic thresholds: The concept and its implications. *Institute of British Geographers Transactions* 4:485–515.

Schumm, S. A., and G. R. Brakenridge. 1987. River responses. *In* Ruddiman, W. F, and H. E. Wright Jr., eds, North America and adjacent oceans during the last deglaciation. Boulder, Colo.: The Geological Society of America, The Geology of North America, vol. K-3:221–40.

Shimek, B. 1908. Nebraska "Loess Man". *Geological Society of America Bulletin* 19:243–54.

Sterns, F. H. 1915. A stratification of cultures in eastern Nebraska. *American Anthropologist* New Series 17:121–27.

Strong, W. D. 1935. An introduction to Nebraska archeology. Washington, D.C.: Smithsonian Miscellaneous Collections, vol. 93, no. 10.

Thompson, D. M., and E. A. Bettis III. 1980. Archeology and Holocene landscape evolution in the Missouri drainage of Iowa. *Journal of the Iowa Archaeological Society* 27:1–60.

———. 1981. Out of sight, out of planning: Assessing and protecting cultural resources in evolving landscapes. *Contracts Abstracts and CRM Archaeology* 2:16–22.

Van Nest, J. 1993. Geoarchaeology of dissected loess uplands in western Illinois. *Geoarchaeology* 8:281–311.

———. 1997. Late Quaternary geology, archeology and vegetation in West-Central Illinois: A study in geoarcheology. Ph.D. diss., Iowa City, The University of Iowa.

Van Nest, J., and E. A. Bettis III. 1990. Postglacial responses of a stream in central Iowa to changes in climate and drainage basin factors. *Quaternary Research* 33:73–85.

Van Zant, K. L. 1979. Late-glacial and postglacial pollen and plant macrofossils from Lake West Okoboji, northwestern Iowa. *Quaternary Research* 12:358–80.

Wedel, W. R. 1941. Environment and native subsistence economy in the central Great Plains. Washington, D.C.: Smithsonian Miscellaneous Collections 110:1–29.

Wedel, W. R. 1943. Archeological Investigations in Platte and Clay Counties, Missouri. Washington, D.C.: U.S. National Museum, Bulletin 183.

Winchell, N. H. 1902. Editorial comment: The Lansing skeleton. *American Geologist* 30:189–94.

Wood, W. R., and D. L. Johnson. 1978. A survey of disturbance processes in archaeological site formation. *Advances in Archaeological Method and Theory* 1:315–83.

Wood, W. R., and R. B. McMillan, eds. 1976. Prehistoric Man and his environments: A case study in the Ozark Highland. New York: Academic Press.

CHAPTER SIX

Geoarchaeological Research in Nebraska

A HISTORICAL PERSPECTIVE

David W. May

INTRODUCTION

From the beginning of systematic paleontological and archaeological surveys in Nebraska in the 1920s, studies of Paleoindian sites (those more than 8,000 years old) have almost always involved a geologist or physical geographer. Many of the Paleoindian sites discovered in Nebraska during the 1920s and 1930s were actually found by paleontologists and subsequently reported to archaeologists. The discovery of many Paleoindian sites in Nebraska by paleontologists was not accidental. Bones of large mammals, often bison, are common at Paleoindian sites. Also, paleontologists often search in deep gullies and at the base of high river banks for fossil bones, and virtually every Paleoindian site that has been discovered in Nebraska has been deeply buried by alluvium, loess, or dune sand. From the 1920s through the 1940s, when the archaeological community questioned the antiquity of deeply buried Paleoindian sites, earth scientists were often consulted to determine the ages of these sites. Over the past seventy years, geoarchaeological investigations in Nebraska have progressed from simply dating newly discovered, buried Paleoindian sites to predicting where buried cultural deposits may be found in the landscape.

Several themes emerge from this review of geoarchaeology in Nebraska. For example, archaeologists have utilized the skills of earth scientists for dating Paleoindian sites. At first geologists and geographers established ages of archaeological sites using relative-dating techniques. These techniques included regional stratigraphic relationships, relative heights of river terraces, the assemblage of fossil mammals found in sedimentary and cultural deposits, and assumptions about rates of landscape erosion and valley sedimentation. With the advent of radiocarbon dating, archaeological sites could be numerically dated using carbon-14 assays of wood, charcoal, bone, and shells. Radiocarbon dating has been an especially important tool in the central Great Plains where trees for tree-ring dating, another numerical-dating technique, are neither abundant nor well preserved.

Geoarchaeologists began utilizing radiocarbon dating to develop chronologies of landscape change that could then be used by archaeologists to predict where buried sites might be found. Initially geoarchaeologists focused on reconstructing local and regional alluvial chronologies of erosion and sedimentation for river valleys because many archaeological sites had been discovered buried in alluvium. Later they used radiocarbon dating to establish regional chronologies of loess accumulation and sand-dune migration.

Most recently, geoarchaeological investigations have become increasingly interdisciplinary; pedologists and palynologists now commonly work with geomorphologists and archaeologists. As a result, great strides have been made in understanding local and regional vegetation changes over time, landform evolution, and the depositional processes at individual sites. Disturbances to archaeological sites by overland flow and infiltrating water, wind, and the burrowing of vertebrate and invertebrate animals are now more clearly understood.

I have organized this chapter into several sections. First, I discuss how the search for paleontological sites by members of the Morrill Paleontological Expedition during the late 1920s and early 1930s led to the discovery of many archaeological sites in western and northwestern Nebraska. The initial collaborations between geologists and archaeologists occurred at sites uncovered during these expeditions. Next, I discuss the reservoir surveys and excavations of the three deeply buried Lime Creek Paleoindian sites during the late 1940s and early 1950s at Harry Strunk Lake (Medicine Creek Reservoir) in southwestern Nebraska. These investigations were important because the ages of these sites were controversial and radiocarbon dating was in its infancy. I then report on collaborations between archaeologists and geomorphologists in the late 1970s and early 1980s. These renewed joint research efforts followed a hiatus in geoarchaeological work that had lasted from the late 1960s until the late 1970s.

The new era of geoarchaeology in Nebraska began when federal waterresources construction projects were funded for the Loup River Basin in central Nebraska in the late 1970s and early 1980s. These projects were important to archaeology in Nebraska because they were the first major federal construction projects in the state after the passage of the National Historic Preservation Act of 1966 and the National Environmental Protection Act of 1969. These two new laws mandated both the development of an inventory of cultural resources on project lands before construction and the mitigation of the impact of project construction on these cultural resources. In practice these laws had the effect of requiring pedestrian surveys to search for archaeological sites, and the subsequent testing of discovered sites, or, in some cases, the complete excavation of threatened sites. Increasingly, geoarchaeologists have become involved with archaeologists in the early phase of pedestrian surveys by developing landform-evolution models that predict where cultural resources may lie buried beneath the surface. In the case of the Loup River Basin projects, geoarchaeologists were involved in both the early pedestrian surveys and the later phases of site-specific research into site-formation processes.

Finally, I summarize the recent, more diverse, geoarchaeological research in Nebraska. Some of this recent research involves reinvestigation of sites, and much of it involves a multidisciplinary approach. Map 6.1 shows the specific sites and areas in Nebraska that are addressed in this chapter.

MORRILL PALEONTOLOGICAL EXPEDITIONS (LATE 1920S AND 1930S)

The first serious collaborations between geologists and archaeologists in Nebraska were the result of a systematic and intense search for large fossils by personnel associated with the University of Nebraska Museum in Lincoln (now the University of Nebraska State Museum). The following account of this intensive search is gleaned from Christianson (1990:94–96).

In 1925 several fossil mastodons and the remains of other large mammals were found near Ainsworth, Nebraska, and were purchased by the Denver

Museum and the American Museum of Natural History in New York. Erwin Hinckley Barbour, then director of the University of Nebraska Museum, was shocked that these fossils were leaving Nebraska. In the spring of 1928 Barbour responded by organizing the Morrill Paleontological Expedition, which was generously funded by Charles H. Morrill, a wealthy landowner and financier. Barbour formed two museum field parties: the North Party was to cover the northern part of Nebraska while the South Party was to cover the southern part of the state. However, they were soon merged into one (referred to as the South Party). The field parties were instructed to collect anything and everything of potential scientific value.

Discoveries in Central and Southwestern Nebraska

In 1929, while members of the South Party were removing fossil mammoth and bison bones from the floor of a tributary valley to the South Loup River near Cumro, two young boys reported finding "elephant knuckles" in a stream bank nearby (map 6.1) (Shultz 1938:354). C. Bertrand Schultz, then a member of the South Party, eventually examined the exposed fossils. They turned out to be part of a fossil bison that was buried sixteen feet below the present surface (Schultz 1932:271). After digging around the bison bones in the cutbank for about an hour, Schultz discovered an artifact (Schultz 1932:271). However, the museum field party did not recognize the significance of the find (a Paleoindian projectile point) at the time (Schultz 1938). It was a year later, when Schultz was working as a part-time student assistant to archaeologist William Duncan Strong, then curator of anthropology in the University of Nebraska State Museum, that Schultz learned the importance of the find. One day Schultz casually showed Strong the artifact that he had collected at the Cumro site; Strong at once recognized the importance of the find and wished to see the site immediately (Schultz 1983).

In 1930 C. Bertrand Schultz and Frank Crabill, another member of the South Party who had helped Schultz originally investigate the Cumro site, met Strong at the site. The purpose of their visit was to work out the general geology of the nearby region and to further excavate the site in the hope of discovering more artifacts (Schultz 1932:272). Thus, it was Schultz who initiated the first formal working relationship between a geologist and a professional archaeologist in Nebraska. During the next few years, members of the South Party excavated additional paleontological sites in central and western Nebraska. Several of these sites were also Paleoindian archaeological sites. In

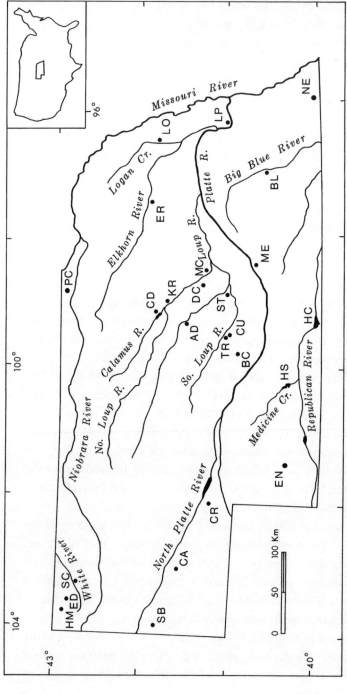

Map 6.1. Map of archaeological sites in Nebraska where geomorphologists have assisted archaeologists. Site abbreviations are as follows: AD = Arcadia Diversion Dam; BC = Buffalo Creek; BL = Blue River basin; CA = Cape; CD = Calamus Dam and Reservoir; CR = Clary Ranch; CU = Cumro; DC = Davis Creek Dam and Reservoir; ED = Everson-Dodd; EN = Enders Reservoir; ER = Elkhorn River; HC = Harlan County Lake; HM = Hudson-Meng; HS = Harry Strunk Lake; KR = Kruml; LO = Logan Creek; LP = Little Pawnee; MC = Moffet Creek; ME = Meserve; NE = Big Nemaha River basin; PC = Ponca Creek and Keya Paha River; SB = Scottsbluff Bison Quarry; SC = Slaughterhouse Creek; ST = Stark; TR = Truman.

1931 they visited the Meserve site along the Platte River near Grand Island (map 6.1) (Schultz 1932:273). This site was discovered by high school students in the spring of 1923. In the summer of 1923 F. G. Meserve, a professor of biology at Grand Island College, partially excavated the site (Schultz 1932:273–74). Meserve recovered a bison skull, a partial bison skeleton, and a "dart point" (Schultz 1932:273–74).

Eight years later in the summer of 1931, the field party from the Nebraska State Museum discovered many more bison bones in the eroding cutbank and "with these a dart point in intimate association" (Schultz 1932:274). In the fall of 1931 associate professor A. L. Lugn of the Department of Geology at the University of Nebraska visited the site to determine its age. Lugn determined that the site might "well be of Peorian age" (Schultz 1932:274).

In 1932 the Morrill Paleontological Expedition's South Party discovered a bone bed near Signal Butte in western Nebraska. The bone bed was exposed along Spring Creek near its junction with Kiowa Creek (Schultz and Eiseley 1935). This site soon became known as the Scottsbluff Bison Quarry site (map 6.1) (also see Albanese, this volume). It is discrete from the nearby Signal Butte site that William Duncan Strong was excavating at the same time.

Also, in the summer of 1932, the first of eight artifacts was found in situ at the Scottsbluff Bison Quarry site (Schultz and Eiseley 1935). Two days after this first artifact was discovered, E. H. Barbour, director of the University of Nebraska State Museum, and Earl Bell, then assistant professor of anthropology at the University of Nebraska, visited the site (Schultz and Eiseley 1935). Again, C. Bertrand Schultz recognized the archaeological significance of the Scottsbluff site and apparently wanted a professional anthropologist involved in the excavation from the beginning. It is important to recognize that the Folsom Paleoindian site had already been excavated in New Mexico, and the Blackwater Draw Paleoindian site in New Mexico and the Dent Paleoindian site in Colorado were being excavated. Thus, the search for the oldest archaeological site in North America was well underway.

The age of the Scottsbluff site was of considerable interest to all involved. Schultz and Eiseley (1935:318) recognized at the time that "varied research" would be needed to determine the age of the site. A. L. Lugn visited the site and concluded that the age of the site was "late mid-Pleistocene, that is, post-Kansas, pre-Wisconsin" (Schultz and Eiseley 1935:310). The age of the site was later revised to late Pleistocene, based on both the vertebrate and invertebrate fossils that were present in the three primary horizons overlying the bones and artifacts (Barbour and Schultz 1936). However, Barbour and Schultz (1936:432) believed that the "Yuma" artifacts from the Scottsbluff Bison Quarry were "representative of a cultural complex definitely antedating all other known cultures in Nebraska."

A decade later, in a study of terraces in the nearby North Platte River valley and tributary valleys, geologists with the U.S. Geological Survey (U.S.G.S.) concluded that the "Yuma points" from the bison quarry were collected from the base of the second terrace in the basin and that the bison quarry site dated to about 10,000 B.P. (Wenzel et al. 1946:41–46). Today we know that the Scottsbluff Bison Quarry site is about 9,200 to 8,400 years old, which is 1,500 to 2,000 years later than the Folsom site in New Mexico (Holen 1995).

Discoveries in Northwestern Nebraska

The Morrill Paleontological Expedition began work in northwest Nebraska in 1929 (Barbour and Schultz 1936:432). Although finds of artifacts in the region had been reported to the Nebraska State Museum as early as 1928, the South Party did not locate artifacts associated with fossil bones in situ until the summer of 1935 (Barbour and Schultz 1936:444). "Yuma artifacts" were found buried as deeply as twenty-five feet in a carbon-stained "soil horizon" (Barbour and Schultz 1936). This site, the Everson site, which is now known as the Everson-Dodd site (Stout et al. 1965), is in the headwaters of the White River drainage (map 6.1) (MacClintock et al. 1936:346–49).

The research in northwestern Nebraska that was conducted by personnel from the Nebraska State Museum during the 1930s is of geoarchaeological importance for two reasons. First, a geomorphologist worked with the Morrill Paleontological Expedition for two summers. Second, C. Bertrand Schultz developed a model of terrace formation for this region of the state, the first of many versions of a generalized model for the central Great Plains.

The Carnegie Institution in Washington, D.C., which was funding much of the archaeological research in the Plains, sent Paul MacClintock, a geology professor and geomorphologist at Princeton University, to Nebraska to spend two summer field seasons with the Morrill Paleontological Expedition (Schultz 1983). He identified "varves" and "slackwater deposits" within what were then considered to be late-Pleistocene geologic sections in the region (MacClintock et al. 1936). The "varves" were viewed as a way of dating the artifact finds in the region (Barbour and Schultz 1936:446). It is historically significant that the members of the Morrill Expedition both recognized the importance of establishing the ages of the artifacts that they discovered and acknowledged the difficulties that they encountered in actually establishing the ages of the deposits containing the artifacts. A decade later geologists from the U.S.G.S. reported that "examination of the laminations fails to support the contention that they are 'varves,' and hence the existence of laminated silts cannot provide any clue as to the age of the deposit" (Wenzel et al. 1946:44). Thus, the possibility that "varves" could be used to date the sites was dismissed in the later study.

The work of the Morrill Paleonotological Expedition South Party in the upper White River Basin in the early and mid-1930s is important in the history of geoarchaeology in Nebraska in another way. It was here that C. Bertrand Schultz (1938) used terrace heights, alluvial and soil stratigraphy, and both artifacts and fossil mammals found in alluvium to develop a regional model of valley evolution for the upper White River drainage of northwestern Nebraska. His primary purpose in developing the model was to make it possible to date the archaeological deposits discovered in valleys throughout the region. Soon after the advent of radiocarbon dating in the late 1940s (Libby 1955), Schultz submitted samples of charcoal collected from buried hearths in Cedar Canyon by members of the Morrill Paleontological Expedition during the 1930s (Libby 1951, 1954a, 1954b, 1955). Once the alluvial deposits had been radiocarbon dated, this artifact-rich valley became the type locality for Terrace 1 in the generalized terrace model for the central Great Plains (Schultz et al. 1948:32–34; 1951:37).

One other archaeological site, the Cape site, was discovered and tested during the 1930s, but not by personnel connected with the Morrill Paleontological Expedition. The Cape site is located in the Nebraska panhandle on a tributary to Pumpkin Creek in the North Platte River basin (map 6.1) (Bell and Van Royen 1936). The landowner discovered the site in 1932, and it was investigated by Earl Bell, Professor of Anthropology in the Department of Sociology at the University of Nebraska-Lincoln, and Willem Van Royen, Professor of Geography in the Department of Geography at the University of Nebraska-Lincoln (Bell and Van Royen 1936). Bell and Van Royen's study of the site included a careful geomorphic and stratigraphic assessment of the artifact-bearing horizons. They were, however, extremely cautious about assigning an age to the site. They apparently had neither vertebrate nor invertebrate fossils to assist them in dating the site. Rather, they suggested an age for the site based on rates at which processes of valley aggradation, soil formation, and erosion might occur in the region and then deduced the time necessary for the site to become buried, a soil to form, and for the entire section to be exposed by erosion (Bell and Van Royen 1936:410–11). They concluded that the Cape site, and other Paleoindian sites in western Nebraska (e.g., Scottsbluff Bison Quarry site), "might well be from 6,000 to 8,000 years old" (Bell and Van Royen 1936:417). Theirs was a novel approach to the critical issue of determining an age for a deeply buried site before radiocarbon dating was available.

SURVEY AND EXCAVATIONS AT THE LIME CREEK SITES DURING THE 1940S AND 1950S

By 1946 the Bureau of Reclamation had decided to construct a dam across Medicine Creek, a major tributary to the Republican River in southwestern Nebraska. This multipurpose dam was part of a massive federal program of reservoir construction in seven states in the Missouri River Basin (Wedel 1949:257). The lake formed by Medicine Creek Dam is now referred to as Harry Strunk Lake (map 6.1). During June of 1946, the University of Nebraska State Museum began a search for paleontological sites in the area that was to be inundated by the lake, and then excavated these sites under a cooperative agreement with the Smithsonian Institution and the National Park Service (Schultz and Frankforter 1948:44). C. Bertrand Schultz, who was by then director and curator of the Nebraska State Museum, was assisted by W. D. Frankforter, who was then assistant curator of paleontology at the museum. Frankforter later completed an important monograph on terraces and the late Quaternary history of the Elkhorn River Valley in eastern Nebraska (Frankforter 1950). Schultz and Frankforter's survey work along Lime Creek and Medicine Creek led to the discovery of three deeply buried archaeological sites that were partly excavated in the late 1940s and early 1950s before inundation. Collectively, these three sites (Red Smoke, Allen, and Lime Creek) are referred to as the Lime Creek sites (Schultz et al. 1948:31).

The Red Smoke archaeological site was discovered during the Nebraska State Museum's reconnaissance work in April 1947, but the Lime Creek and Allen archaeological sites were not discovered until after the disastrous flood of June 22, 1947, which had severely eroded banks along Lime and Medicine Creeks (Schultz and Frankforter 1948:44–46). At all three of these sites, artifacts were discovered near the base of 7.5 meter- to 15 meter-high cutbanks. These sites were immediately excavated during the 1947 field season (Schultz and Frankforter 1948:48) (fig. 6.1). At the Lime Creek site, two Scottsbluff

Fig. 6.1. Excavations at the Lime Creek site (25FT41) along Lime Creek in 1947. Courtesy of the University of Nebraska State Museum.

points were found in situ during test excavations (Schultz and Frankforter 1948:49). However, Schultz's news of deeply buried artifacts at the Lime Creek sites was generally greeted with skepticism by the archaeological community (Davis 1992). To deflect criticism and resolve the controversy over the age of these sites, C. Bertrand Schultz responded by hiring archaeologists for the excavations of these sites.

Fig. 6.2. Excavations at the Allen site (25FT50) along Medicine Creek in 1948. Courtesy of the University of Nebraska State Museum.

Once Schultz convinced Preston Holder, an archaeologist from SUNY at Buffalo, that the artifacts at the base of the cutbank at the Allen site were truly in situ, Holder accepted Schultz's offer of a position with the University of Nebraska State Museum as supervisor of the archaeological excavations at the Allen site (E. Mott Davis, personal communication, 1992; Schultz and Frankforter 1948:56). Holder and his wife, Joyce Wike, supervised the work at the Allen site during the 1948 field season and published a short paper on the results of their work (Holder and Wike 1949:260) (fig. 6.2).

E. Mott Davis, an archaeologist with experience in the American southwest and the lower Mississippi River valley, was employed by the University of Nebraska State Museum in the fall of 1948 to excavate the Lime Creek and Red Smoke sites (Davis 1992). During the 1949 field season and occasional weekends during the fall of 1949 and during the spring and early summer of 1950, Davis was responsible for the archaeological investigations of the three Paleoindian cultural horizons at the Lime Creek site (Davis 1992). In the summers of 1949–1953, Davis excavated the Red Smoke site (Davis 1992) (fig. 6.3).

Fig. 6.3. Excavations at the Red Smoke site (25FT42) along Lime Creek in July 1951. Courtesy of the University of Nebraska State Museum.

Davis and Schultz (1952) published the results of the preliminary research at all three archaeological sites, and Davis (1953) gave a more detailed preliminary report on the Lime Creek and Red Smoke sites. Data from the Red Smoke site formed a part of Davis's (1954) doctoral dissertation. A final report on the Lime Creek site has been published (Davis 1962), but a final report on the Red Smoke site has not yet been published.

C. Bertrand Schultz envisioned an interdisciplinary effort at the three Lime Creek Paleoindian sites. He wanted to include experts traditionally involved in museum-sponsored excavations (archaeologists, geomorphologists, and vertebrate paleontologists), as well as other specialists in the disciplines of sedimentology, invertebrate paleontology, paleobotany, and pedology (Schultz and Frankforter 1948:56). He was partially successful. For instance, Gregory Elias (1949) wrote a master's thesis at the University of Nebraska on the sedimentological properties of the alluvial fills beneath terraces along Medicine Creek. His thesis contains a considerable amount of particle-size data for individual sedimentary units within each of the fills at representative stratigraphic sections. Howard Stacy (1949) also wrote a master's thesis at the University of

Nebraska on invertebrates found in the fills beneath the terraces described in Elias's (1949) thesis. In his thesis, Stacy inferred local climatic conditions and changes in those conditions from the species of invertebrates found in the valley fills. In general, the excavations of the Lime Creek sites were more interdisciplinary than any previous archaeological excavations in Nebraska, although apparently not to the extent that Schultz had originally envisioned.

Radiocarbon dating was in its infancy at the time that the three Lime Creek sites were excavated (see Libby 1955). Schultz was able to obtain some radiocarbon ages (the first for deposits in Nebraska) for three samples from the Allen site, one sample from the Lime Creek site, and one sample from the Red Smoke site. Two charcoal samples from the lower occupation level (I) at the Allen site were dated to 8274 and 10,493 B.P., and a mixture of charcoal from the two "soil bands" associated with occupation levels I and II at the Allen site was dated to only 5256 B.P. (Arnold and Libby 1951:116). The average age of two ages of a charcoal sample from a Paleoindian component at the Lime Creek site was 9524 B.P. (Arnold and Libby 1951:116). The average of two ages of a charcoal sample from the Red Smoke site, cultural zone 92 in Davis (1953), was 8862 B.P. (Libby 1954b:738). Although these ages were determined using the solid-carbon method and are generally dismissed today, they were the first absolute ages for Paleoindian sites in Nebraska.

C. Bertrand Schultz and others (1951) took advantage of the radiocarbon ages of cultural deposits at the Lime Creek sites to assign absolute ages to terraces and valley fills in the region. By using the radiocarbon ages of the Lime Creek Paleoindian components, in conjunction with paleontological data, field surveys of terrace elevations, and soil stratigraphy within valley fills, they revised an earlier terrace and alluvial fill model for the upper Republican River (Schultz et al. 1948:39). The new, detailed model of valley evolution in Nebraska showed stratigraphic positions in which Paleoindian components most likely would be found. The type locality for their Terrace 2A fill in this model is the valley fill at the Lime Creek archaeological site (Schultz et al. 1951:30).

Geoarchaeology in the 1970s and Early 1980s

Following the completion of the original excavations of the Allen, Lime Creek, and Red Smoke sites in the early 1950s, little systematic work was carried out by geoarchaeologists in Nebraska until the 1970s. The reasons for this hiatus are not clear. A reduction in the number of construction projects in valleys, no new discoveries of Paleoindian sites, or perhaps the absence of any concentrated efforts by archaeologists to find new sites may all have played a role. Nevertheless, when federal funding was allocated for construction of two Bureau of Reclamation reservoirs and associated canals in central Nebraska, geoarchaeology in Nebraska was revived. This resurgence of geoarchaeology was also fueled by the discovery of, or initial study of, several Paleoindian sites during the late 1970s and early 1980s.

In the late 1970s the Bureau of Reclamation contracted for extensive archaeological surveys and testing in the areas of two proposed dams and reservoirs in the North Loup River basin: Calamus Dam and Reservoir and the Davis Creek Dam and Reservoir (map 6.1) (King et al. 1981; Sadler and King 1981). Once the initial archaeological survey work was completed (King et al. 1981; Sadler and King 1981), a private consulting company (Gilbert/Commonwealth, Inc.) was awarded a contract for site-specific archaeological investigations at two Protohistoric Pawnee sites in the Calamus Reservoir area (Roper 1989). The geoarchaeological investigation associated with the excavation of these sites was one of the most intensive to date in Nebraska. The fieldwork was directed by Joseph Schuldenrein (1985) and included a variety of earth-science studies of the immediate region. Schuldenrein authored four chapters of the final report on the site (Roper 1989:ch. 15–18). He addressed regional landforms, geomorphic mapping, erosion and sedimentation at the sites, and the chronology of land-forming events at the sites. The Calamus Dam project was probably the first major archaeological project in Nebraska to involve scientists from a variety of disciplines since the investigation of the Lime Creek sites in the late 1940s. This project may also claim the distinction of being the first study in Nebraska to employ a project geomorphologist at a non-Paleoindian archaeological site.

Several Paleoindian sites were investigated by geomorphologists in the 1970s and early 1980s. One of these, the Hudson-Meng site, was discovered in the fall of 1971 and excavated between 1971 and 1977 by Larry Agenbroad, then at Chadron State College (Agenbroad 1978; also see Albanese, this volume). This bison-kill site is located in a buried arroyo on the north slope of the Pine Ridge Escarpment in the northwestern portion of the state less than twenty-five miles from the Wyoming border (map 6.1). C. Vance Haynes Jr., Professor of Geology at the University of Arizona, carried out extensive geoarchaeological investigations during the 1960s just across the western border of Nebraska in southeastern Wyoming (Irwin-Williams et al. 1973). Apparently because of the proximity of the Hudson-Meng site to the Hell Gap sites in Wyoming and his reputation as a thorough and experienced geoarchaeologist, Haynes participated in some of the geologic work at the Hudson-Meng site. Ages were tentatively assigned to the four sedimentary units in the paleo-arroyo (Agenbroad 1978:figs. 41, 44) based on stratigraphic correlations to deposits in Wyoming (Haynes 1968) and to those elsewhere in northwestern Nebraska (Stout et al. 1965).

The Clary Ranch site is another Paleoindian bison-kill site in western Nebraska that was studied in the 1970s (map 6.1). This site was reported to the University of Nebraska State Museum in 1970 (Myers et al. 1981:1). However, the museum did not have an archaeologist on staff at the time, so no further work was done at the site until fall 1978, when the site was tested with a coring tool to determine its extent (Myers et al. 1981:1). In 1979 an extensive excavation of the site took place. Lloyd Tanner, then a member of the University of Nebraska State Museum staff, was responsible for placing the Clary Ranch site in a geomorphic and stratigraphic context. He reported that the site lies "within a remnant of the Terrace 2 (or Kersey) valley fill" (Tanner 1982).

Steven Holen, who was an archaeologist with the Nebraska State Historical Society in the early 1980s, undertook a survey of archaeological sites in the South Loup River Valley in the summer of 1983. After seeking the assistance and recommendations of Quaternary geologists at the University of Nebraska Conservation and Survey Division, he turned to me for geoarchaeological assistance on the project. At the time I was a doctoral student in geography at the University of Wisconsin-Madison. During that summer we investigated two Paleoindian sites in the South Loup River Valley, and during the summer of 1984 we investigated a third Paleoindian site in the North Loup River Valley.

Holen had discovered the Truman archaeological site in the South Loup River valley in 1971 while searching for the nearby Cumro site on which C. Bertrand Schultz had worked in 1929 and 1930 (map 6.1). Holen wanted an estimate of the age of the lowest component at the Truman site; no diagnostic artifacts had been exposed, and the stratigraphic section was very incomplete. When I visited the site in 1983 I suggested that the deepest component at the site was almost 10,000 years old, based on the elevation of the component and on local and regional alluvial and soil stratigraphy. Holen then submitted some bison bones, which he had removed from just below the lowest cultural horizon, for a radiocarbon age. The collagen fraction of these bones had a radiocarbon age of 9780 B.P., which confirmed my estimate of the age of the site (May and Holen 1985:9). Thus began our working relationship.

Local collectors had known about a Paleoindian site (Stark site) in a short tributary to the lower South Loup River (map 6.1) for years before Holen first studied it in 1972. They had recovered Cody Complex (Scottsbluff) projectile points from the site that date from 9200 to 8400 B.P. (S. R. Holen, personal communication, 1984; Holen 1995). After both detailed stratigraphic work and subsurface coring at this site in the summer of 1983, we developed a scenario of landscape evolution for the site (Holen and May 1984). This simple reconstruction included a gully at the site that may have been used as a bison trap.

During the summer of 1984 Holen and I investigated a third Paleoindian site, the Kruml site, in the Loup River Basin (map 6.1). This site consists of two deeply buried Paleoindian components that have been exposed by bank erosion along the North Loup River (Holen and May 1984). My assessment of the site was that the Paleoindian components were on early Holocene floodplain deposits within the Elba Valley Fill (Brice 1964). A thermoluminescence age from the deposits confirmed the age estimate of 10,000–9000 B.P.

The archaeological survey project that Holen and I conducted in the South Loup River valley during the summer of 1983 not only yielded an accounting of archaeological sites in that valley (Holen 1983), but ultimately led to much more geomorphological research in the valley. During the summer and fall of 1984 I mapped river terraces and deciphered alluvial stratigraphy in the valley for a doctoral dissertation in geography at the University of Wisconsin-Madison (May 1986). In the late 1980s, while Assistant Professor of Geography at the University of Northern Iowa, I received several small research grants that funded additional fieldwork and radiocarbon dating of alluvial deposits in the South Loup River valley. These additional studies helped me develop a complete Holocene model of landscape evolution in the valley (May 1989, 1992).

Steven Holen and I have cooperated on several archaeological surveys and site testings since our first collaboration in 1983 in the South Loup River valley. In the summer of 1984 we worked on a highway right-of-way project that involved the testing of the Slaughterhouse Creek site in the Pine Ridge area of northwestern Nebraska (map 6.1) (Bozell and Ludwickson 1988). My geoarchaeological investigation involved describing soils and sediments exposed in one-by-two-meter test pits and in backhoe trenches and then reconstructing the late Holocene evolution of the valley (May 1988a). In 1987 Holen and I worked on a survey for archaeological sites on different landforms in the Buffalo Creek drainage of central Nebraska (map 6.1) (Winham et al. 1988). My contribution to this study included mapping landforms in the project area for the purpose of establishing a proportional, stratified, random sampling for archaeological sites in the project area (May 1988b).

RECENT GEOARCHAEOLOGICAL INVESTIGATIONS IN NEBRASKA

While the early geoarchaeological work was performed primarily by Schultz and other personnel affiliated with the University of Nebraska State Museum, more recent work involving the collaboration of archaeologists and geomorphologists has involved physical geographers, soil scientists, and geologists affiliated with a variety of academic institutions.

In 1991 Steven Holen was working under contract with the Historic Preservation Office of the Nebraska State Historical Society to develop a sample strategy for a partial archaeological survey of the central Elkhorn River valley (map 6.1). The goals of the project were very similar to those of the Buffalo Creek project on which we had collaborated in 1987, so he invited me to work with him on this project (Holen et al. 1992).

The Davis Creek Dam project of the Bureau of Reclamation had also included a related bureau project: the Fullerton-Elba Canal system along the lower North Loup and Loup Rivers. The archaeological survey work on this canal project began in the summer of 1989. As geoarchaeologist on the project, I was responsible for determining the potential for buried archaeological sites along the canal right-of-way. Many cutbanks along tributaries to the North Loup and Loup Rivers were studied, described, and sampled as part of this effort. The result was a report and maps detailing potential for buried archaeological sites beneath different landforms along the canal right-of-way (May 1990).

One of the study localities during the summer of 1989 was a cutbank along Moffet Creek (map 6.1). Here a deeply buried Paleoindian component was discovered during the pedestrian archaeological survey of the canal right-of-way. In the summer of 1991 Holen directed archaeological testing of the multiple cultural components at the Moffet Creek site (fig. 6.4). I assisted by

Fig. 6.4. Cutbank along Moffet Creek at the Moffet Creek archaeological site (25HW59). At top left two individuals are digging down to a Late Archaic cultural horizon (about 4000 B.P.). At bottom right near the ladder a trench has been excavated through a late Paleoindian cultural horizon (about 8500 B.P.). Photograph by David May, May 1991.

determining the ages of the multiple buried soils containing the cultural components and the extent and depth of the buried Paleoindian deposits. This work involved drilling many holes across the site to reconstruct the configuration of the buried Paleoindian horizon. Once the depth and spatial extent of the buried occupational surface was delineated, a large backhoe trench was excavated to expose the deeply buried cultural horizon. The trench was several meters deep and covered nearly one hundred square meters. The sedimentary structures found in the alluvium comprising the low-angle fan revealed that a variety of fluvial and mass-wasting processes had created, buried, and altered the Paleoindian component at the site. A complete report on this site has not yet been published.

During the spring and summer of 1992 Holen, who was now affiliated with the department of anthropology at the University of Nebraska, directed the excavation of threatened cultural resources along the Fullerton canal right-of-way in the Loup River Valley. He invited me to conduct geoarchaeological research at the largest of the threatened archaeological sites in the path of the canal. Geoarchaeological research during the spring and summer of 1992 included describing soils at the site, close-interval sampling of soils and sediments for physical and chemical analyses and radiocarbon assays, and describing the regional geomorphic and stratigraphic context of the site. A complete report on this site is currently being prepared for the Bureau of Reclamation.

As the Corps of Engineers and Bureau of Reclamation have moved away from constructing new, large, multipurpose reservoirs, they have focused on managing cultural resources at their existing reservoirs. This has become an especially important task where shoreline erosion exposes cultural resources each year. These federal agencies are also working to inventory all cultural resources on all of the property that they manage. This includes some upland areas around their reservoirs. Two existing reservoirs in Nebraska received considerable attention from archaeologists and geoarchaeologists in the late 1980s and 1990s: Harlan County Lake (U.S. Army Corps of Engineers) and Harry Strunk Lake (Medicine Creek Reservoir) (Bureau of Reclamation).

In the mid-1980s archaeologists Mary Adair and Kenneth Brown investigated twenty-eight archaeological sites around Harlan County Lake (map 6.1) (Adair and Brown 1987). Geomorphologist Kevin Cornwell (1987) also worked on the project. He mapped the distribution of terraces around the margin of the lake, constructed cross-sections of the Republican River Valley before inundation by Harlan County Lake, and described stratigraphic sections at individual sites around the lake.

A much more intensive and site-specific geoarchaeological investigation took place at the North Cove site at Harlan County Lake in the fall of 1987 as part of an interdisciplinary investigation (Adair 1989). While the archaeological evidence from the site is controversial (see Logan 1989), the site has produced a tremendous amount of paleoecological, soil-stratigraphic, and chronological data for late Quaternary deposits in the middle reaches of the Republican River Valley. William C. Johnson, Professor of Geography at the University of Kansas, was responsible for unraveling the stratigraphy and generating a model of landform evolution at the site (Johnson 1989; Johnson and Logan 1990). As part of his investigation, he collected many samples for radiocarbon dating and described the sediments at the site. Charles W. Martin, a student of Johnson's who worked with him at the site, continued the study of landscape evolution in the region for his doctoral dissertation (Martin 1990).

Paleoindian sites, including pre-Clovis, were the focus of a small project at Harlan County Lake that was initiated by Steven Holen in the fall of 1995

(Holen et al. 1996). While attempting to relocate previously identified sites with Paleoindian components and searching for new Paleoindian sites, Holen involved me as geoarchaeologist. My work consisted of both identifying late Pleistocene stratigraphy around the lake during the pedestrian shoreline survey and making detailed stratigraphic descriptions at newly discovered archaeological sites. This geoarchaeological work was a refinement of Cornwell's (1987) mapping of landforms around the reservoir for the specific purpose of identifying locations along the lakeshore where Paleoindian sites might be exposed during shoreline erosion.

Harry Strunk Lake (Medicine Creek Reservoir) had received considerable attention from archaeologists and geologists before and during the construction of the reservoir in the late 1940s and early 1950s. However, little additional archaeological work was done at the lake until the mid- and late-1980s (Roper 1993:2). A renewed archaeological effort at the lake has been directed by Robert Blasing, archaeologist at the Grand Island office of the Bureau of Reclamation. He has contracted for various site-specific archaeological investigations at Harry Strunk Lake with Donna Roper, Steven Holen, and Douglas Bamforth. He has also involved Donald Blakeslee, Professor of Anthropology, and his students at Wichita State University in a pedestrian archaeological survey of all the federal land around the reservoir.

Donna Roper, who was working for the consulting firm Gilbert/Commonwealth, investigated the Marvin Colson site at Harry Strunk Lake during fall 1985 and fall 1986 (Roper 1993). This is an Upper Republican site that was not investigated during the original Smithsonian Institution River Basin Surveys (Roper 1993). Alison Rautman (1993) was geoarchaeologist during the testing of the site. She used shallow backhoe trenches and augering with manual posthole augers to investigate the sediments in the upper part of the valley fill underlying Terrace 2 (Stockville Terrace) in Medicine Creek Valley. In many ways, her contribution to Nebraska geoarchaeology is similar to that of Joseph Schuldenrein's (1985) at the Calamus Reservoir sites. Both geoarchaeologists were involved in intensive geomorphic and stratigraphic investigations of non-Paleoindian archaeological sites on federal property.

Another major geoarchaeological study at Harry Strunk Lake involved a pre-Clovis mammoth-processing site buried in loess (La Sena site). A brief history of this controversial site is warranted. In 1987 Bureau of Reclamation archaeologist Robert Blasing discovered some fractured mammoth bones and some lithic material lying together on the shore of Harry Strunk Lake. Blasing

Fig. 6.5. View south of the La Sena site (25FT177) at Harry Strunk Lake during the June 1994 excavation. Photograph by David May.

notified Steven Holen, who was an independent consulting archaeologist at the time, and Holen and I investigated the site in 1988. We determined that the pieces of mammoth bone on the lakeshore dated to 18,000 B.P., and that more fragments of mammoth bone were present in situ in the loess deposits form-ing the vertical bluff above the beach where the original bones were found (Holen and May 1989). Given the presence of lithic material with the bones found on the beach and seasonal erosion of the loess bluff, the Bureau of Reclamation sponsored more complete testing of the site in 1989, 1990, 1991, 1993, 1994, 1996, 1997, and 1998 (fig. 6.5). In the fall of 1998 the site was sealed and protected from further wave erosion by a large berm constructed by the Bureau of Reclamation along the eroding loess bluff. Therefore, some of the site has been preserved.

Archaeological testing at the site has uncovered pieces of fractured long bones of mammoth and more fragile rib bones that are still in one piece (May and Holen 1994). Furthermore, the mystery of the associated lithic material has been solved. Holen's careful excavation of the site has demonstrated that lithic material from a Central Plains Tradition site on the modern surface apparently fell down into modern rodent burrows that extend to a depth of as much as four meters, which is the depth of the bed of fractured mammoth bones. Geoarchaeological work at the site has involved coring around the site to determine the local stratigraphy, spatial extent of the bone bed, and slope of the bone bed (fig. 6.6). Also, numerous sediment samples have been collected for laboratory analyses. These samples were collected to answer such questions as the radiocarbon age of the site, the rate of loess deposition, and the degree of soil formation at the depth of the bone bed. Although a full publication of the archaeological evidence has not yet been completed, the stratigraphic context of the site has been described and some of the radiocarbon ages have been included in a short published paper (May and Holen 1993). Radiocarbon ages of 18,860 and 16,730 B.P. have been determined on soil humates just above and in the mammoth bone bed, respectively; the older age is considered the more reliable because of possible modern rootlet contamination of the younger, smaller, soil sample from within the bone bed (May and Holen 1993). The older age of humates in the loess from just above the bone bed is consistent with age (18,000 B.P.) of bone collagen in the large fragment of mammoth bone found on the beach below the loess bluff containing the bone bed (Holen and May 1989). Close-interval sampling (5 cm) through the bone bed has revealed that the bone bed is in a weakly developed buried Bt soil horizon (May and Holen 1993).

Harry Strunk Lake has been the focus of yet another long-term archaeological and multidisciplinary project under the direction of Douglas Bamforth, who is now Associate Professor of Anthropology at the University of Colorado-Boulder. In 1989, when Bamforth was Assistant Professor in the Department of Anthropology at the University of Nebraska, he entered into a cooperative agreement with the Bureau of Reclamation to study the artifacts originally recovered from the three Lime Creek Paleoindian sites at the reservoir (Allen, Lime Creek, and Red Smoke sites) and to collect additional geomorphic, stratigraphic, palynological, and other paleoenvironmental data from the three sites. Although the Allen site is now inundated by Harry Strunk Lake, a tremendous amount of material collected in 1948 from the site was never processed. The only publication to date is Holder and Wike's (1949) brief summary of their work at the site during 1948. Thanks to Bamforth's efforts and those of many experts in a variety of disciplines, the materials that have been in storage for over fifty years have been analyzed. A multidisciplinary volume on the Allen site, edited by Bamforth, will soon be published.

As part of Douglas Bamforth's project, Steven Holen and I conducted a shoreline survey of the alluvial fills exposed in bluffs around the lake by wave erosion. The objective of our reconnaissance during the summer of 1989 was

Fig 6.6. Drill rig owned by the Bureau of Reclamation being used at the La Sena site (25FT177) to determine the spatial limits of the buried bed of fractured mammoth bones. Drill rig is drilling in the northwest corner of the site. Photograph by David May.

to identify the potential for preservation of other Paleoindian sites in the reservoir area. This geoarchaeological work resulted in a map of landforms in the basin, especially the distribution of Schultz and others' (1948, 1951) Terrace 2 or Brice's (1966) Stockville Terrace. We also discovered and studied a nearly complete stratigraphic section of fill underlying Terrace 2 in the upper part of the reservoir area. The sediments exposed at the base of this section are very similar to those described by Schultz et. al. (1948:37–38) and photographed by Schultz and Frankforter (1948) at the base of the Lime Creek stratigraphic section (Davis 1962:27).

Other geoarchaeological research associated with Douglas Bamforth's project at Harry Strunk Lake included drilling the Lime Creek and Red Smoke sites in the fall of 1989, resampling alluvium from the Red Smoke site for radiocarbon assays and pollen analysis in the spring of 1993, and sampling a previously unstudied Paleoindian site (Stafford site) discovered along upper Lime Creek more than twenty years after the lake was filled. Sediment was sampled from the thick alluvial fill at the Stafford site in the summers of 1993 and 1995 for both radiocarbon assays and pollen analyses. A report on this site will be included in Bamforth's edited volume.

Other geoarchaeologists have conducted research in Nebraska during the past several years. For instance, in the fall of 1991 Rolfe Mandel, then Assistant Professor of Geography and Geology at the University of Nebraska at Omaha, reinvestigated the Logan Creek site in northeastern Nebraska (map 6.1) with archaeologist Gayle Carlson of the Nebraska State Historical Society. Mandel (1992, 1995) has reinterpreted the genesis of the alluvial deposits in which artifacts have been found and has greatly expanded the original chronology for sedimentation at the site (Crane and Griffin 1960:40, 1962:195).

Rolfe Mandel (1993) also worked on an intensive archaeological survey of the Blue River drainage in southeastern Nebraska (map 6.1) in 1992 and 1993 with archaeologists Edward J. Lueck and R. Peter Winham from the Archeology Laboratory of Augustana College in Sioux Falls, South Dakota. This project was funded by the State Historic Preservation Office of the Nebraska State Historical Society. Mandel developed a landscape-evolution model to predict the occurrence of cultural deposits of different ages on particular landforms and within particular alluvial valley fills along portions of both the Big Blue and Little Blue River valleys (map 6.1). Mandel (1994) has also worked in eastern Nebraska on a highway archaeology project with archaeologists John Bozell and John Ludwickson of the Nebraska State Historical

Society. As part of this project, Mandel developed a landscape-evolution model for Little Pawnee Creek (map 6.1).

More recently Mandel (1996) conducted a thorough investigation of landforms and alluvial stratigraphy within the Big Nemaha River valley (map 6.1) in conjunction with an archaeological survey headed by Steven Holen (University of Nebraska State Museum) and sponsored by the Historic Preservation Office of the Nebraska State Historical Society. Mandel identified two terraces (T1 and T2) and a variety of landform features associated with the modern floodplain (T0). He reported that Terrace 1 is the dominant terrace in the Big Nemaha River valley and that cutbanks up to eight meters high expose the alluvium beneath this terrace. Mandel assigned this alluvium to the DeForest Formation, which was originally recognized in western Iowa (see Bettis, this volume), and learned that the eight-meter-deep base of the Late Gunder Member of the DeForest Formation is as old as about 4400 B.P.

Most recently, Mandel (1997) participated in an archaeological survey of the Ponca Creek and Keya Paha River valleys with archaeologist Steven Holen (map 6.1). He focused on late Quaternary landscape evolution in the valleys. Mandel provided a detailed soil-stratigraphic framework for the cultural deposits that were found in the project area, and he determined the geologic potential for buried archaeological materials in Holocene valley fills.

Lawrence Todd of Colorado State University, Dave Rapson of the University of Wyoming, and Lou Redmond of the Nebraska National Forest have recently reopened the Hudson-Meng Paleoindian site in northwestern Nebraska (map 6.1). As part of the reinvestigation, professors E. F. Kelly of the Department of Agronomy and Evelyn E. Wohl of the Department of Earth Resources at Colorado State University have characterized the fluvial and eolian processes responsible for the development of the site (Kelly and Wohl 1994). They have provided detailed descriptions of buried soils; particle-size analyses of sediments; and laboratory analyses of pollen, phytoliths, organic carbon, and pedogenic carbonate. One significant result of their reinvestigation of the site is a detailed reconstruction of the paleoclimate of the site.

Finally, I have been involved with Steven Holen in two recent projects in 1997 and 1998; both have been funded by the Bureau of Reclamation. The first was a project to conduct an archaeological survey of the Arcadia Diversion Dam and Sherman Reservoir (map 6.1). The Arcadia Diversion Dam is along the Middle Loup River. A portion of the federal land on the west side of the river includes two early Holocene terrace remnants containing Paleoindian and Early Archaic cultural components. Here a combination of geoarchaeological stratigraphic investigative methods have been used to reach the deeply buried cultural deposits and to laterally trace buried soils and cultural materials (May 1999). A hydraulic soil-coring device was used in conjunction with several deep backhoe trenches and hand-augered holes to develop a three-dimensional model of the buried deposits. The second project was an archaeological survey of Enders Reservoir in southwestern Nebraska (map 6.1). Several terraces are present around this reservoir and many surface archaeological deposits were discovered, but only a few, shallowly buried cultural materials were identified (May 1998).

CONCLUSIONS

Geoarchaeological research in Nebraska in the 1930s and 1940s was usually initiated by geologists, especially paleontologists, and was almost exclusively concerned with establishing the age of Paleoindian sites using stratigraphic and terrace correlations. C. Bertrand Schultz, who was affiliated with the University of Nebraska State Museum in various capacities from the late 1920s until his death in 1995, was largely responsible for many of the early discoveries of Paleoindian sites in Nebraska and for getting professional archaeologists involved in the excavations of these sites. He also was responsible for initiating interdisciplinary research during excavation of the Lime Creek sites and for developing the first model of valley evolution in Nebraska.

Since the mid-1980s, the U.S. Bureau of Reclamation and U.S. Army Corps of Engineers have funded reinvestigations of previously discovered archaeological sites, as well as complete pedestrian surveys of all cultural deposits on federal land around their reservoirs. Also, during this time the State Preservation Office of the Nebraska State Historical Society has contracted for archaeological surveys within selected drainage basins. These studies have involved stratified sampling based on landform distribution and age. During these studies, geomorphologists have become more intimately involved in the discovery of archaeological sites. Usually they are asked to assess the likelihood of finding buried cultural deposits beneath different landforms. Archaeologists then tailor their pedestrian surveys accordingly.

Today the roles that geoarchaeologists play in archaeological projects in Nebraska are more varied than in the past. Whereas in the past geoarchaeologists were invited to assess the age of deeply buried sites, today they are often involved in helping predict where buried sites might be found. At individual sites geoarchaeologists usually describe sediments and buried soils in detail. Then they infer the depositional environment of the sediments and cultural deposits and causes of postdepositional modifications of cultural deposits and sediments. Thus, today geoarchaeologists recognize and map a broad spectrum of landforms in the entire landscape, determine absolute ages of individual landforms and buried land surfaces, construct chronologies of landscape change, and interpret site-specific sedimentation and site-disturbance patterns.

ACKNOWLEDGMENTS

I thank Douglas Bamforth, E. Mott Davis, and Steven Holen for their helpful reviews of earlier versions of this chapter. Their comments were very helpful in making the chapter more complete and accurate. I thank Susan Boley-May for her many hours of editorial assistance on earlier drafts of this chapter. I thank Rolfe Mandel for taking the initiative to organize the session at the Plains Conference in Lincoln on which this volume is based, for editing this chapter and the entire volume, and for his perseverance in completing this book.

REFERENCES

Adair, M. J., ed. 1989. Archaeological investigations at the North Cove site, Harlan County Lake, Harlan County, Nebraska. Kansas City, Kans.: U.S. Army Corps of Engineers.

Adair, M. J., and K. L. Brown, eds. 1987. Prehistoric and historic cultural resources of selected sites at Harlan County Lake, Harlan County, Nebraska. Kansas City, Kans.: U.S. Army Corps of Engineers.

Agenbroad, L. D. 1978. The Hudson-Meng Site: An Alberta bison kill in the Nebraska high plains. Washington, D.C.: University of America Press.

Arnold, J. R., and W. F. Libby. 1951. Radiocarbon dates. *Science* 113, no. 2927: 111–20.

Barbour, E. H., and C. B. Schultz. 1936. Palaeontologic and geologic consideration of Early Man in Nebraska. *The Nebraska State Museum Bulletin* 45, vol. 1:431–49.

Bell, E. H., and W. Van Royen. 1936. Some considerations regarding the possible age of an ancient site in western Nebraska. *In* Bell, E. H., ed., *Chapters in Nebraska Archaeology* 1, no. 6:400–19. Lincoln: The University of Nebraska.

Bozell, J. R., and Ludwickson, J. 1988. Highway archeological investigations at the Slaughterhouse Creek site and other cultural resources in the Pine Ridge area. Lincoln: Nebraska State Historical Society.

Brice, J. C. 1964. Channel patterns and terraces of the Loup Rivers in Nebraska, chap. D of Physiographic and hydraulic studies of rivers. U.S. Geological Survey Professional Paper 422:D1–D41.

———. 1966. Erosion and deposition in the loess-mantled Great Plains, Medicine Creek drainage basin, Nebraska, chap. H of Erosion and sedimentation in a semiarid environment. U.S. Geological Survey Professional Paper 352-H:255–339.

Christianson, G. E. 1990. Fox at the wood's edge: A biography of Loren Eiseley. New York: Henry Holt and Company.

Cornwell, K. J. 1987. Geomorphology and soils. In Adair, M. J., and K. L. Brown, eds., Prehistoric and historic cultural resources of selected sites at Harlan County Lake, Harlan County, Nebraska: Test excavations and determination of significance for 28 sites, 29–46. Kansas City, Kans.: U.S. Army Corps of Engineers.

Crane, H. R., and J. B. Griffin. 1960. University of Michigan radiocarbon dates V. American Journal of Science Radiocarbon Supplement 2:31–48.

———. 1962. University of Michigan Radiocarbon Dates VII. Radiocarbon 4:183–203.

Davis, E. M. 1953. Recent data from two Paleo-Indian sites on Medicine Creek, Nebraska. American Antiquity 18:380–86.

———. 1954. The culture history of the central Great Plains prior to the introduction of pottery. Ph.D. diss., Harvard University, Cambridge.

———. 1962. The archeology of the Lime Creek site in southwestern Nebraska. Special publication of the University of Nebraska State Museum, no. 3.

———. 1992. Manuscript for volume in preparation on the Allen site. In Bamforth, D., ed., forthcoming. Albuquerque: University of New Mexico Press.

Davis, E. M., and C. Bertrand Schultz. 1952. The archaeological and paleontological salvage program at the Medicine Creek Reservoir, Frontier County, Nebraska. Science 115:288–90.

Elias, G. K. 1949. The sedimentation and geologic history of certain terraces in Frontier County, Nebraska. Master's thesis, University of Nebraska, Lincoln.

Frankforter, W. D. 1950. The Pleistocene geology of the middle portion of the Elkhorn River Valley. Lincoln: University of Nebraska Studies no. 5.

Haynes, C. V. 1968. Geochronology of Late-Quaternary alluvium. In Morrison, R. B., and H. E. Wright Jr., eds., Means of correlations of Quaternary successions, 591–631. Salt Lake City: University of Utah Press.

Holder, P., and J. Wike. 1949. The Frontier Culture Complex, a preliminary report on a prehistoric hunters' camp in southwestern Nebraska. American Antiquity 14, no. 4:260–66, 340–43.

Holen, S. R. 1983. A preliminary report on the South Loup River Survey. Lincoln: Nebraska State Historical Society, Historic Preservation Office.

———. 1995. Evidence of the first humans in Nebraska. Museum Notes, University of Nebraska State Museum, Lincoln, no. 90.

Holen, S. R., and D. W. May. 1984. The archeology and geomorphology of three early Holocene sites in the Loup River drainage [abs.]. Program and Abstracts: 25. Forty-second annual Plains Anthropological Conference, Lincoln, Nebraska.

———. 1989. Report on preliminary investigations at 25FT177: A probable late Pleistocene man/mammoth association. Grand Island, Nebr.: U.S. Bureau of Reclamation, Open-file Report.

Holen, S. R., T. Barton, S. M. Parks, and D. W. May. 1992. Geoarchaeology and culture history of the central Elkhorn River Valley: A preliminary survey. Lincoln: University of Nebraska, Department of Anthropology, Technical Report no. 92-01.

Holen, S. R., D. W. May, and P. M. Prettyman. 1996., An archaeological and geomorphic survey of paleoindian sites at Harlan County Lake, Harlan County, Nebraska. Lincoln: University of Nebraska State Museum, Nebraska Archaeological Survey, Technical Report 96-01.

Irwin-Williams, C., H. Irwin, G. Agogino, and C. V. Haynes Jr. 1973. Hell Gap: Paleo-Indian occupation on the High Plains. *Plains Anthropologist* 18, no. 59:40–53.

Johnson, W. C. 1989. Stratigraphy and late-Quaternary landscape evolution. *In* Adair, M. J., ed., Archaeological investigations at the North Cove site, Harlan County Lake, Harlan County, Nebraska, 22–52. Kansas City, Kans.: U.S. Army Corps of Engineers.

Johnson, W. C., and B. Logan. 1990. Geoarchaeology of the Kansas River basin, central Great Plains. *In* Lasca, N. P., and J. Donahue, eds., Archaeological geology of North America. Boulder, Colo.: The Geological Society of America, Centennial Special vol. 4:267–99.

Kelly, E. F., and E. E. Wohl. 1994. Integration of palynological, pedological, and geomorphological analyses: Paleoenvironmental significance at the Hudson-Meng site, Sioux County, Nebraska. Fort Collins: Colorado State University, Departments of Agronomy and Earth Sciences, Final report prepared for the Hudson-Meng Research Group.

King, N. S., R. E. Pepperl, and C. R. Falk. 1981. Archeological investigations: Calamus project area. *In* King, N. S., R. E. Pepperl, C. R. Falk, P. Sadler, J. S. Smith, M. R. Vorrhies, R. Hartley, and D. Henning, eds., Cultural and paleontological resource investigations within the Calamus and Davis Creek reservoir areas, Nebraska, Appendix A. Lincoln, Nebr.: Division of Archeological Research, Department of Anthropology, University of Nebraska, Technical Report no. 80-04, section 1.

Libby, W. F. 1951. Radiocarbon dates, II. *Science* 114, no. 2960: p. 673–81.

————. 1954a. Chicago radiocarbon dates, IV. *Science* 119, no. 3083:135–40.

————. 1954b.Chicago radiocarbon dates V. *Science* 120, no. 3123:733–42.

————. 1955. Radiocarbon dating, 2d ed. Chicago: University of Chicago Press.

Logan, B. R. 1989. Lithic artifacts from the North Cove site: The pre-Clovis problem in the Central Plains. *In* Adair, M. J., ed., Archaeological investigations at the North Cove site, Harlan County Lake, Harlan County, Nebraska, 81–91. Kansas City, Mo.: U.S. Army Corps of Engineers.

MacClintock, P., E. H. Barbour, C. B. Schultz, and A. L. Lugn. 1936. A Pleistocene lake in the White River Valley. *American Naturalist* 70:346–60.

Mandel, R. D. 1992. Geomorphology and stratigraphy of the Logan Creek site (25BT3), northeastern Nebraska. Lincoln: Nebraska State Historical Society, 50th Plains Anthropological Conference, Program and Abstracts: 70–71.

————. 1993. Holocene landscape evolution in the Big Blue and Little Blue River Valleys, eastern Nebraska: Implications for archaeological research. *In* Lueck, E. J., and P. Winham, eds., Blue River drainage intensive archaeological survey 1992–1993, Seward and Thayer Counties, Nebraska, vol. 2:H1–H79. Sioux Falls, S.Dak.: Archeology Laboratory, Augustana College, Archeological Contract Series number 84.

————. 1994. Geomorphology and stratigraphy of the Little Pawnee Creek site. *In* Bozell, J. R., and J. Ludwickson, eds., Nebraska Phase archeology in the South Bend locality, 193–206. Lincoln: Nebraska State Historical Society, Highway Archeology Program Report.

————. 1995. Geomorphic controls of the Archaic record in the Central Plains of the United States. *In* Bettis, E. A., III, ed., Archaeological geology of the Archaic period in North America. Boulder, Colo.: The Geological Society of America, Special Paper 297:37–66.

————. 1996. Geomorphology of the South Fork Big Nemaha River valley, southeastern Nebraska. *In* Holen, S. R., and D. R. Watson, eds., A geoarchaeological survey of the South Fork Big Nemaha Drainage, Pawnee and Richardson counties, Nebraska. Lincoln: University of Nebraska State Museum, Nebraska Archaeological Survey, Technical Report 95-02: 26–81.

————. 1997. Geormophology and late Quaternary stratigraphy of Ponca Creek and the Key Paha River valley. *In* Holen, S. R. and Watson, D. R., eds, An archaeological survey of Ponca Creek and the Keya Paha River Drainages in Nebraska. Lincoln: University of Nebraska State Museum, Nebraska Archeological Survey, Technical Report 97-02:20–73.

Martin, C. W. 1990. Late Quaternary landform evolution in the Republican River basin, Nebraska. Ph.D. diss., Lawrence, University of Kansas.

May, D. W. 1986. Holocene alluviation, soil genesis, and erosion in the South Loup Valley, Nebraska. Ph.D. diss., Madison, University of Wisconsin.

————. 1988a. Sedimentary history. *In* Bozell, J. R., and J. Ludwickson, Highway archeological investigations at the Slaughterhouse Creek site and other cultural resources in the Pine Ridge area. Lincoln: Nebraska State Historical Society, Report:28–30.

———. 1988b. Landforms in the Buffalo and French Creek Drainage Basins. *In* Winham, R. P., S. R. Holen, E. J. Lueck, and L. A. Hannus, eds., Archeological sample survey of selected lands in the Buffalo Creek drainage, Dawson and Custer Counties, Nebraska, vol.1:10–25. Sioux Falls, S.Dak.: Archeology Laboratory of the Center for Western Studies, Augustana College, Archeological Contract Series, no. 41.

———. 1989. Holocene alluvial fills in the South Loup Valley, Nebraska. *Quaternary Research* 32:117–20.

———. 1990. The potential for buried archaeological sites along the Fullerton Canal, North Loup and Loup River valleys, Nebraska. Grand Island, Nebr.: U.S. Department of the Interior, Bureau of Reclamation, Open-file Report.

———. 1992. Late Holocene valley-bottom aggradation and erosion in the South Loup River Valley, Nebraska. *Physical Geography* 13:115–32.

———. 1998. Geomorphology of the project area. *In* Holen, S. R., and D. R. Watson, eds., A phase I archaeological survey of Enders Reservoir, Chase County, Nebraska. Lincoln: University of Nebraska State Museum, Nebraska Archaeological Survey, Technical Report 98-06: 12–33.

———. 1999. Geoarchaeology of the Arcadia diversion dam, Middle Loup River. *In* Phase I survey and phase II testing of archaeological sites at the Arcadia diversion dam lands on the Middle Loup River, Custer County, Nebraska. Lincoln: University of Nebraska State Museum, Nebraska Archaeological Survey, Technical Report 99-01: 122–52.

May, D. W., and S. R. Holen. 1985. A chronology of Holocene erosion and sedimentation in the South Loup Valley, Nebraska. *Geographical Perspectives* 56:8–12.

———. 1993. Radiocarbon ages of soils and charcoal in late Wisconsinan loess, south-central Nebraska. *Quaternary Research* 39:55–58.

———. 1994. Two mammoth-bone processing sites without lithics in late-Wisconsinan loess in Nebraska. Boulder, Colo.: The Geological Society of America, *Abstracts with Programs* 26, no. 7:341.

Myers, T. P., R. G. Corner, and L. G. Tanner. 1981. Preliminary report on the 1979 excavations at the Clary Ranch site. *Transactions of the Nebraska Academy of Science* 9:1–7.

Rautman, A. 1993. Geomorphic context. *In* Roper, D. C., ed., Archaeological investigations at the Marvin Colson Site, 25FT158, Frontier County, Nebraska. Grand Island, Nebr.: U.S. Department of the Interior, Bureau of Reclamation, Great Plains Region, Open-file Report: 73–84.

Roper, D. C. 1989. Proto-Historic Pawnee hunting in the Nebraska Sand Hills: Archeological investigations at two sites in the Calamus Reservoir. Grand Island, Nebr.: U.S. Department of the Interior, Bureau of Reclamation, Great Plains Region, Open-file Report.

————. 1993. Archaeological investigations at the Marvin Colson Site, 25FT158, Frontier County, Nebraska. Grand Island, Nebr.: U.S. Department of the Interior, Bureau of Reclamation, Great Plains Region, Open-file Report.

Sadler, P. A., and N. S. King. 1981. Archeological investigations: Davis Creek project area. In King, N. S., R. E. Pepperl, C. R. Falk, P. Sadler, J. S. Smith, M. R. Vorrhies, R. Hartley, and D. Henning. Cultural and paleontological resource investigations within the Calamus and Davis Creek reservoir areas, Nebraska, Appendix A. Lincoln, Nebr.: Division of Archeological Research, Department of Anthropology, University of Nebraska, Technical Report no. 80-04, section 2.

Schuldenrein, J. 1985. Geological and cultural sedimentation patterns at the Royel Goodenow site. Iowa City: 43rd Plains Anthropological Conference, Program and Abstracts:39.

Schultz, C. B. 1932. Association of artifacts and extinct mammals in Nebraska. Bulletin of the University of Nebraska State Museum 1, no. 33:271–82.

————. 1938. The first Americans. Natural History 42, no. 5:346–56, 378.

————. 1983. Early Man and the Quaternary: Initial research in Nebraska. Transactions of the Nebraska Academy of Sciences 11:129–36.

Schultz, C. B., and L. C. Eiseley. 1935. Paleonotological evidence for the antiquity of the Scottsbluff Bison Quarry and its associated artifacts. American Anthropologist 37, no. 2:306–18.

Schultz, C. B., and W. D. Frankforter. 1948. Preliminary report on the Lime Creek sites: New evidence of Early Man in southwestern Nebraska. Lincoln: Bulletin of the University of Nebraska State Museum 3, no. 4, pt. 2:43–62.

Schultz, C. B., G. C. Lueninghoener, and W. D. Frankforter. 1948. Preliminary geomorphological studies of the Lime Creek area. Lincoln: Bulletin of the University of Nebraska State Museum 3, no. 4, pt. 1:31–42.

————. 1951. A graphic resume of the Pleistocene of Nebraska (with notes on the fossil mammalian remains). Lincoln: Bulletin of the University of Nebraska State Museum 3, no. 6:1–41.

Stacy, H. E. 1949. Invertebrate paleontology and paleoecology of the Late Pleistocene of the Lower Medicine Creek Valley, Nebraska. Master's thesis, University of Nebraska, Lincoln.

Stout, T. M., V. H. Dreeszen, and W. W. Caldwell. 1965. Central Great Plains, International Association for Quaternary Research VIIth Congress Guidebook for Field Conference D. Lincoln: Nebraska Academy of Sciences.

Tanner, L. G. 1982. Geologic relations at the Clary Ranch site, Ash Hollow, Garden County, Nebraska. Lincoln: Proceedings of the Nebraska Academy of Science 92nd Annual Meeting:52.

Wedel, W. R. 1949. Archaeological researches in the Missouri Basin by the Smithsonian River Basin Surveys and cooperating agencies. American Antiquity 14:257–59.

Wenzel, L. K., R. C. Cady, and H. A. Waite. 1946. Geology and ground-water resources of Scottsbluff County, Nebraska. Washington, D.C.: U.S. Geological Survey Water-Supply Paper 943.

Winham, R. P., S. R. Holen, S.R., E. J. Lueck, E.J., and L. A. Hannus. 1988. Archeological sample survey of selected lands in the Buffalo Creek drainage, Dawson and Custer Counties, Nebraska, vol. 1. Sioux Falls, S.Dak.: Archeology Laboratory of the Center for Western Studies, Augustana College, Archeological Contract Series no. 41.

CHAPTER SEVEN

Resumé of Geoarchaeological Research on the Northwestern Plains

John Albanese

INTRODUCTION

Archaeological geology, also referred to as geoarchaeology, developed as an offshoot of Quaternary geology in the 1930s following the discovery in 1926 of the Folsom site in New Mexico, where extinct bison and associated projectile points were found in situ. The site was excavated by J. D. Figgins, a vertebrate paleontologist associated with the Colorado Museum of Natural History (now the Denver Museum of Natural History). Figgins expended much effort to convince the archaeological community of the validity of the association between artifacts and extinct bison. Two subsequent field seasons and visitations by notables in the profession, including Barnum Brown of the American Museum of Natural History, Frank H. H. Roberts Jr. of the Smithsonian Institution, and A. V. Kidder of Phillips Academy, finally resulted in the acceptance by the archaeological community of the antiquity of humans in North America (Wormington 1957:23–25).

Following the Folsom discovery, archaeologists and geologists realized that it was mutually beneficial to cooperate in site investigations. The archaeologists gained knowledge of the relative age of prehistoric sites and some insight into past climates, while the geologists benefited by gathering data that allowed reconstruction of a regional alluvial chronology, an endeavor being pursued in the southwestern United States in the 1920s (see Haynes 1969:592). Before the advent of radiocarbon dating in 1949 (Libby et al 1949), the main effort in the geologic investigation of a prehistoric site was to determine the site's age. This effort involved a stratigraphic-geomorphic approach through which, ideally, strata within the site could be traced laterally into nearby mountains and placed in a stratigraphic context relative to an existing glacial sequence. There were, however, many problems with this approach. In some cases, site strata could not be traced laterally into equivalent sediment, or terrace treads that were being traced disappeared. Another problem was that even if correlations could be made between strata in a site and a glacial sequence, opinions varied on the relative ages of the glacial sequences and their synchroniety.

Another difficulty was the confusion concerning projectile point names, equivalent typologies, and chronology. Currently, most Paleoindian projectile points can be differentiated on the basis of appearance. A fluted Folsom point, dated at 10,800 radiocarbon years, has a completely different form than a Hell Gap point, dated at 10,000 years. However, in the 1930s and early 1940s these differences were not recognized by all, and the term "Yuma Point" (named after Yuma County in northeastern Colorado), was used to encompass all Paleoindian point types other than Folsom. This practice resulted in confusion and caused consternation among archaeologists. It was not until the late 1940s that Marie Wormington (1948, 1957) finally brought order to Paleoindian projectile point classification.

Although archaeological sites often yielded the remains of animals, the late Pleistocene and Holocene vertebrate fossil sequence was not defined well enough in the 1930s and 1940s to allow its use in dating a site. The fossil record and its interpretation have improved greatly over the past fifty years. Kirk Bryan (1951) presented a cogent discussion of the pitfalls in determining the relative ages of sites.

The introduction of radiocarbon dating in 1949 (Libby et al. 1949) had a profound effect on the fields of archaeology and Quaternary geology. The dating of sediments became less arduous and far more accurate. This new data also led to the understanding that landscapes and associated deposits were more complicated than previously thought. For example, geomorphologists realized that the age of sediment beneath the surface of an alluvial terrace could vary considerably across a valley floor and within a drainage basin.

The geographic area under discussion in this chapter includes the northwestern portion of the Great Plains and adjacent basins and mountain ranges (map 7.1). It encompasses those portions of Wyoming, Montana, and northern Colorado that lie east of the Continental Divide, as well as western Nebraska and western North and South Dakota. It largely coincides with the Northwestern Plains as define d by Frison (1991: 5). It is a large area (approximately 950 x 550 km) and contains very diverse topography and biological communities. The centers of some basins receive as little as 15 cm of precipitation per year, while mountainous areas, some of which exceed 4,100 m in height, can receive as much as 80 cm per year. It is a land of extremes. The climate of the Northwestern Plains is generally harsher than it is in areas to the east, though it is unwise to make generalizations about the area, particularly when one is considering prehistoric ecotones (see Albanese and Frison 1995). The region has a relatively low population, a situation that probably also existed in prehistoric times.

Before the 1970s the investigation of archaeological sites within the Northwestern Plains was primarily an activity performed by the academic community. However, a combination of events during the late 1960s resulted in the expansion of the archaeological profession. These events included the passage of two federal laws: the National Historic Preservation Act (NHPA) of 1966 and the National Environmental Protection Act of 1969 (NEPA). Both laws required the mitigation of cultural resources that would be affected by a federal action.

In addition, an energy boom occurred in the late 1970s and early 1980s and involved large-scale development of oil, gas, coal, and uranium resources. The area within the Northwestern Plains most affected was Wyoming, which is richly endowed with energy resources and where the federal government owns approximately 50 percent of the land. Federal agencies began to require that cultural resource surveys be conducted on affected public lands and that any impacted sites be mitigated.

As a consequence, government bureaus became larger, and a whole new industry evolved: contract archaeology. A prime example of the economic law of supply and demand subsequently developed. The number of archaeologists rose dramatically to satisfy the needs of the contract archaeology business. This rise was accompanied by an increase in the size of anthropology departments in colleges and universities. The nature of the archaeological profession also changed dramatically. Specifically, more than half of its practitioners were now engaged in consultation work for industry. This was in contrast to prior years, when only a small group of academic researchers predominated. It is perhaps a

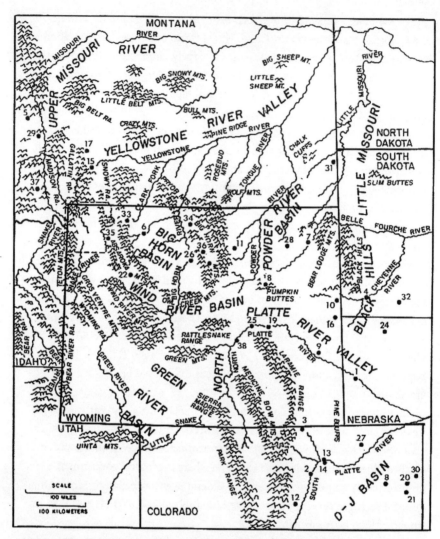

Map 7.1. The Northwestern Plains, showing locations of sites listed in text: 1) Scottsbluff; 2) Dent; 3) Lindenmeier; 4) Ray Long; 5) MacHaffie; 6) Horner; 7) McKean; 8) Claypool; 9) Hell Gap; 10) Agate Basin; 11) Sisters Hill; 12) Lamb Spring; 13) Jurgens; 14) Frazier; 15) Myers-Hindman; 16) Betty Greene; 17) Anzick; 18) Ruby; 19) Glenrock Buffalo Jump; 20) Selby; 21) Dutton; 22) Lookingbill; 23) Little Canyon Creek Cave; 24) Hudson-Meng; 25) Casper; 26) Colby; 27) Frasca; 28) Carter-Kerr McGee; 29) Indian Creek; 30) Jones-Miller; 31) Milliron; 32) Lange-Ferguson; 33) Dead Indian; 34) Hanson; 35) Mummy Cave; 36) Medicine Lodge Creek; 37) Barton Gulch; 38) Dunlap-McMurray.

natural development that educational institutions, as well as private firms, became involved with contract archaeology. At the University of Wyoming, where George Frison was both department head and state archaeologist, a large contract group evolved within the Office of the Wyoming State Archaeologist. Contract archaeology groups also formed at Colorado State University at Fort Collins, Western Wyoming College at Rock Springs, University of Northern Colorado at Greeley, and Montana State University at Bozeman. The differences between academic researcher and consultant became blurred. Most of the academic contract groups are still in operation.

The meteoric rise during the 1970s and 1980s of the number of field archaeologists was accompanied by an increase in the number of people engaged in archaeological geology. However, the number of archaeological geologists working in the Northwestern Plains has always been small. Before the late 1960s there were a few academicians, all of whom were associated with universities or colleges located outside the region (e.g., John Moss, of Franklin and Marshall College in Pennsylvania, and C. Vance Haynes, at the University of Arizona). Things have changed somewhat over the past two decades; there are now five individuals other than myself who currently live in the area and are actively engaged in geoarchaeology.

The initial impetus for geoarchaeological studies in the Northwestern Plains was the investigation of Paleoindian sites. Few sites of younger age were geologically investigated before the 1970s. In his authoritative and comprehensive review of archaeology on the Northwestern Plains, Frison (1991) lists a total of 54 stratified sites with a Paleoindian component, of which 31 (57 percent) are located in Wyoming. Information gleaned from the literature and my own personal files indicated that 36 (67 percent) of them were subjected to a geologic study. Frison's (1991) selective listing includes 133 excavated sites younger than Paleoindian. Of these 31 (23 percent) were investigated by a geoarchaeologist. The bulk of these investigations occurred after 1970.

Much of the remainder of this chapter is a chronicle of past geoarchaeological activity on the Northwestern Plains. It will be concerned mainly with personalities and events. Most of the information is taken from the literature, though some is also derived from personal acquaintance with many of the principal characters. For ease in discussion, the historical review is divided into five main time periods: 1930–42, 1946–59, 1960–69, 1970–79, and 1980–89. I will not attempt to include an account of all site investigations, but will emphasize geoarchaeologic activities at the more significant sites.

PERIOD 1930–1942

Probably the first detailed description of a stratigraphic column at a Paleo-indian site located in the Northwestern Plains occurred in 1932 with the publication of a paper describing the occurrence of both artifacts and extinct bison at the Scottsbluff Bison Quarry site situated in extreme northwestern Nebraska (map 7.1) (Barbour and Schultz 1932; Schultz and Eiseley 1935; May, this volume). Bison bone and eight artifacts, including a Scottsbluff type projectile point, were found within a 60–120-centimeter-thick gravel deposit, overlain by silt and sand, which in turn were overlain by loess (Wormington 1957:118).

According to Wormington (1957:43), "The first generally accepted discovery of a fluted point unmistakably associated with articulated mammoth remains was made near Dent, Colorado in 1932" (map 7.1). After a flood, the bone bed was discovered lying next to railroad tracks by Frank Garner, a section foreman with the Union Pacific Railroad. Garner reported the find to Father Conrad Bilgery of Regis College, who identified the bone as mammoth and began excavating the site, aided by some of his students. He recovered a large projectile point beneath the pelvis of one of the animals. Father Bilgery turned over the project to J. D. Figgins of the Colorado Museum of Natural History, who continued to excavate during the 1933 field season. Two projectile points and the remains of twelve mammoths were recovered during the two seasons of excavations (Wormington 1957:44). However, geologic studies were not attempted during these excavations.

In 1954 Harold Malde of the United States Geological Survey (U.S.G.S.) investigated the geologic setting of the Dent site. He felt that "the bones and artifacts were emplaced during a glacial phase, possibly the Mankato, or an early phase of glacial recessional time" (Wormington 1957:44).

The site was reexamined in the early 1970s by Frank Frazier and Linda Spikard of the University of Colorado Museum, who concluded that the bone and projectile points had been redeposited—a conclusion already reached by Father Bilgery, the original investigator (Cassels 1983:47). An unpublished manuscript about the Dent site was filed at the University of Colorado Museum (Spikard 1972). In 1973 the Dent site was revisited by Joe Ben Wheat, an archaeologist with the University of Colorado Museum, and C. Vance Haynes, a geoarchaeologist from the University of Arizona. Their investigation revealed the presence of an additional mammoth, bringing the total to thirteen. Haynes again visited the site in 1992, accompanied by Michael McFaul, a soils scientist from Laramie, Wyoming, who conducted core-hole testing. According to Haynes (personal communication, 1995), the site lies on a remnant of the Kersey Terrace. The mammoth bones are within a thin deposit of fluvial sands and gravels that overlie the main Pleistocene gravel that caps the terrace. Bedding within the bone deposit led Haynes to conclude that the bones had been redeposited, but he suggested that they had been transported only a short distance. The site is currently being reexamined by Robert Brunswick, an archaeologist associated with the University of Northern Colorado at nearby Greeley (Haynes, personal communication, 1995).

One of the premier Paleoindian sites in North America is the Lindenmeier site located in northeastern Colorado (map 7.1). Most of the information concerning this major Folsom site was derived from Wormington (1957) and Wilmsen and Roberts (1978), who proclaimed: "Lindenmeier is by any measure, the largest Paleolithic site yet discovered in the Western Hemisphere. The quantity and variety of materials preserved here is greater than that yet found at any other site of comparable age in The New World" (Wilmsen and Roberts 1978:17). The site, discovered in 1924 by members of the Coffin family, lies 2.8 km south of the Wyoming state line and 43 km due north of the city of Fort Collins. It was excavated each year from 1934 to 1940 by Frank H. H. Roberts Jr. of the Smithsonian Institution. Interestingly enough, adjoining excavations were conducted in 1936 and 1937 by members of the Coffin family and in 1935 by a team from the Colorado Museum of Natural History (now the Denver Museum of Natural History). The site was visited in 1935 by Kirk Bryan, Professor of Geology at Harvard, pioneer geoarchaeologist, and one of the foremost Quaternary investigators in the western United States. Bryan returned to Lindenmeier in 1936 with one of his graduate students, Louis Ray. Although Bryan started the geologic investigation in 1935, most of the project work was done by Ray from 1936 to 1938 and was the subject of his doctoral thesis. The main thrust of the investigation was to correlate the sediments at the site with the Pleistocene sequence in the nearby Front Range of the Rocky Mountains, the foothills of which lie only 5 km due west of the Lindenmeier site. The construction of a geomorphic and stratigraphic sequence and chronology to use to determine the relative age of the site, entailed the tracing of the Pleistocene terrace system present in the site area into the glacial morainal sequence present in the high mountain core. This is not a simple task, and it has severe limitations because an association between stratigraphic units cannot always be established. The results of this work were published by Bryan and Ray (1940), who concluded that the Folsom occupation at the Lindenmeier site occurred in post-Mankato time, which marks the end of the Pleistocene period (Wormington 1957:39). Charcoal from the Folsom horizon at the site yielded a radiocarbon age of 10,780 ± 135 (I-141) (Haynes and Agogino 1960). Bryan and Ray (1943) also investigated the stratigraphy at the site and described three Quaternary units above the Brule Formation (Oligocene bedrock). Haynes and Agogino (1960) reexamined the sediments at the site and recognized seven depositional units above bedrock, separated by either unconformities or disconformities. Geologic investigations at Lindenmeier were renewed in the summer of 1995, when Vance T. Holliday, a geomorphologist at the University of Wisconsin, and Vance Haynes drilled a number of core holes in the site area.

Period 1946–1960

Shortly after World War II, excavation was initiated at the MacHaffie site near Helena, Montana (map 7.1). This site, which contained Folsom and Scottsbluff cultural horizons, was examined by professional archaeologists in 1949 and 1950 and excavated in 1951 under the direction of Richard Forbis of Columbia University (Forbis and Sperry 1952). The initial investigations at the site were conducted without the aid of a geologist. The MacHaffie site was reentered years later, in 1989, and was excavated by Montana State University, under the direction of Leslie Davis. I was brought into the project as a consulting geoarchaeologist in 1989. The site is unusual because it is located within the modern channel area of a fourth-order ephemeral stream (Albanese 1991). The Paleoindian horizons are associated with an alluvial sequence, and an overlying colluvial unit contains at least six cultural horizons dating to the Archaic and Late Prehistoric periods.

The year 1946 was marked by the initiation of a program that included widespread cultural resource surveys of the Missouri River drainage system. Emphasis was placed on locales that were the proposed sites for major dams. This survey and mitigation effort was directed by the Smithsonian Institution. In 1947 the Ray Long site was discovered near Hot Springs, South Dakota (map 7.1), by J. M. Shippee, a member of a Smithsonian Institution Missouri River Basin Survey team. The crew was investigating the area of the proposed Angostura Reservoir, along the Cheyenne River. Here, the river cuts across the southern end of the Black Hills. Excavation work at the Ray Long site occurred from 1948 to 1951, mainly under the direction of Richard P. Wheeler of the Smithsonian Institution. A cultural horizon was encountered that yielded a late Paleoindian, Angostura-type projectile point (Hughes 1948). However, few artifacts were recovered from the site. A stratigraphic succession was identified and correlated throughout the site by the work crew (Wheeler n.d.). In addition, a study of the terrace system and sediment adjacent to the Cheyenne River was carried out by White and Hughes (n.d.). They concluded that much of the sediment at the site was colluvium derived from the adjoining bedrock of the Pierre Shale (Upper Cretaceous).

The Ray Long site is currently being reinvestigated under the direction of Adrian Hannus of Augustana College in Sioux Falls, South Dakota. Excavation and exploratory trenching were carried out in 1985 and from 1991 to 1995. I conducted geologic investigations at the site in conjunction with the archaeological studies. The evidence secured from this effort indicates that the four cultural levels at the Ray Long site are incorporated in deposits of a complex alluvial fan system that developed in the Cheyenne River valley between 10,300 and 7000 radiocarbon years B.P. (Hannus et al 1993).

The Horner site, the type site of the Cody Complex, was discovered by Jimmy Allen in 1939. It is situated on the northwestern margin of the Bighorn Basin just east of the town of Cody, Wyoming (map 7.1). Allen showed the site to Dr. Glenn Jepsen, Professor of Vertebrate Paleontology at Princeton University, in 1948. Jepsen began excavation at the site in 1949, inaugurating an excavation program that lasted through 1952, though it is uncertain just how much excavation work was carried out in 1950 and 1951 (Wedel 1987). The University of Pennsylvania was invited to join the venture in 1948, before excavation. Pennsylvania accepted, and their representative was Loren C. Eiseley, chairman of the anthropology department. The partnership between the two institutions lasted until the late 1950s, when the University of Pennsylvania withdrew from the project because of conflict between Jepsen and Eiseley.

The Horner site was visited by Kirk Bryan on a number of occasions. He and Jepsen corresponded early in 1950, and some of the correspondence concerned the problems between Jepsen and Eiseley. Bryan wrote as follows on March 11:

> I am not sure that I am a success at the diplomacy necessary with archaeologists. They depend on patronage and fight for it. They are divided

into fighting groups. If you are friends with one group, you have trouble
with others. All I do is play the dumb geologist. I never admit that I
know anything about anthropology or archaeology. I never quote one
archaeologist to another if I can avoid it, and I have a few other rules.
Mainly I am just a blundering and dumb geologist.... Does all this help
you? Gossip is highly prevalent in this field and much more common
than among us. Every one of these sites is chewed over in private correspondence and by word of mouth to an extent that is hard to realize.
(Wedel 1987).

It is sad that, while later visiting the Horner site, Kirk Bryan died unexpect-
edly in Cody on August 22, 1950 (Schullinger 1951).

Other geologists visited and worked at the site, mainly during 1950.
Sheldon Judson spent five days at the site during June 1950. He presented the
results of his work in an unpublished paper (Judson 1950). John Schullinger,
an undergraduate student at Princeton, spent the summer of 1950 carrying
out geologic studies at the site, including drilling 130 auger holes and excavating five profile trenches. He described the results of his work in an unpublished senior thesis (Schullinger 1951) submitted to the Princeton University
Department of Geology. The quality of the fieldwork was excellent by the
standards of 1950 and even by present standards would be regarded as quality
work. Interestingly enough, Schullinger was not a geology major but took geology courses to satisfy the science requirements in the curriculum he was taking for entry into medical school.

John Moss, of Franklin and Marshall College, and two students brought a
drilling rig to the Horner Site during the summer of 1950. Schullinger (1951)
reports that Moss drilled core holes and excavated trenches within and adjacent to the Horner site. Some of the recovered sediment samples were sent
back to the Princeton geologic laboratory for analysis. According to Wedel
(1987), Moss was also at the Horner site in 1952 and "made extensive test borings on the site terrace." Unfortunately, none of the results of Moss's investigations in the specific area of the site were ever reported. However, the results
of Moss's regional investigation of the Pleistocene terraces along the
Shoshone River later appeared in two publications: Moss and Bonini (1961)
and Moss (1974).

Arthur Montgomery, of Lafayette College, studied Pleistocene terrace gravels in and around the Horner site during a visit to the area in 1952. Montgomery's main interest was the identification of the various rock types within

the gravels and their specific sources. He presented the results of this research in a report submitted to Jepsen (Montgomery 1953).

Excavation at the Horner site was completed at the end of the 1952 field season. Waldo Wedel, of the Smithsonian Institution, was the archaeologist at the site during the last field season. Wedel (1987) has presented a detailed account of the history of excavations at the Horner site, particularly on the activities of the various individuals involved with the project and correspondence between them. Much of this account concerning the history of the site was taken from Wedel's 1987 summary.

According to Judson (1950) and Schullinger (1951), the cultural horizons at Horner are associated with floodplain deposits of the Shoshone River, the present channel of which lies 296 meters northwest of the site. The river drains through a 43-meter-deep, 183-meter-wide, steep-sided canyon. If Judson and Schullinger are correct, the present canyon has formed in less than 8,500 years, which was the period of the initial prehistoric occupation in the area excavated by Princeton University.

George Frison (University of Wyoming) reentered the project, and he began excavating at the Horner site in 1977 and continued excavations during 1978 and 1980. Much of the impetus for reentering the site came from the lack of published data. A formal report giving the results of Princeton's four years of investigation was never issued. Only a few brief accounts concerning excavations had been published, one of which was contained in a Princeton Alumni Newsletter (Jepsen 1953). In addition to the Cody Complex occupation, which dated to approximately 8500–6600 B.P. (Frison and Todd 1987: 98), Frison uncovered a lower and older bison bone bed with associated artifacts that yielded radiocarbon ages of 9875 ± 85 B.P. (SI-4851 A) and 10,060 ± 220 B.P. (I-10900). This lower Alberta/Cody horizon rests directly on Pleistocene gravels (Frison and Todd 1987:98).

Multidisciplinary investigations conducted at the site included studies of the geology, soils, and opal phytoliths, as well as vertebrate and invertebrate fossils. I conducted the geologic studies, and the soils were studied by Richard Reider of the University of Wyoming. The results of these studies indicate that the terrain in the area has changed little during the past 10,000 years; the Shoshone Canyon appeared much the same at the time of the Paleoindian occupations as it does today (Albanese 1987:325). The sedimentology and stratigraphy at Horner indicate that the site was situated on the edge of a playa during much of the time of the Cody Complex occupation (Albanese 1987:

Fig. 7.1. The Horner site, 1977. View to the north. Photograph by George Frison.

279–326). Additional information concerning the Horner site can be found in figures 7.1 and 7.2 and map 7.2.

Excavations were begun at a number of other archeological sites in the early 1950s, including the McKean site located in northeastern Wyoming and the Claypool site in northeastern Colorado (map 7.1). The McKean site was discovered by a Smithsonian Missouri River Basin crew in 1948, the same year in which the Ray Long site was found. The McKean site is the type site for the Middle Archaic cultural complex, which suddenly and dramatically appeared over all of the northern Plains approximately 5,000 years ago (Frison 1991:24). The site is in the northern part of the Black Hills where the Belle Fourche River has cut a canyon through the outcrops of the Fall River (Dakota) Sandstone.

The McKean site was excavated by William Mulloy (University of Wyoming) in 1951–1952, before it was inundated by the waters of Keyhole Reservoir. Mulloy joined the faculty of the University of Wyoming in 1949 while he was completing work on a doctorate from the University of Chicago. The same year Jimmy Allen (discoverer of the Horner site) directed Mulloy's attention to a late Paleoindian location (the James Allen site) in the Laramie Basin of southeastern Wyoming. Mulloy and students excavated the site in 1951, 1953, and 1954 (Mulloy 1959a). Mulloy also worked at other sites in Wyoming and

Fig. 7.2. The Horner II bison bone bed excavated in 1977–78 by the University of Wyoming at the Horner site (see map 7.2 for location). Photograph by George Frison.

Montana and subsequently developed a cultural chronology for the Northwestern Plains (Mulloy 1958). This chronology is still the fundamental framework, although subsequent modifications have been made.

Mulloy's report (1954) on the McKean site lacked information on stratigraphy and sediments. A map of the Holocene terrace system present in the area of the site was prepared by Brainard Mears, geomorphologist at the University of Wyoming, although no discussion of the geomorphology of the area accompanied the map. The site lies on the highest Holocene Terrace (T3) at the channel of the Belle Fourche River. Sandstone outcrops of the Fall River Formation lie adjacent to the T3 terrace tread (Albanese 1985)

The McKean site was reinvestigated in 1983 by George Frison. Several years of drought had resulted in much lowering of the level of Keyhole Reservoir and exposing of the area in the vicinity of the McKean site. The Bureau of

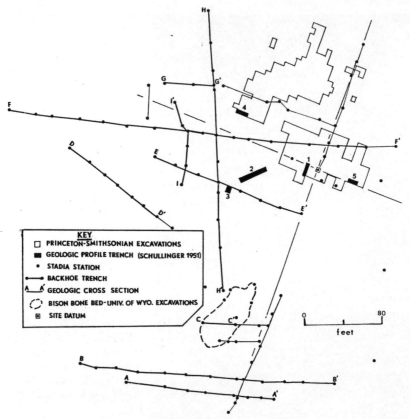

Map 7.2. Map showing locations of excavated areas, geologic profile trenches, and cross sections at the Horner site (from Albanese 1987:fig. 8.1). Courtesy of Academic Press.

Reclamation decided that the site should be revisited and sponsored Frison's investigation. The 1983 investigation was a multidisciplinary effort that was reported upon by Kornfeld and Todd (1985). The report included my geologic study and a pedological study by Richard Reider (University of Wyoming). In his original studies, Mulloy delineated two cultural horizons: a lower McKean layer (Middle Archaic) and an upper horizon containing artifacts of Late Archaic style. Both horizons were marked by a dark gray color and were separated by light colored sediment. Mulloy attributed the dark color in both horizons to staining by charcoal as a result of human activity, even though individual charcoal grains were rare (Mulloy 1954:436). The results of the 1983

investigations led to the conclusion that the dark-colored horizons were actually the A horizons of soils that are developed within a sandy colluvial sequence
that comprises the bulk of the Holocene sediment at the site (Albanese 1985:54).
I present this latter interpretation not to impugn the previous work at the
McKean site, but merely to show that interpretations change with time.

Located in Washington County, the Claypool site was the first stratified
Cody Complex occupation to be excavated in eastern Colorado. The site occurs
within an elongate, blowout depression in eolian sheet sand. It is located on
the western edge of a large, northeast-trending dune field that extends into
Yuma County, the home of the "Yuma Point," a generic term used in the 1930s
to describe most post-Folsom age, Paleoindian projectile points. During the
early 1950s, a mammoth bone and Clovis point were discovered in a blowout
at Claypool. In 1953 Herbert W. Dick (University of Colorado Museum) excavated the site and discovered both Scottsbluff and Eden projectile points, a
Cody knife, and other artifacts, as well as bone. All were obtained from the
same stratigraphic horizon called the "B" soil. A graver was also found at the
surface "5 feet" west of the mammoth bones that had been found earlier (Dick
and Mountain 1960:233–43).

The Claypool site was first examined geologically in 1941 by Paul H.
Gerhard, a consultant who attempted to determine the stratigraphic relationships of artifacts in Yuma County (Gerhard 1949:132–43). In 1954, following
the University of Colorado Museum excavation, Harold Malde of the U.S.G.S.
conducted a geological investigation of the site. Malde concluded that the
Cody Complex artifacts occurred within eolian sands deposited "under conditions that were cool and dry, . . . possibly during the retreat of Valders ice
that began about 10,000 years ago." He suggested that a moderately mature
"Brown Soil" about five feet thick developed on the surface of the sand-sheet
about 7,000 to 5,000 years ago during a moist phase of the Thermal Max-
imum, and that the underlying artifacts were 10,000 to 7,000 years old (Malde
1960:236). Malde's age estimates were made without the benefit of radiocarbon dates. The mammoth bones were found in a marl bed below the earlier
sand-sheet. Malde correlated the marl with the Grand Island Formation
(Kansan) and the Sappa Formation (early Yarmouthian). Hence he concluded
that the bones were too old to be associated with the Clovis projectile point
and nearby graver.

The Claypool site was revisited in 1975 when the Smithsonian Institution
conducted archaeological and geological investigations under the direction of

Dennis Stanford. Exploratory backhoe trenches totaling 30 meters in length
were excavated as well as 60 square meters of site area. I carried out the geologic work, and Richard Reider (University of Wyoming) studied the soils.
The 1975 excavations were located to the west of the original 1953 work area.
Debitage and four chert artifacts, including a Cody knife, were recovered. The
evidence was in agreement with Dick's original conclusion that the site was a
camp and not a bison kill. However, the geologic evidence secured in 1975
indicated that some of the Cody Complex artifacts were not in situ but were
redeposited by postoccupation deflation. Dick's "B" soil that envelops the
main Cody Complex horizon probably is a Udipsamment. It has a 0.75 meter-
thick, brown-to-dark-brown (10YR) A horizon that may be a product of a
lush or long-term growth of grasses (Reider 1990:340). Evidence obtained in
1975 also suggested that the marl layer containing the mammoth bones may
date to the late Pleistocene. Therefore, the association of mammoth bone and
Clovis artifacts might not be fortuitous (Stanford and Albanese 1975:28).

A geologic publication that had a major effect on archaeological perspective within Wyoming and adjacent areas was published in 1954. This was
U.S.G.S. Water Supply Paper 1261, "A Post Glacial Chronology for Some
Alluvial Valleys in Wyoming," by Luna Leopold and John Miller. This paper
described the Holocene terrace system in eastern and central Wyoming, with
emphasis on the Powder River drainage system. Leopold and Miller recognized a three-tiered, paired-terrace system along the Powder, Belle Fourche,
Cheyenne, Big Horn, and Popo Agie Rivers. The three terraces, in ascending
order, were named the Lightning, Moorcroft, and Kaycee. Along the Powder
River, the Lightning terrace lies 1.2 to 2.0 meters above the river's floodplain;
the age of the alluvial fill beneath the terrace tread was estimated at 800 B.P.
The Moorecroft terrace lies 3.6 to 5 meters above the floodplain and was dated
at 2500–1000 B.P. The earliest terrace, the Kaycee, lies 6 to 15 meters above the
floodplain and its alluvial fill was dated at 4000–2500 B.P. These estimates
were made without the benefit of radiocarbon ages because much of the fieldwork was conducted prior to the advent of radiocarbon dating.

Leopold and Miller believed that the terraces and associated alluvium
could be correlated over large areas, and that the geologic events that led to
terrace formation were also regionally synchronous. This hypothesis of regional
synchroniety captured the imagination of archaeologists, who recognized that
at long last a tool was available that would allow the determination of the ages
of archaeological sites over a large area. Jack Hughes, an investigator at the Ray

Long site, had attempted to correlate projectile point typology with a terrace sequence along the Cheyenne River in South Dakota (Hughes 1950). Efforts were made to date sites and sediment using the Leopold and Miller model (e.g., Haynes and Grey 1965). Even today, one occasionally hears an investigator place a name on a specific terrace using the Leopold and Miller terminology and then attempt to use it to infer the age of a prehistoric feature associated with the terrace.

Unfortunately, the real world is more complicated. With the advent of radiocarbon dating and more extensive field data, it became apparent that the Leopold and Miller model was too simplistic. Hadley and Schumm (1961) determined that the number of terraces can vary along a given drainage system and that alluviation and erosion can also occur simultaneously along different portions of an individual stream channel. Studies also revealed that, within the same drainage basin, the age of sediment beneath a given terrace tread can vary considerably from one location to another (Albanese and Wilson 1974:8–18; Albanese 1978:375–89).

PERIOD 1960–1969

The decade of the 1960s was marked by a dramatic increase in the excavations of Paleoindian sites and the use of the multidisciplinary approach to site investigation. Soil scientists became part of the investigative team, and discussions of soils became increasingly common in site reports. The trend to a multidisciplinary approach arose because archaeologists realized that an understanding of past human activity required knowledge of the biological and climatic environment in which prehistoric peoples lived. This knowledge could only be obtained by combining information derived from other disciplines (geology, soils science, paleobotany, vertebrate paleontology, etc.).

The emphasis on the multidisciplinary approach to site interpretation was evident at the Hell Gap site, a premier Paleoindian site located within the Precambrian core of the Hartville Uplift in eastern Wyoming (map 7.1). The site was discovered in 1959 by James Duguid and Charles McKnight, amateur collectors, and reported to George Agogino, then at the University of Wyoming. The results of testing by Agogino and C. Vance Haynes (University of Arizona) in 1959 and 1960 led to full-scale excavations by Harvard University and the University of Wyoming during the period 1961–1966. The investigative team included archaeologists Cynthia Irwin-Williams, Henry Irwin, and George Agogino, as well as geologist C. Vance Haynes, palynologist P. J. Mehringer, and paleontologist Michael Roberts.

The Hell Gap site lies within the south-trending Hell Gap Valley, which is drained by a fourth-order, ephemeral stream. Four localities, spread over about 700 meters of stream bank, were excavated. Eight Paleoindian occupations, which yielded Goshen, Folsom, Midland, Hell Gap, Alberta, Cody, Frederick, and Lusk style projectile points, were documented at the site. C. Vance Haynes identified seven stratigraphic units of alluvial, colluvial, and eolian origin, as well as several paleosols. The two basal stratigraphic units are Pleistocene while the overlying units range from early to late Holocene. The oldest radiocarbon age secured from the basal Holocene unit is 10,840 ± 200 B.P. (A-303) (Irwin-Williams et al. 1973:44). A detailed report concerning the results of the excavation at Hell Gap was never published. The only published information is contained in a summary article in an issue of the *Plains Anthropologist* (Irwin-Williams et al. 1973:40–53).

In 1995 George Frison secured a substantial grant from the National Endowment for the Humanities to synthesize all of the information previously gathered at Hell Gap. In addition new information, including radiocarbon ages and other multidisciplinary data, is being acquired as a result of recent excavations. C. Vance Haynes is part of the present investigative team and is updating the work he did at the site in the 1960s. This update includes the acquisition of many more radiocarbon ages to develop a more detailed geochronology.

In 1960, in addition to working at Hell Gap, Haynes and Agogino carried out excavations at the Sister's Hill site located on the northwestern flank of the Powder River Basin (map 7.1). The bases of three Hell Gap projectile points, as well as stone tools, were secured from a sandy silt interbedded with carbonaceous horizons (Agogino and Galloway 1965:191). Haynes recognized the three-tiered alluvial terrace system of Leopold and Miller (1954) along an ephemeral tributary to Sand Creek, which passes through the site area. He also recognized eight depositional units, of which the basal one is Pleistocene. The succeeding five units appear to be early Holocene and yielded radiocarbon ages of 9600 ± 241 B.P. (I-221) and 9650 ± 250 B.P. (I-221). The uppermost two units are middle and late Holocene in age. Haynes also analyzed a pollen column that was dominated by pine, suggesting that the vegetative ecotone present in the foothills of the Big Horn Mountains has remained much the same during the past 10,000 years (Haynes and Grey 1965:196–211). The foothills lie only five kilometers to the west of the site.

The Sister's Hill site was reentered in 1978 by George Frison. I examined the sediments in the new excavation pits and backhoe trenches, while Richard Reider (University of Wyoming) carried out soil studies. A complete Hell Gap point and associated stone artifacts were recovered in the new excavations. Reider (1983:117–27) concluded that the Hell Gap cultural layer lies within an Aquoll soil (Humic Gley) that formed under a high water table present along the stream that flows adjacent to the site, which resulted in strong gleying and mottling in subsoils. He also recognized a calcareous Altithermal paleosol in sediments above the Hell Gap cultural layer. This change in soil types is interpreted by Reider to have resulted from a climatic change from cool-moist conditions to a warm-dry regime.

In 1968 C. Vance Haynes published a paper titled "Geochronology of the Late Quaternary Alluvium" (Haynes 1968:591–631). This was a revision of previous chronologies by Bryan (1941), Antevs (1948, 1955) and Miller (1958), of which all but the last study was formulated without the benefit of radiocarbon ages. Within the late Pleistocene and Holocene strata of the western Plains, Haynes recognized five depositional units separated by unconformities. On the basis of stratigraphic succession and radiocarbon ages, these units were traced from Wyoming southward through Colorado, New Mexico, and Arizona. Much of the data were derived from his own studies.

The Lamb Spring site, located south of Denver and 3.2 kilometers east of the foothills of the Front Range, was excavated in 1961–1962 by Waldo Wedel of the Smithsonian Institution. The site was discovered in 1960 by Charles Lamb, who noticed fossil mammal bones while excavating a stock pond at the spring. He notified the U.S.G.S. and the site was subsequently visited by Glenn Scott, a geologist, and C. Edward Lewis, a paleontologist. They noted the presence of an extinct Pleistocene fauna, including mammoth, horse, camel, bison, and antilocaprid. While conducting hand auger tests, they found a number of worked chert flakes. The possibility of an association between humans and extinct fauna was obvious, so the Smithsonian Institution was invited to investigate.

National Science Foundation funding was secured for Lamb Spring, and Waldo Wedel subsequently arrived with a field assistant, George Metcalf. Other members of the field team were Glen Scott and Holmes Semken, both geologists, and paleontologists G. L. Gazing of the Smithsonian, Bertrand

Schultz of the Nebraska State Museum, and C. Edward Lewis. An extensive buried bison bone bed and two associated Cody Complex projectiles were found adjacent to the spring vent. A Duncan (Middle Archaic) point was found in an overlying stratum. Two other artifact-bearing horizons were found above the Duncan horizon. The package of Quaternary sediment is approximately 3 meters thick, and the microstratigraphy is complex, probably because of mixing by spring action. A radiocarbon age of 13,140 ± 1000 B.P. (M1464) was determined on collagen from a bone recovered at the base of the Quaternary sequence. Although no stone artifacts were found at the bottom of the sequence, a number of flaked mammoth and camel bones were recovered. The possibility of a pre-Clovis occupation led to a retesting of the site in 1979 by Dennis Stanford of the Smithsonian Institution. The remains of three mammoths were found in a backhoe trench. During the following 1980 field season, additional mammoth remains were discovered, bringing the total to two dozen mammoths. Other animal remains included horse, camel, and a coyote-sized canid (Stanford et al. 1981:14–27). The conclusions reached after the 1981 field season were that two major unconformities existed, each defined by a channel. The Cody Complex and younger artifacts lie in the upper channel, while the remains of the mammoth lie within the lower channel. It was also noted that the upper channel cut into the lower one. Some stone artifacts were found in the lower mammoth bed, but the relationship to the mammoth remains is ambiguous (Rancier et al. 1982).

In 1963 John H. Moss returned to northwestern Wyoming to conduct geologic studies at the Mummy Cave site. The site is located 19 kilometers east of Yellowstone Park on the banks of the North Fork of the Shoshone River (map 7.1). It lies within the Absaroka Mountain range, which has a volcanic-igneous origin. This is a major site with thirty-eight cultural horizons that yielded radiocarbon ages that ranged between 9230 B.P. and 370 B.P. An abundance of perishable material (e.g., leather and feathers) was also encountered in the cultural horizons contained within 8.5 meters of detrital sediment. This sediment filled a large overhang cut into volcanic bedrock by the channel of the North Fork of the Shoshone River (Wedel et al. 1968:184–86). The excavation was carried out during 1963 and 1964 under the direction of the Whitney Museum of Art (Cody, Wyoming), and the National Geographic Society provided financial support during 1964. The investigative team included Wilfred Husted, an archaeologist with the Smithsonian River Basin Surveys. Husted had spent the 1962–69 field seasons excavating overhangs in the nearby Bighorn River Canyon, which contained Paleoindian cultural horizons. Waldo Wedel, who had worked at the Horner site, was the principal adviser. In addition, the team included H. E. Wright, pollen analysis; John Moss, geologist; William Mulloy, adviser; and Robert Edgar, excavation field foreman. The project director was Harold McCracken, an art historian and director of the Buffalo Bill Historic Center (McCracken et al. 1978). McCracken did not participate in the field excavation per se but, according to participants, did enjoy the publicity associated with the project. One such episode occurred when a complete, clothed, mummified, male body was encountered with burial goods, including bow and arrows. The burial is radiocarbon dated at 1216 ± 110 B.P.

The overhang at Mummy Cave that contains the archaeological horizons is approximately 45 meters wide and 12 meters deep. The sediment that filled it accumulated by the exfoliation of igneous bedrock (fragmental andesite tuff-breccia), which exhibits sheet jointing (Moss 1978:35–40). In 1967 Moss returned to Mummy Cave and dug a trench to bedrock using power equipment. Money for this project was obtained from the National Science Foundation. An interesting aspect of Moss's investigation was the conclusion that the channel of the North Fork of the Shoshone has remained at its present elevation for at least the past 10,000 years.

In the late 1960s the momentum in Paleoindian studies moved southward into Colorado to the vicinity of the town of Kersey and the nearby Kersey Terrace of the South Platte River. Two sites, Jurgens and Frazier, located 1.6 kilometers apart, are situated on top of the terrace in an area located 26 kilometers downstream from the previously discussed Dent site (map 7.1). The Jurgens site was discovered in 1965 by Frank Frazier, a geologist who was investigating gravel deposits along the South Platte River. The site was excavated in 1968 and 1970 under the auspices of the National Science Foundation and the supervision of Joe Ben Wheat of the University of Colorado Museum and Marie Wormington, research associate at the museum. Harold Malde of the U.S.G.S., who had previously worked at the Claypool and Dent sites, was project geologist. The Jurgens site was a composite camp and bison kill site that contained Cody Complex artifacts. The prehistoric artifacts and bone are contained within a thin succession (less than 1 meter thick) of sand and clay lenses that fill a swale-like depression atop Pleistocene gravels (Wheat 1979). Marie Wormington had excavated the Frazier site in 1967. It contained bison bone and Agate Basin style artifacts (Wormington 1984:12–13).

Harold Malde also studied the geology of the Frazier site (Wheat 1979: 151–53). The stratigraphic succession at this site was the same as at Jurgens. The interesting thing about both sites is the thinness of the early Holocene stratigraphic column and the lack of a geomorphic feature that could serve as a natural trap for containing bison.

Not all significant Paleoindian sites excavated during the 1960s received a detailed geologic examination. Although there are various reasons for the absence of geologic assessments at some important sites, it was often due to restricted funding or lack of access to a geologist. Restricted funding was the case at the Myers-Hindman site near Livingston, Montana (Lahren 1976), and there was no access to a geologist at the Betty Greene site (Greene 1967) located in eastern Wyoming, approximately 40 kilometers south of the Agate Basin site (map 7.1).

The Anzick site, located in south-central Montana, exemplifies another problem researchers encountered (map 7.1). This Clovis burial site yielded the skeletal remains of two subadults plus approximately one hundred stone and bone artifacts (Lahren and Bonnichsen 1974; Wilke et al. 1991). It was discovered in May 1968 by two workmen who were using power machinery to gather fill material from a talus slope. They noted a flaked stone artifact and dug into the burial with shovels, unearthing some ninety bone and stone artifacts, as well as human skeletal material coated with red ochre (Lahren and Bonnichsen 1972). Shortly afterward D. C. Taylor and a crew from the University of Montana arrived on the scene and spent two weeks excavating. Taylor concluded that the original context had been thoroughly mixed and disturbed and that the original stratigraphic relationships were not decipherable because nothing had been left in situ (Taylor 1969).

In 1971 the Anzick site was reinvestigated by Lahren and Bonnichsen, who dug a series of trenches adjacent to the burial and one pit at the burial. The trenches outside the burial area penetrated archaeological material that yielded a radiocarbon age of 1,160 ± 90 B.P. (Gak 3287). In the burial area, they unearthed the clavicle of a one-year-old child covered with red ochre. Their investigation concluded that the Clovis artifacts and human remains were contained in "an extremely dry zone consisting of sandy clay and small angular rubble immediately above bedrock" (Lahren and Bonnichsen 1972). I visited the site in 1981 and carried out a geologic investigation in collaboration with Lahren and Bonnichsen. The Clovis material had been contained in a small rock shelter located at the base of a steep, high slope that lies adjacent to the south bank of Flathead Creek. By 1981 all of the original Quaternary sediment had been dug and removed from the rock shelter. Backhoe trenches were dug in the areas peripheral to the rock shelter. However, the trenches only penetrated sediment of late Holocene age.

Not all geoarchaeological investigations carried out in the Northwestern Plains during the 1960s were concerned with Paleoindian sites. I investigated two sites of more recent vintage in 1968–69 and 1969–70. These were the first archaeological sites that I worked on. The first site was the Ruby site, a Late Archaic (Besant) bison kill in the Powder River Basin of Wyoming (Frison 1971) (map 7.1). The second site was the Glenrock Buffalo Jump, a Late Prehistoric bison jump located on the southern rim of the Powder River Basin (Frison 1970) (map 7.1). The principal investigator at both sites was George Frison (University of Wyoming). The Ruby site was interesting from both archaeological and geological viewpoints. It contains post molds that are the remnants of a former bison "holding pen" structure. It was evident that a major regional cycle of stream incision had occurred after the site was last occupied around 1600 B.P. (Albanese 1971). An interesting sidelight concerning the Glenrock Buffalo Jump was a problem about determining its age. Radiocarbon ages of 260 ± 100 B.P. (M 2349) and 190 ± 100 B.P. (M 2350) were secured from two horizons within the bone bed. Alluvium of late Holocene age, which contains redeposited bison bone derived from the site, lies adjacent to the site within a channel depression that formed after the site was occupied. If the young radiocarbon ages secured from the site were valid, they indicated that major geomorphic changes had occurred along the nearby North Platte River during historic time. Using age estimates of terrace development by Leopold and Miller (1954), as well as those of Haynes and Grey (1965) at Sisters Hill, it was estimated that the site must be at least 450 to 750 years old (Albanese 1970:62). This estimate was made before the advent of calibration curves for correction of radiocarbon dates. Using present-day corrections, the original radiocarbon dates and geologic age estimates are compatible.

PERIOD 1970–1979

During the 1970s archaeological geology was accepted by other geologists as a legitimate endeavor. The first Geological Society of America (GSA) symposium concerning archaeological geology was held in Dallas, Texas, on November

12, 1973. The session was cochaired by C. Vance Haynes and Harold E. Malde. Seven papers were presented, including my own on the Casper site. The GSA meeting was typical in that it was well attended and had many sessions. However, almost the only attention that it received from the Dallas newspapers was a feature article concerning a paper in the archaeological symposium, in which Virginia Steen-McIntyre, Ronald Fryxell, and Harold Malde advocated a 245,000 year age for an archaeological site in Valsequillo, Mexico.

The decade of the 1970s was also one of change in the fields of archaeology and archaeological geology. A new set of academic players arrived early on the scene, later to be augmented by a large contingent of contract archaeologists. The discovery of bone tools, dated at 27,000 years B.P., in the Old Crow area of the Canadian Yukon (Irving and Harrington 1973:335–40) created a lot of excitement in the archaeological community, and the search for pre-Clovis was on. This enthusiasm extended into the Northwestern Plains. It was most evident in northeastern Colorado, where Dennis Stanford of the Smithsonian Institution, in addition to conducting research at a number of Paleoindian sites, also excavated three sites with evidence that suggested the possibility of pre-Clovis occupation.

Stanford's efforts included the excavation of the Jones-Miller site, a Hell Gap bison kill with the skeletal remains of around three hundred animals; a reentry into the Claypool, Cody Complex site; the investigation of the Frasca site, a Cody Complex bison kill; the excavation of the Dutton and Selby sites; and reentry into the Lamb Spring site (see table 7.1 for dates of excavations). The main incentive for investigating the Dutton, Selby, and Lamb Spring sites was the possibility that all three sites were occupied by humans before the entry of the Clovis people into North America.

The critical point in interpreting what happened at the Lamb Spring site is whether the mammoth bone modification was due to human or natural causes. The evidence is equivocal (Rancier et al. 1982:1–17; Fisher 1992:51–82).

The Dutton and Selby sites lie 27 kilometers apart and are located within 25 kilometers of the eastern border of Colorado. Both were accidentally discovered in the fall of 1975 as a result of the machine excavation of water storage pits. The presence of the skeletal remains of a late Pleistocene fauna at both locales, some of which appeared to have been stacked, led to investigation by the Smithsonian field crew, then working at the Jones-Miller site (Stanford 1979:101–24). Excavations at both sites continued through the 1978 field season. Both Dutton and Selby lie within closed topographic depressions that contained a playa pond, and the stratigraphy at both locales was essentially the same. The playa depressions were incised into Peorian Loess and subsequently filled with lacustrine sediment. A thick, dark gray surface soil (Holocene) that is underlain by a gley soil was also present at both sites (Reider 1978). Clovis artifacts were recovered from the Holocene soil at Dutton. The gley soil contained mammoth bone at Selby, but at Dutton much of the soil had been removed by machinery. The lacustrine unit at both locales contains an abundant megafauna, including mammoth, horse, camel, bison, sloth, peccary, deer, and antelope bones. The remains of smaller animals were also found. The Peoria Loess is the lowest stratigraphic unit examined at both locations, and it contains remains of grassland herbivores such as horse, camel, and bison. Mammoth bones were not recovered from the Peoria Loess at either site (Stanford 1979:104).

The vertebrate remains at the Dutton and Selby sites were analyzed by Russell Graham of the Illinois State Museum. Graham concluded that almost all of the megafaunal species at Dutton and Selby are grazers characteristic of an open grassland (Graham 1981). The age of the Peorian Loess in nearby Nebraska ranges from about 23,000 B.P. at the base to 12,000– 11,000 B.P. near the top (Johnson et al. 1993). Items made from bone, which could be interpreted as artifacts, were recovered at both sites, particularly in the lacustrine unit. At Dutton the lacustrine unit also yielded seven tiny, impact flakes (Stanford 1979:113–15). Stanford in 1979 (ibid.) felt that the evidence leaned towards a human origin for the recovered "bone tools." However, in 1983, based on natural bone modification research by Gary Haynes, he slightly altered his view and stated, "but at present a clear and simple resolution is not possible" (Stanford 1983:69).

References to possible pre-Clovis occupation sites outside of northern Colorado are rare. One exception is the Little Canyon Creek rock shelter site located in the Bighorn Basin of Wyoming (map 7.1). Within the sediment column that fills this overhang, lithic artifacts lie at the same stratigraphic position as bones of musk ox, collared lemming, and a large canid. An unconformity is present above the zone of artifacts and bone. Radiocarbon ages of 8790 ± 210 B.P. (RL 640) and 10,170 ± 250 B.P. (RL 641) were secured above the unconformity (Shaw and Frison 1979).

Table 7.1 presents a list of some of the prehistoric sites within the region that were subjected to scrutiny by a geologist and/or pedologist during the 1970s. Several of the listed sites have been described elsewhere in this chapter. From a

Table 7.1 Sites Excavated During the 1970s in the Northwestern Plains

Site Name	Principal Investigator	Year of Excavation	Geologist	Soils Scientist	Site Reference	Geology/Soils Reference	Remarks
Casper, WY	G. C. Frison	1971	John Albanese		Frison (1974)	Albanese (1974)	The skeletal parts of 77 Bison Antiquus and Hell Gap style projectile points were recovered from the blowout portion of a parabolic sand dune.
Dead Indian, WY	G. C. Frison	1972	John Albanese	Richard Reider	Frison and Walker (1984)	Albanese (1984) Reider (1984)	Middle Archaic camp site located on third Holocene terrace above Dead Indian Creek. Site contains well developed "Altithermal soil."
Hudson-Meng, NE	L. Agenbroad	1971–77	Larry Agenbroad		Agenbroad (1978)	Agenbroad (1978)	Bison bone bed with skeletal remains of approximately 600 animals. Contains Alberta cultural material. Postulated to be bison jump. Site reentered in 1991, by investigators L. Todd and D. Rapson, sponsored by U. S. Forest Service.
Lookingbill, WY	G. C. Frison	1972–92	James Miller	Richard Reider	Frison (1983)	Reider (1990)	Campsite at spring in mountainous area. Occupied from Paleoindian through late Prehistoric time.
Jones-Miller, CO	D. Stanford	1973–75	John Albanese	Richard Reider	Stanford (1978)	Albanese (1976) Reider (1976, 1990) Stanford (1978)	Bison bone bed with remains of approximately 300 bison with associated Hell Gap artifacts. Located on third Holocene terrace above Arikaree River.

Table 7.1 Sites Excavated During the 1970s in the Northwestern Plains (*continued*)

Site Name	Principal Investigator	Year of Excavation	Geologist	Soils Scientist	Site Reference	Geology/ Soils Reference	Remarks
Hanson, WY	G. C. Frison	1973–76	John Albanese	Richard Reider J. P. Moore	Frison and Bradley (1980)	Moore (1976)	Folsom camp site, located within alluvial sediments beneath T3 terrace adjacuent to Davis Draw. Site reentered in 1987–88 by Eric Ingbar.
Claypool, CO	D. Stanford	1975 (reentry)	John Aalbanese	Richard Reider	Stanford and Albanese (1975)	Reider (1990) Albanese (1980)	Cody Complex cultural horizon contained within eolian sheet sands; camp site; deflated.
Dutton, CO	D. Stanford	1975–78	John Albanese David Bannan	Richard Reider	Stanford (1979)	Bannan (1980) Reider (1978, 1990) Stanford (1979)	Playa in Peoria Loess. Late Pleistocene fauna are contained in both late Pleistocene lacustrine sediment of pond and in Peoria Loess. Clovis artifacts recovered from surface sedimant. Evidence for human occupation during late Pleistocene is equivocal.
Selby, CO	D. Stanford	1975–78	John Albanese David Bannan	Richard Reider	Stanford (179)	Bannan (1980) Reider (1978, 1990) Stanford (1979)	Playa in Peoria Loess. Late Pleistocene fauna are contained in both late Pleistocene lacustrine sediment of pond and in Peoria Loess. Evidence for human occupation during late Pleistocene is equivocal.
Colby, WY	G. C. Frison	1973–78	John Albanese		Frison and Todd (1986)	Albanese (1986a)	Skeletal remains of 7 mammoth and associated Clovis artifacts were contained within the basal portion of an abandoned arroyo that was originally 11 m deep with a floor width of ±10m.

Table 7.1 Sites Excavated During the 1970s in the Northwestern Plains (*continued*)

Site Name	Principal Investigator	Year of Excavation	Geologist	Soils Scientist	Site Reference	Geology/ Soils Reference	Remarks
Dunlap-McMurray Burial, WY	G. Ziemens	1975	John Albanese		Ziemens et al. (1976)	Ziemens et al. (1976)	An early Plains Archaic burial and campground lie within ephemeral stream sediments. Burial is dated at 5250 ±150 RCYBP.
Lamb Spring, CO	D. Stanford	1979–81 (reentry)	Glenn R. Scott		Stanford et al. (1981) Stanford (1983) Rancier et al. (1982) Fisher (1992)	Stanford et al. (1981) Stanford (1983) Rancier et al. (1982) Fisher (1992)	Spring area with upper archaeological horizons (Cody Complex and younger) and lower mammoth bone horizon with ±40 individual animals.
Carter-Kerr McGee, WY	G. C. Frison	1977	John Albanese	Richard Reider	Frison (1984)	Reider (1980a, 1990)	Multicomponent paleoindian site (Goshen through Cody Complex); cultural horizons enclosed in colluvium that accumulated in first-order ephemeral stream draw.
Agate Basin, WY	G. C. Frison	1972, 1975–80 (reentry)	John Albanese	Richard Reider	Frison and Stanford (1982)	Albanese (1982) Reider (1982a, 1982b, 1990)	Multicomponent paleoindian site complex (Clovis-Hell Gap), preserved in ephemeral stream sediments within abandoned (captured) arroyo segement of Moss Agate Draw.
Laddie Creek, WY	G. C. Frison	1976	John Albanese	Eric Karlstrom and Richard Reider	Larson (1990)	Karlstrom (1977) Reider and Karlstrom (1987) Albanese (1977)	Middle Archaic site with Cody Complex and late Prehistoric components. Cultural horizons lie within colluvial and alluvial sediments on T2 terrace, abundant springs in area; well developed "spring" soils.

Table 7.1 Sites Excavated During the 1970s in the Northwestern Plains (*continued*)

Site Name	Principal Investigator	Year of Excavation	Geologist	Soils Scientist	Site Reference	Geology/ Soils Reference	Remarks
Medicine Lodge Creek, WY	G. C. Frison	1974–75	Charles Love	1973–75	Frison (1976)		Multicomponent site (Paleoindian through late Prehistoric) within alluvial-colluvial sequence beneath T3 terrace, adjacent to large overhang.
Copper Mountain, WY	C. Zier	1978–79	John Albanese	Richard Reider	Zier et al. (1987)	Albanese (1980b) Reider (1980b) Zier et al. (1987)	Large sale cultural resources management project. Multiple archaeological horizons ranging in age from 10,000 B.P. to late Archaic, enclosed in alluvial sediment.
Sisters Hill, WY	G. C. Frison	1978 (reentry)	John Albanese	Richard Reider		Reider (1983, 1990)	Buried Hell Gap cultural horizon in alluvial sequence. previously excavated by Agogino and Haynes (see text).
Frasca, CO	D. Stanford	1979–80	John Albanese		Fulgham and Stanford (1982)		The site is a Cody Complex bison kill. The remains of approximately 56 bison were recovered from the narrow bottom remnant of a former arroyo.

Table 7.1. List of sites excavated during the 1970s in the northwestern Plains, in which archaeological geology studies were carried out (see Map 7.1 for locations).

geoarchaeological viewpoint, some of the more interesting sites are Casper, Hudson-Meng, Lookingbill, Colby, Agate Basin, and Carter-Kerr McGee.

The Casper site, which lies at the edge of the city of Casper, Wyoming (map 7.1), was discovered April 2, 1971, by two amateur archaeologists (R. Laird and D. Egolf). George Frison and a crew arrived at the site the next day (Frison 1974:57). The site was a Hell Gap bison kill, where at least seventy-four *Bison antiquus* were trapped and killed in a blowout of a parabolic sand dune (see figs. 7.3, 7.4). A playa pond formed at the site after the Hell Gap bison kill. The pond sediment formed a seal that prevented further deflation and resulted in preservation of bison remains. The site lies within the Casper Dune Field, one of the three major sand dune fields within the state (Albanese 1974:173–90). This is the first documented case in the region of a natural geomorphic feature in a sand dune being used as a bison trap by Paleoindians. Several years later, George Frison reentered the site because it was going to be destroyed by building construction. The archaeological salvage operation yielded bison bone plus the skeletal remains of a camel (George Frison, personal communication, 1980).

The Hudson-Meng site, located in southwestern Nebraska (map 7.1), was excavated between 1971–77 by Larry Agenbroad of Chadron State College (see May, this volume). Alberta style, Paleoindian artifacts were found associated with a large bison bone bed that contains the remains of approximately six hundred animals. Agenbroad (1978) postulated that the site was a bison jump. The site was reentered in 1991 by Lawrence Todd of Colorado State University and David Rapson of the University of Wyoming under the sponsorship of the U.S. Forest Service, which plans to construct a large visitor center at the site. The new investigation includes excavation of the bone bed, as well as the large-scale exposure by machinery of sediment outside the bone bed area, to secure an understanding of the paleogeomorphology of the site. In addition, extensive studies of the taphonomy of the bone bed have also been undertaken. The evidence secured from these studies to date suggests that the physiography required for a bison jump is not present and that most of the approximately six hundred bison died of natural causes (Redmond 1994). Just what the natural phenomenon was that caused the sudden death of such a large number of bison is open to speculation.

The Lookingbill site is located within the Bridger Mountains of northwestern Wyoming. It is an extensive campsite that contains numerous cultural horizons that span Paleoindian, Early Archaic (Altithermal), Middle and Late Archaic, and Late Prehistoric periods. It lies within and adjacent to a moun-

Fig. 7.3. The Casper site. There is a windrow of bison bone (Hell Gap horizon, Unit B) exposed in a blowout depression at the bottom of an ancient parabolic dune. Photograph by George Frison.

tain meadow with associated springs and perennial stream. Based on soil evidence, a wet meadow has existed in the area nearly continuously since the late Pleistocene (Reider 1990:349). The position of the interface between the two main lithologic facies at the site (colluvium and alluvium) has remained nearly constant throughout the same time period. This interface is less than two meters wide (Reider 1990:349; and Albanese, field notes, 1988). From a geomorphic viewpoint the site area has been remarkably stable for more than 10,000 years. The permanent nature of the springs, which emanate from the Madison Limestone of Mississippian age, has undoubtedly been an important factor in maintaining a stable ecologic and geomorphic environment.

The Colby site, located on the eastern side of the Bighorn Basin of Wyoming, contained the remains of seven mammoths and some associated Clovis artifacts. The bones and artifacts were found on the floor of an abandoned steep-sided arroyo (see map 7.3, fig. 7.5) that was originally ten meters wide at

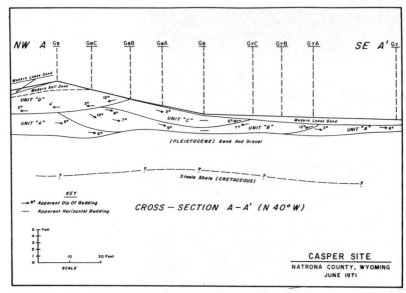

Fig. 7.4. Cross Section A-A' at the Casper Site (from Albanese 1974:fig. 4.4). The Hell Gap bison bone bed lies within Unit B. Courtesy of Academic Press.

its base and eleven meters high (Albanese 1986a:143–64). The bones and artifacts are contained within approximately two meters of preserved ephemeral stream sediment. Some of the mammoth bone has obviously been redeposited, but hydraulic forces were not strong enough to destroy two stacked piles of mammoth bones (see fig. 7.5), which have been interpreted as meat caches (Frison and Todd 1986:139–40). The lack of paleosols and the containment of bone within ephemeral stream sediments suggests that climatic conditions were dry—a situation that would support C. Vance Haynes's hypothesis of drought conditions over much of the United States during the time of Clovis occupation (Haynes 1991:438–50).

The Agate Basin site is one of the most significant Paleoindian sites in the Northwestern Plains. It is located in Wyoming, but lies only 270 meters from the South Dakota border (map 7.1). It is a multicomponent Paleoindian site (Clovis, Folsom, Agate Basin, and Hell Gap) that has had a long and varied investigative history. The site was discovered in 1916 by William Spencer, a rancher who lived near Edgemont, South Dakota. A chance social meeting in 1941 between Spencer and R. E. Frison, a Wyoming game warden, resulted in their visiting the site in 1942. Frison subsequently sent a projectile point and

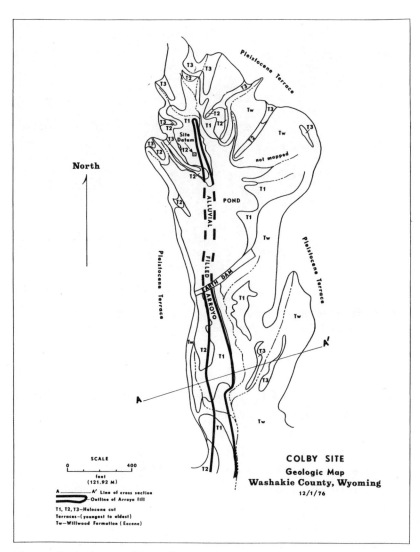

Map 7.3. Geologic map of the Colby Site (from Albanese 1986a: fig. A1.1). The main excavation area is located in vicinity of site datum. Courtesy of the University of New Mexico Press.

Fig. 7.5. Stacked mammoth bone Pile No. 2 at the Colby Site. The bone pile has slumped into an ancient stream channel due to undercutting of the bank. Photograph by George Frison.

some bison teeth to Frank H. H. Roberts (Smithsonian Institution). Roberts tested the site in 1942 and published a brief note concerning the results (Roberts 1943). In 1959 a portion of the site area was investigated by George Agogino, C. Vance Haynes, and W. D. Frankforter, a paleontologist (University of Nebraska Museum). The small test area, named the Brewster site, contained a Folsom horizon (Agogino and Frankforter 1960). Haynes described the stratigraphy and record of sedimentation at the site. This was the first geologic investigation in the Agate Basin site area.

In 1961 Frank H. H. Roberts returned to the Agate Basin site, accompanied by William M. Bass of the University of Kansas. They conducted the first major excavation at the site, but unfortunately they had been preceded by artifact collectors, who had inflicted heavy damage on the Agate Basin cultural horizon. Much of the 1961 field season was spent cleaning up the site, so that excavation could proceed. Regretably, Roberts and Bass did not return to the area. Their excavation pits were not filled and thus provided a guide to projectile point collectors, who then demolished that portion of the site (Frison and Stanford 1982:14). In 1972 the site was visited by George Frison (University of

Wyoming), who tested it and decided that a portion of the site was still intact. Frison again visited the site in 1973 and in 1975 and noted evidence of new and extensive looting. Excavation work was subsequently carried out each summer from 1975 through 1980. This extended study was a multidisciplinary effort that included geologic studies by me and investigation of soils by Richard Reider (University of Wyoming) and Thomas Lee Boyd (University of Wyoming graduate student). The geologic and soil studies indicated that the Paleoindian horizons are preserved in ephemeral stream sediments contained within an abandoned arroyo (Frison and Stanford 1982). The Paleoindian horizons are associated with organic-rich paleosols (Aquolls)(Reider 1982a, 1982b). There is a marked change in types of soils and sediments at the transition from early to middle Holocene that indicates a shift from moist to dry climatic conditions in post-Paleoindian time. The arroyo was no longer an active watercourse due to stream capture by Moss Agate Arroyo during late Holocene time (Albanese 1982:309–30). The spatial relationships between the early Holocene and the modern drainage systems, plus stratigraphy, are shown in map 7.4 and figures 7.6 and 7.7.

The Carter-Kerr McGee site is a multicomponent Paleoindian site (Goshen, Folsom, Agate Basin, and Cody Complex) located in the Powder River Basin of Wyoming (map 7.1). What makes it unusual is that the cultural horizons are contained within a one- to two-meter-thick unit of colluvium that has filled the channel of a minor, first-order, ephemeral stream that still drains the hillside. Aquoll soils are associated with the cultural horizons (Reider 1980a: 301–15). One wonders how such a minor accumulation of sediment survived while exposed at or near the surface for 9,000 years.

PERIOD 1980–1989

The 1980s was a decade of great activity for archaeologists working in the Northwestern Plains. Contract archaeology dominated the profession, both in numbers of people employed and amounts of money expended. The differences between academic and contractor became blurred. College professors commonly worked on contract projects for government or private agencies. A prime example of this occurred at the Milliron site in southeastern Montana (map 7.1). There, from 1985 through 1989, George Frison and a University of Wyoming field crew excavated an 11,000-year-old Goshen campsite. The work

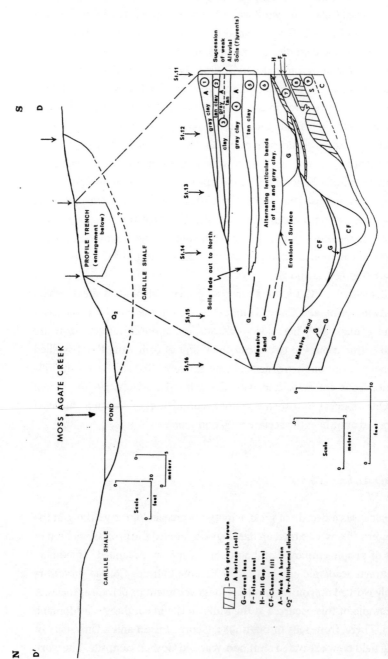

Map 7.4. Agate Basin site, Cross Section D-D'; Hell Gap and Folsom horizons are labeled H and F. (from Albanese 1982: fig. 5.8). The cross section trends south through the approximate center of "Brewster site," which is located on right side of the view shown in fig. 7.6, beyond the pond. Courtesy of Academic Press.

Fig. 7.6. Agate Basin site, view looking south. Moss Agate Creek lies in the approximate center of the photo. The main excavation area lies just beyond the creek, in approximately the center of the photo. Photograph by George Frison.

was done under contract with the Bureau of Land Management as federal mitigator.

The 1980s were also marked by the advent of major contractor mitigation efforts with large industrial projects (usually oil, gas, or coal mine development). Two examples are the Exxon Pipeline Company gas plant project in the Opal Dune Field of southwestern Wyoming and the Bairoil Project, an oil field development project in south-central Wyoming, where in the late 1980s more than one million dollars was spent on cultural resource mitigation (personal communication from Amoco Oil Company manager, 1989). Much of this large-scale archaeological contract work was centered in southwestern Wyoming and in the Powder River Basin of Wyoming and Montana; both areas were affected by extensive oil and gas development. In addition, coal was strip-mined on a large scale in the Powder River Basin.

With all of this activity, one would have expected an explosion in geoarchaeological studies. However, this did not occur. Most cultural resource management consulting firms operating in the Northwestern Plains during the 1980s did not employ geoarchaeologists, because few were available.

Fig. 7.7. Agate Basin site, Hell Gap bone bed in main site area. Photograph by George Frison.

Federal agencies were also not as stringent in regard to a multidisciplinary approach to excavation as they are now. One geoarchaeologist employed by contractors during the 1980s was Dennis Grasso. Grasso had extensive experience in the area and worked on many projects; however, most of the results were not published and the records currently reside in the files of federal agencies. Grasso subsequently received a Ph.D. from the University of Wyoming and is presently employed by the U.S.G.S.

Another geoarchaeologist who spent much time working for the archaeological contracting section of Western Wyoming College was James C. Miller. Much of his experience was in southwestern Wyoming, where the mechanical grain size analysis of eolian sands is standard procedure on many sites because many of the prehistoric sites in that region occur within sand dunes. Miller has also worked as a consultant in the Northwestern Plains and is currently

(1998) pursuing a Ph.D. at the University of Wyoming. A third consulting geoarchaeologist, who worked in Wyoming and Montana during the late 1980s and still maintains an active consulting business in both states, is William Eckerle, who resides in Salt Lake City.

The locus of Paleoindian research shifted away from Wyoming and Colorado during the 1980s. Excavation was initiated at two sites in southwestern Montana: Indian Creek (1982–86) and Barton Gulch (1987–90). The MacHaffie site was also reentered in 1989–90. Leslie Davis of Montana State University directed all three projects. The Milliron site, located in southeastern Montana (map 7.1), was excavated by George Frison. In western South Dakota Adrian Hannus of Augustana College conducted excavations at the Lange-Ferguson site (1980–84), and in 1985 he reentered the Ray Long site.

An interesting aspect of the geologic studies of sites located in the mountainous area of southwestern Montana was an apparent change in sedimentation patterns along valley floors during the transition from early to middle Holocene time. Specifically, the accumulation of alluvial floodplain sediments gave way to alluvial fan and/or colluvial deposition. The transition from floodplain to alluvial fan deposition took place at the Barton Gulch site at approximately 9000 B.P. Alluvial fan deposition persisted until sometime after 3000–2000 B.P. (Eckerle 1988a). The two Paleoindian occupations at Barton Gulch date to 9400 B.P. and 8800 B.P. (Davis et al. 1989).

At the Indian Creek site, located 100 kilometers to the north of Barton Gulch (map 7.1), the same sedimentation pattern occurred, with alluvial fan deposition predominating from 8300–4000 B.P. (Albanese 1986b). The pollen record indicates that the change in sedimentary regime at 8300 B.P. coincides with a transition from coniferous forest to sagebrush steppe. A return to more mesic conditions about 4000 B.P. resulted in the creation of a mixed sagebrush steppe-subalpine coniferous forest (Fredlund and Bozarth 1987). Approximately 8.5 meters of sediment is exposed at Indian Creek, within which are twenty-eight cultural horizons ranging from Folsom to Late Archaic. Both the Glacier Peak layer G and Mazama volcanic ashes can be seen in the steep valley walls created by placer mining operations (Davis and Greiser 1992:235–83).

At the MacHaffie site, located 45 kilometers northwest of the Indian Creek site (both sites lie within the Elkhorn Mountain range), an abrupt change from braided-stream deposition to colluviation also occurred shortly after 8300 B.P. (Albanese 1991). Colluviation was the dominant sedimentary process through the remainder of the Holocene. The approximately 1.5-meter-thick exposure of alluvium contained four Paleoindian horizons: two Folsom and two overlying Cody Complex. Cultural horizons within the upper 1.2-meter-thick deposit of colluvium range from Early to Late Archaic. Pollen analysis indicates that a sagebrush steppe predominated in the general area throughout the Holocene. The valley floor itself was covered by riparian vegetation before 8230 B.P. "Increases in sagebrush pollen immediately thereafter mark the onset of mid-Holocene Altithermal conditions" (Davis et al. 1991).

At the Mill Iron site, located 11.9 kilometers west of the Montana-South Dakota boundary (map 7.1), an 11,000-year-old Goshen cultural horizon lies atop the crest of a butte that stands 25 meters above fourth-order Humbolt Creek. At the time of the Goshen occupation, the land surface was at grade to the channel of Humbolt Creek, which lay 275 meters to the southwest. Since that time, the valley floor has been lowered approximately 18 meters with the resultant development of six terrace surfaces, of which the lower four are strath (erosional) terraces. Sedimentation patterns have remained relatively constant throughout the past 11,000 years with colluvial deposition on valley slopes, alluviation on valley floors, and intermittent episodes of eolian sand accumulation on ridge crests (Albanese 1996). The correlation present in southwestern Montana, between change in type of sedimentation and Holocene climate, is not evident at the Mill Iron site.

In 1980–84, Adrien Hannus excavated at the Lange-Ferguson site in the White River Badlands of southwestern South Dakota (map 7.1). The partial remains of at least two mammoths (Martin 1987:314–32), as well as Clovis artifacts, including two complete points and one partial projectile point, were recovered (Hannus 1990:91). A radiocarbon age of 10,670 ± 300 B.P. (I-11, 710) was secured from an organic-rich soil horizon that lies just above the mammoth bone horizon (Hannus 1990:86). The vertebrate fossils at the site were analyzed by James Martin (South Dakota School of Mines), while the geology of the site was studied by C. Vance Haynes. On the basis of geology and vertebrate fauna, Martin (1987:328) postulated that a pond surrounded by brush and/or woodlands was present at the site during the Clovis occupation.

Haynes (1991:445) reports that the Clovis occupation lies on a buried surface that is erosional in some places and nonerosional in others. The associated mammoth bones are in the laminated, calcareous, diatomaceous silt (Unit C) deposited in a spring-fed pond that lies adjacent to the dry land surface containing the Clovis points and other artifacts. A radiocarbon age of approximately 11,140 ± 140 B.P. (AA-905) was obtained on carbonized plant remains (insoluble residue) from Unit C. Haynes describes the organic-rich soil from which the radiocarbon age was secured as a "gray, wet-meadow soil" that reflects a rebound of the local water table following a brief but significant decline. The decline may have resulted from a prolonged drought that coincided with the time of the Clovis occupation (11,300–10,900 B.P.). According to Haynes (1991:447) this "Clovis drought" occurred throughout much of the United States.

CONCLUSIONS

From the time of the first geologic study of sediment at an archaeological site, which occurred at the Scottsbluff site in 1932, the driving force behind archaeological geologic studies in the Northwestern Plains has been the investigation of Paleoindian sites. Originally, one of the main reasons for carrying out these studies was to determine the age of the site. A prime example of this approach was the fieldwork conducted by Bryan and Ray at the Lindenmeir site from 1935–38. With the advent of radiocarbon dating in 1949, determining the age of a site by geologic techniques became less important and emphasis shifted to the study of geomorphic and sedimentary changes during the Holocene and the development of a regional, stratigraphic chronology as exemplified by the work of C. Vance Haynes in the 1960s. The emphasis on a multidisciplinary approach to site excavation increased in the 1960s and became commonplace thereafter.

The explosion in contract archaeology, occasioned by the energy boom of the late 1970s and early 1980s, resulted in an increase in both the number of geologic investigations and the number of practitioners. Sites other than Paleoindian became common subjects of study by a geologist and/or soils scientist. However, even today, when essentially no Paleoindian site escapes investigation by a multidisciplinary team, many younger sites of consequence are still neglected.

Within the Northwestern Plains, the discipline of geoarchaeology is still in its infancy or, more accurately, is still in the embryonic stage. A very large area contains very little data. Nearly all of the information on the chronology of Holocene sedimentation and pedogenesis has been derived from the study of individual archaeological sites. As yet, no individual drainage basin has been subjected to a detailed analysis of patterns and ages of Holocene sedimentation and terrace development, as has been attempted in the Central Plains (Mandel 1995:37–66) or in the Upper Midwest (Bettis and Hajic 1995:87–114). We do not know the critical factors in the preservation and distribution of early and middle Holocene sediments that would allow us to prospect for Paleoindian and Early Archaic sites, or at least delineate broad areas where they might occur. While carrying out cultural resource management surveys and geoarchaeological work in the Powder River Basin of Wyoming, I have noticed that most exposures of sediment that lie above bedrock are late Holocene in age (Albanese 1990). This anecdotal line of evidence is based on the lack of Aquoll and well-developed calcic soils, each of which are, respectively, diagnostic of early- and middle-Holocene soils (Reider 1990:335–59). The Powder River Basin has enough data, largely derived from extensive cultural resource management surveys and mitigation, to allow the initiation of a detailed study of a drainage basin such as that of the Belle Fourche River.

The formulation of a regional alluvial chronology by Haynes (1968:591–631) and a regional pedogenic synthesis and chronology by Reider (1990:335–59) are the beginnings of an effort that should be expanded in the future. The evidence concerning the synchroniety of climatic, sedimentary, pedogenic, and geomorphic events during the Holocene is ambiguous. The pollen record does not indicate that climatic events were synchronous within the region (Albanese and Frison 1995:4–6). In fact, the past climate record can vary greatly within such a small geographic area as Yellowstone Park (Whitlock and Bartlein 1993:231–38). A divergence in response to climatic change is also seen regionally within the Holocene stratigraphic record (Albanese and Frison 1995:6–10).

However, other lines of evidence suggest that regional "time markers" do exist, and that they can be correlated over large areas. One such marker unit is a Haplargid (argillic) soil associated with eolian dune fields and first identified by Eckerle (1988b) as occurring throughout much of central Wyoming. I have found the same soil in contiguous areas and in sedimentary contexts other than eolian. The soil formed in the period 3500 to 2000 B.P. (Albanese 1995). Another marker is geomorphic and occurred approximately 1,000 years ago. It is a pronounced episode of stream incision that marked the initiation of the Holocene terrace system throughout eastern Wyoming (Albanese 1990). This event may very well correlate with a similar regional episode of stream incision that occurred at the same time in Oklahoma and Texas (Hall 1990:342–45) and Nebraska (Martin 1992:315–22). Obviously, we are only beginning to understand what happened geologically during the Holocene within the Northwestern Plains.

ACKNOWLEDGMENTS

I thank reviewers George C. Frison and David May, and editor Rolfe Mandel for their helpful comments and suggestions, all of which resulted in text clarification and improvement.

REFERENCES

Agenbroad, L. D. 1978. The Hudson-Meng site: An Alberta bison kill in the Nebraska High Plains. Washington, D.C.: University Press of America.

Agogino, G. A., and W. D. Frankforter. 1960. The Brewster site: An Agate Basin-Folsom multiple component site in eastern Wyoming. *The Masterkey* 34:102–107.

Agogino, G. A., and E. Galloway. 1965. The Sisters Hill site: A Hell Gap site in north-central Wyoming. *Plains Anthropologist* 10:190–95.

Albanese, J. P. 1970. Geology of the Glenrock site area. *In* The Glenrock Buffalo Jump: Late prehistoric period of buffalo procurement and butchering on the Northeastern Plains. *Plains Anthropologist Memoir* no. 7:56–66.

———. 1971. Geology of the Ruby site area, Wyoming, 48CA302. *American Antiquity* 36:91–95.

———. 1974. Geology of the Casper archaeological site. *In* Frison, G. C. ed., The Casper site: A Hell Gap bison kill on the High Plains, 173–90. New York: Academic Press.

———. 1976. Geology of the Jones-Miller archaeological site. Washington, D.C.: Department of Anthropology, Smithsonian Institution, unpublished manuscript on file.

———. 1977. Geology of the Laddie Creek archaeological site area, Big Horn County, Wyoming. Laramie, Wyo., Department of Anthropology, University of Wyoming, unpublished manuscript on file.

———. 1978. Archaeology of the Northwestern Plains. *In* Frison, G. C., ed., Prehistoric hunters of the High Plains, 375–89. New York: Academic Press.

———. 1980a. Geology of the Claypool archaeological site, Washington County Colorado. Washington, D.C., Department of Anthropology, Smithsonian Institution, unpublished manuscript on file.

———. 1980b. Geologic report on 48FR579 archaeological site area, Appendix 1. *In* Zier, A., and C. J. Zier, eds., Final report of archaeological survey and test excavations at the Copper Mountain development project, Fremont County, Wyoming, 152–59. Denver: Powers Elevation Company.

———. 1982. Geologic investigation. *In* Frison, G. C., and D. J. Stanford, eds., The Agate Basin site: A record of the Paleoindian occupation of the northwestern High Plains, 309–30. New York: Academic Press.

———. 1984. Geology of the Dead Indian Creek site. *In* Frison, G. C., and D. Walker, eds. Dead Indian Creek site, an Achaic occupation in the Absoroka Mountains of Northeastern, Wyoming. *The Wyoming Archaeologist* 27:101–10.

———. 1985. Geology of the McKean site 48CK7. *In* Kornfeld, M., and L. C. Todd, eds., McKean/Middle Plains Archaic: Current research. Laramie: Office of the Wyoming State Archaeologist, Occasional Papers on Wyoming Archaeology no. 4:63–78.

———. 1986a. The geology and soils of the Colby site. *In* Frison, G. C. and L. C. Todd, eds., The Colby mammoth site: Taphonomy and archaeology of a Clovis kill site in northern Wyoming, 143–64. Albuquerque: University of New Mexico Press.

———. 1986b. Geologic investigation of the Indian Creek archaeological site (24BW626), Broadwater County, Montana. Bozeman, Department of Sociology, Montana State University, unpublished manuscript on file.

———. 1987. Geologic investigations. *In* Frison, G. C. and L. C. Todd, eds., Horner: The type site of the Cody Complex, 279–326. New York: Academic Press.

———. 1990. The geoarchaeology of the eastern Powder River Basin. Cheyenne, State Historic Preservation Office, Wyoming Archives Museums and Historical Department, unpublished manuscript on file.

———. 1991. Geologic investigation, MacHaffie site 24JF4, Jefferson County, Montana. Bozeman, Department of Sociology, Montana State University, unpublished manuscript on file.

———. 1995. A widespread Late Archaic pedogenic marker in Wyoming: An archaeological tool. Plains Anthropological Society, 53rd Anthropological Conference, Program and Abstracts:55.

———. 1996. Geology of the Milliron site. *In* Frison, G. C. ed., The Milliron site, 25–41. Albuquerque: University of New Mexico Press.

Albanese, J. P., and G. C. Frison. 1995. Cultural and landscape change during the middle Holocene, Rocky Mountain area, Wyoming and Montana. *In* Bettis, E. A., III, ed., Archaeological geology and the Archaic period in North America. Boulder, Colo.: The Geological Society of America, Special Paper 297:1–20.

Albanese, J. P., and M. Wilson. 1974. Preliminary description of the terraces of the North Platte River at Casper, Wyoming. *In* Wilson, M. ed., Applied geology and archaeology: The Holocene history of Wyoming. Laramie: Geological Survey of Wyoming, Report of Investigations no. 10:8–18.

Antevs, E. 1948. Climatic changes and pre-white man in the Great Basin, with emphasis on glacial and post-glacial times. *University of Utah Bulletin* 33:168–91.

———. 1955. Geologic-climate dating in the West. *American Antiquity* 20:317–35.

Bannan, D. 1980. Stratigraphy and sedimentology of late Quaternary sediments in the high plains depressions of Yuma and Kit Carson counties, Colorado. Master's thesis, Davis, The University of California.

Barbour, E. H., and B. C. Schultz. 1932. The Scottsbluff bison quarry and its artifacts. Lincoln: Nebraska State Museum, *Bulletin 34* 1:283–86.

Bettis, E. A., III, and E. R. Hajic. 1995. Landscape development and location of evidence of Archaic Cultures in the upper Midwest. *In* Bettis, E, A. III, ed., Archaeological geology of the Archaic period in North America. Boulder, Colo.: The Geological Society of America, Special Paper 297:87–114.

Bryan, K. 1941. Geologic antiquity of man in America. *Science* 62:338–44.

———. 1951. Forward. *In* Moss, J. H. ed., Early man in the Eden Valley. Philadelphia: University of Pennsylvania Museum Monograph 6:1–4.

Bryan, K., and L. L. Ray. 1940. Geologic antiquity of the Lindenmeier site in Colorado. Washington, D.C.: Smithsonian Miscellaneous Collections 99, no. 2.

Cassells, S. E. 1983. The archaeology of Colorado. Boulder, Colo.: Johnson Books.

Davis, L. B., S. A. Aaberg, W. P. Eckerle, J. W. Fisher Jr., and S. T. Greiser. 1989. Montana Paleoindian occupation of the Barton Gulch site, Ruby Valley, southwestern Montana. *Current Research in the Pleistocene 6:7–9.*

Davis, L. B., J. P. Albanese, L. S. Cummings, and J. W. Fisher Jr. 1991. Reappraisal of the MacHaffie site Paleoindian sequence. *Current Research in the Pleistocene* 8:121–22.

Davis, L. B., and S. T. Greiser. 1992. Indian Creek Paleoindians: Early occupation of the Elkhorn Mountains southeast flank, west-central Montana. *In* Stanford, D. J., and J. S. Day, eds., Ice Age hunters of the Rockies, 253–283. Denver: Denver Museum of Natural History and University Press of Colorado.

Dick, H. W., and B. Mountain. 1960. The Claypool site: A Cody Complex site in northeastern Colorado. *American Antiquity* 26:223–35.

Eckerle, W. 1988a. Geoarchaeological analysis of 42MA171: Locality B, 1988 excavation area, early Holocene section. Bozeman, Department of Sociology, Montana State University, unpublished manuscript on file.

———. 1988b. Geoarchaeology of Altithermal sand dunes: Adaptation to eolian environments during the Early Plains Archaic. Master's thesis, Laramie, University of Wyoming.

Fisher, J. W., Jr. 1992. Observations on the late Pleistocene bone assemblage from the Lamb Spring site, Colorado. *In* Stanford, D. J., and J. S. Day, eds., Ice Age hunters of the Rockies, 51–82. Denver: Denver Museum of Natural History and University Press of Colorado.

Forbis, R. G. and J. D. Sperry. 1952. An early man site in Montana. *American Antiquity* 2:127–32.

Fredlund, G. G., and S. Bozarth. 1987. A late Pleistocene and Holocene alluvial record from the Indian Creek archaeological site, Montana. Bozeman, Mont.: Department of Sociology, Montana State University, unpublished manuscript on file.

Frison, G. C. 1970. The Glenrock Buffalo Jump, 48CO304: Late Prehistoric buffalo procurement and butchering. *Plains Anthropologist Memoir* no. 7.

———. 1971. The buffalo pound in Northwestern Plains prehistory: Site 48CA302, Wyoming. *American Antiquity* 36:77–90.

———. 1974. The Casper site: A Hell Gap bison kill on the High Plains. New York: Academic Press.

———. 1976. The chronology of Paleoindian and Altithermal Period groups in the Bighorn Basin, Wyoming. *In* Cleveland, C. E., ed., Cultural change and continuity: Essays in honor of James Bennett Griffin, 147–73. New York: Academic Press.

———. 1983. The Lookingbill site, Wyoming 48FR308. *Tebiwa* 20:1–16.

———. 1984. The Carter/Kerr McGee Paleoindian site: Cultural resource management and archaeological research. *American Antiquity* 49:288–314.

———, ed. 1991. Prehistoric hunters of the High Plains, 2d ed. New York: Academic Press.

Frison, G. C., and B. A. Bradley. 1980. Folsom tools and technology at the Hanson site, Wyoming. Albuquerque: University of New Mexico Press.

Frison, G. C., and D. J. Stanford. 1982. The Agate Basin site: A record of the Paleoindian occupation of the Northwestern Plains. New York: Academic Press.

Frison, G. C., and D. N. Walker. 1984. The Dead Indian Creek site: An Archaic occupation in the Absaroka Mountains of northwestern Wyoming. *The Wyoming Archaeologist* 27:15–122.

Frison, G. C., and L. C. Todd. 1986. The Colby mammoth site: Taphonomy and archaeology of a Clovis kill in northwestern Wyoming. Albuquerque: University of New Mexico Press.

———. The Horner site: The type site of the Cody cultural complex. New York: Academic Press.

Fulgham, T., and D. Stanford. 1982. The Frasca site: A preliminary report. *Southwestern Lore* 48:1–9.

Gerhard, P. H. 1949. An archaeological survey of the blowouts of Yuma County, Colorado. *American Antiquity* 15:132–43.

Greene, A. M. 1967. The Betty Green site: A late Paleoindian site in eastern Wyoming. Master's thesis, Philadelphia, University of Pennsylvania.

Graham, R. W. 1981. Preliminary report on late Pleistocene vertebrates from the Selby and Dutton archaeological/paleontological sites, Yuma County, Colorado. *Contributions to Geology* 20:33–56.

Hadley, R. F., and S. A. Schumm. 1961. Sediment sources and drainage basin characteristics in upper Cheyenne River Basin. Washington, D.C.: U.S. Geological Survey Water Supply Paper 1531-B.

Hall, S. A. 1990. Channel trenching and climatic change in the southern U.S., Great Plains. *Geology* 18:342–45.

Hannus, A. 1990. The Lange-Ferguson site: A case for mammoth bone-butchering tools. *In* Agenbroad, L., J. I. Mead, and L. W. Nelson, eds., Megafauna and Man: Discovery of America's heartland. Hot Springs, S.Dak.: The Mammoth site of Hot Springs South Dakota Inc. *Scientific Papers* 1:86–99.

Hannus, L. A., P. R. Winham, and J. P. Albanese. 1993. Preliminary report, 1992 archaeological investigations at the Ray Long site (39FA65), Angostura Reservoir, South Dakota. Sioux Falls, S.Dak.: Augustana College, Archeological Laboratory, Archeological Contract Series no. 66.

Haynes, C. V., Jr. 1968. Geochronology of the late Quaternary alluvium. *In* Morrison, R. B. and H. E. Wright Jr., eds., Means of correlation of Quaternary successions, 591–631. Salt Lake City: University of Utah Press.

————. 1991. Geoarchaeological and paleohydrological evidence for a Clovis-Age drought in North America and its bearing on extinction. *Quaternary Research* 35:438–50.

Haynes, C. V. Jr., and G. Agogino. 1960. Geological significance of a new radiocarbon date from the Lindenmeier site. Denver: Denver Museum of Natural History, *Proceedings* 9:23.

Haynes, C. V., Jr., and D. C. Grey. 1965. The Sisters Hill site and its bearing on the Wyoming postglacial chronology. *Plains Anthropologist* 10:196–211.

Hughes, J. T. 1949. Investigations in western South Dakota and northeastern Wyoming. *American Antiquity* 14:266–77.

————. 1950. An experiment in the relative dating of archaeological remains by stream terraces. *Bulletin of the Texas Archaeological and Paleontological Society* 21:98–104.

Irving, W. N., and C. R. Harrington. 1973. Upper Pleistocene radiocarbon-dated artifacts from the northern Yukon. *Science* 179:335–40.

Irwin-Williams, C., H. Irwin, G. Agogino, and C. V. Haynes. 1973. Hell Gap: Paleoindian occupation on the High Plains. *Plains Anthropologist* 18:40–53.

Jepsen, G. L. 1953. Ancient buffalo hunters. *Princeton Alumni Weekly* 53:10–12.

Johnson, W. C., D. W. May, and E. Diekmeyer. 1993. A 600 k (?) record of loess deposition and soil development. Lawrence, Kans.: Kansas Geological Survey, Open File Report 93-30:1–21.

Judson, S. 1950. Geology of the Sage Creek (Horner) site, Park County, Wyoming—A preliminary report. Madison, State Historical Society of Wisconsin, unpublished manuscript on file.

Karlstrom, E. T. 1977. Genesis, morphology and stratigraphy of soils at the Laddie Creek archaeological site, Big Horn Mountains, Wyoming. Master's thesis, Laramie, University of Wyoming.

Kornfeld, M., and L. C. Todd. 1985. McKean/Middle Plains Archaic: Current research. Laramie: Office of the Wyoming State Archaeologist, Occasional Papers on Wyoming Archaeology, no.4.

Lahren, L. A. 1976. The Myers-Hindman site: An exploratory study of human occupation patterns in the upper Yellowstone valley from 7000 B.P. to A.D. 1200. Livingston, Mont.: Anthropologus Researches Incorporated.

Lahren, L. A., and R. Bonnichsen. 1972. The Anzick site: A Llano Complex burial in southwestern Montana. Unpublished paper.

———. 1974. Bone foreshafts from a Clovis burial in southwestern Montana. *Science* 186:147–150.

Larson, M. L. 1990. The Archaic of the Bighorn Mountains, Wyoming. Ph.D. diss., Santa Barbara, University of California at Santa Barbara.

Leopold, L. B., and J. P. Miller. 1954. A postgalcial chronology for some alluvial valleys in Wyoming. Washington, D.C.: U.S. Geological Survey Water-Supply Paper 1261.

Libby, W. F., E. C. Anderson, and J. R. Arnold. 1949. Age determination by radiocarbon content: World-wide assay of natural radiocarbon. *Science* 109:227–28.

McCraken, H., W. Wedel, R. Edgar, J. H. Moss, H. E. Wright Jr., W. M. Husted, and W. Mulloy. 1978. The mummy cave project in northwestern Wyoming. Cody, Wyo.: The Buffalo Bill Historical Center.

Malde, H. E. 1960. Geological age of the Claypool site, northeastern Colorado. *American Antiquity* 26:236–43.

Mandel, R. D. 1995. Geomorphic controls of the Archaic record in the Central Plains of the United States. *In* Bettis, E. A., III, ed., Archaeological geology of the Archaic period in North America. Boulder, Colo.: The Geological Society of America, Special Paper 297:37–66.

Martin, C. W. 1992. Late Holocene alluvial chronology and climate change in the Central Great Plains. *Quaternary Research* 37: 315–22.

Martin, J. E. 1987. Paleoenvironment of the Lange/Ferguson Clovis kill site in the bad lands of South Dakota. *In* Graham, R. W., H. A. Semken Jr., M. Graham, eds., Late Quaternary biogeography of the Great Plains and Prairies. Springfield, Ill.: Illinois State Museum Scientific Papers 2:314–32.

Miller, J. P. 1958. Problems of the Pleistocene in Cordillera North America as related to reconstruction of environmental changes that effected early man. *In* Smiley, T. L., ed., Climate and Man in the Southwest, 19–41. Tucson: University of Arizona Press.

Montgomery, A. 1953. Untitled paper concerning pebble counts on terraces and streams in the northwestern Bighorn Basin. Princeton, N.J.: Princeton University, unpublished manuscript on file.

Moore, J. P. 1976. Soil morphology and stratigraphy at the Hanson archaeological site, Big Horn Basin, Wyoming. Master's thesis, Laramie, University of Wyoming.

Moss, J. H. 1974. The relationship of terrace river formation to glaciation in the Shoshone River basin of western Wyoming. *In* Coates, P. R. ed., Pluvial geomorphology. Binghamton: State University of New York *Publications in Geomorphology* 293–314.

————. 1978. The geology of Mummy Cave. *In* McCraken, H., ed., The Mummy Cave project in northwestern Wyoming, 35–42. Cody, Wyo.: The Buffalo Bill Historical Center.

Moss, J. H., and W. E. Bonini. 1961. Seismic evidence supporting a new interpretation of the Cody Terrace near Cody, Wyoming. *Geological Society of America Bulletin* 72:547–56.

Mulloy, W. T. 1954. The McKean site in northeastern Wyoming. *Southwestern Journal of Anthropology* 10:432–60.

————. 1958. A preliminary historical outline for the Northwestern Plains. Laramie: University of Wyoming Publications, no. 31.

————. 1959. The James Allen site near Laramie Wyoming. *American Antiquity* 25:11–16.

Rancier, J., G. Haynes, and D. Stanford. 1982. 1981 investigations at the Lamb Spring site. *Southwestern Lore* 48:1–17.

Redmond, L. A. 1994. Excavations in the non-bonebed area of the Hudson-Meng site, Fiddle Creek, update. Third Annual Island in the Plains Archaeological Symposium, Program and Abstracts:11.

Reider, R. G. 1976. Soil morphology and pedogenesis at the Jones-Miller (Hell Gap) archaeological site, Yuma County, Colorado. Washington, D.C.: Department of Anthropology, Smithsonian Institution, unpublished manuscript on file.

————. 1978. Paleopedology of the Selby and Dutton sites, High Plains, eastern Colorado. Washington, D.C.: Department of Anthropology, Smithsonian Institution, unpublished manuscript on file.

————. 1980a. Late Pleistocene and Holocene soils of the Carter/Kerr McGee archaeological site, Powder River Basin, Wyoming. *Catena* 7:301–15.

————. 1980b. Paleopedology of the 48FR579 (Guffey Peak II) archaeological site, Fremont County, Wyoming, Appendix 11. *In* Zier, A., and C. J. Zier, eds., Final report of archaeological survey and test excavations at the Copper Mountain development project, Fremont County, Wyoming, 160–73. Denver: Powers Elevation Company.

————. 1982a. Soil development and paleoenvironments. *In* Frison, G. C., and D. J. Stanford, eds., The Agate Basin site: A record of Paleoindian occupation of the northwestern High Plains, 331–44. New York: Academic Press.

————. 1982b. The soil of Clovis age at the Sheaman archaeological site, eastern Wyoming. *Contributions to Geology* 21:195–200.

————. 1983. Soils and late Pleistocene-Holocene environments of the Sisters Hill archaeological site near Buffalo, Wyoming. *Contributions to Geology* 22:117–27.

————. 1984. An observation on soil development at the Dead Indian Creek Site. *In* Frison, G. C., and D. Walker, eds., The Dead Indian Creek site, an Archaic occupation in the Absoroka Mountains of northeastern, Wyoming. *The Wyoming Archaeologist* 27:99–100.

————. 1990. Late Pleistocene and Holocene pedogenic and environmental trends in archaeological sites in plains and mountain areas of Colorado and Wyoming. *In* Lasca, N. P., and J. Donahue, eds., Archaeological geology of North America. Boulder, Colo.: The Geological Society of America, Centennial Special 4:335–60.

Reider, R. G., and E. T. Karlstrom. 1987. Soils and stratigraphy of the Laddie Creek site 48BH345, an Altithermal-age occupation in the Big Horn Mountains, Wyoming. *Geoarchaeology: An International Journal* 2:29–47.

Roberts, F. H. H. 1943. A new site. *American Antiquity* 8:100.

Schullinger, J. N. 1951. Geology and chronology at the Horner site, Park County, Wyoming. Senior thesis, Princeton, N.J., Department of Geology, Princeton University.

Schultz, C. B., and L. C. Eiseley. 1935. Paleontological evidence of the antiquity of the Scottsbluff Basin Quarry and its associated artifacts. *American Anthropologist* New Series 3: 306–318.

Shaw, L., and G. C. Frison. 1979. Evidence for pre-Clovis in the Bighorn Basin. Washington, D.C.: Society for American Archaeology, 44th Annual Meeting, Program and Abstracts:72.

Spikard, L. 1972. Progress report of a Dent site investigation. Boulder, Colo.: University of Colorado Museum.

Stanford, D. J. 1978. The Jones-Miller site: An example of Hell Gap bison procurement strategy. *In* Davis, L. B., and M. Wilson, eds., Bison procurement and utilization, a symposium. *Plains Anthropologist Memoir* 14:90–97.

————. 1979. The Selby and Dutton Sites: Evidence for a possible pre-Clovis occupation of the High Plains. *In* Humphrey, R. L., and D. J. Stanford, eds., Pre-Llano cultures of the Americas: Paradoxes and possibilities, 101–24. Washington, D.C.: The Anthropological Society of Washington.

————. 1983. Pre-Clovis occupation south of the ice sheets. *In* Shutler, R., Jr., ed., Early Man in the New World, 65–72. Beverly Hills, Calif.: Sage Publications.

Stanford, D. J., and J. P. Albanese. 1975. Preliminary results of the Smithsonian Institution excavation at the Claypool site, Washington County, Colorado. *Southwestern Lore* 41:22–28.

Stanford, D. J., W. R. Wedel, and G. R. Scott. 1981. Archaeological investigation at the Lamb Spring site. *Southwestern Lore* 47:14–27.

Taylor, D. C. 1969. The Wilsall Site: An exercise in frustration. *Proceedings of the Montana Academy of Science* 29:147–49.

Wedel, W. R. 1987. History of the Princeton and Smithsonian investigations at the Horner Site, the type site of the Cody cultural complex. *In* Frison, G.

C., and L. C. Todd, eds., Horner: The type site of the Cody Complex, 19–38. New York: Academic Press.

Wedel, W. R., W. M. Husted, and J. Moss. 1968. Mummy Cave: Prehistoric record from the Rocky Mountains of Wyoming. *Science* 160:184–86.

Wheat, J. B. 1979. The Jurgens site. *Plains Anthropologist Memoir* 15.

Wheeler, R. P. n.d. Archaeological remains in the Angostura Reservoir area, South Dakota, and in the Keyhole and Boysen Reservoir areas, Wyoming, 501–88. Washington, D.C.: Smithsonian Institution, River Basin Surveys, unpublished manuscript on file.

White, T. E., and J. T. Hughes. n.d. A preliminary appraisal of the physiographic history of Horsehead Creek in the vicinity of 39FA65. Washington, D.C.: Smithsonian Institution, Missouri Valley Project Basin Surveys.

Whitlock, C., and P. J. Bartlein. 1993. Spatial variations of Holocene climatic change in the Yellowstone region. *Quaternary Research* 39:231–38.

Wilke, P. J., J. J. Flenniken, and T. L. Ozbun. 1991. Clovis Technology at the Anzick site, Montana. *Journal of California and Great Basin Anthropology* 13:242–72.

Wilmsen, E. N., and F. H. H. Roberts. 1978. Lindenmeier 1934–1974. Washington, D.C.: Smithsonian Institution, Contributions to Anthropology, no. 24.

Wormington, H. M. 1948. A proposed revision of Yuma Point terminology. *Proceedings of the Colorado Museum of Natural History* 18.

———. 1957. Ancient Man in North America, 4th ed. Denver: The Denver Museum of Natural History, Popular Series no. 4.

———. 1984. The Frazier site, Colorado. *In* Anderson, A. B., ed., Paleoindian sites of the Colorado Pediment. Boulder, Colo.: American Quaternary Association Field Trip Guidebook:12–13.

Ziemens, G. N., D. Walker, T. K. Larson, J. Albanese, and G. W. Gill. 1976. The Dunlap-McMurray burial 48NA67, Natrona County, Wyoming. *Wyoming Archaeologist* 22:15–25.

Zier, C. J., A. G. Hummer, J. P. Albanese, and R. G. Reider. 1987. The Copper Mountain Site: A 10,000 year occupation in the Owl Creek Mountains of central Wyoming. *In* Osborn, A. J., and R. C. Hassler, eds., Perspectives on archaeological resources management, 299–322. Omaha, Nebr.: I and O Publishing Company.

CHAPTER EIGHT

Archaeology and the Earth Sciences on the Northern Plains

Joe Alan Artz

INTRODUCTION

The earth sciences—in particular geology, pedology, and geomorphology—have always played a role in how archaeology was conducted on the Northern Plains, serving primarily as a set of tools or techniques for establishing the sequence, chronology, and environmental context of prehistoric cultures. Prior to the 1970s, however, most archaeological research in the region was anthropological in orientation, focusing on cultural history, cultural evolution, and cultural process. Collaboration with earth scientists was sporadic. Only in recent years have the earth sciences started to play a major role in archaeological excavation and survey projects.

The focus of this chapter is historical trends that marked the emergence and development of geoarchaeology in a portion of the Northern Plains that includes North Dakota, South Dakota, and southern Manitoba and Saskatchewan (map 8.1). However, developments in this region cannot be considered independently of broader historical patterns in the development of archaeology and the earth sciences. For this reason, the chapter begins and ends with a discussion of events and processes that, although occurring outside the Northern Plains, established an intellectual milieu for geoarchaeology in the region and set the pace at which the subdiscipline would slowly develop.

Historical Background

During the 1930s and 1940s many archaeologists working in the Great Plains realized that the earth sciences would play an important role in Plains archaeology. Geological evidence had already proven valuable in demonstrating the antiquity of humans on the Plains (and in all of North America) by helping to establish the stratigraphic association of fluted points and extinct fauna at sites such as Folsom and Clovis (e.g., Figgins 1927; Howard 1935). Other intriguing archaeological occurrences in the Central Plains also held potential for interdisciplinary collaboration. At sites like Signal Butte in Nebraska, William Duncan Strong (1935) found that prehistoric occupational layers often coincided with the A horizons of buried soils. The soils, which he knew represented former stable land surfaces, were overlain by deposits of eolian sediment. Elsewhere in Nebraska, along the Republican River, Waldo R. Wedel found the remains of small agricultural hamlets of the Central Plains Tradition—the abandoned lodges capped over with windblown dust (Wedel 1941).

With the environmental ravages of the "Dirty Thirties" fresh in memory, Wedel and Strong understood the severe challenges that eolian sedimentation and climate change could pose for humans living on the Plains (Wedel 1982:158). Wedel, in particular, was convinced that archaeological and geological records, viewed together, provided evidence that Plains prehistory was one of human adaptation to dynamic oscillations between dry and moist climates (Wedel 1941, 1947, 1953).

In 1953, Wedel issued a strong call for interdisciplinary collaboration, writing:

We will need the full cooperation of competent workers in geology, pedology, and climatology. The climates of the period preceding instrumental observations will have to be determined largely from the land itself, as expressed in terrace and cave fills, soil profiles, and otherwise. These prehistoric soils and surfaces ought to be datable from the archaeological materials in or on them (Wedel 1953).

Wedel and his colleagues envisioned a role for the earth sciences that went beyond the traditional tasks of describing strata and establishing sequence and relative chronology. The geological record was to be used to establish the ecological context of prehistoric cultures on the Plains and to reconstruct the dynamic environments to which human culture had adapted.

The perceived importance at mid-century of interdisciplinary studies is nowhere more evident than in the published proceedings of the Sixth Plains Anthropological Conference, held in 1948. In two back-to-back sessions, archaeologists, geologists, soil scientists, and climatologists discussed what was known about postglacial climates on the Plains. Archaeologists discussed prehistoric sites in buried soils and valley fills. Earth scientists debated terrace sequences and the processes and chronologies of their formation (Jennings 1950; Bettis, this volume). One gets the impression of a group of researchers on the verge of a major advance in interdisciplinary science.

The advance, however, did not happen immediately. Twenty to thirty years would pass before a sustained, productive collaboration between archaeologists and earth scientists emerged in the Great Plains. This chapter seeks to demonstrate that in the Northern Plains of the Dakotas, Manitoba, and Saskatchewan, productive collaboration did not begin until the various disciplines each reached a certain level of sophistication in their individual realms of study.

THE DEVELOPMENT OF GEOARCHAEOLOGY ON THE NORTHERN PLAINS

This review emphasizes projects, events, and publications that are relevant to the realm of study that we today call "geoarchaeology," defined as "the application of concepts and methods of the geosciences to archaeological research" (Waters 1992:3). The chapter focuses on studies that have employed earth science principles to establish the stratigraphic, geomorphic, or geochronologic context of archaeological sites as components of prehistoric landscapes (Butzer 1978, 1982). Geoarchaeology, of course, encompasses a broader spectrum of endeavor. An important aspect of geoarchaeology on the Northern Plains, the characterization of lithic raw materials, is not dealt with here (but see Porter 1962; Clayton et al. 1970; Leonoff 1970; Ahler 1977; Campling 1980; Van Nest 1985; Christensen 1991; Low 1996; Nowak and Hannus 1985), nor are the important efforts at geophysical remote sensing in the region (e.g., Weymouth 1976; Weymouth and Nickel 1977).

The study region selected for this paper (map 8.1), although considered within the Northern Plains by most archaeologists working in the region, actually overlaps the boundary between the Central Lowlands and Great Plains

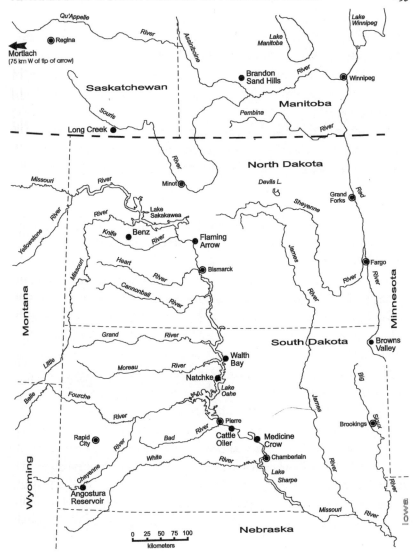

Map 8.1. The Northern Plains of North and South Dakota and adjoining states and provinces, showing locations of archaeological sites and study areas mentioned in text.

physiographic provinces (Fenneman 1931; Osterkamp et al. 1987:164–65). Despite its environmental diversity, the region is characterized by a generally similar environment (rolling, open grassland) that supported broadly similar adaptive systems (an emphasis on bison hunting) throughout prehistory. Archaeologists refer to the Great Plains portion of this region (primarily the Missouri Plateau section of Fenneman 1931) as the "Northwestern Plains" (Frison 1991; Wedel 1961) and to the Central Lowlands portion as the "Northeastern Periphery" (Wedel 1961) or, more recently, "Northeastern Plains" (Schneider 1982). The Middle Missouri subarea of the Great Plains, as defined by archaeologists, refers to the deeply incised valley of the Missouri River in the Dakotas (Wedel 1961; Lehmer 1971).

The following narrative is organized chronologically in four periods, each characterized by differences in the kinds and intensity of archaeological field-work and in the attention that archaeologists have given to geological concerns.

Prior to the 1950s

Prior to the 1950s little work resembling geoarchaeology was done in the Northern Plains. Archaeological studies, beginning in the late nineteenth century, emphasized surface-visible cultural features, such as burial mounds, earth-lodge villages, and boulder outlines, hundreds of which were present in the region (Will 1933; Wedel 1961:212–20, 228–34, 1982:91; Helgevold 1981:8–15; Mayer-Oakes 1967:341). Geologists working in North Dakota and Manitoba in the late nineteenth century sometimes made observations on prehistoric burial mounds and ancient village sites in the course of geological surveys (e.g., Upham 1895). Tyrrell (1892:95, cited by Pettipas and Buchner 1983:426), identified a site on a former Lake Agassiz shoreline where possible chipped stone artifacts occurred in association with moose or elk bone.

Direct collaboration between archaeologists and geoscientists was rare during this period. The few examples include the investigations by Jenks (1936, 1937) of a human burial and associated lanceolate projectile points discovered at Browns Valley, Minnesota (map 8.1). A geologist, Frank Leverett, made observations on the geological context of the find with respect to the shorelines and southern outlets of Lake Agassiz that were relevant to establishing the Paleoindian age of the remains (Leverett 1932; Wormington 1957: 143–44), an inference substantiated by a radiocarbon age of 9094 ± 82 B.P. on bone from the Browns Valley skeleton (Shane 1991).

The lack of collaboration between archaeologists and geoscientists on the Northern Plains stands in contrast to the situation on the Southern Plains. In that region, geologists including Kirk Bryan, Ernst Antevs, and E. H. Sellards made important contributions to Paleoindian studies beginning in the 1920s (Haynes 1990; Ferring 1994; Holliday, this volume). By the 1930s on the Central Plains, the vertebrate paleontologist C. Bertrand Schultz was actively involved in documenting associations between human artifacts and extinct bison (Haynes 1990:63). However, few if any pre-1950s Quaternary scientists developed a deep interest in the Northern Plains archaeological record. Although Antevs and Bryan, among others, argued the antiquity of deeply buried human remains discovered near Fergus Falls, Minnesota, east of the region considered in this paper, their interest in the region appears to have been as brief as their debate was inconclusive (Haynes 1990:59; Bettis, this volume).

Among the earliest examples from the Northern Plains of the use of earth science principles to establish the context of archaeological remains is a report by Sheldon (1905) on prehistoric Indian hearths buried in valley fill sediments in the South Dakota badlands. The hearths, contained in pits and filled with burned rock and charcoal, were exposed in the banks of a tributary of the White River. Sheldon observed that the prehistoric features and associated artifact scatters were contained within "a stratum of a black humus material" buried beneath 2.4 to 3 meters of stratified sediments. He correctly interpreted this stratum as a formerly stable ground surface on which the prehistoric occupations had occurred. He also recognized that the overlying sediments were fluvial in origin and that aggradation had been followed by an episode of downcutting, exposing the hearths. Neither Sheldon nor J. E. Todd, the South Dakota State Geologist with whom he corresponded about the exposures, could guess the age of the features.

Two important workers of this period were George F. Will, in North Dakota, and William H. Over, in South Dakota. Will, educated in botany and anthropology at Harvard University, was a Bismarck businessman and member of the State Historical Society of North Dakota who published prolifically on North Dakota history and prehistory (Robinson 1966:511). His archaeological work was strongly ethnohistorical in its orientation, seeking to establish connections between earthlodge village sites of the Missouri Trench and the Mandan, Hidatsa, and Arikara, the region's village-dwelling Native American tribes (Will and Spinden 1906; Will 1911, 1924, 1933; Will and Hecker 1944). Will made cross-disciplinary studies in the fields of ethnobiology (Will and Hyde 1917) and dendrochronology (e.g., Will 1946), but none of his many contributions can be considered geoarchaeological in scope.

W. H. Over, curator of the University of South Dakota Museum from 1919 to 1949, was also active in the excavation of village sites on the Missouri River and in eastern South Dakota. Like Will, his major interest in archaeology was tracing the living village cultures to their prehistoric antecedents (Sigstad and

Sigstad 1973; Helgevold 1981:17–38; Zimmerman 1985:20–22). Over also conducted excavations in rock shelters in western South Dakota (e.g., Over 1936) and published on a variety of other subjects, including several studies of the state's wildlife (e.g., Over and Thomas 1921; Over 1923; Over and Churchill 1945).

One of Over's endeavors dealt indirectly with geoarchaeology. Along the Missouri River north of Pierre, South Dakota (map 8.1), Over recorded several sites where distinctive prehistoric ceramics were associated with exposures of a buried soil found at depths of 0.5 to 2.5 meters below the surface of a Missouri River terrace (fig. 8.1). He referred to this manifestation as the "Old Soil Zone Culture" (Sigstad and Sigstad 1973:318–22). In 1931 he led participants in the First Plains Conference to an exposure of the "Old Soil Zone" north of Pierre (Wedel 1977), and in 1944 he corresponded with James B. Griffin of the University of Michigan about its ceramics (Sigstad and Sigstad 1973:323–24). Although Over had no training as an earth scientist, his identification of the Old Soil Zone conformed to stratigraphic principles. Implicit in Over's descriptions is his observation that the buried soil could be correlated laterally among exposures on the basis of its physical properties and stratigraphic relationships. He must also have realized that the cultural similarities indicated by artifacts from the buried soil supported the stratigraphic correlation of exposures and afforded evidence for dating the stratum.

Interestingly, Over's Old Soil Zone has reemerged in the archaeological literature as the "Big Bend paleosol," a soil-stratigraphic unit informally defined by Toom (1992:197–98). The soil formed in eolian sediments that mantle the MT-2 terrace of the Missouri River in the Big Bend region between Chamberlain and Pierre (map 8.1). The A horizon of the soil yields archaeological remains dating to the Plains Woodland through Initial Middle Missouri periods and probably formed between approximately 920 and 700 B.P. (Toom et al. 1990:417–18; Toom 1992:320).

The 1930s–1950s

The amount of archaeological study accomplished in the Dakotas increased dramatically in the mid-1930s as a result of excavations funded by the Works Progress Administration (WPA). The era of WPA excavation, 1934–1941 (Wedel 1982:101), was followed in the years after World War II by the even more intensive and extensive River Basin Surveys (RBS). The latter surveys were carried out between 1946 and 1969 (Wedel 1982:103; Jennings 1986; Glenn 1994;

Fig. 8.1. Arrows point to a buried soil, the "Big Bend paleosol," exposed in a lake-eroded cutbank at the Cattle Oiler site (39SST224), Stanley County, South Dakota. In 1931 W. H. Over led participants in the first Plains Conference to a similar exposure to observe archaeological remains he referred to as the "Old Soil Zone Culture." Photograph by Dennis Toom, University of North Dakota.

Thiessen 1994). Both the WPA and RBS efforts focused, for very good reason, on the earthlodge villages of the Missouri Trench. These were the region's most spectacular archaeological resource and were also obviously and imminently threatened by construction of federal reservoirs along the whole length of the upper Missouri River, from Fort Randall, South Dakota, to Fort Peck, Montana (Lehmer 1971; Helgevold 1981: 40–41).

The River Basin Surveys also sponsored investigations at proposed reservoirs in the eastern and western Dakotas (e.g., Hughes 1949; Cooper 1958; Wheeler 1963; Banks 1994; Del Bene 1994), and a number of pre–Plains Village and pre-ceramic sites were investigated in the Missouri Trench itself (e.g., Neuman 1964, 1975). However, analysis and publication of the Plains Village materials tended to take precedence over the pre-ceramic sites. This was an unfortunate but perhaps unavoidable consequence of prevailing research priorities and constraints of funding and staff. Many of the pre-ceramic sites, and sites in reservoirs off the Missouri Trench, have become the object of "backlog analysis" studies (e.g., Wheeler and Johnson 1985; Ahler and Toom 1989:5; Wheeler 1995) that the National Park Service, through its Midwest Archaeological Center, has funded since the 1970s (Jennings 1985:295).

The pre-ceramic sites were often buried by eolian, alluvial, or colluvial sediments, and their interpretation required geological expertise. However, neither the WPA nor RBS programs were explicitly interdisciplinary in scope. Fortunately several RBS archaeologists appear to have had prior training in the earth sciences. For example, in 1958, William N. Irving directed excavations of Archaic components at the Medicine Crow site, in Buffalo County, South Dakota (map 8.1). The components are buried in eolian silt, one to two meters thick, that overlies outwash gravels on the MT-2 terrace of the Missouri River. Irving prepared two unpublished manuscripts describing the stratigraphy and geologic setting of the site. The manuscripts, on file at the Midwest Archaeological Center, Lincoln, Nebraska, were indispensable to Ahler and Toom (1989) in their analysis of the site. As another example, in the course of his RBS surveys in the Angostura Reservoir area of southwestern South Dakota (map 8.1), Jack T. Hughes, in collaboration with Theodore E. White, prepared a manuscript on stream terrace and alluvial fan sediments observed on the Cheyenne River and its tributary Horsehead Creek. In addition to topographic mapping and cutbank inspections, White and Hughes (n.d.) determined the thickness of valley fill by hand augering to depths of five to eleven meters.

Theodore E. White, a vertebrate paleontologist, was the only member of the Missouri Basin Program of the RBS with professional credentials in the geosciences (W. Raymond Wood, personal communication, 1995). However, his published contributions to the program dealt exclusively with studies of faunal remains from Plains Village sites, which are considered pioneering efforts in the field of zooarchaeology (Falk 1977: 152).

Professional expertise outside the RBS was sometimes available. In 1948 RBS surveyors discovered the Ray Long site, a late Paleoindian campsite complex in the Angostura Reservoir area of extreme southwestern South Dakota (Hughes 1949). In 1949 a field party of United States Department of Agriculture soil scientists working in the area "graciously consented" (Wheeler 1995) to describe and sample soils at the site. James Thorp, the leader of the party, reported his observations in a letter to Richard Wheeler (Wheeler 1995). In 1956, Dwight Crandell, a geologist with the United States Geological Survey, provided a geological interpretation of the Natche site on the Missouri River in Dewey County, South Dakota (map 8.1), where buried soils yielded Plains Woodland cultural material (Wheeler and Johnson 1985).

In contrast to these serendipitous contacts with earth scientists, the RBS in 1958 funded a geological study for the explicit purpose of providing a context for deeply buried archaeological remains that had been encountered along the Missouri Trench in South Dakota. The study was undertaken by Alan Coogan, then of the Department of Geology at Cornell College, Mount Vernon, Iowa, with assistance from William Irving of the RBS. Using archaeological evidence from Medicine Crow and other archaeological sites, Coogan and Irving (1959) conclusively demonstrated the Holocene age of the eolian sediments that mantled the first two terraces (MT-1 and MT-2) above the flood plain (MT-0) and also identified Holocene valley fills in a small-order tributary of the Missouri River (Coogan 1960).

Coogan's use of geoarchaeological evidence to date the eolian mantle along the Missouri River was a significant advance for geology. As late as 1955 many geologists were still writing of these sediments and their buried soils as Pleistocene in age, based on presumed correspondences with glacial and interglacial periods (Flint 1955), despite the growing abundance of archaeological evidence to the contrary. However, the study had little immediate effect on archaeological studies in the Northern Plains. As long as research remained focused on the Plains Village period, the study was of interest primarily as environmental background. Coogan and Irving's study received only passing mention in archaeological studies, including Lehmer's (1971) synthesis of the RBS program.

In the 1950s, while the River Basin Surveys were progressing in the Dakotas, major archaeological surveys were undertaken in southern Manitoba and Saskatchewan. Richard MacNeish tested several multicomponent sites buried in alluvium of the Red River in southern Manitoba (MacNeish 1958). Wilson (1990:61) observes that MacNeish, while on the faculty of the University of Calgary, was a strong proponent of interdisciplinary collaboration. However, papers that MacNeish published on his work in Manitoba focused primarily on establishing a culture historical sequence. The stratigraphy of the sites is described, but not related to the surrounding landscape. The sites provided an important baseline for the culture history of southeastern Manitoba, but little if any geologically relevant information can be gleaned from the work.

Meanwhile, in Saskatchewan, Boyd Wettlaufer undertook studies that were characterized by a detailed consideration of geological context. In 1954 Wettlaufer excavated at the Mortlach site on a Saskatchewan River tributary near

Moosejaw (map 8.1). In 1957 he worked at the Long Creek site, on a Souris River tributary of the same name, near Estevan (map 8.1). Both sites contained stratified components ranging in age from less than 200 to 3500 B.P., buried in Holocene alluvium (Wettlaufer 1955; Wettlaufer and Mayer-Oakes 1960).

Specialists from the Saskatchewan Soil Survey described and interpreted the geomorphology and stratigraphy of both sites (Moss 1955; Clayton and Janzen 1960). They found evidence of a series of fining upward sequences, each sequence ending with a relatively brief soil-forming episode. Clayton and Janzen (1960) suggested that the basal, coarse-textured part of each sequence was deposited by high magnitude floods, while the upper, finer-textured parts were deposited either in waning flood stages or by local colluviation during episodes of flood plain stability.

In a decade when specialists' contributions were commonly relegated without comment to the appendices of reports (Willey and Sabloff 1993:183), Wettlaufer integrated the soil scientists' conclusions with his own archaeological interpretations. Citing Antevs's recently published "Geologic Climatic Dating in the West" (Antevs 1955), Wettlaufer suggested that the coarse-textured flood deposits represented moist climatic episodes, when the local stream carried sufficient water to overtop its banks. The buried soils, by contrast, were evidence of flood plain stability, equated with reduced flooding and drought. He noted that most cultural levels at the Mortlach site coincided with the A horizons of buried soils, and he attempted to correlate these with major drought periods identified by Antevs (Wettlaufer 1955: 73–77). He speculated that, in moist climatic intervals between soil-forming episodes, valley floors were too flood prone and muddy for human habitation (Wettlaufer 1955:75; Wettlaufer and Mayer-Oakes 1960:83). The abundance of fragmented bison bone in cultural levels at the sites suggested to him that drought-plagued people were reduced to cracking open bones for sustenance (Wettlaufer and Mayer-Oakes 1960:83).

The correlations that Wettlaufer drew between climate and alluvial stratigraphy are oversimplistic. Many factors in addition to climate influence cycles of aggradation, stability, and erosion in fluvial systems. His cultural inferences concerning fragmented bison bone are also somewhat exaggerated. Marrow and bone grease, the products obtained by bone-cracking, are important sources of fat in hunter-gatherer diets, not simply starvation foods (Vehik 1977; Leechman 1951; Speth 1983). These criticisms, however, do not detract from the overall importance of the Mortlach and Long Creek studies as the first truly interdisciplinary studies involving the earth sciences in the Northern Plains. As noted by Wilson (1990:61), "These excellent studies more strongly exemplified the geoarchaeology ideal than many that followed."

Wettlaufer concluded the Mortlach report with a series of remarkably far-sighted recommendations. Noting that buried sites like Mortlach were likely to occur elsewhere in Saskatchewan, he recommended that future archaeological surveys be "directed where possible by the results of geologic research" (Wettlaufer 1955). He advocated collaboration with Quaternary scientists to locate the geologic contexts most likely to have been inhabited by prehistoric people, an approach that has become basic methodology in modern geoarchaeology on the Plains (e.g., Artz 1985; Bettis and Benn 1985; Bettis 1992; Mandel 1994). He also called for the routine use of posthole augers to probe for buried cultural deposits, a procedure advocated in recent years by several geoarchaeologists (e.g., Stein 1986; Abbott and Neidig 1993; Stafford 1995).

The 1960s and Early 1970s

During the 1960s, although interest in Plains Village cultures of the Missouri Trench remained strong, areas outside the Missouri Trench received increasing attention. Archaeologists also took stock of the knowledge gained in preceding decades to produce important syntheses of archaeology and culture history, the most significant of which, in terms of its geographic and temporal scope, was Wedel's *Prehistoric Man on the Great Plains* (Wedel 1961). Syntheses specifically relevant to the Northern Plains were published by Mulloy (1958), Wormington and Forbis (1965), Hlady (1970), Reeves (1970), and Lehmer (1971). Other works provided reviews of archaeological knowledge at smaller spatial and temporal scales. For example, Johnson (1962) provided an overview of the prehistory of the Red River Valley in eastern North Dakota and western Minnesota, and Syms (1969) produced a detailed synthesis of a single Middle Archaic cultural taxon, the McKean complex.

The Holocene geological record of the Northern Plains received increasing attention from earth scientists. White (1966) described eolian sedimentation on cliff dunes in South Dakota and commented on its importance as an archaeological site formation process. Brophy (1966) reported a radiocarbon age and paleontological data on bison bones deeply buried in alluvium from a Knife River tributary in North Dakota. Harksen (1974) reported two radiocarbon ages on hearths in the South Dakota Badlands and discussed their geological significance in establishing the late Holocene age and depositional complexity of alluvial fills in the valley of a Cheyenne River tributary. The hearths were similar to those reported in 1905 by Sheldon. Hamilton (1967), Everitt (1968), and Tinker (1971) reported on very recent ages of alluvium and colluvium in the Little Missouri Badlands of North Dakota. Clayton et al. (1970) mapped prehistoric flint quarry pits that were visible on aerial photographs of the Knife River basin and offered the first petrographic analysis of Knife River flint, an important prehistoric stone tool material.

The 1960s and early 1970s also witnessed the publication of important multidisciplinary syntheses in the earth sciences (e.g., Wright and Frey 1965; Dort and Jones 1970). Archaeologists contributed to these syntheses, reflecting their growing concern with problems of environmental reconstruction and an increasing awareness of the value of interdisciplinary collaboration.

As geoscientists advanced their understanding of the region, archaeologists used the newly available data to develop increasingly sophisticated perspectives on the archaeological record as a component of regional landscapes. For example, detailed mapping and radiocarbon dating of the Laurentide ice sheet margins (Christiansen 1965; Clayton and Freers 1967) and of Glacial Lake Agassiz shorelines (e.g., Elson 1967) provided Kehoe (1966) and Pettipas (1967), respectively, with essential data for examining the northward expansion of Paleoindian peoples into the deglaciated landscapes of southern Saskatchewan and Manitoba.

In a paper of considerable geoarchaeological importance, Reeves (1973) exhaustively reviewed the archaeological, paleontological, and geological literature to pose a solution to a perplexing archaeological problem. Several researchers, including Mulloy (1958) and Hurt (1966), had posited widespread abandonment of the Plains during the Altithermal, a middle Holocene episode of arid climate. Reeves concluded that the perceived absence of a middle Holocene archaeological record on the Plains was due to sampling bias and to the widespread burial or erosion of sediments of this age, a view substantiated to a considerable degree by subsequent researchers (Root and Ahler 1987; Mandel 1992; Sheehan 1995; Artz 1996).

An important sign of increased collaboration on the Northern Plains between archaeologists and researchers from other disciplines was the Conference on Environmental Studies of the Glacial Lake Agassiz Region, convened in 1966 at the University of Manitoba in Winnipeg. The conference assembled a cross section of scientists that rivaled the Sixth Plains Conference in disciplinary diversity, including participants from geology, hydrology, paleoecology, paleoclimatology, and archaeology. An archaeologist, William Mayer-Oakes, both organized the conference and edited its proceedings (Mayer-Oakes 1967). Morgan Tamplin, also an archaeologist, wrote an introductory paper on the history of geological studies of Lake Agassiz. His perception of the significance of the conference is reflected in the following remark: "It may be thought odd that a department of Anthropology should presume to bring together geologists, botanists, zoologists, geographers, and archaeologists, but such an interdisciplinary fusion is essential to understand the early human occupation and its relationship to the environment of the lake basin" (Tamplin 1967:34).

Like the Sixth Plains Conference in 1948, the Lake Agassiz conference included contributors from many disciplines within the natural sciences. There is a great difference, however, in the general tone of the papers presented. While participants in the Sixth Plains Conference primarily expressed excitement about the potential for forthcoming advances in their respective disciplines, the Lake Agassiz conference participants presented substantive summaries of progress that had been made in all aspects of regional paleoenvironmental study. The conference reflected real progress toward a holistic understanding of the environment at many scales of space and time. It reflected not only the sophistication of the individual disciplines but also a common desire for continued interdisciplinary communication and collaboration.

Mid-1970s to the Present

The threshold event in the emergence of geoarchaeology on the Northern Plains was the publication of a brief paper entitled "Stratigraphy, Origin, and Climatic Implications of Late Quaternary Upland Silt in North Dakota," by Clayton et al. (1976). At the time, Lee Clayton and his coworkers were involved in mapping Quaternary deposits in that state for the North Dakota State Geological Survey. They recognized that eolian sediments of terminal Wisconsinan and Holocene age mantled uplands throughout the state. They assigned these deposits to a single, formally defined lithostratigraphic unit, the Oahe Formation, which they subdivided into the Mallard Island, Aggie Brown, Pick City, and Riverdale members. Buried soils formed in the Aggie Brown and Riverdale members (fig. 8.2) were informally named the Leonard and Thompson paleosols, respectively (Clayton et al. 1976).

Lacking data for directly dating the Oahe Formation, Clayton and his colleagues proposed a geoclimatic model that linked the four members to dated paleoecological records (Clayton et al. 1976). The model (fig. 8.3) proposed that

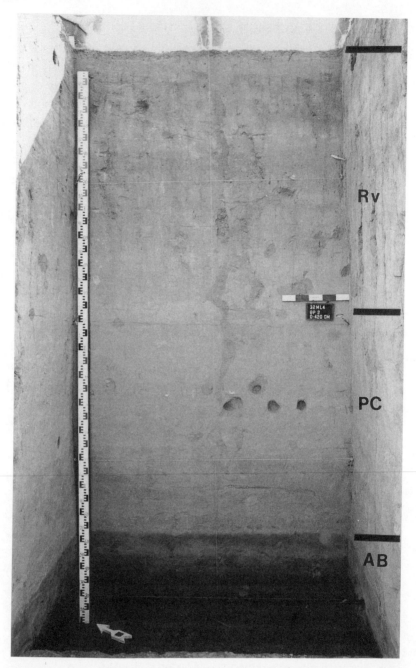

Fig. 8.2. A 4.2-meter-high profile at the Flaming Arrow site (32ML4), McLean County, North Dakota, exposes the upper three members of the Oahe Formation: Riverdale (Rv), Pick City (PC), and Aggie Brown (AB). Two buried soils are formed in the Riverdale Member, and a thick, dark-colored soil is formed in the Aggie Brown Member. Photograph by Dennis Toom, University of North Dakota.

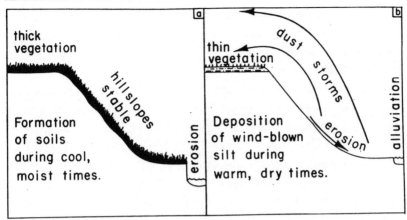

Fig. 8.3. Clayton et al. (1976) proposed a simple geoclimatic model to explain the alternating episodes of deposition and stability/soil formation evident in the uplands silts of the Oahe Formation (from Clayton et al. 1976:9).

the buried soils formed during relatively moist climatic episodes, when uplands were stabilized by prairie vegetation. During dry episodes, sparsely vegetated hill slopes provided a sediment source for rapid eolian sedimentation. They suggested that the Leonard paleosol formed during the cool, moist climates of the terminal Wisconsinan and early Holocene; that the Pick City Member dated to the warm, dry middle Holocene; and that paleosols in the Riverdale Member formed during relatively moist intervals of the late Holocene (Clayton et al. 1976).

Publication of this model coincided with an unprecedented opportunity to test its chronological implications. The 1970s and 1980s witnessed a virtual explosion in archaeological studies related to cultural resource management on the Northern Plains. Federal historic preservation legislation mandated that archaeological surveys be conducted in advance of development projects funded in whole or in part with federal money. Also implemented was a mandate for the inventory of cultural resources on federal land. The 1970s witnessed a boom of federally regulated energy development in the oil, natural gas, and coal fields of North Dakota and the development of mineral and timber resources on federal lands in the Black Hills of South Dakota. Irrigation and municipal water projects in both the eastern and western Dakotas were also planned and implemented with federal funding assistance and often entailed archaeological surveys. Consequently, during the 1970s and 1980s, vast quantities of archaeological data were generated on the Northern Plains. By the mid-1980s geological studies undertaken in support of archaeology were becoming relatively routine components of most major survey and excavation projects (e.g., Coogan 1983; Reiten 1983; Wyckoff 1984; Albanese 1985; Jorstad et al. 1986; Kuehn et al. 1987).

Several published papers, in addition to a host of poorly disseminated proprietary and technical reports not cited here, presented archaeological or radiocarbon evidence for the ages of upland eolian sediments of the Oahe Formation. These studies largely supported the chronology postulated by Clayton et al. (1976). Ahler et al. (1974) reported on an interdisciplinary project that documented stratified Paleoindian through Plains Village components in windblown sediments at Walth Bay on the Missouri River in South Dakota (map 8.1). Root and Ahler (1984) reported on the Benz site, a late Paleoindian occupation buried in the Leonard paleosol in Dunn County, North Dakota (map 8.1). The site yielded Scottsbluff and Alberta projectile points in association with radiocarbon ages of 8,000 to 9,300 years before the present. Toom (1988) reported a radiocarbon age on the Leonard paleosol at the Flaming Arrow site on the Missouri Trench (map 8.1, fig. 8.2). Wyckoff (1984) and Jorstad et al. (1986) documented the association of archaeological sites with buried soils of the Riverdale Member in western North Dakota. Kuehn et al. (1987) and Root and Ahler (1987) documented the somewhat sporadic occurrence of archaeological materials in middle Holocene, Pick City member deposits of western North Dakota. From the Brandon Sand Hills of southwestern Manitoba (map 8.1), David (1971) reported late Holocene ages on buried soils that are equivalent to the Riverdale Member of the Oahe Formation.

While these and other studies largely supported the chronology postulated by Clayton et al. (1976), other aspects of the initial model proved more difficult to confirm. Coogan (1983, 1987) documented that the entire Oahe Formation package described by Clayton et al. (1976) is rarely preserved in any one locality because the Holocene geological record in uplands of the region is primarily erosional, not depositional (fig. 8.4). Evidence to confirm the paleoclimatic implications suggested by Clayton and his coworkers also proved elusive (Barnosky et al. 1987). Archaeologists, although actively gathering empirical evidence for the age and depositional environments of Holocene sediments, have tended to infer paleoclimates by extrapolation from a few sites along the eastern fringes of the region (e.g., Reeves 1973) or by reference to global climate-change models (e.g., Toom 1992).

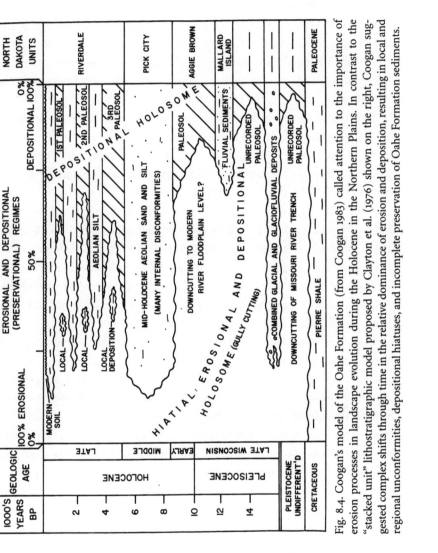

Fig. 8.4. Coogan's model of the Oahe Formation (from Coogan 1983) called attention to the importance of erosion processes in landscape evolution during the Holocene in the Northern Plains. In contrast to the "stacked unit" lithostratigraphic model proposed by Clayton et al. (1976) shown on the right, Coogan suggested complex shifts through time in the relative dominance of erosion and deposition, resulting in local and regional unconformities, depositional hiatuses, and incomplete preservation of Oahe Formation sediments.

In 1979 the North Dakota Geological Survey expanded the definition of the Oahe Formation to include all postglacial sediments in North Dakota. Alluvial and paludal/lacustrine sediments thus also became part of the formation (Clayton and Moran 1979; Clayton et al. 1980). A formal lithostratigraphy has not been developed for Holocene alluvium in the region, although terrace sequences and alluvial fills have been described for a number of drainage basins and drainage basin segments (e.g., Reiten 1983; White and Hannus 1985; Gonzalez 1987; McFaul 1990; Kuehn 1993, 1998; Picha and Gregg 1993; Van Nest 1995).

Artz (1995) reviewed advances in understanding the Holocene geological record of North Dakota and adjacent states and provinces since about 1970, and they are summarized as follows. In the uplands, erosion has produced large gaps in local geological and archaeological records (Coogan 1983, 1987). The entire Oahe Formation package described by Clayton et al. (1976) is rarely preserved in any one locality because the Holocene geological record in uplands of the region is primarily erosional, not depositional (fig. 8.4). The eolian record in many localities appears to be entirely late Holocene in age (e.g., David 1971; Muhs et al. 1997). Early to middle Holocene records are most often preserved in settings that are conducive to trapping eolian and colluvial sediment, such as topographic lows, and on the lee sides of knolls and ridges (Kuehn et al. 1987; Artz 1995).

In stream valleys late Holocene alluvial fills often consist of vertical accretion deposits that contain multiple, weakly developed buried soils (e.g., McFaul 1990; Picha and Gregg 1993). These fills indicate that late Holocene vertical accretion was highly episodic. In large valleys early-to-middle Holocene alluvium is thought to be deeply buried or removed by erosion. Alluvium from these periods has proved easier to find in the valleys of tributaries to the major streams, such as Spring Creek in the Knife River basin (e.g., Root et al. 1986; Artz and Ahler 1989), and Long Creek in the Souris River basin (e.g., Wettlaufer and Mayer-Oakes 1960). Early-to-middle Holocene deposits are perhaps less deeply buried, or less extensively eroded, in these smaller streams. In eastern North Dakota alluvial fans along the margins of late Wisconsinan spillways have a high potential for early to middle Holocene records (e.g., Boettger 1986; Running 1995).

The geoarchaeology of the Northern Plains will surely become much better known and understood in the coming decades. Archaeologists have begun to advance beyond the generalities of regional models like those of Clayton et al.

(1976) and Knox (1984). These advances represent successful efforts to establish local stratigraphic and geomorphological frameworks as a spatiotemporal context for the prehistoric archaeological record (e.g., Reiten 1983; Coogan 1987; McFaul 1990; Toom 1992; Kuehn 1993, 1998; Picha and Gregg 1993; Van Nest 1995). Others (Artz 1995, 1996; Waters and Kuehn 1996; Kuehn 1997) have examined the effects of geological processes on the differential preservation of archaeological sites across the Northern Plains landscape. Geoarchaeological studies have also contributed to extending the time depth spanned by the prehistoric archaeological record. In the western Dakotas, recognition of paleosols dating to the terminal Wisconsinan and early Holocene has contributed to successful searches for Paleoindian occupation (e.g., Ahler 1992; Donohue 1992; Kuehn 1993; Root 1993). In the Red River valley, where previous archaeological syntheses professed only scanty knowledge of prehistory prior to the Late Archaic (Johnson 1962; Michlovic 1988), geoarchaeological studies have contributed to the identification and interpretation of significant Early Archaic occupation sites (McFaul 1991; Running 1995). The past decade has also witnessed significant advances in paleolimnological and paleoecological research on the Northern Plains (e.g., Schwalb and Dean 1998; Yansa 1998), advances that have begun to influence archaeological models of human adaptations to Holocene environments (e.g., Beaudoin 1993, 1998).

SUMMARY

Archaeologists in the Central and Northern Plains became aware of the need for a geoarchaeological approach in the 1930s and 1940s. On the Northern Plains, several studies in the 1950s combined archaeological and geological knowledge and expertise, but true interdisciplinary collaboration was infrequent before the 1960s and did not become commonplace until the 1970s and 1980s. The threshold event in the emergence of geoarchaeology on the Northern Plains was the definition of the Oahe Formation by Clayton et al. (1976). This stratigraphic framework, and the geoclimatic model that underlies it, can be criticized as too simplistic (Coogan 1983, 1987), but simplicity was the key to its success among archaeologists. Without extensive training in the earth sciences, archaeologists could use the model to interpret the natural stratigraphy of archaeological sites, estimate their relative ages, and even attempt paleoclimatic inferences. The Oahe Formation model served to "demystify" the

Holocene geological record for archaeologists. This occurred at precisely the same time that archaeologists were beginning to explore in earnest the upland archaeological record of the region. Archaeological data provided an important test of the model's chronological applications, but the paleoclimatic and process-response aspects of the model have yet to be adequately tested.

DISCUSSION

Increased collaboration between archaeologists and earth scientists in the past few decades laid the foundation for the emergence of geoarchaeology as an active field of endeavor on the Northern Plains. Actual collaboration was made possible in part by increased levels of funding for archaeological research that accompanied the expansion of cultural resource management studies in the 1970s and 1980s. It would be a mistake, however, to say that the emergence of geoarchaeology was due solely to increased levels of funding or even to increased levels of interest in the topic.

Public funding of archaeology rapidly expanded at least twice before the 1970s on the Plains: once in the 1930s with the availability of WPA funds and again in the 1950s with the inception of the RBS. By the 1940s Plains archaeologists were aware of the importance of collaboration with the earth sciences, and at least one conference, the Sixth Plains Conference, was convened to promote such collaboration. Yet despite the perceived need, virtually no WPA funds and relatively few RBS dollars were spent to actively foster interaction between archaeologists and earth scientists on the Northern Plains. To account for the twenty to thirty year hiatus in the emergence of geoarchaeology, one is led to a consideration of historical factors that were shaping archaeology and the earth sciences throughout this period.

Throughout the twentieth century American archaeology has been firmly subsumed within the broader social science of anthropology (Dunnell 1986; Willey and Sabloff 1993). Many of the early archaeologists on the Northern and Central Plains, including Wedel and Strong, held degrees from departments of anthropology on the east and west coasts, where they received strong backgrounds in Native American ethnography (Wedel 1977, 1982:4–5, 154–59). Their archaeological work therefore reflected deep interests in the region's ethnohistory. Beginning as early as the work by Will and Spinden (1906), archaeological research on the Central and Northern Plains was guided by a methodology that came to be known as the direct historic approach (Strong 1935; Wedel 1938, 1982:161–63). The methodology attempts to work backward from the ethnographically documented material culture of the known tribes, tracing its origins to protohistoric and prehistoric antecedents. Given the ethnographic interests of the early archaeologists, the imminent perils posed by reservoir construction, and the strong ethnohistoric emphasis of the direct historic approach, it was virtually inevitable that an almost preemptive concern with Plains Village cultures would come to dominate Northern Plains archaeology. The focus of fieldwork on the Plains Village period kept scientific attention and public funding channeled toward relatively recent, and predominantly near-surface, geological contexts. The emphasis on problems of culture history focused interest on artifacts and not on their sedimentary matrices.

This theoretical and methodological focus was an important factor that delayed the emergence of geoarchaeology on the Northern Plains. Within this paradigm, archaeologists required little knowledge of geological concepts other than a common-sense understanding of the Law of Superposition. Indeed, ethnographic analogies were often as useful as geoscience concepts in interpreting the stratigraphy of an earthlodge village, with its complex associations of constructed cultural features, such as house floors, postmolds, and storage pits. The development of consistent and rigorous archaeological field techniques aimed at elucidating questions of culture history was viewed as a major accomplishment of the WPA and RBS excavations. As Alex Krieger, a participant in the Sixth Plains Conference, remarked, "Field techniques in archaeology have reached the point of perfection. On the whole, American archaeologists can be proud of the careful and precise work done in the field" (Jennings 1950:35).

At no time in the history of the RBS, or of Northern Plains archaeology as a whole, was the focus on Plains Village cultures exclusive. During the two and a half decades of the RBS, fieldwork was undertaken throughout the region, and a great deal of data was accumulated about pre-ceramic cultures and cultures of the plains and prairies east and west of the Missouri Trench. The amassing of this regional database coincided with a shift in North American archaeology toward a greater interest in problems of cultural process, cultural evolution, and cultural ecology as means of explaining the patterns manifested by culture history (Jennings 1986:58–59; Willey and Sabloff 1993:176–82). Wedel's early papers on the impacts of environmental change on prehistoric cultures were the forerunners of this important paradigm shift, and as he had correctly foreseen (Wedel 1953), the earth sciences would come to play an important role.

272   JOE ALAN ARTZ

Willey and Sabloff (1993:182–87) observe that American archaeology after about 1940 was increasingly stimulated by "scientific aids from other disciplines," most notably radiocarbon dating but also including the earth sciences. They note, however, that before about 1960 archaeologists often lacked the conceptual tools to work with data from outside their own discipline. Thus, Coogan's study of Missouri River terraces, although an important contribution to both the archaeology and geology of the region, contributed only marginally to archaeological studies at the time.

Davidson (1985) notes that the geosciences, and in particular geomorphology, had little impact on archaeology until archaeologists began to think of sites as components of dynamic landscapes. In the 1960s and 1970s archaeologists developed a strong interest in the physical structure of archaeological sites and site formation processes (e.g., Binford et al. 1970; Schiffer 1987). Increased interest in the paleoenvironmental context of sites (e.g., Butzer 1964; Flannery 1968) and in the geologic history of sites (e.g., Butzer 1977) contributed to the development of geoarchaeology.

The emergence of geoarchaeology on the Northern Plains was also conditioned by the timing of developments in the earth sciences. In the 1940s, when Plains archaeologists were inviting collaboration (Jennings 1950; Wedel 1953), geoscientists on the Plains were still grappling with fundamental problems of stratigraphy and chronology. In the two decades following World War II, great advances were made in the understanding of Quaternary geology and geomorphology on the northern North American midcontinent, culminating in the 1960s with the publication of several important syntheses (e.g., Wright and Frey 1965; Mayer-Oakes 1967; Dort and Jones 1970; Ruhe 1969). Process-oriented research, grounded in quantitative methods, came to the forefront in the earth sciences after World War II and represented a profound paradigm shift in those disciplines (Tinkler 1985; Vitek and Ritter 1993). The lack of a grasp on process posed very real obstacles to Northern Plains geologists. For example, in 1962–63 the North Dakota Geological Survey dispatched a field party to Alaska to study modern glacial processes after realizing that "a knowledge of glacial deposits resulting from ablation of stagnant ice was going to be essential to the understanding of the surficial deposits which covered most of the state" (Folsom 1980:29).

The advances in interdisciplinary collaboration that began in the 1970s were therefore dependent on advances in the individual disciplines, without which interdisciplinary work was not possible. For example, a fundamental component of Clayton et al.'s (1976) model was that the lithostratigraphic members of the Oahe Formation formed in response to Holocene climatic fluctuations. Their model of this relationship was based on geoclimatic concepts that, although expressed qualitatively in the early part of the century, only gained quantitative confirmation in process-response models developed in the 1950s and 1960s by Schumm and others (e.g., Langbein and Schumm 1958). In addition, their age estimates for the Oahe Formation were derived largely from palynological evidence from the Northern Plains and upper Midwest, much of which was also a product of work conducted in the 1950s and 1960s (e.g., Watts and Wright 1966; McAndrews 1966, 1967; McAndrews et al. 1967).

CONCLUSIONS

Before geoarchaeology could be established on the Northern Plains as a sustainable, collaborative venture, the participating disciplines had to each individually attain a certain degree of sophistication in their realms of study. Archaeologists had to work out a regional cultural chronology, a task that was essentially complete by about 1970 (Lehmer 1971; Mulloy 1958; Wedel 1961). Archaeologists also had to begin to formulate questions and advance concepts about settlement patterns, cultural ecology, and human land use in prehistory. Geoscientists had to come to grips with the Quaternary stratigraphic sequence and develop an understanding of the processes that were responsible for its formation. Archaeologists and earth scientists alike would have welcomed an integrated interdisciplinary approach to Holocene studies in the 1940s, but postponement was inevitable. The disciplines, as individual sciences, were not yet ready for fruitful collaboration. Fifty years later, such collaboration among researchers is not only possible but is well under way.

ACKNOWLEDGMENTS

Parts of this chapter began nearly twenty years ago as a section on Plains geoarchaeology that I excised from a draft of my master's thesis. I am grateful to Rolfe Mandel for the opportunity to return to those old notes. My concepts of historical trends have evolved through exposure to the work, libraries, and camaraderie of many colleagues. These include my too-brief association with Bob Alex, Alice Tratebas, and Tom Haberman in South Dakota, and my longer and immensely pleasurable time with many colleagues in North Dakota, including Stan Ahler, Mike Gregg, Paul Picha, Dennis Toom, Matt Root, Fred Schneider, and Dave Kuehn. In preparing this paper, I am indebted to Kuehn, Picha, Mike Metcalf, Peter Winham, and Mark Luther for providing references and manuscripts. I benefited from comments by Lynn Alex, Bill Green, Dave Kuehn, Marlin Hawley, Vance Holliday, Marvin Kay, Rolfe Mandel, Mike Michlovic, Paul Picha, Garry Running, Fred Schneider, Dennis Toom, Ray Wood, and Don Wyckoff. This is Iowa Quaternary Studies Group Contribution no. 67.

REFERENCES

Abbott, L. R., and C. A. Neidig. 1993. Archaeological postholing: A proposed sub-surface survey and site-testing methodology. *Illinois Archaeology* 5:38–45.
Ahler, S. A. 1977. Lithic resource utilization patterns in the Middle Missouri subarea. *In* Wood, W. R., ed., Trends in Middle Missouri prehistory: A festschrift honoring the contributions of Donald J. Lehmer. Lincoln, Nebr.: Plains Anthropological Society, Memoir 13:132–50.
———. 1992. Phase II cultural resource investigations associated with proposed dam safety modifications at Lake Ilo National Wildlife Refuge, Dunn County, North Dakota. Grand Forks: University of North Dakota, Department of Anthropology.
Ahler, S. A., and D. L. Toom. 1989. Archaeology of the Medicine Crow site complex (39BF2), Buffalo County, South Dakota, vol. 1. Springfield: Illinois State Museum Society.
Ahler, S. A., D. K. Davies, C. R. Falk, and D. B. Madsen. 1974. Holocene stratigraphy and archaeology in the middle Missouri River trench, South Dakota. *Science* 184:905–908.
Albanese, J. 1985. Geologic investigation of prehistoric sites 39HN152, 39HN157/158, and 39HN163, Harding County, South Dakota. *In* Metcalf, M. D., and K. D. Black, Archaeological investigations at three sites in the North Cave Hills, Hardin County, South Dakota, 202–48. Eagle, Colo.: Metcalf Archaeological Consultants.
Antevs, E. 1955. Geologic-climatic dating in the west. *American Antiquity* 20:317–35.
Artz, J. A. 1985. A soil-geomorphic approach to the location of Late Archaic sites in northeastern Oklahoma. *American Archaeology* 5:142–50.

————. 1995. Geological contexts of the early and middle Holocene archaeo-
logical record in North Dakota and adjoining areas of the Northern Plains.
In Bettis, E. A., III, ed., Archaeological geology of the Archaic period in
North America. Boulder, Colo.: The Geological Society of America, Special
Paper 297:67–86.

————. 1996. Cultural response or geological process? A comment on Sheehan.
Plains Anthropologist 41:383–93.

Artz, J. A., and S. A. Ahler. 1989. Further evaluation of the Alkali Creek archaeological site, 32DU336-SEE, Dunn County, North Dakota. Grand Forks:
University of North Dakota, Department of Anthropology.

Banks, K. M. 1994. Lord of the rings: Forty years of archaeology at Lone Tree
Reservoir, North Dakota. *In* Banks, K. M., ed., Forty something: The River
Basin Surveys. *North Dakota Archaeological Society Journal* 5:97–116.

Barnosky, C. W., E. C. Grimm, and H. E. Wright Jr. 1987. Towards a postglacial
history of the northern Great Plains: A review of the paleoecologic problems. Pittsburgh: *Carnegie Museum Annals* 56:259–73.

Beaudoin, A. B. 1993. A compendium and evaluation of postglacial pollen
records in Alberta. *Canadian Journal of Archaeology* 17:92–112.

————. 1998. Holocene climatic variability on the interior plains of Canada:
Contrasting the context for Eurocanadian settlement with that for previous human occupation. Boulder, Colo.: Annual Meeting of the Geological Society of America, *Abstracts with Program* 30, no. 7:A-251.

Bettis, E. A., III. 1992. Soil morphologic properties and weathering zone characteristics as age indicators in Holocene alluvium in the Upper Midwest.
In Holliday, V. T., ed., Soils in archaeology: Landscape evolution and
human occupation, 119–44. Washington, D.C.: Smithsonian Institution
Press.

Bettis, E. A., III, and D. W. Benn. 1985. An archaeological and geomorphological survey in the central Des Moines River valley, Iowa. *Plains Anthropologist* 29:211–27.

Binford, L. R., S. R. Binford, R. Whallon, and M. A. Hardin. 1970. Archaeology
at Hatchery West. Washington, D.C.: *American Antiquity*, Memoir 24.

Boettger, W. M. 1986. Origin and stratigraphy of Holocene sediments, Souris
and Des Lacs glacial-lake spillways, north-central North Dakota. Master's
thesis, Grand Forks, University of North Dakota.

Brophy, J. A. 1966. A possible *Bison (Superbison) crassicornis* of mid-Hypsi-
thermal age from Mercer County, North Dakota. North Dakota Academy
of Science, *Proceedings* 19:214–23.

Butzer, K. W. 1964. Environment and archaeology: An introduction to Pleistocene geography. Chicago: Aldine.

————. 1977. Geomorphology of the lower Illinois valley as a spatial-temporal
context for the Koster Archaic site, Illinois. Springfield: Illinois State
Museum, *Reports of Investigation* 34.

————. 1978. Toward an integrated, contextual approach in archaeology: A personal view. *Journal of Archaeological Science* 5:191–93.

————. 1982. Archaeology as human ecology. London: Cambridge University Press.

Campling, N. R. 1980. Identification of Swan River chert. *In* Pettipas, L., ed., Directions in Manitoba prehistory, 291–301. Winnipeg: Manitoba Archaeological Society.

Christensen, R. C. 1991. Instrumental neutron activation analysis of Knife River Flint from the primary source area: Phase I: elemental description and statement of variability. Master's thesis, Oxford, University of Mississippi.

Christiansen, E. A. 1965. Ice frontal positions in Saskatchewan. Saskatoon: Saskatchewan Research Council, Geology Division, Map 2, scale 1:1,520,000.

Clayton, L., and T. F. Freers, eds. 1967. Glacial geology of the Missouri Coteau and adjacent areas. Grand Forks: North Dakota Geological Survey, Miscellaneous Series 30.

Clayton, L., and S. R. Moran. 1979. Oahe Formation. *In* Groenewold, G. H., L. R. Hemish, J. A. Cherry, B. W. Rehm, G. N. Meyer, and L. M. Winczewski, eds., Geology and geohydrology of the Knife River basin and adjacent areas of west-central North Dakota. Grand Forks: North Dakota Geological Survey, Report of Investigations 64:337–39.

Clayton, L., W. B. Bickley Jr., and W. J. Stone. 1970. Knife River flint. *Plains Anthropologist* 15:282–90.

Clayton, L., S. R. Moran, and W. B. Bickley Jr. 1976. Stratigraphy, chronology, and climatic implications of late Quaternary upland silt in North Dakota. Grand Forks: North Dakota Geological Survey, Miscellaneous Series 54.

Clayton, L., S. R. Moran, and J. P. Bluemle. 1980. Explanatory text to accompany the geologic map of North Dakota. Grand Forks: North Dakota Geological Survey, Report of Investigation 69.

Clayton, J. S., and W. K. Janzen. 1960. Soils of the Long Creek archaeological site. *In* Wettlaufer, B., and W. J. Mayer-Oakes, eds., The Long Creek site. Regina: Saskatchewan Museum of Natural History, Anthropological Series 2:75–81.

Coogan, A. H. 1960. Geological age of Soldier Creek, Buffalo County, South Dakota. *Iowa Academy of Science Proceedings* 67:314–25.

————. 1983. Geology and geological history of the site locality. *In* Toom, D. L., and M. L. Gregg, eds., Archaeological excavations at the Mondrian Tree site (32MZ58), Missouri River, McKenzie County, North Dakota. Grand Forks: University of North Dakota, Department of Anthropology, Contribution 193:7.1–7.49.

————. 1987. Holocene geomorphic and stratigraphic framework of archaeological sites along the Missouri River, central South Dakota. Omaha, Nebr.: U.S. Army Corps of Engineers.

Coogan, A. H., and W. N. Irving. 1959. Late Pleistocene and Recent Missouri River terraces in the Big Bend Reservoir, South Dakota. *Iowa Academy of Science Proceedings* 66:317–27.

Cooper, P. L. 1958. Archaeological investigations in the Heart Butte Reservoir area, North Dakota. Washington, D.C.: Smithsonian Institution, Bureau of American Ethnology Bulletin 169:1–40.

David, P. P. 1971. The Brookdale Road section and its significance in the chronological studies of dune activities in the Brandon Sand Hills of Manitoba. Ottawa: Geological Survey of Canada, Special Paper 9:293–99.

Davidson, D. A. 1985. Geomorphology and archaeology. In Gifford, J. A., and G. Rapp, eds., Archaeological geology, 24–55. New Haven: Yale University Press.

Del Bene, T. A. 1994. Heart condition: A synthesis of archaeological investigations at Heart Butte Reservoir in North Dakota. In Banks, K. M., ed., Forty something: The River Basin Surveys. North Dakota Archaeological Society Journal 5:51–66.

Donohue, J. 1992. Geoarchaeological investigations of sites buried in upland loess deposits in western South Dakota. Lincoln: Nebraska State Historical Society, Abstracts of the 50th Annual Meeting of the Plains Anthropological Society:42.

Dort, W., Jr., and J. K. Jones Jr., eds. 1970. Pleistocene and Recent environments of the central Great Plains. Lawrence: University of Kansas Press, Special Publication 3.

Dunnell, R. C. 1986. Five decades of American archaeology. In Meltzer, D. J., D. D. Fowler, and J. A. Sabloff, American archaeology, past and future: A celebration of the Society for American Archaeology, 1935–1985, 23–49. Washington, D.C.: Smithsonian Institution Press.

Elson, J. A. 1967. Geology of Glacial Lake Agassiz. In Mayer-Oakes, W. J., ed., Life, land, and water, 97–106. Winnipeg: University of Manitoba Press.

Everitt, B. L. 1968. Use of the cottonwood in an investigation of the recent history of a flood plain. American Journal of Science 266:417–34.

Falk, C. R. 1977. Analysis of unmodified vertebrate fauna from sites in the Middle Missouri subarea. In Wood, W. R., ed., Trends in Middle Missouri prehistory: A festschrift honoring the contributions of Donald J. Lehmer. Lincoln, Nebr.: Plains Anthropological Society, Memoir 13:151–61.

Fenneman, N. M. 1931. Physiography of the western United States. New York: McGraw Hill.

Ferring, C. R. 1994. The role of geoarchaeology in Paleoindian research. In Bonnichsen, R., and D. G. Steele, eds., Method and theory for investigating the peopling of the Americas, 57–72. Corvallis, Ore.: Center for the Study of the First Americans.

Figgins, J. D. 1927. The antiquity of man in America. Natural History 27:229–39.

Flannery, K. V. 1968. Archaeological systems theory and early Mesoamerica. In Meggers, B. J., ed., Anthropological archaeology in the Americas, 67–87. Washington, D.C.: Anthropological Society of Washington.

Flint, R. F. 1955. Pleistocene geology of eastern South Dakota. Washington, D.C.: United States Geological Survey, Professional Paper 262.

Folsom, C. B., Jr. 1980. A history of the North Dakota Geological Survey. Grand Forks: North Dakota Geological Survey, Miscellaneous Series 58.

Frison, G. C. 1991. Prehistoric hunters of the High Plains, 2nd ed. New York: Academic Press.

Glenn, J. R. 1994. The River Basin Surveys program. *In* Banks, K. M., ed., Forty something: The River Basin Surveys. *North Dakota Archaeological Society Journal* 5:5–14.

Gonzalez, M. A. 1987. Fluvial geomorphology of Paddock Creek, Little Missouri Badlands, southwestern North Dakota. Master's thesis, Madison, University of Wisconsin.

Hamilton, T. M. 1967. Recent fluvial geology in western North Dakota. Master's thesis, Grand Forks, University of North Dakota.

Harksen, J. C. 1974. Radiocarbon dating of terraces along Bear Creek, Pennington County, South Dakota. Rapid City: South Dakota Geological Survey, Report of Investigations 108.

Haynes, C. V. 1990. The Antevs-Bryan years and the legacy for Paleoindian geochronology. *In* Laporte, L. F., ed., Establishment of a geologic framework for paleoanthropology. Boulder, Colo.: The Geological Society of America, Special Paper 242:55–68.

Helgevold, M. K. 1981. A history of South Dakota archaeology. South Dakota Archaeological Society, Special Publication 3.

Hlady, W., ed. 1970. Ten thousand years: Archaeology in Manitoba. Winnipeg: Manitoba Archaeological Society.

Howard, E. B. 1935. Evidence of early man in America. *Museum Journal* 24: 53–171.

Hughes, J. T. 1949. Investigations in western South Dakota and northeastern Wyoming. *American Antiquity* 14:266–77.

Hurt, W. 1966. The Altithermal and the prehistory of the Northern Plains. *Quaternaria* 8:101–13.

Jenks, A. E. 1936. Pleistocene man in Minnesota: A fossil *Homo sapiens*. Minneapolis: University of Minnesota Press.

————. 1937. Minnesota's Browns Valley Man and associated burial artifacts. American Anthropological Association, Memoir 49.

Jennings, J. D., ed. 1950. Proceedings of the sixth Plains Archaeological Conference (1948). Salt Lake City: University of Utah, Anthropological Papers 11.

Jennings, J. D. 1985. River Basin Surveys: Origins, operations, and results, 1945–1969. *American Antiquity* 50:281–96.

————. 1986. American archaeology, 1930–1985. *In* Meltzer, D. J., D. D. Fowler, D. D., and J. A. Sabloff, eds., American archaeology, past and future: A celebration of the Society for American Archaeology, 1935–1985, 53–62. Washington, D.C.: Smithsonian Institution Press.

Johnson, E. 1962. The prehistory of the Red River Valley. *Minnesota History* 38:157–65.

Jorstad, T., T. East, J. M. Adovasio, J. Donahue, and R. Stuckenrath. 1986. Paleosols and prehistoric populations in the High Plains. *Geoarchaeology* 1:163–81.

Kehoe, T. F. 1966. The distribution and implications of fluted points in Saskatchewan. *American Antiquity* 31:530–39.

Knox, J. C. 1984. Responses of river systems to Holocene climates. *In* Wright, H. E., Jr., ed., Late Quaternary environments of the United States: Vol. 2, the Holocene, 26–41. Minneapolis: University of Minnesota Press.

Kuehn, D. D. 1993. Landform and archaeological site location in the Little Missouri Badlands: A new look at some well established patterns. *Geoarchaeology* 8:313–23.

———. 1997. A geoarchaeological assessment of bison kill site preservation in the Little Missouri badlands. *Plains Anthropologist* 42:319–28.

———. 1998. Preliminary geoarchaeological reconnaissance in Badlands National Park, South Dakota. Lincoln, Nebr.: Midwest Archaeological Center.

Kuehn, D. D., L. J. Scott, and J. W. Wyckoff. 1987. Late mid-Holocene paleoenvironments at the Tysver-Olson site. *In* McKinnon, N. A., and G. S. L. Stuart, eds., Man and the mid-Holocene climatic optimum, 71–84. Calgary: University of Calgary Archaeological Association.

Langbein, W. B., and S. A. Schumm. 1958. Yield of sediment in relation to mean annual precipitation. *American Geophysical Union, Transactions* 39:1076–84.

Leechman, D. 1951. Bone grease. *American Antiquity* 16:355–56.

Lehmer, D. L. 1971. Introduction to Middle Missouri archaeology. Washington, D.C.: National Park Service, Anthropological Papers 1.

Leonoff, L. M. 1970. The identification, distribution, and sources of lithic raw materials in Manitoba archaeological sites. Master's thesis, Winnipeg, University of Manitoba.

Leverett, F. 1932. Quaternary geology of Minnesota and parts of adjacent states. Washington, D.C.: United States Geological Survey Professional Paper 161.

Low, B. 1996. Swan River chert. *Plains Anthropologist* 41:165–74.

McAndrews, J. H. 1966. Postglacial history of prairie, savanna, and forest in northwestern Minnesota. Torrey Botanical Club, *Memoirs* 22:1–72.

McAndrews, J. H. 1967. Paleoecology of the Seminary and Mirror Pool peat deposits. Winnipeg: University of Manitoba, Department of Anthropology, Occasional Papers 1:253–69.

McAndrews, J. H., R. E. Stewart, and R. C. Bright. 1967. Paleoecology of a prairie pothole: A preliminary report. *In* Clayton, L., and T. F. Freers, eds., Glacial geology of the Missouri Coteau and adjacent areas. Grand Forks: North Dakota Geological Survey, Miscellaneous Series 30: 101–13.

McFaul, M. 1990. Geoarchaeological potential of Souris River terrains, Renville County, North Dakota. *North Dakota Archaeological Society Journal* 4:17–42.

McFaul, M. 1991. Physiography and soil/sediment relationships. *In* Larson, T. K., and D. M. Penny, eds., The Smilden-Rostberg site: An Early Archaic component on the Northeastern Plains, 34–49. Laramie, Wyo.: Larson-Tibesar Associates.

MacNeish, R. S. 1958. An introduction to the archaeology of southeast Manitoba. Ottawa: National Museum of Canada, Bulletin 157.

Mandel, R. D. 1992. Soils and Holocene landscape evolution in central and southwestern Kansas: Implications for archaeological research. *In* Holliday, V. T., ed., Soils in archaeology: Landscape evolution and human occupation, 101–19. Washington, D.C.: Smithsonian Institution Press.

———. 1994. Holocene landscape evolution in the Pawnee River valley, southwestern Kansas. Lawrence: Kansas Geological Survey, Bulletin 236.

Mayer-Oakes, W. J., ed. 1967. Life, land, and water. Winnipeg: University of Manitoba Press.

Michlovic, M. G. 1988. The archaeology of the Red River valley. *Minnesota History* 51:55–62.

Moss, H. C. 1955. Physical features and soils of the Mortlach archaeological area. *In* Wettlaufer, B. N., The Mortlach site in the Besant Valley of central Saskatchewan. Regina: Saskatchewan, Department of Natural Resources, Anthropological Series 1:61–70.

Muhs, D. R., T. W. Stafford Jr., J. Been, S. A. Mahan, J. Burdett, G. Skipp, and Z. M. Rowland. 1997. Holocene eolian activity in the Minot dune field, North Dakota. *Canadian Journal of Earth Sciences* 34:1442–59.

Mulloy, W. T. 1958. A preliminary historical outline for the Northwestern Plains. Laramie: University of Wyoming *Publications in Science* 22, no. 1.

Neuman, R. W. 1964. Projectile points from preceramic occupations near Fort Thompson, South Dakota: A preliminary report. *Plains Anthropologist* 9:173–89.

———. 1975. Sonota complex and associated sites on the northern Great Plains. Lincoln: Nebraska State Historical Society, *Publications in Anthropology* 6.

Nowak, T. R., and L. A. Hannus. 1985. Lithic raw materials from the West Horse Creek quarry site (39SH37). *South Dakota Archaeological Society Journal* 8–9:98–114.

Osterkamp, W. R., M. M. Fenton, T. C. Gustavson, R. F. Hadley, V. T. Holliday, R. B. Morrison, and T. J. Toy. 1987. Great Plains. *In* Graf, W. L., ed., Geomorphic systems of North America. Boulder, Colo.: The Geological Society of America, Centennial Special 2:163–210..

Over, W. H. 1923. Amphibians and reptiles of South Dakota. Vermillion: South Dakota State Geological Survey, Bulletin 12.

———. 1936. The archaeology of Ludlow Cave and its significance. *American Antiquity* 2:126–29.

Over, W. H., and E. P. Churchill. 1945. Mammals of South Dakota. Vermillion: University of South Dakota, The Museum.

Over, W. H., and C. S. Thomas. 1921. Birds of South Dakota. Vermillion: South Dakota Geological and Natural History Survey Bulletin 21, no.9.

Pettipas, L. 1967. Paleo-Indian manifestations in Manitoba: Their spatial and temporal relationships with the Campbell strandline. Master's thesis, Winnipeg, University of Manitoba.

Pettipas, L. F., and A. P. Buchner. 1983. Paleo-Indian prehistory of the Glacial Lake Agassiz region in Manitoba, 11,500 to 6500 B.P. In Teller, J. T., and L. Clayton, eds., Glacial Lake Agassiz. St. John's, Newfoundland: Geological Society of Canada Special Paper 26:421–51.

Picha, P. R., and M. L. Gregg. 1993. Chronostratigraphy of upper James River flood plain sediments: Implications for southeastern North Dakota archaeology. Geoarchaeology 8: 203–15.

Porter, J. W. 1962. Notes on four lithic types found in archaeological sites near Mobridge, South Dakota. Plains Anthropologist 7:267–69.

Reeves, B. O. K. 1970. Culture change in the Northern Plains: 1000 B.C.–A.D. 1000. Ph.D. diss., Calgary, Alberta, University of Calgary.

———. 1973. The concept of an Altithermal cultural hiatus in Northern Plains prehistory. American Anthropologist 75:1221–53.

Reiten, J. 1983. Quaternary geology of the Knife River Indian Villages National Historic Site. Master's thesis, Grand Forks, University of North Dakota.

Robinson, E. B. 1966. History of North Dakota. Lincoln: University of Nebraska Press.

Root, M. J., ed. 1993. Site 32DU955A: Folsom occupation of the Knife River flint primary source area. Pullman: Washington State University, Center for Northwest Anthropology Project Report 22.

Root, M. J., and S. A. Ahler. 1984. Early man at the Knife River flint quarries. North Dakota History 51:54.

———. 1987. Middle Holocene occupation and technological change in the Knife River flint primary source area. In McKinnon, N. A., and G. S. L. Stuart, eds., Man and the mid-Holocene climatic optimum, 85–109. Calgary: University of Calgary Archaeological Association.

Root, M. J., S. A. Ahler, C. R. Falk, J. E. Foss, H. Haas, and J. A. Artz. 1986. Archaeological investigations in the Knife River flint primary source area, Dunn County, North Dakota: 1982–1986 program. Grand Forks: University of North Dakota, Department of Anthropology, Contribution 234.

Ruhe, R. V. 1969. Quaternary landscapes in Iowa. Ames: Iowa State University Press.

Running, G. L., IV. 1995. Archaeological geology of the Rustad Quarry (32RI775): An Early Archaic site in southeastern North Dakota. Geoarchaeology 10:183–204.

Schiffer, M. B. 1987. Formation processes of the archaeological record. Albuquerque: University of Mexico Press.

Schneider, F. 1982. Recent research in the Northeastern Plains. *North Dakota Archaeological Society Journal* 1:63.

Schwalb, A., and W. E. Dean. 1998. Stable isotopes and sediments from Pickerel Lake, South Dakota, USA: A 12ky record of environmental changes. *Journal of Paleolimnology* 19:15–30.

Shane, O. C., III. 1991. Final report to the Minnesota Historical Society: Radiocarbon assays of bone from the Browns Valley skeleton. Minneapolis: Science Museum of Minnesota.

Sheehan, M. S. 1995. Cultural responses to the Altithermal or inadequate sampling. *Plains Anthropologist* 40:261–70.

Sheldon, A. E. 1905. Ancient Indian fireplaces in South Dakota bad-lands. *American Antiquity* 7:44–48.

Sigstad, J. S., and J. K. Sigstad. 1973. Archaeological field notes of W. H. Over. Rapid City: South Dakota Archaeological Research Center, *Bulletin* 1.

Speth, J. D. 1983. Bison kills and bone counts: Decision making by ancient hunters. Chicago: University of Chicago Press.

Stafford, C. R. 1995. Geoarchaeological perspectives on paleolandscapes and regional subsurface archaeology. *Journal of Archaeological Method and Theory* 2:69–104.

Stein, J. K. 1986. Coring archaeological sites. *American Antiquity* 51:505–27.

Strong, W. D. 1935. An introduction to Nebraska archaeology. Washington, D.C.: Smithsonian Institution, Miscellaneous Collections 93, no. 10.

Syms, E. L. 1969. The McKean complex as a horizon marker in Manitoba and on the northern Great Plains. Master's thesis, Winnipeg, University of Manitoba.

Tamplin, M. 1967. A brief summary of Glacial Lake Agassiz studies. *In* Mayer-Oakes, W. J., ed. Life, land, and water, 27–36. Winnipeg: University of Manitoba Press.

Thiessen, T. D. 1994. The National Park Service and the Interagency Archaeological Salvage Program in the Missouri River mainstem reservoirs. *In* Banks, K. M., ed., Forty something: The River Basin Surveys. *North Dakota Archaeological Society Journal* 5:15–26.

Tinker, J. R., Jr. 1971. Rates of hillslope lowering in the badlands of North Dakota. Boulder, Colo.: The Geological Society of America, *Abstracts with Programs* 3.

Tinkler, K. J. 1985. A short history of geomorphology. London: Croom Helm.

Toom, D. L. 1988. A preliminary statement on the archaeology and radiocarbon dating of the Flaming Arrow site (23ML34), McLean County, North Dakota. *North Dakota Archaeological Association Journal* 3:51–73.

———. 1992. Climate and sedentism in the Middle Missouri subarea of the plains. Ph.D. diss., Boulder, University of Colorado.

Toom, D. L., M. A. Van Ness, C. W. Wheeler, and P. R. Picha. 1990. Archaeological test excavations at eight sites in the Lake Sharpe project area of

Hughes, Lyman, and Stanley counties, South Dakota, 1987. Omaha, Nebr.: U.S. Army Corps of Engineers.

Tyrrell, J. B. 1892. Report on north-western Manitoba with portions of the adjacent districts of Assiniboia and Saskatchewan. Ottawa: Geological Survey of Canada, Annual Report 5: pt. 1, sect. E.

Upham, W. 1895. The Glacial Lake Agassiz. Washington, D.C.: United States Geological Survey Monograph 25.

Van Nest, J. 1985. Patination of Knife River flint artifacts. *Plains Anthropologist* 30:325–39.

———. 1995. Geology of the Alkali Creek site. *In* Metcalf, M. D., and S. A. Ahler, eds., Alkali Creek: A stratified record of prehistoric flint mining in North Dakota, 51–109. Bismarck: United States Department of Agriculture, Natural Resources Conservation Service.

Vehik, S. C. 1977. Bone fragments and bone grease manufacturing: A review of their archaeological use and potential. *Plains Anthropologist* 21:199–206.

Vitek, J. D., and D. F. Ritter. 1993. Geomorphology in the U.S.A. *In* Walker, H. J., and W. E. Grabau, eds., The evolution of geomorphology: A nation-by-nation summary of development, 469–82. New York: John Wiley.

Waters, M. R. 1992. Principles of geoarchaeology: A North American perspective. Tucson: University of Arizona Press.

Waters, M. R., and D. D. Kuehn. 1996. The geoarchaeology of place: The effect of geological processes on the preservation and interpretation of the archaeological record.*American Antiquity* 61:483–98.

Watts, W. A., and H. E. Wright Jr. 1966. Late-Wisconsin pollen and seed analysis from the Nebraska Sand Hills. *Ecology* 47:202–10.

Wedel, W. R. 1938. The direct historic approach in Pawnee archaeology. Washington, D.C.: Smithsonian Institution, Miscellaneous Collections 47, no. 7:1–21.

———. 1941. Environment and native subsistence economies in the central Great Plains. Washington, D.C.: Smithsonian Institution, Miscellaneous Collections 101, no. 3:1–29.

———. 1947. Prehistory and environment in the central Great Plains. Kansas Academy of Science *Transactions* 50: 1–18.

———. 1953. Some aspects of human ecology in the Central Plains. *American Anthropologist* 55:499–514.

———. 1961. Prehistoric man on the Great Plains. Norman: University of Oklahoma Press.

———. 1977. The education of a Plains anthropologist. *Plains Anthropologist* 22:1–11.

———. 1982. Essays in the history of Plains archaeology. Lincoln, Nebr.: J & L Reprints.

Wettlaufer, B. N. 1955. The Mortlach site in the Besant Valley of central Saskatchewan. Regina, Saskatchewan: Department of Natural Resources, Anthropological Series 1.

Wettlaufer, B. N., and W. J. Mayer-Oakes, eds. 1960. The Long Creek site. Regina: Saskatchewan Museum of Natural History, Anthropological Series 2.

Weymouth, J. W. 1976. A magnetic survey of the Walth Bay site (39WW203). Lincoln, Nebr.: Midwest Archaeological Center, Occasional Studies in Anthropology 3.

Weymouth, J. W., and R. Nickel. 1977. A magnetometer survey of the Knife River Indian villages. Plains Anthropological Society, Memoir 13:104–18.

Wheeler, R. P. 1963. The Stutsman Focus: An aboriginal cultural complex in the Jamestown Reservoir area, North Dakota. Washington, D.C.: Smithsonian Institution, Bureau of American Ethnology, Bulletin 185.

————. 1995. Archaeological investigations in three reservoir areas in South Dakota and Wyoming. Lincoln, Nebr.: J&L Reprints, *Reprints in Anthropology* 46.

Wheeler, R. P., and A. M. Johnson. 1985. A stratified Woodland site in the Oahe Reservoir area, South Dakota. *South Dakota Archaeological Society Journal* 8–9:80–91.

White, E. M. 1966. Conditions for cliff dune formation and the climatic implications. *Plains Anthropologist* 11:80–82.

White, E. M., and L. A. Hannus. 1985. Holocene alluviation and erosion in the White River badlands, South Dakota. South Dakota Academy of Science *Proceedings* 64:82–94.

White, T. E., and J. T. Hughes. n.d. A preliminary appraisal of the physiographic history of Horsehead Creek in the vicinity of 39FA65. Lincoln, Nebr.: Midwest Archaeological Center.

Will, G. F. 1911. A new feature in the archaeology of the Missouri Valley in North Dakota. *American Anthropologist* 13:585–88.

————. 1924. Archaeology of the Missouri River valley. American Museum of Natural History, Anthropological Papers 22, no. 6.

————. 1933. A resume of North Dakota archaeology. *North Dakota Historical Quarterly* 7:150–61.

————. 1946. Tree ring studies in North Dakota. Fargo: North Dakota Agricultural Experiment Station, *Bulletin* 338.

Will, G. F., and T. C. Hecker. 1944. The Upper Missouri River Valley aboriginal culture in North Dakota. *North Dakota Historical Quarterly* 11, no. 1–2:5–126.

Will, G. F., and G. E. Hyde. 1917. Corn among the Indians of the upper Missouri. Lincoln: University of Nebraska Press.

Will, G. F., and H. J. Spinden. 1906. The Mandans: A study of their culture, archaeology, and language. Cambridge, Mass.: Peabody Museum of American Archaeology and Ethnology, Papers 3, no. 4.

Willey, G. R., and J. A. Sabloff. 1993. A history of American archaeology, 3rd ed. San Francisco: W. H. Freeman.

Wilson, M. C. 1990. Archaeological geology in western Canada: Techniques, approaches, and integrative themes. *In* Lasca, N. P., and J. Donahue, J., Archaeological geology of North America. Boulder, Colo.: The Geological Society of America, Centennial Special 4:61–86.

Wormington, H. M. 1957. Ancient man in North America, 7th ed. Denver Museum of Natural History, Popular Series 4.

Wormington, H. M., and R. G. Forbis. 1965. An introduction to the archaeology of Alberta, Canada. Denver Museum of Natural History, *Proceedings* 11.

Wright, H. E., Jr., and D. G. Frey, eds. 1965. The Quaternary of the United States. Princeton, N.J.: Princeton University Press.

Wyckoff, J. W. 1984. A late Holocene environmental record from the Knife River region, North Dakota. North Dakota Academy of Science, *Proceedings* 38:24.

Yansa, C. H. 1998. Holocene paleovegetation and paleohydrology of a prairie pothole in southern Saskatchewan, Canada. *Journal of Paleolimnology* 19:429–41.

Zimmerman, L. J. 1985. Peoples of prehistoric South Dakota. Lincoln: University of Nebraska Press.

CHAPTER NINE

The Past, Present, and Future

A SUMMARY OF GEOARCHAEOLOGICAL
RESEARCH IN THE GREAT PLAINS

Rolfe D. Mandel

THE PAST

The essays in this volume describe the history of geoarchaeological research for different regions of the Great Plains. As one would expect, this approach reveals differences and similarities in the historical development of geoarchaeology among the regions.

Geoarcheology emerged and developed diachronically in the Plains, and the intensity of geoarchaeological research varied among the regions. For example, interdisciplinary archaeology was underway in the Southern Plains as early as 1933 with the discovery of the Clovis type site, and geoarchaeological research was in full force in that region by the 1950s. By contrast, geoarchaeological research faltered in the Central Plains of Kansas after H. T. U. Smith and Loren Eiseley's 1937–38 collaborations at the Spring Creek site, and it did not reemerge and develop until the 1970s.

The Osage Plains and the Eastern Plains and Prairies are similar in the historical development of geoarchaeology. Throughout the 1930s, a number of archaeological studies in the Southern Osage Plains included geologic assessments, but the application of geoarchaeology waned in this region between 1940 and 1965 and interest in it did not redevelop until the late 1960s. Beginning as early as 1915, archaeological investigations in the Eastern Plains and

Prairies involved geologic interpretations, but geoarchaeology was slow to develop in this region and it did not reach fruition until the late 1960s.

Beginning in the 1920s and continuing on through the 1950s, systematic archaeological surveys in Nebraska have almost always involved a geoscientist. The hiatus in geoarchaeological research that lasted from the late 1960s until the late 1970s was followed by numerous cultural resource management (CRM)-related collaborations between geomorphologists and archaeologists.

The early history of geoarchaeology in the Northwestern Plains is similar to that in Nebraska during the first half of the twentieth century. In the Northwestern Plains, geoarchaeological research emerged in 1932 at the Scottsbluff site and quickly intensified with the discovery of numerous other early sites. As with the evolution of geoarchaeology in the Southern Plains, the development of geoarchaeology in this region has remained closely tied to Paleoindian archaeology. Despite its long history, geoarchaeology in the Northwestern Plains has not developed much beyond the site-assessment level because of the emphasis on Paleoindian occupations.

On the Northern Plains the earliest example of the use of earth science principles in an archaeological investigation was in 1905, and archaeologists and geologists occasionally interacted during the 1930s. However, true collaboration between geoscientists and archaeologists was rare before the 1960s, and did not become commonplace until the 1970s and 1980s.

Although geoarchaeology did not emerge and develop simultaneously in various regions across the Great Plains, several research themes brought geoscientists and archaeologists together on the Plains during certain periods in the nineteenth and twentieth centuries. From the 1860s through the 1930s the controversy over the antiquity of humans in the New World dominated North American archaeology, and many sites in the Plains (e.g., Frederick, 12 Mile Creek, Clovis, Lindenmeier, "Nebraska Loess Man," Lansing, Scottsbluff) were at the center of this debate. Lacking a numerical-dating technique that could resolve the controversy, archaeologists turned to geoscientists to corroborate or refute evidence that suggested peopling of the Americas during the last (Wisconsin) glacial period. As Bettis (this volume) notes, geoscientists were intrigued with the debate and agreed that geologic proof was the key to demonstrating the antiquity of human presence on the continent. During this period archaeologists considered geologic information important, but only in situations in which great antiquity was suspected. Hence, geoscientists were rarely invited to participate in archaeological investigations unless artifacts were found with the remains of extinct fauna or human skeletal remains were enclosed in deposits presumed to date to the last glacial period.

In the early 1900s collaboration between geoscientists and archaeologists in North America was hindered by developments in both disciplines. Archaeology was shifting from a natural to a more social science (Daniel 1975:239–42; Gifford and Rapp 1985: 419). Also, this was a time when both archaeology and the geosciences were developing into more strictly defined fields with boundaries that were rarely crossed. Artz (this volume) notes that productive collaboration between archaeologists and earth scientists did not emerge until the separate disciplines had individually reached a "certain level of sophistication" in their own realms of study.

A threshold event in the development of geoarchaeology was the arrival of radiocarbon dating, which was developed by Frank Willard Libby in the late 1940s. Geoscientists were no longer tethered to "early man" sites. Moreover, radiocarbon dating opened the door for another research theme: reconstructing paleoenvironments contemporary with prehistoric human activity at a given time and place.

In some areas of the Great Plains, particularly the Central Plains of Kansas and northern Oklahoma, the Eastern Plains and Prairies, and the Northern Plains, collaboration between archaeologists and geologists waned between 1940 and 1965. Many archaeologists working in the Plains during this period focused on Late Prehistoric sites, and their research reflected deep interests in the region's ethnohistory. Consequently, they were primarily concerned with the cultural significance of artifacts; the geologic context of archaeological materials was considered irrelevant (Artz, this volume; Mandel, this volume). Also, those involved with Late Prehistoric sites usually assumed that the landscape has not changed much over the past millennium, and therefore the landscape contexts of cultural deposits were readily interpreted without the need for an earth-science specialist (Bettis, this volume). Given these perceptual barriers, it is not surprising that geoarchaeology stagnated in many areas of the Plains during the mid-twentieth century.

The emergence of processual and environmental archaeology during the mid- to late 1960s caused a resurgence in Plains geoarchaeology. Louis Binford and Karl Butzer were instrumental in changing the modus operandi of North American archaeology, as they steered it towards hypothesis testing and interdisciplinary research, respectively (Butzer 1964; Binford 1968). Archaeologists began to think of sites as components of dynamic landscapes, and they developed a strong interest in the physical structure of sites (Artz, this volume). This interest, combined with increased concern for the paleoenvironmental context of cultural deposits, caused archaeologists to seek out specialists among other disciplines, especially geography and geology.

The most important events shaping contemporary North American geoarchaeology were the passage of the National Historic Preservation Act of 1966, the National Environmental Policy Act of 1969, and the Moss-Bennett Act of 1974. These acts, along with subsequent laws and regulations, established federal mandates for large-scale cultural resource surveys and for the mitigation of the impacts of development on significant cultural resources. Cultural resource management (CRM), which emerged in response to the federal mandates, has been the principal driving force behind Plains geoarchaeology since 1970. During the first decade of CRM, geoscientists were often limited to describing soil profiles at archaeological sites and/or providing terrain analysis for archaeological survey areas. However, by the 1980s geoarchaeology moved beyond the descriptive stage: geoscientists were providing archaeologists with insights about the nature of the archaeological record. Today, earth-science specialists are often called upon to map landform sediment assemblages and determine the geologic potential for buried cultural resources. At individual sites, they are usually expected to interpret depositional environments, site-formation processes, and postdepositional modification of archaeological deposits and sediments (Mandel, this volume). Bettis (this volume) places modern geoarchaeology in a historical perspective, noting that it has "graduated from something done only by a specialist at an old or deeply buried site to a cooperative effort among archaeologists and earth-science specialists (often with archaeological training) in a wide variety of archaeological contexts."

In order to fully understand the development of Plains geoarchaeology, it is necessary to look beyond the research themes and consider the practitioners. Several individuals, including Kirk Bryan, Ernst Antevs, E. H. Sellards, and C. Bertrand Schultz, played key roles in the development of Plains geoarchaeology during the first half of the twentieth century. Although each of these scholars made significant contributions that are often cited in chronicles of geoarchaeological research, Kirk Bryan stands out. From 1925 to 1950 he dominated research and teaching at the interface between geology and archaeology in North America (Gifford and Rapp 1985). For most of his professional career, Bryan was Professor of Physiography in the Department of Geology at Harvard University. His involvement with archaeology began in the American

Southwest, but he quickly developed an interest in the geologic setting of Folsom and other early sites on the Plains (Haynes 1990). This interest took him to several world-class Paleoindian sites, including Lindenmeier and Horner, where he focused on the geologic context of the archaeological deposits (see Albanese, this volume). Gifford and Rapp (1985:418) noted that Bryan influenced much of the American work done in geoarchaeology shortly after World War II and that by the time he died in 1950, he had "effected a convergence of Pleistocene studies and archaeological geology through an explicit paleogeographic approach to archaeology."

Kirk Bryan's influence on Plains geoarchaeology can also be measured through the accomplishments of his graduate students. This is exemplified by the works of Louis Ray and Sheldon Judson. Ray provided a detailed Pleistocene chronology for the Cache la Poudre drainage basin in northern Colorado as a means of geologically dating the Lindenmeier site (Bryan and Ray 1941; Albanese, this volume). Judson focused on the stratigraphy and sedimentary history of the San Jon site, a Cody/Firstview occupation in the Southern Plains (Judson 1953; Hill et al. 1995; Holliday, this volume).

There were other graduate students at Harvard who either studied under Bryan or interacted with him before they became involved in archaeological projects on the Plains. Among them were H. T. U. Smith (see Mandel, this volume), Claude C. Albritton Jr. (see Ferring, this volume), E. Mott Davis (see May, this volume), and Fred Wendorf (see Holliday, this volume). Bryan's influence on these individuals is apparent in their contributions to Plains archaeology. Also, there are many Plains geoarchaeologists who never studied under Bryan, including C. Vance Haynes Jr. and the contributors to this volume, but have been strongly influenced by his work.

THE PRESENT

Over the past several years, two trends have emerged in Plains geoarchaeology: First, the increasing involvement of geoscientists in studies of previously excavated archaeological sites, and second, geoscientists and archaeologists working together on Geographic Information Systems (GIS). The participation of geoscientists in studies of previously excavated sites has been fostered by both philosophical changes and technological developments. For example, archaeologists now realize that the theoretical approaches of the 1970s were not matched with methodologies that would guide recovery of the field data that is essential for interpreting the archaeological record. Also, archaeologists have become increasingly sensitive to site formation processes. Before the 1980s many archaeologists focused on the recovery of artifacts and did not consider either the geological context of cultural materials or the nature of the deposits containing the artifacts. These were major oversights because the geologic deposits that harbor the archaeological materials contain many clues about the cultural processes responsible for the formation and subsequent history of the site. Armed with new and improved analytical methods, such as micromorphological analysis and accelerator mass spectrometry (AMS) dating, researchers now have the capability to learn more about the age and geologic history of previously excavated sites in the Plains.

A recent study of material from the Plainview and Olsen-Chubbuck sites in the Southern Plains is a good example of an effort to glean new information from previously excavated sites. Plainview was excavated in the mid- and late 1940s, and Olsen-Chubbuck was initially tested in 1958 and then fully excavated in 1958 and 1960. Unfortunately, both of these important sites lacked good radiocarbon control, and this has led to some confusion regarding the history of Paleoindian occupations throughout the Great Plains (Hofman 1989; Holliday 1997). In an attempt to resolve this problem, geomorphologist Vance T. Holliday, archaeologist Eileen Johnson (Museum of Texas Tech University), and geochronologist Thomas W. Stafford (Stafford Research Laboratories, Inc.) used AMS-radiocarbon dating of specific amino acids from bone associated with the type Plainview and Firstview artifact assemblages from the Plainview and Olsen-Chubbuck sites, respectively (Holliday et al. 1999). The new ages clarify some issues of post-Folsom artifact chronologies but also raise some new questions about artifact typology. In addition, the relatively new analytical method used in this study demonstrates both the advantages and disadvantages of AMS-radiocarbon dating of bone (Holliday et al. 1999).

Other investigations of previously excavated sites in the Southern Plains include ongoing geoarchaeological studies at the Folsom, Nall, and San Jon sites. Vance Holliday is working with archaeologist David Meltzer (Southern Methodist University) at Folsom and Nall. The Folsom site in New Mexico is one of the most famous sites in the history of North American archaeology because of the role it played in demonstrating the antiquity of humans in the Western Hemisphere (Meltzer 1983, 1991). The work at the site from 1926 to

1928 was, however, never fully reported (e.g., Cook 1927, 1928; Figgins 1927). The current work is intended to enhance understanding of the original investigations and the bone bed, as well as document the stratigraphy and geochronology of the site (Meltzer et al. 1998). Nall, in the Oklahoma Panhandle, produced a large surface collection of Paleoindian artifacts that was only briefly reported some decades ago (Baker et al. 1957; see Mandel, this volume). New work at the site is intended to assess the state of the site and document the stratigraphic and paleogeographic context of an important collection. At San Jon, New Mexico, Holliday and archaeologist Eileen Johnson, based on initial reinvestigation by Hill et al. (1995), are following on the original archaeological work of Roberts (1942) and geologic investigations by Judson (1953). The current work is aimed at understanding the nature and context of the Paleoindian and Late Prehistoric bison bone beds originally examined at the site, as well as investigating more recently discovered Paleoindian and Archaic levels and, more generally, attempting to understand prehistoric use of the ubiquitous playa basins of the High Plains.

In the Central Plains of Nebraska, geomorphologist David May has been working with archaeologist Douglas Bamforth (University of Colorado) at two Paleoindian sites that were excavated in the late 1940s and early 1950s: Lime Creek and Red Smoke (see May, this volume). Their investigations are yielding new temporal, stratigraphic, and paleoenvironmental information for the sites.

One of the most rapidly evolving trends in Plains geoarchaeology is the integration of geologic, geophysic, paleontologic, ecologic, pedologic, hydrologic, climatic, geographic, topographic, and archaeological data within Geographic Information Systems. Application of GIS to the field of geoarchaeology provides earth scientists with a powerful tool for organizing, analyzing, and presenting spatial and temporal data sets, which might otherwise be unmanageable or difficult to comprehend. In some cases the role of geoarchaeologists is limited to the collection of data that are entered into a GIS. However, they are becoming more involved in designing the research systems and preprocessing, manipulating, and analyzing the data.

An ongoing geoarchaeological research project at Fort Riley in northeastern Kansas provides a good example of the potential for GIS applications in the Plains. ARC/INFO and ArcView (Environmental Systems Research Institute, Inc.) systems are being used to apply various attributes to the landscape through the compilation of a series of data layers. Data being collected by geomorphol-

ogist William Johnson (University of Kansas) include standard sedimentological information, soil and sediment field descriptions, stable carbon isotope
ratios, opal phytoliths, rock magnetics, and radiocarbon ages. Temporal and
lithostratigraphic data entered into the GIS are being used to develop areal
probabilities for burial of archaeological materials according to cultural period
(e.g., Paleoindian, Early Archaic, Late Woodland, Protohistoric, Historic),
including depth.

THE FUTURE

As we look ahead in the twenty-first century, geoarchaeological research
in the Great Plains is likely to involve new and rapidly evolving field and laboratory methods. For example, noninvasive geophysical techniques, such as
magnetometry, electrical resistivity, electromagnetic conductivity, magnetic
susceptibility, and ground-penetrating radar (GPR), will probably become
more widely used. The application of these techniques will be largely driven
by the rising costs of archaeological surveys and excavations and by the need
to collect information using the least destructive methods. In the western
United States, GPR surveys have already proven effective in the rapid, nonde-
structive discovery and mapping of buried archaeological deposits (Goodman et al. 1995; Conyers and Goodman 1997; Conyers and Cameron 1998).

It is also likely that innovations from the field of geochronology will influence archaeological research in the Great Plains during the twenty-first century. While some of the new numerical-dating techniques may be used to
determine the age of archaeological materials directly, others will be used to
date the sediments associated with cultural deposits, thereby providing an
indirect estimate of the age of archaeological materials. A number of relatively
new dating techniques, including electron spin resonance (ESR), thermoluminescence (TL), optical stimulated luminescence (OSL), infrared stimulated
luminescence (IRSL), and oxidizable carbon ratio (OCR) analysis, are available, but some have not been used, and others have not been adequately
tested, at archaeological sites in the Plains. As these techniques are improved,
they may become as common as radiocarbon dating is today.

Cultural resource management will probably continue to be a major driving force in bringing archaeologists and geoscientists together in the Great
Plains. However, as archaeologists become engaged in new quests, such as the

search for Pre-Clovis sites, geoarchaeological investigations unrelated to CRM will most likely increase in the region.

Archaeological studies in the Plains and elsewhere are becoming more interdisciplinary, as well as being multidisciplinary. Although their training has broadened and often crosses into other disciplines, most American archaeologists depend on consultants for interpretation of nonarchaeological evidence. Hence, archaeologists and earth scientists are interacting more frequently to resolve problems related to the human past, and this trend is likely to continue.

REFERENCES

Baker, W. E., G. L. Evans, and T. N. Campbell. 1957. The Nall site: Evidence of Early Man in the Oklahoma Panhandle. *Bulletin of the Oklahoma Anthropological Society* 5:1–20.

Binford, L. R. 1968. Archaeological perspectives. *In* Binford, S. R., and L. R. Binford, eds., New perspectives in archaeology, 5–32. Chicago: Aldine.

Butzer, K. W. 1964. Environment and archaeology: An introduction to Pleistocene geography. Chicago: Aldine.

Conyers, L. D., and C. M. Cameron. 1998. Ground-penetrating radar techniques and three-dimensional computer mapping in the American Southwest. *Journal of Field Archaeology* 25:417–30.

Conyers, L. D., and D. Goodman. 1997. Ground-penetrating radar: An introduction for archaeologists. Walnut Creek, Calif.: AltaMira Press.

Cook, H. J. 1927. New geological and paleontological evidence bearing on the antiquity of mankind in America. *Natural History* 27:240–47.

———. 1928. Glacial age man in New Mexico. *Scientific American* 139:38–40.

Daniel, G. 1975. A hundred and fifty years of archaeology. London: Duckworth.

Figgins, J. D. 1927. The antiquity of man in America. *Natural History* 27:229–39.

Goodman, D., Y. Nishimura, and J. D. Rogers. 1995. Time-slices in archaeological prospection. *Archaeological Prospection* 2:85–89.

Haynes, C. V., Jr. 1990. The Antevs-Bryan years and the legacy for Paleoindian geochronology. *In* Laporte, L. F., ed., Establishment of a geologic framework for paleoanthropology. Boulder, Colo.: The Geological Society of America, Special Paper 242:55–68.

Hill, M. G., V. T. Holliday, and D. J. Stanford. 1995. A further evaluation of the San Jon site, New Mexico. *Plains Anthropologist* 40:369–90.

Holliday, V. T. 1997. Paleoindian geoarchaeology of the Southern High Plains. Austin: University of Texas Press.

Holliday, V. T., E. Johnson, and T. W. Stafford. 1999. AMS radiocarbon dating of the type Plainview and Firstview (Paleoindian) assemblages: The agony and the ecstasy. *American Antiquity* 64: 444–54.

Hofman, J. L. 1989. Prehistoric cultural history—Hunters and gatherers in the Southern Great Plains. *In* Hofman, J. L., et al., eds., From Clovis to Comanchero: Archaeological overview of the Southern Great Plains. Fayetteville: Arkansas Archaeological Survey, Research Series 35:25–60.

Judson, S. 1953. Geology of the San Jon Site, eastern New Mexico. Washington, D.C.: Smithsonian Miscellaneous Collection 121.

Meltzer, D. J. 1983. The antiquity of man and the development of American archaeology. *Advances in Archaeological Method and Theory* 6:1–51.

———. 1991. On "paradigms" and "paradigm bias" in controversies over human antiquity in America. *In* Dillehay, T. D., and D. J. Meltzer, eds., The first Americans: Search and research, 13–49. Boca Raton, Fla.: CRC Press.

Meltzer, D. J., V. T. Holliday, and L. C. Todd. 1998. Recent field reserch at the Folsom site (29CX1), New Mexico. *Current Research in the Pleitocene* 15:42–45.

Rapp, G., Jr., and C. L. Hill. 1998. Geoarchaeology: The Earth-science approach to archaeological interpretations. New Haven, Conn.: Yale University Press.

Roberts, F. H. H. 1942. Archaeological and geological investigations in the San Jon District, eastern New Mexico. Washington, D.C.: Smithsonian Miscellaneous Collections 103, no. 4.

Contributors

ROLFE D. MANDEL is Adjunct Professor, Department of Geography, University of Kansas, and a consulting geomorphologist. He has spent over twenty years working with archaeologists on projects throughout the United States and the eastern Mediterranean. However, during the past ten years, his research has focused on the Central Plains of North America. Especially interested in the effects of geologic processes on the archaeological record, he has published work in a number of books and professional journals. Mandel is the Editor-in-Chief of *Geoarchaeology:An International Journal.*

VANCE T. HOLLIDAY is Professor, Geography Department, University of Wisconsin at Madison. A leading authority on the geoarchaeology of the Southern High Plains, Holiday is best known for his research at the Lubbock Lake Paleoindian site in northwest Texas. His recent publications include *Paleoindian Geoarchaeology of the Southern High Plains,* and his research papers have been published in nearly all of the major geoscience and archaeological journals.

C. REID FERRING is Professor, Department of Geography, University of North Texas. Ferring is one of the few people in the United States who has earned doctorates in geology and anthropology. He is best known for his research in the Southern Osage Plains of Texas and Oklahoma. Ferring recently gained national attention with his discovery of the Aubrey Paleoindian site near Denton, Texas.

JOHN ALBANESE is Adjunct Professor, Department of Geology, University of Wyoming, and a consulting geologist. Albanese is a leading authority on the geoarchaeology of the Northwestern Plains of the United States. He has studied nearly all of the major Paleoindian sites in that region, and he frequently collaborates with George Frison, one of the most distinguished archaeologists in North America. Albanese recently received the Geological Society of America's Rip Rapp Archaeological Geology Award.

E. ARTHUR BETTIS III is Assistant Professor, Department of Geoscience, University of Iowa. Bettis, a leading authority on the geoarchaeology of the Eastern Plains of North America, has degrees in anthropology, pedology, and geology. Most of his geoarchaeological research has focused on stream valleys in western Iowa, and his work has been published in many books and professional journals.

DAVID W. MAY is Associate Professor, Geography Department, University of Northern Iowa. He is a leading authority on the geoarchaeology of the Central and Western Plains of Nebraska. In addition to spending more than twenty years studying the late-Quaternary geologic history of that region, May has been working with archaeologists who are reinvestigating a number of important Paleoindian sites that were excavated during the 1940s.

JOE A. ARTZ is Geographic Information Coordinator, Iowa Office of the State Archaeologist, University of Iowa. He is a leading authority on the geoarchaeology of the Northern Plains, and has worked as an archaeologist and geomorphologist on many projects in the Dakotas. Artz is best known for his studies of buried archaeological sites in the Holocene loess that covers large areas of the Northern Plains.

Index

Abbott, Charles, 88–89
Abbott, Larry R., 157
Academic institutions: Augustana College, 109, 189, 207, 237; Baylor University, 57; Chadron State College, 179, 228; Colorado State University, 190, 203, 228; Franklin and Marshall College, 203, 208; Harvard University, 79, 89, 205, 215–16, 289, 290; Iowa State University, 147, 151; Kansas State University, 85; Luther College, 151, 154; Montana State University, 203, 206, 237; Oklahoma State University, 57, 62, 116, 118; Princeton University, 207, 209; Southern Methodist University, 57, 61, 68, 291; Texas A&M University, 57, 62, 68; Texas Tech University, 16, 17, 62, 291; University of Arizona, 149, 179, 203, 204, 215; University of Chicago, 92; University of Colorado, 187, 213, 219, 292; University of Iowa, 92, 114, 139, 143, 147; University of Kansas, 87, 93, 94, 101–102, 103, 104, 109, 111, 112, 113–14, 184, 232, 293; University of Minnesota, 92; University of Missouri, 149; University of Montana, 220; University of Nebraska/State Museum, 7, 148, 168–69, 171, 172, 173, 174, 176, 180, 182, 183, 187, 189, 191, 218, 232; University of Northern Colorado, 203, 205; University of North Texas, 62; University of Oklahoma, 57, 62, 114, 115; University of Pennsylvania, 14, 207; University of Texas, 15, 55, 57, 61, 86, 97, 99; University of Tulsa, 98; University of Wisconsin, 148, 149, 180, 181; University of Wyoming, 190, 203, 209, 210, 214, 215–16, 217, 221, 228, 232–33; Washington State University, 149; Western Wyoming College, 203, 236
Academy of Natural Sciences, 14, 141
Adair, Mary, 104, 105, 184
Adovasio, J. M., 266
Agenbroad, Larry, 179, 228
Agogino, George A., 17, 27, 206, 215, 216, 232
Ahler, S. A., 258, 266
Albanese, John, 7–8, 207, 209, 212, 214, 217, 220–21, 222, 233, 238

Albritton, Claude C., Jr., 3, 11, 16, 22, 26, 57, 60, 61, 290
Allen, D. C., 54
Allen, James, 207, 210
American Museum of Natural History, 79, 169, 199
Anderson, Adrian, 59–60
Antevs, Ernst, 3, 51, 53, 69, 141, 217, 254, 255, 260, 289; on Altithermal drought, 21, 26, 29–30
ARC/INFO, 292–93
ArcView, 292–93
Artz, Joe Alan, 8–9, 99–100, 112–13, 268, 288, 289

Baerreis, D. A., 47, 57
Baerreis, David, 149
Baker, Victor, 61
Baker, William E., 97
Bamforth, Douglas, 187, 189, 292
Banks, Larry D., 67
Barbour, Erwin H., 139–40, 169, 171–72
Bass, William M., 93, 232
Baumgardner, Robert, 62
Bell, Earl, 173–74
Bell, Robert E., 47, 57, 59–60, 92
Bement, Leland, 119
Benn, David W., 151, 154
Bettis, E. Arthur, III, 6–7, 98, 106, 114, 151–52, 154–55, 287, 288, 289
Bilgery, Conrad, 204
Binford, Lewis, 59, 288
Blakeslee, Donald J., 104
Blasing, Robert, 185–86
Blum, Michael, 61, 64, 67–68
Bode, F. D., 21, 27
Bonini, W. E., 208
Bonnichsen, R., 220
Bousman, Britt, 61, 66
Boyd, Thomas Lee, 233
Bozarth, Steven, 104, 105
Bozell, John, 189
Brackenridge, G. R., 60
Brakenridge, Robert, 67, 115, 117, 120
Brice, J. C., 189
Broilo, Frank, 22
Brooks, Robert, 67

Brophy, J. A., 261
Brown, Barnum, 199
Brown, Kenneth, 184
Brunswick, Robert, 205
Bryan, Kirk, 3, 15, 61, 69, 94, 200, 217, 254, 255, 289–90; at Horner site, 207–208, 290; at Lindenmeier site, 205–206, 239, 290; at McLean site, 54; at "Spanish Diggings," 96–97
Bryant, Vaughn, 62
Bryson, Reid A., 148–49
Butzer, Karl W., 58–59, 61, 68, 288

Calvin, Samuel, 93
Campbell, T. N., 97
Caran, Chris, 62, 64
Carlson, D. L., 64
Carlson, Gayle, 189
Carter, Brian J., 62, 64, 67, 115, 116, 117, 118–19, 120
Central Plains, 79–122; Afton Springs site, 91–92; alluvial deposits, 99–100, 102, 103, 104–105, 106, 107, 108–109, 110–11, 112–13, 114, 115, 116, 119, 120; Archaic period, 93, 100, 102, 105, 111; Arkansas City Country Club site, 86; Birch Creek, 99, 100; bison remains, 90, 91, 116–17, 118–19; Burnham site, 111, 116–18; Cherokee Turnpike Project, 100; Clinton Lake sites, 104–105; Cloud County, Kans. site, 85; Coffee site, 101–102; Cooper site, 118, 119; Copan Lake, 98–99, 100; Copple Mound, 115; dating, 81, 91, 92–93, 99, 100, 102, 103, 104, 106, 107, 111, 113, 116, 118, 119, 293; Deer Creek basin, 119–20; Delaware River Basin, 107; Doyle Creek Basin, 107; El Cuartelejo, 87–88; El Dorado Lake, 102–103, 112, 113; eolian deposits, 112; Folsom Complex, 118, 119; Fort Riley site, 292–93; Fort Scott Lake, 103; geologists in, 79–81, 86–87, 89–90, 92, 120; Great Bend Prairie, 112; Hajny site, 116; Holocene formations, 99–100, 103, 104–105, 106, 109, 110, 112–13, 120; Hominy Creek, 99–100; Jenks/Bixby Project, 100–101; Kanopolis Lake, 107; Lansing Man site, 87, 92–93, 120, 139, 287; Laverty Ditch, 115; Little Caney River, 99, 100; loess deposits in, 92–93, 96, 120; macrofloral analyses, 104, 105; mammoth remains in, 91, 92, 116; Maple City chert quarries, 86; mastodon remains, 91, 92; Melvern Lake, 103–104; Milford Lake, 103–104; Mill Creek valley, 109–10; Nall site, 96–97, 291, 292; Norton Bone Bed site, 112; Packard site, 114–15; Paint Creek Village site, 85; paleoenvironments, 99, 100, 104, 112, 118; Paleoindian sites, 88–94, 121; Pawnee River Basin, 105–106; Penokee figure, 87; Peoria Quarry/"Spanish Diggings," 88, 96–97;

Perry Lake, 103–104, 105; phytolith analyses, 104, 105, 293; Pleistocene fauna associated with humans, 90–92, 116–17, 118–19, 120; Pleistocene formations, 92–93, 96, 100, 112–13, 116–17, 120; Pomona Lake, 103–104; Rice County, Kans. site, 85; Riley County, Kans. site, 85; Site 14RC102, 114; Site 14RY38, 109; Skiatook Lake, 99–100; Southeast Kansas Highway Corridor Project, 108; Spring Creek site, 6, 81, 94–95, 96–97, 121, 286; Stigenwalt site, 105; Sutter site, 111; Timbered Mounds, 86; Tuttle Creek, 103–104; 12 Mile Creek site, 87, 90–91, 114, 120, 287; U.S. Highway 166 Corridor Project, 108; Walnut River valley, 110–11, 112–13; Waugh site, 118; Whitewater River Basin, 107; Wilson Lake, 104
Chamberlain, Thomas C., 89, 92–93
Champe, John, 142–43, 147, 154, 155
Cheatum, Elmer, 54
Christianson, G. E., 168
Clark, Carroll, 95
Clark, J. G. D., 59
Clarke, W. T., 21
Clayton, J. S., 260
Clayton, Lee, 8, 262, 263, 265, 266, 268–69, 273
Clovis Complex, 24, 213, 214, 220–21, 223, 229-30, 238–39; Clovis site, 22, 27, 31, 32, 33, 251, 286, 287
Cody Complex, 181, 207–10, 213–14, 218, 219, 222, 233, 238, 290
Coe, Michael, 59
Collaboration between geoscientists and archaeologists, 251–52, 290–91, 293–94; Central Plains, 6, 79-81, 94–97, 98, 114, 115–16, 117–22, 286, 288, 291–92; Eastern Plains and Prairies, 6, 137–39, 140, 141, 145–46, 147, 149-50, 155, 157–58, 286–87, 288; Nebraska, 7, 166, 167–68, 169, 171, 172–73, 175–78, 179, 180–87, 189–92, 287, 292; Northern Plains, 250, 254, 259, 261, 262–63, 269, 270, 272–73, 287, 288; Northwestern Plains, 8, 199-200, 206, 207–208, 212–14, 215–21, 223, 232, 238, 239, 287; Southern High Plains, 254–55, 291–92; Southern Osage Plains, 44, 47, 57, 64, 68–69, 286
Collins, M. B., 30, 55, 62, 66
Colorado Museum of Natural History, 168–69, 199, 204, 205
Conference on Environmental Studies, 262–63
Coogan, Alan H., 259, 266, 272
Cook, Harold J., 48, 49-50, 68–69
Cope, Edward, 85
Cornwell, Kevin, 184, 185
Corps of Engineers. See U.S. Army Corps of Engineers
Cotter, John L., 14, 31
Crabill, Frank, 169, 171

Crandell, Dwight, 258
Crook, Wilson, 54–55, 69
Cultural Resource Management (CRM), 58, 289, 293–94; Central Plains, 6, 80, 81, 98–111, 113–14, 121; Eastern Plains and Prairies, 7, 148, 150, 151, 155; Nebraska, 7, 287; Northern Plains, 265–66, 270; Northwestern Plains, 8, 201, 203, 206–207, 235–36, 240; Southern Osage Plains, 6, 62–63, 64–68, 69
Cummings, L. S., 238

Daniels, Raymond B., 152
Darwin, Robert, 66
Dating, 58–59; of Paleoindian sites, 5, 6, 47–49, 68–69, 81, 88–94, 120, 121, 138–41, 143, 145, 199-200, 222, 251, 287–88, 291–92, 294; radiocarbon dating, 32–33, 167, 173, 178, 200, 272, 288, 291, 293; recent techniques, 293; and stratigraphy, 21, 60, 81, 88, 106, 120, 167, 173, 190, 191, 200, 205–206, 213, 214–15, 217, 251, 256, 287–88. *See also under specific regions*
David, P. P., 266
Davidson, D. A., 272
Davis, E. Mott, 143, 176–77, 290
Davis, Leslie B., 206, 237, 238
Denver Museum of Natural History, 168–69, 199, 204, 205
Dick, Herbert, 213, 214
Direct Historical Method, 147
Dixon, John, 100–101
Donahue, J., 266
Dort, Wakefield, Jr., 106, 111–12, 113, 115, 116, 117
Drass, Richard, 120
Drew, Darrell L., 102–103, 112, 113
Duguid, James, 215

Eastern Plains and Prairies, 6–7, 137–58; Akers site, 152, 153; alluvial deposits, 142, 149, 151–52, 154, 155–56; Archaic period, 145, 151; Ash Hollow Cave, 142; Cherokee Sewer site, 151; dating, 141, 143, 145; Denison site, 152, 154; Harry Truman Dam and Reservoir Project, 148, 149-50; Hill site, 145–46; Holocene formations, 145, 149, 151–52, 155–57; Little Platte Drainage, 151; Little Platte River, 151; loess region, 154–55; Logan Creek site, 145–46; MAD sites, 152, 153; Mahaphy site, 152, 154; mastodon remains, 149; Mill Creek Culture Study, 148–49; Minnesota Man, 140–41; Nebraska Loess Man, 139-40, 287; Nebraska phase, 142–43; paleoenvironments, 148–49; Paleoindian sites, 6, 137–41, 151, 156; Pleistocene formations, 149; Pleistocene formations associated with humans, 138–41, 143, 145; Rainbow site, 151–52; River Basins Survey, 141, 147, 149; Rogers Shelter, 149;

Simonson site, 145–46; Turin site, 143, 145; Walker-Gilmore site, 141–42; Woodland period, 141–43, 147, 151
Eckerle, William, 237, 240
Eden culture, 213
Edgar, Robert, 219
Egolf, D., 228
Eiseley, Loren C., 97, 171, 207–208; at Spring Creek site, 6, 81, 94–95, 121, 286
Elias, Gregory, 177–78
Environmental Systems Analysis, 103
Evans, Glen L., 11, 15, 16, 18, 24, 30, 31, 32; at Lubbock Lake site, 21, 97
Evans, Oren F., 50, 114
Everitt, B. L., 262

Fenenga, Franklin, 143
Fergus Falls site, Minn., 255
Ferring, C. Reid, 5–6, 47, 61, 62, 65, 66, 67
Figgins, J. D., 48, 199, 204
Fisher, J. W., Jr., 238
Flannery, Kent, 59
Flynn, Peggy, 116
Folsom Complex, 32, 33, 55, 94, 118, 119, 200, 206, 230, 232, 233, 238; at Clovis site, 22, 31; at Folsom site, 10, 48, 91, 171, 172, 199, 251, 290, 291–92; at Lindenmeier site, 8, 15, 205–206
Forbis, Richard, 206, 261
Fowke, Gerald, 92, 93
Frankforter, W. D., 143–46, 174–76, 189, 232
Frazier, Frank, 204, 219
Frederick, C. D., 67
Fredlund, Glen, 104
Friends of the Pleistocene (FOP), 63–64
Frison, George C., 201, 203, 209, 211–12, 216, 217, 221, 228; at Agate Basin site, 232–33; at Milliron site, 233, 235, 237
Fryxell, Ronald, 222

Garner, Frank, 204
Gazing, G. L., 217
Geoarchaeology: definition of, 3, 252
Geochronology, 3, 5, 16, 17, 33, 151, 292, 293
Geographic Information Systems (GIS), 290, 292–93
Geological Society of America (GSA), 89, 221–22
Geomorphology, 3, 5, 200, 250, 289; Central Plains, 80, 89, 95, 99, 100–101, 102, 103–104, 105–111, 113, 114, 115, 116, 120; Eastern Plains and Prairies, 139, 146, 149, 155; Nebraska, 167, 172, 173, 177, 178, 179, 181–82, 184, 185, 187, 189-90, 191–92; Northern Plains, 260, 269, 272; Northwestern Plains, 205, 220, 221, 228, 239, 240; Southern High Plains, 18; Southern Osage Plains, 60, 61, 66, 67–68
Gerhard, Paul H., 213
Gifford, J. A., 290
Gilbert, G. K., 88

Gilder, R. F., 139
Gile, Lee, 64
Gladfelter, B. G., 59
Goshen points, 32, 233–34, 238
Gould, Charles N., 50, 81, 86
Graham, Russell, 223
Grasso, Dennis, 236
Green, F. Earl, 11, 17, 18, 26–27, 30
Grey, D. C., 221
Griffin, James B., 256
Grim, R. E., 53
Grosser, R. D., 98
Ground-penetrating radar (GPR), 293
Gustavson, Thomas, 62

Haag, W. G., 58
Hadley, R. F., 215
Hall, Stephen A., 61, 99-100
Hamilton, T. M., 262
Hannus, Adrian, 207, 237, 238
Harksen, J. C., 261–62
Harris, King, 54
Hassan, Fekri A., 59, 61
Hawley, John, 64
Hawley, Marlin H., 110
Haynes, C. Vance, Jr., 3, 11, 24, 30, 61, 62, 149,
    179-80, 203, 206, 217, 221, 222, 230, 240,
    290; at Agate Basin site, 232; at Clovis site,
    17, 26, 27; at Dent site, 204–205; at Hell
    Gap site, 215, 216; at Lange-Ferguson site,
    238–39
Haynes, Gary, 223
Hay, O. P., 49-50, 68–69
Hell Gap Complex, 8, 180, 200, 215–17, 222,
    228, 230
Henry, Donald O., 61, 65, 99
Hester, James J., 11, 14
Hibben, Frank, 15
High Plains Paleoecology Project (HPPP),
    16–17, 26
Hill, A. T., 142
Hill, M. G., 24, 292
Hill, Robert T., 47
Hlady, W., 261
Hodge, Frederick W., 87
Hofman, Jack L., 24, 47, 60, 112, 114, 118,
    119–20
Holder, Preston, 176, 187
Holen, Steven, 180–85, 186–87, 189, 190–91
Holliday, Vance T., 5, 17, 18, 22, 24, 33, 62, 64,
    206, 291, 292
Holmes, William Henry, 88, 89, 91–92, 93,
    97
Howard, E. B., 11, 14, 19, 21
Howells, W. W., 47
Hrdlička, Ales, 89, 93–94
Hughes, J. T., 207, 214–15, 258
Humphrey, J. D., 67
Hurley, W. M., 147
Hurt, W., 262
Husted, Wilfred, 218–19

Iowa Geological Survey, 139
Iowa State Historic Preservation Office, 154
Irving, William N., 258, 259
Irwin, Henry, 216
Irwin-Williams, Cynthia, 216

Janzen, W. K., 260
Jelks, E. B., 58
Jenks, A. E., 254
Jepson, Glenn, 207–208, 209
Johnson, C. A., 18
Johnson, Donald L., 149, 157
Johnson, Eileen, 11, 18, 33, 64, 261, 291, 292
Johnson, William C., 105, 111, 112, 184, 293
Jorstad, T., 266
Judson, Sheldon, 15, 24, 208, 209, 290, 292

Kansas Department of Transportation
    (KDOT), 106–107, 108, 109, 110
Kansas Geological Survey, 81, 85, 106
Kansas State Historical Preservation Office,
    106
Kansas State Historical Society, 105, 106, 109,
    110
Katz, Paul R., 111
Kay, M., 100
Kehoe, T. F., 262
Kelley, J. H., 18
Kelly, E. F., 190
Kidder, A. V., 199
King, James E., 103, 149
Kivett, Marvin, 143
Knox, James C., 112, 269
Koch, A. K., 88
Kornfeld, M., 212
Krieger, A. D., 16, 22, 26, 57–58, 271
Kuehn, D. D., 266

Lahren, L. A., 220
Laird, R., 228
Lamb, Charles, 217
Leaf, G. R., 102
Lehmer, D. L., 259, 261
Leighton, M. M., 51, 53, 147
Leonhardy, Frank C., 115
Leopold, Luna B., 214–15, 216, 221
Leverett, Frank, 254
Lewis, C. Edward, 217, 218
Libby, Frank Willard, 32–33, 178, 200, 288
Logan, Brad, 104–105
Lohman, K. E., 21
Ludwickson, John, 189
Lueck, Edward J., 189
Lugn, A. L., 171
Lull, R. S., 47
Lyell, C., 88

MacClintock, Paul, 172
McCracken, Harold, 219
McFaul, Michael, 205
McGregor, Dan, 67

McKean Complex, 261
McKern, W. C., 57, 58
McKnight, Charles, 215
McMillan, R. Bruce, 149
MacNeish, Richard, 259
Malde, Harold E., 204, 213, 219, 220, 222
Mallam, R. Clark, 114
Mandel, Rolfe, 62, 64, 68, 103, 106, 108–111, 112, 113–14, 189–90, 289
Marsh, O. C., 85, 86
Martin, Charles W., 184
Martin, Handel T., 87, 90–91
Martin, James, 238
Martin, Larry D., 111, 112, 115, 116, 117
May, David W., 7, 104, 180–84, 185, 186–87, 189, 190–91, 292
Mayer-Oakes, William, 263
Meade, Grayson E., 11, 15, 16, 31
Mears, Barinard, 211
Mehringer, P. J., 149, 216
Melton, Frank, 49
Meltzer, David J., 30, 291
Merserve, F. G., 171
Metcalf, George S., 96, 217
Midvale site, Idaho, 111
Midwestern Taxonomic System, 57, 58
Miller, James C., 236–37
Miller, John P., 214–15, 216, 217, 221
Montgomery, Arthur, 208–209
Morrill, Charles H., 169
Moss, John H., 203, 208, 218, 219
Moss-Bennett Act of 1974, 58, 65, 98, 148, 289
Mound, Gilder, 139
Mudge, Benjamin F., 81, 85
Mulloy, William, 210–11, 212, 219, 261, 262
Museum of New Mexico, 16
Museum of the Great Plains, 59
Muto, Guy, 115

National Advisory Council for Historic Preservation, 65
National Endowment for the Humanities, 216
National Environmental Policy Act of 1969, 58, 98, 148, 168, 201, 289
National Geographic Society, 117, 218
National Historic Preservation Act of 1966, 58, 98, 148, 168, 201, 289
National Park Service, 55, 65, 67, 102, 174, 257
National Science Foundation (NSF), 6, 58, 59, 117, 148, 217, 219
Natural Resource Conservation Service, 106–107, 152, 154–55
Nebraska, 166–92; Allen site, 174, 176, 178, 187; alluvial deposits, 166, 167, 173, 177, 178, 180, 181, 183, 187, 189, 190; Arcadia Diversion Dam and Sherman Reservoir, 190–91; Archaic period, 190–91; Big Blue River valley, 189; Big Nemaha River valley, 190; Buffalo Creek, 182, 192; Calamus Dam and Reservoir, 179, 185; Cape site, 173–74; Cedar Canyon, 173; Clary Ranch

site, 180; Cumro site, 169, 180; dating in, 7, 166–68, 171–74, 178, 179, 180–81, 183, 184, 187, 189, 190, 191, 192, 223; Davis Creek Dam and Reservoir, 179, 182; DeForest Formation, 190; dunes in, 166, 167; Elkhorn River valley, 182; Enders Reservoir, 191; eolian deposits, 190, 251; Everson-Dodd site, 172; Harlan County Lake, 184; Harry Strunk Lake, 167–68, 174, 185–87; Holocene formations, 181–82, 190–91; Hudson-Meng site, 179-80, 190, 228; Keya Paha River, 190; Kruml site, 181; La Sena site, 185–87; Lime Creek sites, 7, 167–68, 174–78, 187, 189, 191, 292; Little Blue River valley, 189; Little Pawnee Creek, 190; loess, 166, 167, 185–87; Logan Creek site, 189; Loup River Basin, 168, 169, 179, 180–81, 182–84, 190–91; mammoth remains, 169, 185–87; Marvin Colson site, 185; mastodon remains, 168–69; Medicine Creek site, 7; Meserve site, 171; Moffet Creek site, 182–83; Morrill Paleontological Expedition, 7, 167, 168–73; North Cove site, 184; North Platte River valley, 172; paleoenvironments, 184, 187, 190, 292; Paleoindian sites in, 7, 166–68, 169, 171, 172–78, 179-83, 184–87, 189, 190–91, 292; phytoliths, 190; Pleistocene formations, 172, 185; Ponca Creek, 190; Red Smoke site, 174, 176–77, 178, 187, 189, 292; River Basins Surveys, 185; Scottsbluff Bison Quarry site, 171–72, 204, 287; Scottsbluff points, 174–75, 181, 204; Signal Butte site, 171, 251; Slaughterhouse Creek site, 181–82; Stafford site, 189; Stark site, 181; Truman site, 180; White River Basin, 173
Nebraska National Forest, 190
Nebraska State Historical Society, 182, 189-90, 191
Newman, Jay, 67
Nichols, J. D., 60
Nordt, Lee, 62, 66–67
North Dakota Geological Survey, 268, 272
Northern Plains, 8–9, 250–73; Alberta points, 266; alluvial deposits, 255, 259, 260, 261–62, 268; Altithermal drought in, 262; Archaic period, 258, 261, 269; Benz site, 266; colluvial deposits, 260, 262, 268; dating in, 254, 256, 259, 260, 261, 262, 263, 266, 272; description, 252–54; eolian deposits, 256, 259, 261, 265, 266, 268; Flaming Arrow site, 266; Glacial Lake Agassiz, 262–63; Holocene formations, 259, 260, 261–62, 263, 265, 266, 268–70, 273; Knife River basin, 262, 268; lacrustine deposits, 268; Long Creek site, 260–61; Missouri Trench, 254, 257–58, 259, 261, 266, 271; Mortlach site, 259-61; Natche site, 258; Oahe Formation, 8, 263, 265, 266, 268–70, 273; Old Soil Zone Culture,

Northern Plains (*continued*)
256; paleoenvironments, 238, 260, 262, 266, 269-70, 271, 273; Paleoindian sites, 254, 258, 266, 269; paludal deposits, 268; Pleistocene formations, 265, 269; Ray Long site, 258; Red River sites, 259, 269; Scottsbluff points, 266; Souris River basin, 268; Woodland period, 256, 258
Northwestern Plains, 199-241; Agate Basin site, 220, 230, 232–33; alluvial deposits, 205, 206, 207, 208–209, 214, 215, 216, 217, 221, 229, 237–38, 238, 240; Altithermal drought in, 238; Anzick site, 220–21; Archaic period, 206, 210, 212, 218–20, 221, 228–29, 238, 240; Barton Gulch site, 237; Betty Greene site, 220; bison remains, 204, 222, 228; Brewster site, 232; Carter-Kerr McGee site, 233; Casper site, 228; Claypool site, 8, 210, 213–14, 219, 222; Clovis Complex, 213, 214, 220–21, 223, 229-30, 238–39; Cody Complex, 207–10, 213–14, 218, 219, 222, 233; Colby site, 229-30; colluvial deposits, 206, 207, 216, 229, 233, 237, 238; contract archaeology in, 203, 222, 235–37, 239; dating in, 8, 205–206, 209, 213, 214–15, 216, 217, 218, 220, 221, 223, 237, 238–39, 240, 290; Dent site, 8, 31, 171, 204–205, 219; Dutton site, 222–23; eolian deposits, 216, 236, 238, 240; Folsom Complex, 205–206, 230, 232, 233, 238; Frasca site, 222; Frazier site, 219-20; Glenrock Buffalo Jump, 221; Goshen points, 233–34, 238; Grand Island Formation, 213; Hell Gap site/style, 8, 180, 200, 215–17, 222, 228, 230; Holocene formations, 211, 213, 214–15, 216–17, 220, 221, 223, 233, 237–38, 239-41; Horner site, 8, 207–10, 290; Hudson-Meng site, 228; Indian Creek site, 237; James Allen site, 210; Jones-Miller site, 222; Jurgens site, 219; lacrustine deposits, 223; Lamb Spring site, 217–18, 222; Lange-Ferguson site, 237, 238; Late Prehistoric Period, 206, 221, 228–29; Lindenmeier site, 8, 15, 205–206, 239, 287, 290; Little Canyon Creek shelter site, 223; loess, 223; Lookingbill site, 228–29; MacHaffie site, 8, 206, 237–38; mammoth remains, 204–205, 213, 214, 218, 222, 229-30, 238; McKean site, 210–13; Milliron site, 233, 235, 237, 238; Mummy Cave site, 218–19; Myers-Hindman site, 220; Paleoindian sites, 8, 203, 204–221, 222, 228–30, 233, 237–39, 240, 287, 290; phytoliths, 209; Pleistocene fauna associated with humans, 217, 222–23, 228, 229-30; Pleistocene formations, 205–206, 216–17, 219, 223; Ray Long site, 8, 206–207, 214–15, 237, 258; Ruby site, 221; Sappa Formation, 213; Scottsbluff Bison Quarry site, 7–8, 171–72, 204, 239, 287; Scottsbluff points, 206, 213;

Selby site, 222–23; Sister's Hill site, 216–17, 221; Sutton site, 222

Oakley, K. P., 47
O'Brien, Patricia, 102
Oklahoma Archaeological Survey, 62, 67, 115, 116, 117, 118, 119
Old Crow site, Can., 222
Oldfield, F., 17
Over, William H., 255–56
Overton, T. R., 90

Paleobotany, 18, 138, 177
Paleontology: Central Plains, 81, 85, 91, 116, 120; Eastern Plains and Prairies, 138; Nebraska, 166, 169, 171, 177, 179, 191; Northern Plains, 258, 261; Northwestern Plains, 209, 216, 217, 232, 238; Southern High Plains, 11, 15, 18
Palynology: Eastern Plains and Prairies, 149, 151; Nebraska, 167, 187, 189; Northern Plains, 216–17, 219, 237, 238, 240, 273; Southern High Plains, 26
Patillo, L. G., 57
Patrick, R., 21
Peabody Museum of Natural History, 86, 89
Pedology, 3, 58–59, 250; Central Plains, 80, 100, 102, 103, 104, 105, 110, 112–13, 114, 115, 116, 118–19, 120, 240, 293; Eastern Plains and Prairies, 138, 139, 146, 147, 149, 151, 155–56, 157; Nebraska, 167, 173, 177, 181–82, 183, 184–87, 190, 192; Northern Plains, 209, 212, 213, 214, 215, 217, 223, 233, 239-40, 263, 265, 266, 269; Southern High Plains, 11, 18, 30; Southern Osage Plains, 51, 53, 60, 61, 62, 66, 67–68
Peterson, J. F., 64
Pettipas, L., 262
Pheasant, David, 61, 65
Phetteplace, Ivan, 95
Phillips, P., 58
Phillips Academy, 199
Plainview style, 31–32
Portales Complex, 32
Priestly, F. G., 47–48
Putnam, Frederic Ward, 89

Rainey, Mary, 61
Rapp, J. R., 290
Rapson, David, 190, 228
Rautman, Alison, 185
Ray, Cyrus N., 51, 53–54, 69
Ray, Louis, 205–206, 290
Redder, Al, 55
Redmond, Lou, 190
Reeves, B. O. K., 261, 262
Reeves, C. C., 64
Reid, K. C., 100
Reider, Richard, 209, 212, 214, 217, 233, 240
Retallick, H. J., 60
Ringstaff, C., 67, 184

River Basin Surveys (RBS), 55, 101, 114, 141, 147, 185, 206–207, 210, 218, 256–59, 270, 271

Roberts, Frank H. H., Jr., 11, 15, 24, 54, 199, 205, 292; at Agate Basin site, 232

Roberts, Michael, 216

Rogers, Richard, 112, 113

Root, M. J., 266

Roper, Donna, 185

Ruppé, Ronald J., 143

Sabloff, J. A., 272

Salisbury, Rollin D., 92, 93

Sampson, Garth, 61

Saunders, J.J., 17

Sayles, E. B., 51

Schmits, Larry J., 102, 103

Schoenwetter, J., 17

Schuldenrein, Joseph, 179, 185

Schullinger, John, 208, 209

Schultz, C. Bertrand, 3, 7, 112, 169, 173, 180, 182, 189, 191, 217–18, 254–55, 289; at Lime Creek sites, 174–77, 178; at Scottsbluff site, 171–72

Schumm, S. A., 149, 215, 273

Scott, Glenn, 217

Scott, Karen, 67

Scott, Robert, 65, 67

Scottsbluff points, 174–75, 181, 204, 206, 213, 266

Sedimentology, 3, 200, 289, 293; Central Plains, 102, 104, 105, 120, 121, 293; Nebraska, 167, 177, 179, 181–82, 183, 184, 185, 187, 189, 190, 192, 251; Northern Plains, 255, 256, 261, 263, 265, 266, 268; Northwestern Plains, 205–206, 207, 208–209, 213, 217, 218, 219, 223, 230, 232, 233, 237–38, 239–40; Southern High Plains, 13–14, 27, 29-30, 290; Southern Osage Plains, 67–68

Seifert, M., 54

Sellards, E. H., 3, 11, 16, 18, 26, 50, 68–69, 97, 254, 289; at Clovis site, 21–22, 24, 31, 32; at Miami site, 15

Semken, Holmes, 217

Sheldon, A. E., 255, 262

Shimek, Bohumil, 92, 93, 139-40

Shippee, J. M., 101, 206

Shor, E. N., 86

Shriver site, Mo., 111

Shuler, Ellis, 47, 49, 50–51

Sixth Plains Anthropological Conference, 252, 262, 263, 270, 271

Slaughter, B. H., 54

Smith, Carlyle S., 96, 102

Smith, G. Hubert, 143

Smith, Harold T. U., 6, 81, 94–95, 121, 286, 290

Smithsonian Institution, 79, 93, 94, 174, 199, 205, 209, 213–14, 217, 222–23; Bureau of American Ethnology (BAE), 87, 88. See also River Basin Surveys

Soil Conservation Service, 106–107, 152, 154–55

Solecki, Ralph S., 101

Sorenson, Curtis, 112

Southern High Plains, 10–34; alluvial deposits, 13, 14; Altithermal drought in, 21, 24, 26, 29-30, 34; Anderson Basin site, 21, 26; Archaic period, 18, 21, 30, 34, 292; bison remains, 24, 292; Blackwater Draw Formation, 13–14, 17, 19, 27, 29; Blanco Formation, 13–14; Clovis points, 24, 27, 31, 32; Clovis site, 5, 14, 16, 17, 18, 19, 21–22, 24, 26, 27, 29, 30, 31, 32–33, 286, 287; Cody Complex, 290; dating in, 11, 18, 21, 26, 29, 32–33, 292; description, 11–14; draws in, 13, 14, 19, 26, 27, 29, 33; eolian deposits, 13, 14, 21, 24, 29-30; Goshen points, 32; High Plains Paleoecology Project, 16–17, 26–27; Holocene formations, 16, 19, 21, 26–27, 29-30, 33; Horace Rivers site, 32; lacrustine deposits, 13, 14, 26, 29; Lake Theo site, 18; Late Prehistoric Period, 292; Lipscomb site, 18; Lubbock Lake site, 5, 15–16, 17–18, 19, 21–22, 24, 26, 27, 29, 30, 32–33, 97; mammoth remains in, 15, 24, 31; Marks Beach site, 17; Miami site, 5, 15, 18, 19, 24, 31; Midland site, 5, 16, 17, 18, 19, 22, 24, 26–27, 30, 33, 97; Milnesand site, 16, 18; Monahans Draw, 16, 26; Mustang Springs site, 18, 19, 29, 30; Ogallala Formation, 13–14; Olsen-Chubbuck site, 291; paleoenvironments, 5, 10, 11, 16–17, 18–19, 21–22, 26, 27, 29-30, 33–34; Paleoindian sites, 10, 14–15, 16, 18–19, 21, 24, 29, 32–33, 34, 291, 292; Palo Duro Creek, 18; paludal deposits, 14, 29; Plainview site, 5, 16, 18, 24, 26, 31–32, 291; playas in, 19, 24; Pleistocene fauna associated with humans, 5, 10, 14, 15, 21, 24, 31, 255, 292; Pleistocene formations in, 13–14, 16, 19, 21, 26–27, 33; Portales Complex, 32; Rex Rodgers site, 18; San Jon site, 5, 15, 19, 24, 26, 30, 290, 291, 292; Sulphur Springs Draw, 18

Southern Osage Plains, 5–6, 44–70; Acton site, 54; alluvial deposits, 45; Aubrey site, 67; Clovis Complex in, 54, 55, 59–60, 67; Cooper Reservoir, 66, 68; Cooperton site, 60; dating in, 54, 57–58, 60, 66, 68; Delaware Canyon, 64, 65; description, 45–47; Domebo site, 59-60, 64, 116; eolian deposits, 54; Finley Fan, 68; Folsom Complex in, 55; Fort Hood site, 64, 66–67; Frederick site, 5, 47–51, 86, 287; Holocene formations, 55; Horn Shelter site, 55; Justiceberg Reservoir, 67–68; Lagow Sand Pit site, 5, 47, 49; Lake Grapevine, 55; Lake Lewisville, 67; Lake Ray Roberts, 67; Lava Creek Ash, 64; Lewisville site, 54–55; Lone Wolf Creek site, 48; mammoth remains,

Southern Osage Plains (*continued*)
53, 54, 57, 60; McLean site, 54;
paleoenvironments, 51, 60, 68;
Paleoindian sites, 6, 47–51, 57, 67;
Pleistocene fauna associated with humans
in, 5, 47–51, 54–55, 54, 68; Red River, 45, 54,
68; South Bend Project, 68; Sulfur River,
61, 68; Trinity River, 47, 54–55, 57, 65;
Valley Branch Project, 68
Spencer, William, 230
Spier, Leslie, 49-50, 69
Spikard, Linda, 204
Spinden, H. J., 270–71
Stacy, Howard, 177–78
Stafford, Thomas W., 18, 291
Stanford, Dennis J., 17, 22, 24, 214, 218, 222,
292
Steen-McIntyre, Virginia, 222
Stephenson, Robert, 55
Sterns, F. H., 141–42, 154
Steward, Julian, 59
Stewart, T. D., 16, 22, 26
Stock, C., 21, 27
Story, D. A., 47
Stratigraphy, 3, 58–59, 88, 200; Central Plains,
80, 81, 92–93, 99-100, 103, 105, 106, 107,
108–109, 110–11, 112–13, 115, 116,
118–19, 120, 121; Eastern Plains and
Prairies, 137, 142–43, 146, 149, 151;
Nebraska, 167, 173, 177–78, 180–81, 183,
184, 185, 187, 189, 190–91, 292; Northern
Plains, 256, 259, 260, 269, 273;
Northwestern Plains, 205–206, 207, 209,
217, 218, 223, 232, 233, 240–41; Southern
High Plains, 5, 11, 15, 16, 17, 18, 19, 21–22,
24, 25, 26–27, 29–30, 31, 32, 33, 290, 292;
Southern Osage Plains, 51, 54, 60
Strong, William Duncan, 96, 142, 154, 171,
251, 270
Struever, Stewart, 59
Stuckenrath, R., 266
Suhm, D. A., 58
Syms, E. L., 261

Tamplin, Morgan, 263
Tanner, Lloyd, 180
Taylor, D. C., 220
Taylor, Walter, 58
Texas Archaeological Research Laboratory,
62
Texas Memorial Museum (TMM), 15, 21, 24,
244
Theler, James, 116
Thompson, Dean M., 106, 155
Thorp, James, 258
Timberlake, Robert D., 106
Tinker, J. R., 262
Todd, J. E., 255
Todd, Lawrence C., 190, 212, 228

Tong, Marvin, 59–60
Toom, D. L., 258, 266
Toomey, R. S., III, 64
Tyrrell, J. B., 254

Udden, Johan A., 81, 85–86
Upham, Warren, 92
U.S. Army Corps of Engineers, 65–66, 67,
102–103, 104, 105, 106–107, 110, 184, 191
U.S. Bureau of Reclamation, 174, 179, 182,
184, 185, 186, 187, 190, 191, 211–12
U.S. Geological Survey, 88, 92, 172, 173, 204,
213, 214, 217, 219, 258
U.S. National Museum. *See* Smithsonian
Institution

Valsequillo site, Mex., 222
Van Royen, Willem, 173–74
Vero site, Fla., 15

Ward, P. A., 64
Wasden site, Idaho, 111
Waters, Michael R., 3, 62, 252
Wedel, Waldo R., 46, 79–80, 85, 86, 91, 94, 96,
97, 143, 147, 251, 261, 270, 271; at Horner
site, 209; at Lamb Creek site, 217–18; at
Mummy Cave site, 219
Wendorf, Fred, 11, 16, 17, 22, 26, 30, 59, 61,
290
Wettlaufer, Boyd, 259–61
Wheat, J. B., 15–16, 18, 30, 204, 219
Wheeler, Richard P., 207, 258
White, E. M., 261
White, J. E., 207
White, Theodore E., 258
Whitney, J. D., 88
Whitney Museum of Art, 218
Wike, Joyce, 176, 187
Will, George F., 255, 270–71
Willey, G. R., 58, 69, 272
Williston, Samuel W., 81, 86–87, 90–91, 92,
120
Wilmsen, E. N., 205
Wilson, M. C., 259, 261
Winchell, Newton Horace, 89–90, 92
Winham, R. Peter, 189
Witte, Adolf, 54, 69
Wohl, Evelyn E., 190
Wood, W. Raymond, 149
Works Progress Administration (WPA), 8,
15–16, 55, 256–58, 270, 271
Wormington, H. M., 31, 143, 200, 204, 205,
219, 261
Wright, G. Frederick, 92
Wright, H. E., 219
Wyckoff, Don G., 62, 67, 112, 114–15, 116–17,
266

"Yuma Point" type, 200, 213